SOMEBODY TO LOVE

THE LIFE, DEATH AND LEGACY OF
FREDDIE MERCURY

MATT RICHARDS & MARK LANGTHORNE

BLINK

bringing you closer

Matt Richards
is an award-winning film director, television
producer and screenwriter, who has written
and directed numerous documentaries
and series in the UK and the US.

Mark Langthorne
is CEO of Roland Mouret and has previously
worked in the music industry with stars such
as Kanye West and Annie Lennox.

Praise for *Somebody to Love*:

'One of the greatest rock biographies ever written'
Marc Almond

'This book should be on any Queen fan's bookshelf'
Get Ready To Rock

'*Somebody to Love* is a worthy and moving read with
new information unknown to even ardent fans'
Advocate

'Meticulous biography… packed with detail'
Belfast Telegraph

Published by Blink Publishing
3.08, The Plaza,
535 Kings Road,
Chelsea Harbour,
London, SW10 0SZ

www.blinkpublishing.co.uk

facebook.com/blinkpublishing
twitter.com/blinkpublishing

Hardback – 978-1-911274-02-5
Paperback – 978-1-911600-04-6
Ebook – 978-1-911274-03-2

A CIP catalogue of this book is available from the British Library.

Design and typeset by seagulls.net
Printed and bound by Clays Ltd, St. Ives Plc

1 3 5 7 9 10 8 6 4 2

Blink Publishing is an imprint of the Bonnier Publishing Group
www.bonnierpublishing.com

By Matt Richards and Mark Langthorne

*83 Minutes: The Doctor, The Damage and
The Shocking Death of Michael Jackson*

*Somebody to Love: The Life, Death and
Legacy of Freddie Mercury*

To Rhoda Charlotte, who has brought so much joy
in such a short time and continues to do so
– Matt

This book is dedicated to my very special friend,
Misha Kucherenko, who is extraordinary in so many ways
– Mark

To Richard and Leigh, thank you for believing
in this book, and for all your support

The unexamined life is not worth living.

SOCRATES

Prologue

November 1991.

London, Sunday 10th. The weather in the capital is typically gloomy. The weekend newspapers are rife with speculation over the death, just days earlier, of the controversial newspaper mogul Robert Maxwell off the coast of Tenerife. Church of England envoy Terry Waite has just been released from captivity in Lebanon. The films *Terminator 2: Judgment Day* and *Robin Hood: Prince of Thieves* are battling it out to rule the British box office. And Labour's hopes of election success, under Neil Kinnock, are boosted by a MORI poll that shows them six points ahead of John Major's ruling Conservatives.

None of this likely matters to the frail passenger inside the private jet as it touches down on British soil after a short flight from Switzerland. Unable to walk unassisted and with his eyesight beginning to fail, he is carefully led down the steps of the aircraft. He is afforded special exemption to bypass the queues at customs, meaning he avoids the public, the press, and the waiting cameras. Once through passport control the passenger is ushered into a waiting Mercedes, the tinted windows helping to preserve his anonymity. Just over an hour later, the car drops him off at his Kensington mansion, the electronic security gates closing him off to the world outside.

And the world to him.

In the spacious hallway, bedecked with beautiful Dresden porcelain, a number of prints have recently been rehung on the walls, and the huge adjoining galleried rooms are full of Japanese furniture and art, oil paintings and exquisite Lalique vases. In the music room, a grand piano rests on the wooden floors, upon it the silver photo frames displaying images from a life unseen by so many. The fallboard of the piano is closed.

The stairway wends its way upwards, the banister a crucial aid to the ailing man in his ever-decreasing quest to reach the master bedroom. Even the days of him coming down in the morning for his cup of tea are far fewer. He spends his time in his bedroom. Upstairs, the smell of air freshener cut with disinfectant lingers. All around is a sense of empty hours.

Within the master bedroom the once pristine bright yellow walls are now sickly-looking and faded. Facing the grand window is the bed, its headboard built into the wall and guarded on either side by two individually made chests of drawers in mahogany, inlaid with delicate marquetry. Bow-fronted French display cabinets from the Second Empire stand against the walls, containing expensive collections of crystal sculptures and Venezia bowls.

A boudoir is on the right-hand side of the bedroom; in it an Edwardian *chaise longue* and a *fauteuil* from the 17th century ready to receive friends and guests. But visitors are fewer now. Those who come don't expect grand revelry and partying, as they once did, simply reminiscences. The drip stand to the right of the bed – there to enable blood transfusions – betrays the illness that now inhabits this house.

The patient on the bed is half sleeping. He rides on limited breath. The anti-emetic prescribed is suppressing the nausea and the painkiller, infused earlier by a member of the loyal household staff who remains by his side night and day, is beginning to work. The assortment of drugs is introduced via a Hickman line implant, a cannula inserted into a vein in the neck. This simple operation was performed several months earlier, thus facilitating easier administration of the medication required to keep the patient alive, or, at least living and free from pain. It also solves the problem of having a nurse on hand to insert Venflons every time access to a vein is required, which is presently at least twice a day. This is not helped by the patient's allergy to morphine, normally the ideal sedative used for the treatment of pain in a case such as this.

The man who lives here would be unrecognisable now to most of us, yet almost all of us know his identity. Virtually incapacitated now, his bed is a raft, like a broken piece of salvage, and he is a prisoner within the walls of his home. Beyond the sanctuary of his Japanese garden, outside the walls of the property a frenzy is being conducted by the press and paparazzi, who permanently prowl, seeking out any rumour, gossip or whisper with which to create headlines for a public growing increasingly insatiable for news of developments within the house. They lay siege and wait. Such is their presence that he can hear the noise of them, blathering and jabbering there, while he lays in his bed. He can hear them just on the other side of the wall, and sometimes he can see the blue curls of smoke from their cigarettes rise upwards.

But they are only one of the reasons the man in the bedroom is prevented from ever leaving his home. The other, principal reason, being that he has AIDS. The hope of a cure, a half-belief in treatments that could extend life, is gone to him. The medical experts have backed away – they have nothing more to offer.

In fact, within weeks he won't ever come downstairs again, let alone even contemplate leaving the walled confines of the house.

No longer able to eat regularly, he exists on less than the minimum. Rice, always fried, never boiled. And liquids: water and tea made with milk. Sometimes, but less frequently now, he has some fresh fruit.

There is no space reserved for hope, no longer any means by which he can rescue himself from the past. His immune system is so compromised that it has rendered the body effectively helpless against the threat of infection. His doctor makes regular phone calls, and he visits every other day, but the patient requires apparatus to assist his breathing now, and has almost entirely lost the use of his muscles.

On the television a video is playing of the 1959 film *Imitation of Life*, a particular favourite of his starring Lana Turner. In the past he would be reduced to tears at the denouement of this movie, his emotions cajoled by the director in the same manner he himself would manipulate the emotions of those who listened to his music over the previous two decades. Except this time he doesn't weep. The change in his condition since he was last in London is significant. It concerns those closest to him, those who surround him. But his decline has been hastened by the decision he made less than a week ago: to come off medication.

The drugs he has taken over the last three years, an experimental and ultimately lethal cocktail, have done little to postpone the inevitable. They have served not as a hope, as he had assumed they would, but as a destructive regime that has reduced the quality of what little life he has remaining.

The hope of a miracle has not transpired. Now it is no longer a question of *if* he was going to die, simply *when*. This is how his life ended.

And how his dying began.

Part One

1

Everything has a beginning.

Our beginning is in the Belgian Congo, deep in the heart of Africa. The year is 1908 and the country is attempting to rebuild itself following the brutal regime of King Leopold II.

This was the year the Congo Free State was abolished and annexed as a colony of Belgium, to become known as the Belgian Congo, an area 75 times larger than Belgium itself. King Leopold died a year later, having never once set foot in the Congo region.

Before long the Belgian Congo had become, to many, a 'model colony' and the transfer of responsibility to Brussels had ensured much of the wealth produced in the Congo was reinvested within the region. Missionaries arrived and built hospitals and clinics and the Church ran schools. An infrastructure of railways, ports and roads underwent construction and mining companies provided homes for their staff as well as welfare and technical training.

But while this had great benefits for the citizens of cities and towns such as Boma and Leopoldville[1], for those inhabitants deep in the rainforest, the tentacles of progress barely touched them. These tribal people continued to exist as they had done for thousands of years, surviving through hunting and gathering before heading to a nearby village or town to trade bush meat or the prized honey they had collected from the rainforest's canopy. A number of tribes existed within the vast Congo rainforest. The most famous were the 'Pygmies', known as the Mbuti of the Ituri Forest in northern Congo, but there were also the Aka, the Twa and the Baka tribes and their taller and more dominant neighbours, the Bantu. And among the Bantu tribe lived a young hunter.

Our hunter lives deep within the Congolese jungle as part of the small ethnic Bantu group that inhabits the upper Sangha river basin. Nomadic in nature, the Bantu survive by hunting bush meat within the forest. Being young, fit and muscular, he is one of the best hunters within the tribe and, not only does he hunt, but he has been entrusted to take the bush meat, carcasses and furs upriver to the city of Leopoldville to trade for the manioc root from which to make cassava bread for the rest of the tribe. However, first he has to catch his prey.

Armed with a long spear, a cast-iron knife and a wire for setting traps, he had crept into the forest the day before to set his snares. He used a twig to pin a lethal loop of wire to the ground, then covered it in leaves. A living sapling bent over by another wire provided the spring that pulls the noose tight. Now, a full night and day since he set his traps, he checks the snares to see what, if anything, he has caught.

Drawing near to his first snare, the hunter hears a disturbance in the undergrowth ahead. He approaches slowly and silently, wary of disturbing the lethal green mamba, bright as blades of grass, who lurk on the rainforest floor and in trees. Finally, he gets close to the snare and, peering through the vine-like tangle of lianas, he sees that he has snared a young male chimpanzee. The animal, once energetic and full of life, now appears exhausted and almost dead.

Moving closer, he notices that it has gnawed off part of its own leg in a struggle to free itself from the snare. He rushes towards the chimp and spears it quickly, but not quick enough. The chimp's teeth sink into his left hand. He recoils as the sharp pain flows up his arm. With his full force he pushes the spear deep into the chimp's chest. It is enough: the chimp releases its grip on life.

He examines his wounded hand. The bite is not too deep as the creature was weak from loss of blood. He cleans up the wound as best he can, then cuts open the dead animal and discards its entrails with an iron knife. Once this job is done, he hoists it across his shoulders and heads back to his boat. The warm blood from the chimp mingles and mixes with his own blood from the open wound.

Unbeknown to him, the chimpanzee he has hunted and killed is carrying a virus. It enters the hunter's bloodstream at the wound, and the virus, in that moment finding his blood to be not so different from the blood of the chimp, takes hold. He is the perfect host, given that chimpanzees and humans share more than 98 per cent sequence identity across their genomes. The virus immediately begins to replicate aggressively. Oblivious to his new infection, the hunter throws the dead chimp into his boat, on top of a pile of carcasses of various animals he has already hunted, species such as pangolins and small antelope, and pushes out from the riverbank. He makes his way on the current towards Leopoldville, a three-day journey down the Sangha river.

Around this time, Leopoldville was a thriving, bustling marketplace with a booming population. While Boma, over 200 miles to the west, was the capital city of the Belgian Congo and residence of the Governor-General, Leopoldville was a sprawling town with single-storey shacks down to the banks of the river Congo, a mighty 3,000-mile expanse of water that curved north and east to Kisangani, more than 600 miles away. Once a fishing village, the recent completion of the Matadi-Leopoldville portage railway meant that it had become a commercial centre. Consequently, it was to Leopoldville that traders, hawkers and hunters from throughout the Belgian Congo would descend to sell their wares. And where there are traders, hawkers and hunters, there are also prostitutes.

After three days on the river, our hunter arrives in Leopoldville. He has made this journey many times before, usually with the same species that he has tracked down and killed in the jungle. This time appears no different. The carcasses he has transported, including the chimpanzee that bit him, are cut up to be sold, cooked or smoked. As a result of this cooking, the chimp meat will likely not infect anyone else. The skins and hides he will exchange with other traders for maize and cassava. But for the bush meat, he manages to make a few Belgian francs – enough money, in fact, to celebrate with a drink and a visit to one of the many prostitutes parading up and down the streets. Either on this, or subsequent visits, the hunter will pass on the virus that lingers unknown within him and that's all that's needed for the virus to begin its spread throughout mankind.[2] The transmission of the virus from chimpanzee to hunter was likely the one and only time this one strain of HIV passed across the species boundary, from chimp to human, and then successfully established itself to become the pandemic we still face today.

In the densely populated Leopoldville, where the ratio of men to women was high and prostitution rife, our hunter's virus was relatively easy to spread. Even more dangerously, the period from infection to death could be, and often was, some years before it compromised the immune system of its host, allowing it ample time to pass silently from the first human victim to the next. The prostitute the hunter spent the night with in Leopoldville, along with other prostitutes he visited on subsequent trips to the city, passed it on to their clients, who then returned home to their wives, girlfriends and partners, and so the fatal cycle slowly began.

2

For a decade after the events of 1908 the chain of infection of the virus was kept alive, though confined to the Congo. The disease that would develop from the virus would not explode as a notable outbreak for a number of decades and would require the perfect alignment of circumstances for the virus to spread rapidly.

That alignment started to occur during a series of well-intended but ill-fated medical campaigns in the Belgian Congo between 1921 and 1959. Colonial health authorities, determined to treat certain debilitating and often deadly tropical diseases such as sleeping sickness, were using, for the first time, mass-produced disposable syringes that enabled them to carry out systemic programmes.

Hypodermic syringes had been around since 1848 but even by the end of World War I they were still only handmade, their components of glass and metal shaped by skilled craftsmen, making them extremely rare. During one medical expedition to the upper Sangha river from 1917–19, the French doctor Eugène Jamot treated over 5,300 cases of sleeping sickness using only six syringes.[1]

It was in the 1920s that the mass manufacture of hypodermic syringes began and changed all that. This was crucial for medical teams working in Africa, particularly the Belgian Congo and neighbouring Cameroon, although resources were still scant – the syringes were not expendable – and sterilisation of the needles or syringes was virtually impossible.

These injection campaigns to combat sleeping sickness were the ideal circumstances for the spread of the virus that the young hunter had unwittingly brought to Leopoldville. The injections were carried out in the Belgian Congo by mobile teams with no formal education and a minimal amount of technical training, who visited patients in their villages to give them their monthly shots in order to treat the villagers, but also to protect the native workforce and colonial administrators. Such was the number of people they had to inject there was no time for boiling and sterilising each needle after use. They were simply rinsed quickly with water and alcohol before being used on the next patient.

Consequently, all too often the syringes retained small quantities of blood. Just the smallest amount of infected blood was all that was required to transmit the disease. Even after 1956, when disposable plastic syringes became available (these were invented by New Zealand pharmacist and veterinarian Colin Murdoch who wanted to develop a method of vaccination that eliminated the risks of infection) they were still likely to have been reused due to cost.

This practice continued unabated and led Jacques Pepin, a Canadian professor of microbiology, to propose in 2011 that the connection between the initial human source and the global pandemic of the virus was the hypodermic syringe.[2] He worked out that around 3.9m injections were given against sleeping sickness, and 74 per cent of these were administered intravenously – right into the vein, not into muscle. This intravenous method of delivery is not only the most direct way of getting a drug into the body it is also the best way to unintentionally transmit a blood-borne virus.[3] Also, before 1950, there were only two colonies in the sub-Sahara region of Africa who had blood transfusion programmes. One was Senegal, which started blood transfusion programmes in 1943, the other was the Belgian Congo, where rudimentary blood transfusion programmes had been in place since 1923 and were used specifically to treat infants with severe anaemia, primarily from malaria. Such was the fear of malaria that it appears the benefits of blood transfusions far outweighed the risk of infection from other diseases or blood-borne viruses such as human immunodeficiency virus (HIV).[4]

There are differing views; some experts doubt that needles were necessary in such a way for HIV to establish itself within humans, suggesting that sexual contact had been enough. But even they agree that injection campaigns, and to a lesser extent blood transfusion programmes, may have played a later role, certainly spreading the virus across Africa once it was established.

According to Pepin, however, it is the injections that might account for the intensification of HIV infections beyond a critical threshold; that is, the moment when the virus had been unintentionally injected into enough people to stop it from burning out naturally, a point whereupon sexual transmission would do the rest. And as travel grew within Africa, thanks to the development of road and rail, so rapid transmission throughout the continent was achieved. From the late 1930s to the early 1950s, the virus spread by rail and river to Mbuji-Mayi and Lubumbashi in the south and Kisangani in the north. At first, it was an infection confined to specific groups of people. But the virus soon broke out into the general population and spread, especially after the Belgian Congo achieved independence on 30th June 1960 and became known as the Democratic Republic of Congo. From here, the virus took hold and formed secondary reservoirs, whereupon it spread to countries in southern and eastern Africa and across the sub-Sahara with an unstoppable momentum.

And, before too long, it had spread to the rest of the world.

3

On 14th December 1908, the same year that the simian immuno-deficiency virus (SIV), which would go on to become HIV, passed from chimp to hunter in the Congo, a woman gave birth to a 6lb 4oz baby boy in a small Indian city to the north of Bombay. The child was named Bomi by his parents and was given the surname of Bulsara after the name of the city of his birth, Bulsar.

Bomi was born into a family of Parsees, a group of religious followers of the Iranian prophet Zoroaster. Meaning 'Persians', the Parsees emigrated to India from Iran to avoid brutal religious persecution by the Muslims in the eighth century and settled predominantly in Bombay and towns and villages to the north of the city.

Developing a flair for commerce, the Parsees were receptive of European influence in India and during the 19th century had become a wealthy community, thanks to Bombay's railway and shipbuilding industries. The Bulsars, however, were not from prosperous Bombay, but lived 120 miles to the north in the state of Gujarat. Here, for many locals, the only realistic source of income was harvesting mangos from the many orchards that dotted the landscape. Consequently, the Parsee community in Gujarat were far from wealthy and many young men from the region were forced to seek work elsewhere, not only in India, but further afield too.

Bomi, one of eight brothers, was no exception. Out of necessity and financial hardship, one by one he and his brothers left India and sailed almost 3,000 miles across the Indian Ocean to the exotically named Zanzibar seeking work.

Upon arrival, Bomi was fortunate and found work almost immediately with the British Government as a high court cashier in Stone Town, settling into life on the island quickly and comfortably, dedicating himself to his work and diligently and slowly building himself a privileged lifestyle. However, he desired a family to share his high standard of living, having arrived in Zanzibar unmarried and alone. Part of Bomi's job meant that he frequently had to travel throughout Zanzibar as well as returning often to India. During one of those return trips to his homeland he met Jer, a bespectacled and dainty young girl, 14 years his junior. It was love at first sight and they married shortly after in Bombay, whereupon Jer left her own family behind to follow her new husband westwards across the Indian Ocean back to Zanzibar, where they hoped to raise a family of their own.

The newlyweds lived in a two-storey apartment that was accessed by a flight of stairs from the busy Shangani Street in Stone Town on the western side of the island. Compared to other Zanzibaris, the Bulsaras enjoyed a high standard of living, with Bomi's salary enabling them to employ a domestic servant and even affording a small family car. Almost 60 years later, Jer Bulsara recalled it as being 'a comfortable life'.[1]

It was on Thursday, 5th September 1946, the Parsee New Year's Day, when the Bulsaras' first child was born at the Government Hospital in Stone Town. The boy, weighing almost seven pounds at birth, was given the name Farrokh Bulsara. One of Farrokh's cousins, Perviz Darukhanawalla, recalled her memories of him years later: 'When he was very young, a small child, very young, that is about three to four years old, when his mother used to go to work, she used to leave him with my mother because my mother was a housewife and because both his parents were working.'[2] Speaking to author Lesley-Ann Jones, Perviz remembered: 'He was so small, like a little pet. Even when he was a very young baby, he used to come to my home with his parents. They used to leave him with my mother and go out. When he was a bit older he would play about in our house. He was such a naughty little one. I was much older than him, and I liked taking care of him. He was such a small boy, a very nice child.'[3]

From the age of five, Farrokh attended the Zanzibar Missionary School, an establishment run by British nuns in Stone Town. Already, according to his mother, Jer, the young boy was showing an interest in music and performing: 'He used to love playing records all the time, and then sing – any sort of music, folk, classical, or Indian music.'[4] When his parents attended various functions or parties, it was always with little Farrokh in tow. It became an accepted routine that, at these parties, he would be asked to sing. Always eager to oblige, perhaps show off even, the small boy would burst into song eagerly and would feel so proud at being able to make everybody feel happy through his singing, even at that young age.

In 1952, Farrokh's sister, Kashmira, was born. 'He was six when I was born, so I only had a year of him, yet I was always aware of my proud older brother protecting me,' she remembers.[5] Why Kashmira only recalls a year of Farrokh is explained by the fact that, in February 1955, he was sent away to boarding school in India. On Valentine's Day of that year, shortly after undergoing the Naojote ceremony or Parsee cleansing ritual, which indoctrinated him into the Zoroastrian faith, Farrokh was enrolled in St Peter's School, an English-style boarding school in Panchgani, an educational facility that was founded in 1902 and established during the dying decades of the British Rule. The school was almost 3,000 miles from Zanzibar, and for the next few years, until 1963, Farrokh would only see his parents once a year, for a month-long period each summer when he returned home.

Farrokh's journey to his new school would begin with a voyage by sea from Zanzibar to Bombay with his parents. The ship would stop in Mombassa and the Seychelles before landing in India from where they travelled on to Bombay and then to Panchgani. For the next few years the school, with its motto of '*Ut Prosim*' ('That I May Serve') was to be Farrokh's home.

'I cried when we left him, but he just mingled with the other boys,' remembers Jer Bulsara, before continuing, 'He was quite happy and saw it as an adventure as some of our friends' children had gone there.'[6]

Whether the young Farrokh was really happy and whether he actually saw his new life at boarding school as an adventure is hard to judge. Any eight-year-old child being sent to school 3,000 miles away from their family could well find it hard to adjust to their new surroundings, not only at the beginning but possibly in later life as well. In his book, *The Making of Them: The British Attitude to Children and the Boarding School System* (Lone Arrow Press, 2000), author Nick Duffell claims that sending a child away to boarding school as young as eight is tantamount to child abuse. He says that he has received thousands of letters from people who 'feel they have been damaged by the experience of being sent away to board as a child. They cannot form bonds with others. Children need to be brought up in the company of people who love them. Teachers, however good they may be, cannot supply that love. Children of this age do not have the emotional intelligence or maturity to deal with this sense of loss. They develop what I call a "strategic survival" personality. On the outside, they are competent and confident. Inside they are private and insecure. For many, the insecurity affects the rest of their lives.'[7]

In later years, when Farrokh Bulsara had become Freddie Mercury, he rarely talked about his schooling and his time boarding in India during interviews. One of Freddie's best friends in his adult life was the singer and West End star Peter Straker, but even to him, Freddie rarely talked about his childhood. 'I have a feeling he didn't go into his childhood too much because he went to school in India and he didn't want to be considered Indian,' suggests Straker. 'Now it wouldn't matter, but at that time it was different. He used to say he was Persian. He liked the idea of being Persian, which I think is much more exotic whether you're a rock and roll star or a wrestler.'[8]

One of the few times Freddie spoke publicly about his schooling was in a 1974 interview. When asked about his school years, he was adamant: 'Have I got upper-class parents who put a lot of money into me? Was I spoilt? – No. My parents were very strict. I wasn't the only one, I've got a sister, I was at boarding school for nine years so I didn't see my parents that often. That background helped me a lot because it taught me to fend for myself.'[9]

In another interview on the subject of boarding school, also in 1974, Freddie would reinforce these views: 'My parents thought boarding school would do me good so they sent me to one when I was seven, dear. I look back on it and I think it was marvellous. You learn to look after yourself and it taught me to have responsibility.'[10]

Naturally, a boarding school environment can sometimes be associated with bullying and sexual abuse, and such actions can often shape the individual in their adult life. Jungian analyst, psychotherapist and supervisor Joy Schaverien PhD suggests that the psychological damage suffered particularly by boys at boarding school, primarily as a result of loss when family is replaced by many same-sex strangers, can have a dramatic effect on sexual development too. She writes: 'Warmth may be sought with the available other, as a new form of sibling group emerges. Sexual experiments may offer solace but may also lead to abuse. This may lead to confusion in development of sexual identity and some boys become uncertain of their primary sexual orientation. Whilst initiating the child into the pleasures of homosexuality the institution proclaims its dangers. This may set a person on a path of covert homosexuality or of proclaimed heterosexuality and emphatic disavowal of homosexuality.'[11]

Whether Farrokh experienced such sexual development at St Peter's is impossible to know, and we'll never know whether it influenced his sexual orientation. Freddie barely touched upon bullying and sexuality at boarding school in his interviews in later life, but he did comment very briefly upon abuse in school in an interview with *NME* in March 1974 when asked about brutish behaviour and homosexual goings-on: 'It's stupid to say there is no such thing in boarding school. All the things they say about them are more or less true. All the bullying and everything else. I've had the odd schoolmaster chasing me. It didn't shock me because somehow, boarding schools, you're not confronted by it, you are just slowly aware of it. It's going through life.' When asked if he was the pretty boy whom everyone wanted to lay, Freddie replied: 'Funnily enough, yes. Anybody goes through that. I was considered the arch poof.' And in response to the question, 'So how about being bent?' Freddie said: 'You're a crafty cow. Let's put it this way, there were times when I was young and green. It's a thing schoolboys go through. I've had my share of schoolboy pranks. I'm not going to elaborate further.'[12]

A former teacher at St Peter's during Farrokh's period there, Peter Patroa, who taught maths, recalls the signs of Freddie Mercury's homosexuality were already well known within the establishment. 'Homosexuality exists in any school,' Patroa said in 2008, 'And it certainly did in St Peter's at the time that Freddie was a student here. When he moved to Mumbai, he was apparently close to a boyfriend there. His father would have been informed and I'm sure was very disappointed. The family had a very rigid background going back generations, and Zoroastrians completely forbid homosexuality.'[13]

A Panchgani schoolmistress, Janet Smith, who resided at St Peter's because her mother taught Freddie art, was also convinced that signs of his homosexuality were evident early on: 'It was obvious that Freddie was different from the other boys. He would run around calling everyone "darling" and he often got over-excited. At that time we didn't understand being gay. I once asked my mother why he was like that and she just told me that some people are different.'[14]

During his early terms at the school, Farrokh was terribly shy, being especially self-conscious about his prominent upper teeth caused by four extra teeth at the back of his mouth that gave him a pronounced overbite. His fellow pupils gave him the nickname 'Bucky'. However, soon he was to adopt another name when the teachers began calling him 'Freddie' as an affectionate term. He seized on this name instantly and from that moment on Farrokh Bulsara became Freddie Bulsara.

Despite being so far away from his parents, Freddie soon got over his homesickness and immersed himself in school activities, particularly sport. 'The school had a very strong emphasis on sport and I ended up doing every single one of them. I did boxing, cricket and table tennis, which I was really good at,' Mercury would later recall.[15] He was also reasonably good at sprinting and hockey, sports of which his mother approved far more than boxing. 'Freddie was excellent at all sports, but when I heard about the boxing, I wrote to him from Zanzibar, where we were living, and told him to stop that. I didn't like the idea, it was too violent,' she remembered.[16]

Eleven-year-old Freddie won the school sports trophy for Junior All Rounder in 1958. Incredibly proud of his achievements, he wrote home to inform his parents:

Dear Mum & Dad, I hope you are all well and Kashmira's cold is better. Don't worry, I'm fine. Me and my friends at the Ashleigh House are like a second family. The teachers are very strict and discipline is most important here at St. Peter's. I'm very happy to tell you that I was awarded the big trophy, Best All Rounder Junior. I received a big trophy and they even took a photograph, which will appear in the annual school magazine. I'm very proud and I hope you are too. Send my love to Kash. I love my little sister as I love you all. Farrokh.[17]

Despite being good at sports, Freddie was increasingly attracted to subjects such as art and literature and, of course, music. He had already been introduced to music – predominantly opera – by his parents in Zanzibar but he had also developed a taste for Western pop, especially the piano-based rock'n'roll sounds of artists such as Little Richard and Fats Domino. While at St Peter's, during which time he joined the school choir and took part in a number of theatrical productions, Freddie also encountered the recordings of Lata Mangeshkar, one of India's best-known and most respected playback singers. Playback singers recorded songs for movie soundtracks for the actors and actress to lip-sync to and Freddie became fascinated with Mangeshkar, attending one of her concerts in Bombay in November 1959. Two years later, she visited St Peter's School and performed at the summer fête in front of Freddie and the other pupils.

In terms of Freddie's own singing, it was his maternal aunt, Sheroo Khory, who first became properly aware of his natural musical gift. 'Once, when I think he was nine years old,' she remembered, 'Freddie used to come running up for breakfast and the radio was on and then, when the music was finished, he went to the [piano] stool and played the tune. I [thought I] must get him some music lessons. He's got an ear for music.'[18] She persuaded his parents to pay for private musical tuition and he subsequently managed to pass his Grade 5 exams in practical and theory, being presented with his Certificate on 7th November 1958 at St Peter's School annual speech day and prize giving. 'I took piano lessons at school,' Freddie would later recall, 'And really enjoyed it. That was my mother's doing. She made sure I stuck at it.'[19]

In 1958, Freddie formed his first band. By then he had developed a close friendship with four other pupils at St Peter's: Bruce Murray, Farang Irani, Derrick Branche and Victory Rana. All fans of Elvis Presley, the five of them decided to form a band and used the art room at St Peter's as a rehearsal studio. Under the name of The Hectics they began thumping out their own rudimentary version of rock'n'roll. For someone who was later to become one of music's most expressive and flamboyant performers, Freddie's role in the fledging band was very much in the background, playing his style of boogie-woogie piano and providing backing vocals while Bruce Murray took on the role of lead singer.

'All we really wanted to do was to impress the girls in the neighbouring girls' school,' Murray recalled. 'We sang hits like "Tutti Frutti", "Yakkety Yak" and "Whole Lotta Lovin". Freddie was an amazing musician. He could play just about anything. And he had the knack of listening to a song on the radio once and being able to play it. The rest of us just made a godawful racket, with cheap guitars, a drum and an old tea chest that we'd converted into a bass with one string. But the band served its intended purpose: the girls really loved us.'[20]

The Hectics, dressed in their rock'n'roll uniform of white shirt, black tie, pleated trousers and perfectly greased hair, soon became star attractions at any school function and also became popular with Panchgani's inhabitants, where they were known as 'The Heretics' because they were so different and so extreme for the time. But when Freddie left Panchgani and St Peter's School on 25th February 1963, having failed his Class 10 examinations, The Hectics were no more and instead he returned to Zanzibar and an uncertain future.

4

Back in Zanzibar and living with his parents, Freddie enrolled at school in Stone Town in an attempt to finish off his education while constantly trying to gather anything connected with pop culture that might somehow find its way onto the island. The Western world, with its music and fashion, was a constant attraction to the teenage Freddie Bulsara, a fact his mother, Jer, was all too aware of: 'He really wanted to come to England. Being a teenager he was aware of these things in Western countries and it attracted him.'[1] Living at home and still in full-time education in the early 1960s, there seemed little prospect of him following his dreams and travelling to England. But significant events were about to cause a massive upheaval in Zanzibar and would ultimately lead to the entire Bulsara family, with their very lives in peril, upping sticks and fleeing to the UK.

At the beginning of the 1960s, Zanzibar had a tremendously varied cultural heritage based upon the extensive ethnic diversity of its population. Over the centuries, trade from Africa, Asia and the Middle East had converged upon Zanzibar, bringing a multitude of influences. Now, in the early part of the decade, tension between ethnic groups was beginning to rise as a result of the Arab population, despite being less than 20 per cent of Zanzibar's population, being dominant both economically and politically. In 1963, when Britain granted Zanzibar independence an election followed which pitted the Afro-Shirazi Party (ASP) against Sultan Jamshid bin Abdullah's Zanzibar Nationalist Party (ZNP). The ZNP were victorious in the election with 54 per cent of the vote, but this only increased feelings of resentment within the black population and a coup led by self-appointed Field Marshal John Okello soon followed. Okello believed he was divinely chosen by God to remove Arabs from power and, on 12th January 1964, with popular support from Zanzibar's oppressed African majority, the revolutionaries fought their way towards Stone Town.

The Bulsaras were still living in their apartment in Stone Town at the time and were all too aware of Okello and his revolutionaries murdering and plundering their way across Zanzibar. It appeared no Arab or Asian was safe. Jer Bulsara remembers this period: 'It was really frightening. And everybody was rushing around and didn't know what to do exactly. And because we had young children, we had to decide too, we had to leave the country.'[2]

Fitting whatever possessions they could carry in two suitcases, the family fled Zanzibar. They could have travelled to India but, owing to the fact that Freddie's father, Bomi Bulsara, had a British passport and that he had worked for the British government in Zanzibar, they chose to fly to England. In May 1964, Bomi, Jer, Freddie and his younger sister Kashmira arrived at Heathrow Airport.

They settled into a four-bedroom house at 22 Gladstone Avenue, Feltham – a suburban town in the west London Borough of Hounslow, directly beneath the Heathrow flight path. Freddie was extremely excited to have finally made it to London, but for his parents, life was tough. They were used to a privileged life in Zanzibar with domestic servants, not to mention the tropical weather. Now they existed under the drab grey London skies with the incessant din of aircraft flying overhead. And Britain itself was not the most welcoming of places towards immigrants in the early 1960s.

Since the late 1940s onwards, the Black and Asian population in Britain had increased through migration from the Caribbean as well as India, Pakistan and Bangladesh. A tide of resentment was beginning to grow and race and immigration had become major domestic political issues. In the summer of 1958 there had been a vicious outbreak of anti-black rioting in London's Notting Hill during which a young black man, 32-year-old Kelso Cochrane, was murdered, and in 1964, the year of the Bulsaras' arrival in the UK, that year's General Election featured the notorious Smethwick by-election in which race became a divisive issue, so much so that a British branch of the Ku Klux Klan was formed later in the year. Against such a tense background, Bomi and Jer Bulsara opted to keep their heads down and simply provide for their family as best they could while they created new lives for themselves in the UK. Finding the cost of living much higher than they had been used to, both parents had to take a job. Bomi found employment as an accountant for a local catering company, while Jer went to work in the local Marks & Spencer store.

For Freddie Bulsara, approaching his 18th birthday, the excitement of finally being in England was tempered by the fact that his life was at something of a crossroads. His education in India and Zanzibar had been a failure but he was keen to revive his studies in London at a local art school. But it wasn't what his parents wanted for him – they were keen he should follow a more established and watertight career. 'He knew we wanted him to be a lawyer or an accountant or something like that, because most of his cousins were,' Jer Bulsara explains. 'But he'd say, "I'm not that clever, Mum. I'm not that clever."'[3] To be seen to be doing something, Freddie would fill out job application forms, but deep inside he hoped they would be unsuccessful.

His desire to go to art school wasn't so much a passion to study painting, sculpture or textiles but a determination to follow a path that many English pop stars had previously trod. While in Zanzibar he had read in the few Western magazines to reach the island that it was almost de rigueur for wannabe pop stars to attend art school first, and he had his heart set on Ealing Technical College & School of Art, as its famous alumni included Ronnie Wood, Roger Ruskin Spear and Pete Townshend. 'He used to talk about that,' his mother, Jer, remembers, 'that so many people from art college had done music, pop music, and I didn't take much notice of that at that time thinking, well, it's one of those things, let us see.'[4]

But Freddie's lack of educational success in India and Zanzibar meant he didn't have the required qualifications to be accepted at Ealing. The only option available to him was to attend a foundation course at another educational establishment. Thirty-five minutes away by bus from Freddie's Feltham home was Isleworth Polytechnic, where in September 1964, he began an arts foundation course. Here, he hoped to get the A-levels he needed to get into Ealing.

Although he was not yet where he wanted to be, Freddie Bulsara had arrived in London. And at just the right time. It was the era of The Beatles, The Kinks and The Rolling Stones, of Mods and Rockers clashing at seaside resorts, of Radio Caroline broadcasting from UK territorial waters, and *Top of the Pops* had just begun on BBC TV. For the first time, Freddie felt he belonged, and he was determined to make the most of the opportunity fate had dealt him.

Little did he know that also living in Feltham, just a few streets away from the Bulsara family, was a 17-year-old physics student. This teenager was a keen guitarist but unable to afford the much-coveted Fender Stratocaster that he so desired. The only solution was to build one himself. So, over the next 18 months with the help of his father, he built an electric guitar to precise specifications.

A few years later, Freddie would be introduced to this teenage guitar wizard during a random meeting in London. It would prove a pivotal moment in music. The life of Freddie Bulsara and the course of pop history would never be the same again, as the foundations of Queen were laid during that very first encounter.

At around the time that the Bulsara family was fleeing Zanzibar for their new lives in London, HIV was beginning its own migration across the world.

For decades, ever since the initial jump of the virus from a chimpanzee to a human sometime around 1908, it had remained, by and large, contained within the Republic of Congo. The country had been granted independence from Belgium in June 1960 and then dispensed with the name of the Belgian Congo. In fact, the year in which Belgium ceded interest and governorship in the region has been identified as a crucial and pivotal mid-century moment of divergence in the spread of HIV globally.

It was the very ambition to develop the west of Africa by the great Western powers that, ultimately, created this situation and provided the routes for HIV to spread beyond the 'Dark Continent'. The desire to plunder the Congo region for its ivory, rubber and diamonds, and the subsequent railway network created to service such intensive industrialisation, produced the perfect environment for the virus to spread. Kinshasa (formerly Leopoldville) rapidly became the best connected of all African cities and, as such, was the perfect conduit from which HIV could spread rapidly. By 1948 over a million people were passing through Kinshasa on the railways every year and this unwittingly enabled HIV-1 to be transmitted throughout the country. At some point between the end of the 1930s and the early 1950s, the virus had spread from its epicentre.

Signs of the virus reaching out were there for all to see, but no one would know what they were looking at, or what they were looking for. As early as the 1930s, Dr Leon Pales, a French military doctor, spent some time observing the soaring death rates among men constructing the Congo-Ocean railway. After conducting autopsies he found in 26 of the deceased workers a wasting condition he named *Mayombe cachexia*. This condition, named after the stretch of the jungle where the men had died, resulted in atrophied brains, swollen bowel lymph nodes and a number of other symptoms that would later become synonymous with HIV. But, during the 1930s, it was simply another unidentified tropical malais.

Therefore, HIV was able to spread extremely quickly across the Democratic Republic of Congo, a country the size of Western Europe, as a result of the railway network and, to a lesser extent, the waterways. The changing sexual habits of the country's population, in particular the rise in the sex trade, also contributed greatly in enabling the virus to become a pandemic. The social changes surrounding independence in 1960 also contributed; a study by Dr Nuno Faria of Oxford University's Department of Zoology states that this year 'saw the virus "break out" from small groups of infected people to infect the wider population and eventually the world'.[1]

As well as medicine and the creation of infrastructure, there remained the most effective method of the virus being transmitted: sex. The sex trade in the Democratic Republic of Congo flourished as a consequence of the building of roads and railways and the increase in industry within the region. The construction workers, miners and administrators who flooded into the region to seek employment were predominantly male (they outnumbered women in the city of Kinshasa by two to one) and they sought out the prostitutes who, taking on a large number of clients and practising unsafe sex, were all unknowingly complicit in helping the virus take hold in the city. From here the virus would spread to neighbouring regions via the very roads and railways these construction workers were building. A study in the journal *Science* suggests that, because of the medical programmes and this increased sex trade, HIV spread from Kinshasa rapidly as infected individuals travelled along their newly constructed railways and roads and even the old waterways. By 1937, HIV had spread four miles from Kinshasa to the nearby city of Brazzaville; by 1946 it had reached Bwamanda, 583 miles away; and by 1953 it had reached Kisangani, over 720 miles from Kinshasa. The authors of the study claim that, by 1960, the spread of the virus had become exponential in West Africa, although no one realised it.[2] How many Africans died of the disease can only be speculated – perhaps, over 80 years, as many as 200m?

Then, sometime in the mid-1960s, HIV crossed the Atlantic and landed in Haiti. The catalyst for this transmission of HIV was yet another goodwill gesture, one that backfired spectacularly. Once independence was granted to the Democratic Republic of Congo in 1960, most – if not all – of the Belgian officials made a hasty retreat from the region, leaving a critical vacuum at the heart of the newborn Republic.

To fill this void UNESCO shipped thousands of Haitian teachers and technocrats to Africa, specifically the Democratic Republic of Congo. A large proportion of these were based in Kinshasa. Ideal recruits to step into the shoes vacated by the Belgians, they were French-speaking, well-educated, black, and more than happy to desert Haiti and the brutal dictatorship of 'Papa Doc' François Duvalier. They spent weeks, months or years working in West Africa, in countries such as the Democratic Republic of Congo, Angola and Cameroon before returning to their homeland. It was when these professionals arrived back home, sometime around 1964, that the HIV-1 subtype reached Haiti.

This timescale corresponds precisely with the thousands of Haitians who went to Africa in 1960 to work and who returned during the mid-to late-1960s and early 1970s once Zaire (the Democratic Republic of Congo had renamed itself Zaire in 1971) had completed the training of local national managers. En masse, Haitians began to leave central Africa after 1968, although many had already returned home. In 1998, J.F. Molez wrote a paper for the *American Journal of Tropical* medicine which states: 'Medical investigations made in Haiti from 1985 to 1988 and clinical observations reported the deaths of retired Haitian managers who had lived and worked in Zaire and then returned to Haiti (and had lived there for a period of 10–15 years) that were suspected to be due to AIDS'. Given the length of time from infection of HIV to death from AIDS in the 1980s was seven to ten years, these dates align perfectly with the theory that Haiti was suffering an AIDS epidemic of its own around 1970 following the return of its workers from Zaire during the late-1960s.

But it wasn't just sexual intercourse in Haiti – be it heterosexual or homosexual – that led to the virus spreading there. Something else was happening in Haiti's capital that exacerbated the problem, a problem no one knew existed at the time, of course. Dr Jacques Pepin claims another of the factors in the rapid expansion of HIV in Haiti was a plasma centre in Port-au-Prince. It only operated for two years, 1971 and 1972, but was known to have low hygiene standards. During those years, impoverished Haitians were being encouraged to sell their blood plasma to the US for derisory sums as America was in desperate need of plasma for transfusions, as well as for the protein elements it contains, such as gamma globulin to inoculate against hepatitis. The US was, apparently, unable to meet its own demand for plasma because there were not enough healthy donors willing to give blood. Part of the reason for this was that most Americans were affluent enough not to be attracted to donate blood whereas the poverty-stricken Haitians were more than willing to sign up for $3 per donation.

A company called Hemo-Caribbean negotiated a ten-year contract with the Haitian Government's Minister of Interior, Luckner Cambronne, leader of the feared Tonton Macoutes secret police and nicknamed the 'Vampire of the Caribbean'.[3] Hemo-Caribbean used a relatively new procedure, which involved the donor giving a litre of blood, from which the amber plasma was harvested out, and then the blood pumped back into the person who donated it. All this for a payment of $3, which could be boosted to $5, if the donor was willing to have a tetanus vaccination, which made their plasma more valuable because additional tetanus shots could then be harvested from the plasma. After this, their own blood was pumped back into them, meaning they could then go back and donate again and again in quick succession without becoming anaemic.

There was a catastrophic problem with this, however, which was that the blood of countless donors was inadvertently mixed together in the plasmapheresis machine before being pumped back into them, thus infecting potentially every donor – and therefore recipient – with any blood-borne virus the donors might be carrying... such as HIV.

But Hemo-Caribbean seemed perfectly happy with the manner in which the plasma was collected. In an interview with the *New York Times* on 28th January 1972, Joseph B. Gorinstein said of his procedures, with a somewhat chilling nonchalance, that the plasma his company processed was 'a hell of a lot cleaner than that which comes from the slums of some American cities'.

It wasn't until later in 1972 that President Richard Nixon asked for an investigation into the blood business in the US, but by that point, with no screening for HIV because it wasn't on anyone's radar, the virus was already circulating around Haiti and, most probably, it had already entered the US either in the infected plasma or via a single infected immigrant who had arrived in a large city such as New York or, more likely, Miami only 700 miles away.

This single migration of HIV from Haiti to the US is called the 'pandemic clade' by investigators and represents a key turning point in the history of the AIDS pandemic. It is called a single migration only when it successfully establishes itself. Individuals with HIV may have crossed into the US and infected several people but the lineage of infection burnt out. The single successful event is estimated to have happened between 1969 and 1972. This would fit the subsequent epidemiology of HIV in the US, as the first cases of AIDS were reported roughly ten years after HIV is thought to have entered the country from Haiti, the precise interval between infection with HIV followed by progression to AIDS and subsequent death.[4] Just as it had before in the Congo, in the decades before mass travel (and colonial medical programmes using a hollow-bore needle), the virus would remain lurking for almost ten years before anyone noticed it.

The death of a teenage boy in St Louis in 1969 of an unspecified illness baffled doctors at Washington University, and suggested to some that the AIDS virus might have already been in the US several times before the epidemic of the 1980s kicked off. The 15-year-old African-American named only as Robert R., but subsequently identified as Robert Rayford, presented himself to a clinic in 1968 suffering from an assortment of ailments including swollen lymph nodes, swelling of the legs, lower torso and genitalia. For 15 months he was treated in three different hospitals but became increasingly exhausted, lost a dramatic amount of weight, and suffered severe chlamydia. None of those treating him in any of the hospitals could diagnose his illness. Eventually he died of bronchial pneumonia and an autopsy found he had Kaposi's sarcoma (KS) lesions throughout the soft tissues of his body, a hallmark we later became aware of AIDS infection.

It wasn't until 1986 that doctors were able to perform specific tests on tissue samples from Robert Rayford. Two tests were conducted:

blot tests of his serum, a precise test for AIDS virus antibodies, and also a test for the P24 antigen, a virus protein that gives further evidence of infection. Both tests came back positive but, crucially, it wasn't the strain that became known in the late 1970s and which spread AIDS worldwide. Doctors remained baffled. Rayford had never had a blood transfusion, didn't do drugs, had never left the area and no other cases had been reported in his vicinity. The general conclusion was that there must have been several different strains of HIV at low level already making incursions into different countries, including the US, and at some point one of these strains became established and spread the pandemic. It is possible that, as in Africa, other people in the US did have HIV and died from it at a much earlier date but that no one had ever connected these deaths to AIDS because no one was looking for a virus they didn't know existed.[5]

Most of the evidence points to the fact that, although various strains of HIV might have already been in existence in the US or, indeed, other parts of the world before the 1970s, the most likely route is that the deadly HIV-1 came to America from Haiti via one migration between 1969 and 1972 and established a foothold within the country then subsequently spread imperceptibly. In the ensuing years, the virus followed certain paths of chance and opportunity in certain subcategories of the American population.

'The virus reached hemophiliacs through the blood supply. It reached drug addicts through shared needles. It reached gay men – reached deeply and devastatingly into their circles of love and acquaintance – by sexual transmission,' suggested David Quammen.[6]

For a dozen years or so it travelled quietly from person to person. Symptoms were slow to arise; death lagged some distance behind. No one knew the cause, and no one associated the deaths.

At some point in the 1970s, someone would give the virus to a Canadian airline steward called Gaëtan Dugas. Then someone would pass it on to the Hollywood actor Rock Hudson.

And just over a decade after it arrived from Haiti, someone else would give it to Freddie Mercury.

On 24th May 2006 at Bonhams auction house in London, a three-minute reel of Super-8mm film came up for auction that attracted a considerable amount of global interest. Lot 474 dated from around 1965 and was significant as it featured rare and unpublished film footage of Freddie Bulsara at Isleworth Polytechnic.

The silent film, shot by one of Freddie's friends, Brian Fanning, shows a group of six young men walking towards or away from the camera, standing in staged positions, and sitting on a park bench smoking or gesticulating towards the sky with their arms. Being silent adds to the eeriness. Dressed in a wine red blazer and white shirt with blue trousers, Freddie is conspicuous by his obvious shyness. Not once does he smile, leading one to speculate his protruding teeth are making him incredibly self-conscious. There is no sign of the showman he is set to become in later life although already his movements and gestures indicate a whimsical nature and an element of camp, particularly when he buries his chin in his shoulder with an embarrassed grin after unravelling his hands theatrically skywards.

Freddie attended the Polytechnic from 1964 to 1966 and in terms of getting him into Ealing School of Art it certainly served its purpose. He had already gained three O-levels in art, history and English and now had the crucial A-level in Art & Fashion. But it offered him more than just that: it gave him a greater exposure to fashion, to films, to the English pop culture of the time and, of course, to music.

The mid-1960s was a turning point for popular culture in the UK. At this time Britain's baby boomers were coming of age and pop culture, art and politics came together to seismically change British society from the bottom up. For the first time, creativity looked to the masses rather than to the higher echelons for validation. The Beatles were showing how pop could be both art and extraordinarily popular at the same time, as well as introducing regional accents to the masses. Films such as *Darling*, *The Knack... and How to Get It*, and Roman Polanski's *Repulsion* starring Catherine Deneuve were redefining British cinema while documentaries like *The War Game* literally blew audiences away with its depiction of the horrors of a nuclear attack. In the world of theatre Frank Marcus' *The Killing of Sister George* opened in London, one of the first British mainstream plays with lesbian characters, and Dirk Bogarde's film *Victim* – notable in film history for being the first English language film to use the word 'homosexual' – also played.

Victim became a highly sociologically significant film as it played an influential role in liberalising attitudes (as well as the laws in Britain). Four years later, Lord Arran proposed the decriminalisation of male homosexual acts, which ultimately led, in 1965, to MP Leo Abse introducing the Sexual Offences Bill. When passed two years later as the Sexual Offences Act, homosexual acts between two men over the age of 21 in private in England and Wales were finally decriminalised. And, if that wasn't enough, 1965 also saw theatre critic Kenneth Tynan spark outrage by uttering the word 'fuck' on BBC1 TV.

Studying at Isleworth Polytechnic and living in London during the Swinging Sixties proved vital to the transition of Freddie Bulsara into Freddie Mercury. He had arrived at just the right time. Bulsara observed and absorbed what was going on around him and, like a magpie, stole that which shone from music, film, dance and fashion. Storing these elements up for future use, he would adapt them into his own music, style and look in the decades that followed. Of course he wasn't the only one doing so, but he was unique in that while others were stealing or borrowing from the blues or skiffle or rock'n'roll, Freddie was stealing from Puccini, Porter and Presley. It was this culturally cluttered mix that would combine in his compositions to create something extraordinary.

But that was all in the future. For now, in 1965, it was taking a while for him to adapt and find his feet. One of his closest friends at Isleworth Polytechnic, Adrian Morrish, recalls how Freddie stood out from early on: 'He dressed weirdly in drainpipe trousers that weren't quite long enough and middle-aged jackets that were slightly too small. I suppose he'd brought those clothes with him from Zanzibar or India. He seemed very gauche, but he desperately wanted to fit in.'[1] His sister, Kashmira, also remembers Freddie's early – and distinct – lack of style: 'Freddie stood out against other boys of his age because at that time the fashion for hairstyles was [the] long and shaggy look, but when we arrived Freddie had that very old-fashioned Cliff Richard look, very shiny, the hair going backwards, standing up, that kind of look, so wherever we would go out together, or come home from a bus stop or something, I'd like to walk behind him because I didn't want people to think I was with him.'[2]

Freddie's determination to 'fit in' led him to join the Polytechnic's youth choir and theatre group and he appeared in a couple of productions, *The Kitchen* and *Spectrum*. But music was still his main passion and he grew restless trying to find an outlet for his musical creativity.

During evenings and weekends he would sometimes join his friends at local pubs, where they'd watch bands and singers such as Rod Stewart and Long John Baldry and occasionally go on to parties afterwards, although Freddie drank little and frequently left early. There appeared little sign of the man who, decades later, would host some of the most outrageous parties in the history of rock'n'roll and though none of his Polytechnic friends recall Freddie having girlfriends during his time at Isleworth, neither do they remember any explicit indication of him being gay. He simply attended his classes, fooled around a little with his friends, earned a bit of extra cash in menial jobs such as washing pots at Heathrow Airport or stacking crates on a nearby industrial estate, and was even paid £5 per session as a nude life model.

By the time he left Isleworth Polytechnic in 1966 Freddie had grown in confidence and he felt more at home in England. Furthermore, his dress sense had improved considerably and he had swapped the outdated clothes he had brought with him from Zanzibar and begun dressing in the more bohemian look of 1960s London. Finally, Freddie Bulsara was beginning to fit in.

In September 1966, enrolling at Ealing School of Art to study a course in fashion design was everything Freddie had dreamed about: the chance to study art and to follow in the footsteps of rock musicians and pop stars who had done the same thing. What's more, he was in London at the height of its cultural power and relevance. What more could he want?

After a while the daily commute from Feltham to Ealing proved to be a drag to Freddie, so he started crashing on the floor of Chris Smith's flat, a college friend who rented a property at 42b Addison

Gardens, Kensington. Despite following his dream, it wasn't long before he became disenchanted with the course at Ealing, where he spent his time studying fabric printing and textile design, and he was already looking at alternatives. But, most of all, Freddie was desperate to follow his musical ambitions. This only intensified on 16th December 1966 when the BBC TV show, *Ready Steady Go!* transmitted the first British television performance by American guitarist Jimi Hendrix. Performing 'Hey Joe', Hendrix announced himself spectacularly with his virtuoso playing style and energetic and wild stage persona. Freddie found himself captivated by everything about Hendrix's performance: the music, the fashion, the hair, and, above all, his command of the stage as an artist.

So captivated was he by Hendrix that Freddie went to see him perform 14 times, including nine nights in a row at pubs all around London. 'I would scour the country to see him whenever he played because he really had everything any rock'n'roll star should have: all the style and the presence,' Freddie would later say. 'He didn't have to force anything. He'd just make an entrance and the whole place would be on fire. He was living out everything I wanted to be.'[3]

Hendrix was less than four years older than Freddie and provided him with the spark to follow his dream. Determined to be a star, Freddie had already started writing songs at home as his mother, Jer, recalls: 'He would write songs from an early age. I kept on saying, as all mothers do, carry on with your studies and clean up your bedroom. Once when I went into his bedroom at our home in Feltham. I told him I was going to clear up all the rubbish including the papers under his pillow. But he said "Don't you dare." He was writing little songs and lyrics then and putting them under his pillow before he slept. It was more music than studying and my husband said he didn't understand what this boy was going to do.'[4]

Freddie knew exactly what he wanted to do, but he needed like-minded musicians around him and, unable to find anyone who shared his passion, ambition and raw talent, he consoled himself by using his time in class to draw images of his idol that he would plaster over his bedroom walls. 'He was a great artist, you know, line drawing, pencil. He had this whole catalogue of stuff. Hendrix, he did a lot of pictures of Hendrix that were brilliant,' remembers one of his college friends at the time, John Taylor.[5]

Sometime between 1967 and 1968, Freddie was asked to leave the fashion design course at Ealing by its principal, James Drew, owing primarily to the fact that he was spending too much time away from college (in part watching Jimi Hendrix) rather than undertaking his studies. Incredibly, he managed to persuade the principal to let him switch courses rather than kick him out and consequently Freddie found himself on the graphics course. It was on this course that he encountered three students who shared his interest in music; as well as Chris Smith – who Freddie already knew – there was Nigel Foster and, perhaps most importantly, Tim Staffell.

Staffell was a more than able musician. He had taken up the harmonica in the early 1960s before moving on to the guitar and then finally settling on the bass guitar as his instrument of choice. One evening in 1964, he was playing harmonica in the wings for a band called Chris & The Whirlwinds at Murray Park in Whitton. In the audience that night was young bass player and a young guitarist who also happened to attend Hampton Grammar School and who had just formed their own band called 1984. The bass player was Dave Dilloway; the young guitarist was the boy from Feltham who had built his own guitar with the help of his father in a workshop. His name was Brian May.

Following the concert, Dilloway and May tracked down Staffell and persuaded him to join their new band as singer and harmonica player and, on 28th October 1964, with Tim Staffell now in the band, 1984 played their first ever gig at St Mary's Church Hall in Twickenham. By 1967, when Freddie Bulsara became friends with Staffell, 1984 had been gigging consistently around London and had even recorded a number of songs at Thames Television Studios. The band also supported Jimi Hendrix on 13th May 1967 when he played at Imperial College London, a concert that, conceivably, Freddie himself attended as an audience member.

Once he had switched courses at Ealing, Freddie quickly fell in with Staffell and the other musically inspired students. 'My first impressions of Freddie were that he was quite straight culturally. That's to say, conservative – I didn't even think about his sexuality. You wouldn't have described him as being at all "in your face". He had a fair degree of humility. Freddie didn't particularly shine. Having said that, though, he was intuitively a performer and his persona was, even then, rapidly developing. As far as being a star was concerned, I personally think he was already in the ascendant. People responded to him,' Staffell remembers.[6]

During the winter of 1967, Staffell's friends were introduced to the band he was fronting, 1984, and Freddie and Chris Smith became regulars in the audience whenever and wherever they played across London. According to Smith, it was fairly obvious that Staffell and May were clearly head and shoulders above the rest of the band in terms of talent. It was to be a prophetic observation as, early in 1968, Brian May abruptly left the band because he wanted to be in a group that performed their own material rather than cover versions and also because he had to devote more time to his studies – he had enrolled at Imperial College in 1965 to study physics and infra-red astronomy, having left Hampton Grammar School with ten O-levels and four A-levels. However, May kept in touch with Staffell after 1984 had split and a few months later they were to join forces again.

In the meantime, when he wasn't living like a gypsy on the floor of Chris Smith's Kensington flat, Freddie continued to compose basic songs or lyrics in the bedroom of his parents' home in Feltham, study at Ealing, and follow Jimi Hendrix around feverishly whenever he could. 'I think Hendrix represented something to him, a goal that he could achieve himself,' suggests Tim Staffell.[7]

But, in 1968, despite the influence of Hendrix, there was still little sign of the flamboyant character Freddie Bulsara would one day become, as classmate John Hibbert remembers: 'With hindsight, looking back you'd think he must have stood out, he must have been the leader of the gang, and he wasn't really, because his nature was actually very kind and gentle and actually relatively quiet.'[8]

Still desperate to get into music somehow, Freddie, for the time being, could only hang onto his friends' coat-tails, so he was fortunate that one of his closest friends at the time, Tim Staffell, was about to form another band.

Staffell and Brian May remained keen to pursue their own musical ambitions after the demise of their previous group, 1984, and, in the autumn term of 1968, May met up with Staffell, who was still at Ealing School of Art, and they decided to form another band. Staffell would provide vocals and play bass while May would play guitar. They needed a drummer to form the musical trio of bass, guitar and drums that was totally in vogue mid-1968, thanks to the popularity of The Jimi Hendrix Experience. So, with that in mind, they posted an advert on the noticeboard at Imperial College, where May was studying, requesting applications for a 'Mitch Mitchell/Ginger Baker type drummer' to join a new band.

The advert was spotted by a number of drummers who all applied; however, none of them were up to the required standard. But fate was to intervene. Passing the noticeboard one day was Imperial College student Les Brown. 'As I remember, the first day back at Imperial College I went to the Student Union Bar, saw the "Drummer Wanted" ad written in hand by Brian, and brought it straight back to the flat,' he recalls.[9]

He wasn't a drummer himself. But his flatmate, Roger Taylor, was.

Roger Taylor had a passion for music from an early age, forming his first skiffle band, The Bubbling-over Boys, while still at primary school. By the age of 12 Taylor had been given his first rudimentary drum kit and would practise diligently in the garage of the family home on the outskirts of Truro, Cornwall. In 1965 he joined a band that was to become known, eventually, as The Reaction, and over the next few years they became well established throughout the Cornish music scene. Despite their provincial success, The Reaction split up in the summer of 1968 and two weeks later, Roger Taylor shared a lift to London in Les Brown's purple Triumph Herald to begin his studies in dentistry at the Royal London Hospital Medical and Dental School.

'I came to London to go to college to meet other people, to be in a band and that was my plan and the college was a way of getting to London and meeting like-minded people,' Taylor recalls.[1]

Roger and Les lived together in a rented ground-floor flat at 19 Sinclair Gardens in Shepherd's Bush and it was to this flat that Les returned one evening with Brian May's advert for a drummer. Roger applied immediately and soon Brian May and Tim Staffell were heading over to his flat with their acoustic guitars for an audition. The three of them struck up an immediate friendship, Roger was hired, and soon afterwards they began rehearsing properly at Imperial College.

'I remember being flabbergasted when Roger set his kit up at Imperial College,' recalls May. 'Just the sound of him tuning his drums was better than I had heard from anyone before. It was amazing.'[2]

The band needed a name. They settled on Smile, suggested by Staffell, and began rehearsing intensively. Not content with playing cover versions, the band, specifically May and Staffell, began composing their own songs too.

The three of them continued with their studies during the day and spent whatever other spare time they could find rehearsing or discussing music. As a result, Taylor's flat in Shepherd's Bush became a frequent meeting place and crash-pad for members of the band and their entourage, which included Freddie Bulsara, who was there by association with his friend and classmate, Staffell. Freddie immediately struck up a friendship with Roger Taylor, which was ignited by their shared passion for Jimi Hendrix, and he became a regular hanger-on at Smile gigs, the first of which was at Imperial College on 26th October 1968 when they supported Pink Floyd.

In February 1969, Smile played their second major gig at Richmond Athletic Club and just a couple of weeks later, played their third major concert (though not the main attraction by any means), which just happened to be at the Royal Albert Hall and was a charity concert for Imperial College. It resulted in Smile's first ever review in which a *Times* journalist referred to them as 'the loudest group in the Western world'.

Following a short tour of Cornwall, Tim Staffell took Freddie along to one of their London rehearsals. 'He came over with Tim one day,' recalls Roger Taylor, 'and he just became one of the circle. He was full of enthusiasm – long, black flowing hair and this great dandy image.'[3]

Freddie immediately liked their sound and started to regularly attend gigs, even taking it upon himself to offer advice, whether it was needed or not. 'Freddie was a very big advocate and appreciator of our talents,' remembers Brian May. 'He had this thing that we were presenting ourselves all wrong. He was into the show as a show, which was a pretty unusual idea in those days because the fashion was that you had to wear jeans and they had to be split and you had to have your back to the audience, otherwise it was pop. Freddie had the idea that rock should be a show, that it should give you something that was overwhelming in every way.'[4]

Freddie was desperate to join Smile but the only room found for him was in the van as he accompanied them to gigs around London and, later in the year, on another tour of Cornwall, where they played venues as diverse as Fowey Royal Regatta, Falmouth Art College and St Minver's Perceval Institute. By now, Roger Taylor had taken a hiatus from his studies to concentrate on his musical career and it appeared his decision might pay off when Smile were offered a one-single deal for the US by Lou Reizner of Mercury Records. In June 1969, Smile decamped to the Trident Recording Studios in London's Soho, where, with producer John Anthony, the band recorded three songs.

To see Smile in the recording studio with a deal for a US release must have been a bitter pill for Freddie to swallow. His route into the band seemed blocked for good and any hopes of a musical career appeared to be diminishing while the possibilities for his friends were potentially limitless. To make matters worse, he had completed his education and his only source of income was from the 'Kasbah' stall he had recently started with Roger Taylor in Kensington Market. 'We had a dream of being in a working band, but the only way to live was to sell the sort of outlandish clothes we loved,' remembers Taylor. 'So we ponced around in velvet capes and tight trousers, and sold the look to other people.'[5]

Eventually, the musical salvation that Freddie hoped for arrived while Smile were awaiting the release of their debut single in America. A band from Liverpool, called Ibex, had arrived in London seeking their own fame and fortune. Like Smile, they were a trio and consisted of Mike Bersin on guitar and vocals, Mick 'Miffer' Smith on drums and John 'Tupp' Taylor on bass. They were managed by 17-year-old Ken Testi, who had accompanied them down from Liverpool. Ken was dating Helen McConnell at the time, whose sister, Pat, knew Roger Taylor and Smile. Consequently, they were all regulars at The Kensington pub and on 31st July 1969, Smile and Ibex found themselves hanging out together there, celebrating Pat's birthday, along with Smile's chief hanger-on, Freddie Bulsara.

Later that evening, everybody decamped to Pat McConnell's flat at 36 Sinclair Road. Here, while the party continued, Brian May began playing the guitar. Before long, an impromptu acoustic Smile gig was underway but this time, rather than shouting suggestions, Freddie simply joined in with the singing. Mike Bersin, the guitarist and lead singer with Ibex, was all too aware of his own limitations as a lead vocalist and realised that Freddie Bulsara might be just the person they were looking for. Their manager, Testi, agreed: 'Ibex were going nowhere fast. They had so much talent though, and it didn't go unnoticed by Freddie.'[6]

One evening, after the bands had met once again at a local pub, Freddie offered a suggestion to Mike Bersin: 'What you guys need is a singer.' Testi was all too aware that Freddie's heart was set on joining Smile, 'but that wasn't going to happen, so that's why he turned his sights on Ibex.'[7]

Soon after, Freddie Bulsara auditioned for Ibex and was quickly accepted into the band as lead singer. 'Once we had Freddie, we were a little rough and ready, but we showed a lot of potential,' remembers drummer Mick 'Miffer' Smith.[8] The mix of three working-class northerners and a London-based dandy originally from Zanzibar was a strange combination but, finally, Freddie was fronting a band. However, as he quickly discovered, Ibex's 17-year-old manager was having no luck finding them any gigs in London. He did, though, have two shows lined up in Bolton and the first of these performances, a lunchtime gig at the Octagon Theatre on 23rd August, was the debut show for Ibex with Freddie Bulsara as lead singer.

Ken Testi remembers Freddie's stagecraft at that first gig more than his vocal performance: 'Freddie was shy off-stage but he knew how to front a show. It was his way of expressing that side of his personality. Everything on-stage later in Queen, he was doing with Ibex at his first gig: marching from one end of the stage to another, from left to right and back again. Stomping about. He brought dynamics, freshness and presentation to the band that had been completely lacking previously.'[9]

After their next gig the following day at an open-air festival in Bolton's Queen's Park, Ibex didn't perform live again until 9th September in Liverpool. The intervening period saw them rehearse whenever possible, practising songs by Rod Stewart, Yes and The Beatles. Most of these rehearsals took place in London and Freddie had, by now, moved out of his parents' house in Feltham and was living in a flat in Ferry Road, Barnes. But he was not alone there; most of Smile and Ibex were also crashing out in any room they could find and their musical instruments and equipment took up any other free space going. In the front bedroom were three single beds, and one of these beds was where Freddie slept, along with any combination of people who happened to find themselves occupying the other two.

Denise Craddock was a student at Maria Assumpta Teacher Training College alongside Pat McConnell, and they were both sharing the house too. She recalls the arrangements at Ferry Road: 'People would just sleep in the sitting room. There were couches and cushions, and other things that could be laid out. It was £25 a month, I think, which sounds nothing now but we had to scratch together as students, and we were not well-off. Freddie was especially struggling to make ends meet. He had very few clothes and his shoes had holes in them.'[10]

Freddie accepted a few commissions as a graphic artist to earn whatever money he could, but his heart was still set on music as a profession. On 9th September, Ibex had their next gig, again in the northwest. It was held at The Sink, a basement venue in Liverpool, and this performance should not have been remarkable except for the fact that, during the encore, Ibex were joined on-stage by two members of the audience: Brian May and Roger Taylor, who were in Liverpool performing with Smile at another venue.

By this point Freddie's stagecraft had improved immeasurably and he had already adopted an on-stage device that would later become one of his signature moves in Queen. 'His mic stand technique, this half mic-stand thing, I think traces back to Ibex,' recalls bass player John Taylor. 'In those days, you're talking 1968, 1969, you know equipment wasn't very good or professional and I think he was just swinging a mic stand around and the bottom fell off and he couldn't get it back on. Nobody had road managers, well, we didn't in those days, so nobody came rushing back with it to fit back to the thing, and he was just prancing around and made the most of it.'[11]

With no performances lined up in London, Freddie and other members of the band were growing tired of the constant driving up and down the motorways of England to perform in Liverpool. For Freddie, London was where he had to be, even though he had little money and life in Ferry Road consisted of constant bed hopping in a marijuana-filled household.

While Smile threw themselves into playing as many shows as they could, Freddie was beginning to plot his next move. He thought that a change of name for Ibex might result in more success. One night he phoned guitarist Mike Berson, who had remained in Liverpool, and suggested they call the band Wreckage. The rest of the band agreed, but not all of them made an appearance at Wreckage's first gig at Ealing College on 31st October 1969. Drummer Mike 'Miffer' Smith had left the band. Smith's decision to leave Wreckage angered Freddie. He wrote a letter to his friend Celine Daley on 26th October in which he laid into Smith: 'Miffer's not with us anymore 'cos the bastard just upped and left one morning saying he was going to be a milkman in Widnes.' The letter continues: 'Miffer, the sod, went and told everyone down here that I had seriously turned into a fully fledged queer.'[12] Certainly, other members in Ibex were making fun at the expense of Freddie's campness, as bassist John Taylor recalls, 'Fred's nickname, within the band, he was quite camp and we all made the most of that. We called him the "old queen".'[13]

Whether or not he was aware of how his bandmates referred to him behind his back, Freddie was almost certainly struggling with his own sexuality at this point. His camp, dandy persona was obvious, but to confuse matters, in 1969 he was dating one of his old Ealing classmates, Rosemary Pearson. She had been drawn to him the first time she saw him – and he to her. 'He didn't do that much work. In the studio he just sang all the time. He was charismatic, dressed outrageously – sometimes in shorts, no top and a fur coat – and was determined to make it as a singer. He was a clown, so much fun to be around. Freddie was also the only truly fearless person I ever met.'[14]

Together they would spend an increasing amount of time together; she would show him around the art galleries of London and he would introduce her to different types of music. 'He always behaved as though he were in front of an audience, even if he was just with me. His gestures were theatrical, and often he'd break into song embarrassingly in the street. Yes, he liked to be the centre of attention, but he was sometimes remorseful about that, and was always genuinely interested in me and my work,' she remembers.[15]

She would accompany him shopping on Portobello Road, they went to parties together, and soon their relationship blossomed. 'We were in a restaurant holding hands and kissing. Next thing I knew we were back at his flat at Barnes. It wasn't like a romantic sweeping me off my feet. I was talking about going to Moscow on my own so we'd be apart and we were feeling really warm about each other and close and comforting. He loved to be affectionate, he'd always put his arm around you and kiss you and be cuddly. It wasn't as though he suddenly made a pass, because we weren't like that anyway,' she recalls.[16]

When they first met, Rosemary had no inkling that Freddie might be gay, but as their relationship grew ever more closer, she began to notice that Freddie showed an increasing interest in her circle of gay friends, which included the film-maker Derek Jarman and the artist David Hockney. Rosemary was the only female invited to their dinner parties and Freddie pestered her to introduce him to the circle. She began to feel confused, especially when Freddie expressed longings to explore gay relationships. 'I felt that if he ever met these people, then that would be it. They would take him from me, and I would be shut out.'[17]

Reluctantly, Rosemary decided to end the relationship in 1970 after a year together. 'It was awful. He begged me not to go, and said he didn't understand. I knew that I could not bear to be simply his friend, hearing about his other relationships. So it had to be the end.'[18] Looking back on the relationship over 35 years later, she said, 'He was a very ardent lover, he was faithful to me, he was devoted to me although we didn't live together. But it wasn't as though we'd just met and it was mad passionate sex, just a very good closeness. I don't think I could say I was passionately in love with him. We weren't ever right for each other.'[19]

Freddie's relationship wasn't the only part of his life that had ended at this point. After playing only ten gigs or so, Wreckage disbanded just before Christmas, 1969. Freddie auditioned for a few other bands and eventually joined Sour Milk Sea after seeing an advert in *Melody Maker*. 'Freddie auditioned with us in a youth club in the crypt of a church in Dorking,' recalls drummer Rob Tyrell. 'We were all blown away. He was very confident. I don't think it was any great surprise to him when we offered him the job.' Rhythm guitarist Jeremy Gallop agrees: 'He had an immense amount of charisma, which was why we chose him.'[20] Guitarist Chris Chesney, also recalls the audition: 'I remember Freddie being really energetic and moving around a lot at the audition, coming up and flashing the mic at me during guitar solos. He was so impressive. There was an immediate vibe. He had a great vocal range. He sang falsetto; nobody else had the bottle to do that.'[21]

Once accepted into the band, Freddie played a number of gigs in and around London but soon his desire for creativity and control became too much for the other members of the band, Chesney remembers: 'When Freddie joined, the band lost its focus. The cohesion between the four of us was significantly weakened. Musically, we were more pastoral than what Freddie was into, he was coming from a different place. He was heavily into Led Zeppelin. I thought the musical frictions were very exciting. We became un-blues based, whereas before we were stuck on that R&B template.'[22]

Jeremy Gallop also recalls the dynamics at the time: 'Freddie very quickly wanted to change us. I can remember him trying to make us learn "Lover". I can still recall how it went. We were all thinking – me especially – "Fucking hell, this isn't the way we want to go!" If only we could relive life again... but Freddie was a very sweet man. He was a very good arbitrator. Chris and I used to argue like hell. I used to have fights with the bass player – and get beaten up – and Fred was always the one who'd cool down the situation with diplomacy. On-stage, Freddie became a different personality – he was as electric as he was in later life. Otherwise he was quite calm. I'll always remember him being strangely quiet and very well-mannered. Extremely well-mannered, in fact. My mum liked him.'[23]

Drummer Rob Tyrell, though fond of Freddie, felt the singer had another agenda with Sour Milk Sea. 'We liked Freddie,' he admits. 'He was fun, but he was quite a schemer in a way. He had other things cooking. I could feel it in my bones he wasn't really interested in us. He knew he was good. He used us as a kind of stepping stone.'

In the spring of 1970, Sour Milk Sea disbanded and Freddie found himself, once again, without a band. He had been through Ibex, Wreckage and Sour Milk Sea in little more than seven months.

Meanwhile, Smile were also struggling. Their US single had disappeared without a trace. Then they played a showcase gig at London's Marquee Club in December 1969, which failed to cause a stir, and were dropped by Mercury Records as a result. To make matters worse, bass player and vocalist Tim Staffell had had enough and quit the band. Suddenly, Brian May and Roger Taylor were left with no group. 'We wondered if we should give up,' remembers May, before adding, 'But then young Freddie Bulsara arrived on the scene.'[24]

Freddie had been on the outer periphery of Smile for a couple of years and watched jealously as they flirted with success. Now, suddenly, he found himself without a band, and Smile found itself without a singer. As May remembers, 'Freddie was always there, you know, Freddie was always saying, "Well, I'll sing, we can do this, you know, put the band together like this, etcetera, etcetera, and we can do this, this, this and this," and we kind of gradually went, well, okay.'[25]

Freddie jumped at the chance to be Smile's vocalist and, in the early part of 1970, although still called Smile, three quarters of what was to become Queen were about to take the stage together for the very first time. Freddie's journey to rock'n'roll stardom had well and truly begun.

'It was exactly right,' says a gracious Tim Staffell. 'Freddie wanted to do the kind of theatrical stuff that Smile was moving towards and I gradually got uncomfortable with it and moved away. Good job I did. I'm glad I got out of the way because if I hadn't, the world wouldn't have had Queen.'[26]

8

At the beginning of 1970, Freddie was 23 years old and, having joined forces with Roger Taylor and Brian May in the band Smile, was about to embark on the next stage of his quest for musical glory. However, whatever convictions he might have had about his talents as a singer and composer, the angst over his sexuality was causing all sorts of confusion, concerns and doubts within his head.

His relationship with Rosemary Pearson had withered once she became aware of his ambiguous and androgynous feelings and, although he was to begin a relationship later in 1970 with another woman, Mary Austin, Freddie was struggling to come to terms with whether he was straight, gay or bisexual. He was not alone; despite the decriminalisation of homosexuality three years previously, any gay man in the UK in 1970 still faced hostility, abuse, and even prison. It was a particularly tough time for someone like Freddie, a young man who had been brought up with values and habits that not only reflected colonial Asia but also his parents' strict Parsee religion, a faith that looked upon homosexuality as a form of demon worship. Consequently, he would have had imprinted on him, by his elders and those within the Parsee faith, a lack of self-esteem and a sense of shame associated with homosexuality. Freddie was, after all, a child of the 1950s when it was a widely held belief that the concept of homosexuality was a mental disease.

Between 1945 and 1955, the number of prosecutions for homosexual behaviour in the UK rose from 800 to 2,500 annually, and 1,000 of these involved custodial sentences. By 1955, 30 per cent of those prosecuted ended up being imprisoned and the irony of imprisoning homosexual men in all-male institutions seemed completely lost on the system.

The increase in numbers of homosexual men being gaoled in the 1950s was as a result of the Home Office pursuing a more vigorous policy of prosecuting offenders, which was also linked to Cold War paranoia, and homosexual men were aware that if they reported a crime and the police suspected they were homosexual, the police would ignore the original crime and concentrate predominantly on *their* aspect of homosexuality. One of the most well-known victims of such an incident was mathematician and Enigma code-breaker, Alan Turing, who called the police to report a break-in, yet was subsequently convicted of gross indecency in 1952, thereby setting off a chain of events that led to Turing's suspected suicide in 1954.

Those who weren't imprisoned were often 'encouraged' to undergo 'aversion therapy' – psychiatry's new toy in the 1950s. This brutal treatment, in which the 'patient' was shown images of naked men and given a series of electric shocks or drugs such as apomorphine to induce him to vomit, was meant to put him off homosexuality forever. To make sure they were 'cured', the men were then shown images of naked women or films of nudist colonies to provide them with relief from the pain. Such aversion therapy continued into the 1960s and, as the decade progressed, homosexuality was viewed not only as a criminal offence but also classified as a mental illness.

When Freddie Bulsara arrived in the UK in 1964, the general social climate was almost unimaginably homophobic, and wherever he looked he could find no openly gay role models and no gay support groups. However, all around him the children of the 1960s had embraced the so-called Summer of Love and young people in the US, the UK and across Europe took the opportunity to cast off not only their clothes but also the conservative social values imprinted on them from their parents' post-war social regimen, and to take the opportunity to experiment freely with drugs and sex. The mid- to late-1960s was a time of sexual awakening and experimentation for many, but for most homosexual men this exhibition of sexual freedom didn't extend to them; they were seen as evidence of moral degradation and, subsequently, many tried to live a 'normal' heterosexual life, concealing their homosexuality.

In 1967, however, a bill to partially legalise homosexual acts was passed in the House of Commons. This followed a decade of bitter campaigning after Sir John Wolfenden's 1957 report had stated homosexuality should not be classified as a crime and that society and law should respect 'individual freedom of actions in matters of private morality'. It had been a long drawn-out affair to get the Bill to this stage and it had endured countless compromises. Consequently, anyone expecting the legal status of heterosexuals and homosexuals to be equal would be disappointed; the Bill didn't even come close to achieving that. And anyone hoping that the arrests would also end was similarly let down. Between 1967 and 2003 some 30,000 gay and bisexual men were convicted on grounds of indecent behaviour, which included holding hands in the street or kissing in public. Crucially, the Bill had only decriminalised homosexuality in private (and then only between two men of 21 years or older) and any exhibition of being openly gay in public could still result in a jail sentence. So while indoors gay men could be out and proud, outside in public they were still outlawed, criminalised and generally perceived as being sick. In fact it was, in effect, illegal to be homosexual anywhere else except behind closed doors and with one other man.

For many at this time the shame attached to being homosexual was almost unbearable. Shame, it is a soul-eating emotion. Letting everyone down. Bringing shame on families, and on their faiths. It is perhaps difficult for anyone born after 1980 to comprehend what that meant, although the stigma of being HIV+ and having AIDS would later come close.

Across the Pond, Americans had taken notice of what was happening in England and Wales (Scotland and Northern Ireland would not decriminalise homosexual acts in private until 1980 and 1982 respectively). In 1969 in the US, the Stonewall riots in New York City ignited the modern gay rights movement in the US. A year later, the first Gay Liberation Day March was held in New York City, the first LGBT (Lesbian, Gay, Bi-sexual and Transgender) parade, billed as the 'Gay Power Parade' was held in Los Angeles and the first 'gay-in' took place in San Francisco. It was also during this time that the first ever cover story featuring gays and lesbians was published in the US. The 1969 story published in *Time* magazine stated that, 'though they seem fairly bizarre to most Americans, homosexuals have never been so visible, vocal or closely scrutinized by research.' It was a period of remarkable transition for gays and lesbians in the US and one that would continue into the early 1970s with an increased visibility for the gay movement. As Rebecca J. Rosen wrote: 'The thick bottle that had contained an entire culture was uncorked in 1969; within a few years it would be shattered into a thousand pieces.'[1]

In England and Wales, the movement struggled to adopt the pace of change seen in America despite the Gay Liberation Front being established at the London School of Economics in 1970. Their slogan was 'Gay Is Good', but prejudice did not vanish from the streets of Britain and in 1971, the Nationwide Festival of Light, supported by Cliff Richard, Mary Whitehouse and Malcolm Muggeridge, was held by British Christians who were anxious to display their growing concern about the development of a permissive society in the UK, with the corrupting influence of homosexuality being a particular focus of angst.

For Freddie Bulsara, and the countless other gay men, it seemed that, despite the passing of the Bill, they would never be able to actually come out. For a flamboyant wannabe rock star like Freddie, with a craving for success and a burning ambition to prove himself, this must have been tortuous inside. After all, his very passions were opera, fashion, ballet and art.

It was one of the reasons Freddie rarely commented on his own sexuality directly. He made witty remarks, delivered double entendres, and spoke in coded tongue to any inquisitive journalist, but he knew that, despite the change in the law, social homosexuality remained taboo and it would continue do so for the next two decades. So, like others masking their true self, he hung out with certain crowds in secure environments of ambiguity to avoid detection and discrimination. He found that showbiz as such would shield him from scrutiny, as it had decades earlier for artists such as Noël Coward, Ivor Novello, Dusty Springfield and Timi Yuro. And maybe that is what Freddie did in the 1970s: became a 1950s gay, behaving outrageously behind closed doors, but not upsetting the status quo, the establishment. Even though times were changing, he wasn't yet confident enough in his own sexuality to make that admission, he couldn't risk it. That would be a decision for another day, another lifetime.

In 1972 the first British Gay Pride rally was held in London and around 700 participants marched from Trafalgar Square to Hyde Park. As well as curious and bewildered onlookers, the marchers faced intimidation, hostility and an aggressive police presence. Arriving in Hyde Park there was food, booze, dope and music and camped-up versions of party games like spin-the-bottle and drop-the-hanky. There was also mass public same-sex kissing, still potentially (depending on the circumstances) illegal in 1972, but, as gay rights campaigner Peter Tatchell – one of the marchers – recalls, 'The cowardly Metropolitan Police would have arrested us if we were lone gay couples kissing, but they dared not arrest 700 of us.'[2]

The year 1972 also saw the launch of *Cosmopolitan*, a magazine aimed at the new breed of ambitious young professional women. The magazine rebranded men as 'vulnerable, dependent and emotional human beings' who were also terrified of being judged solely on their sexual performance. It seemed the gloves were off as challenges to the traditional male role model were becoming apparent. The passing of the Equal Pay Act in 1970, together with the earlier Abortion Act of 1967, helped women become more equal and independent of men, and the whole concept of the male bread-winner and nuclear-family was being questioned, creating an inevitable sense of insecurity and uncertainty among men both in the workplace and in their relationships. The British male's feelings of insecurity at the time were not helped by the fact that British manufacturing was in decline thereby creating a crisis of masculinity as man's dominance within society was eroded.

While the younger generations embraced these attitudes, the older pre- and post-war generations struggled to adapt to the new decade of the 1970s. But now things were changing. Prehistoric attitudes that men didn't wash the dishes or do housework were becoming less acceptable among the newer generation of younger couples, and the first few years of the decade found men from these younger generations spending time with their families and helping out around the house, be it gardening, DIY or going on shopping trips together. This was perfectly illustrated in the various sitcoms of the period such as *Man About the House*.

At the same time there was a seismic shift in men's fashion, with butterfly collars, polyesters, bell-bottoms, skin-tight T-shirts and painstakingly curled hairstyles in vogue. Hats were out and facial hair and gold medallions were very much in. Advertising recognised the shifting attitudes and depicted good-looking, muscular young men, confident and proud, in high-waist pants, floral shirts and cable-knit sweaters, while commercials used celebrities to espouse the appeal of pungent aftershaves, from Denim cologne for '*the man who didn't have to try too hard*' to '*splash it all over*' Brut aftershave.

Fortunately for Freddie, as style boundaries were pushed back, it was popular culture and especially the worlds of music, film and theatre that dared to see just how far they could be stretched. And this was Freddie's world. Salvation came in 1972, in the form of the movie *Cabaret* (based on Christopher Isherwood's 1939 short novel, *Goodbye to Berlin*). Hitting cinema screens across the world, *Cabaret* would shatter the 'saccharine reputation of the movie musical with its edgy take on anti-Semitism, Nazism, abortion and even repressed homosexuality'.[3] The film, set in Berlin in 1931, chronicled the hedonism prevalent during the decline of the Weimar Republic and the rise of the Nazi Party and focuses on the relationship between aspiring actress Sally Bowles and upper-middle class English teacher Brian Roberts. Sally soon discovers that, while Brian adores her personality, he's really in love with the physique of Maximilian von Huene. The trouble is, so is she! The stories behind these characters and their relationship conflicts helped make *Cabaret* a box-office hit, but it was the way it looked, the performances, the score, the groundbreaking choreography and design that would take it on to win eight Academy Awards. More importantly, *Cabaret* was one of the first mainstream films to celebrate homosexuality. It was a film that Freddie adored. 'I like the cabaretish sort of thing,' he said in a 1977 interview. 'In fact, one of my early inspirations came from *Cabaret*. I absolutely adore Liza Minnelli, she's a total wow. The way she delivers her songs, the sheer energy. The way the lights enhance every movement of the show.'[4]

Cabaret would go on to have a profound effect on Freddie, firstly as a young man when he was discovering, and finding himself attracted to, the themes of homosexuality. And, watching the film repeatedly throughout his later life, other themes contained within it would become increasingly relevant and apparent: the futility of false dreams, decadence, loneliness, mortality and the centrality of truth. This is a classical Hollywood musical drawing from the traditions of theatre and literature, arenas that were attractive to Freddie, ones that he already felt a part of. The film's style alternates between naturalism and non-naturalism, drawing on a wide range of musical influences, each one, again, appealing to Freddie's broad spectrum of interests and his innate cultural curiosity. Given the decadence of the film, its broad cultural canvas, the themes of sexual orientation and the fact that *Cabaret* not only allows us to share the lives of the main characters but also places us in the audience, it is easy to see now how much it influenced Freddie on many different levels while at the same time providing him with confidence that he should embrace who he was at that moment in time and be comfortable with the decisions he was making about himself, his present and his future.

Just over a year later, and to Freddie's utter delight, *The Rocky Horror Show* landed in London and in it we can see its cross-dressing elements (just one more example in a long tradition of boys playing girls, from Shakespeare's original plays to men playing women in British pantomime to the later androgyny of British glam rockers, which would soon enough list Freddie Mercury among their members). In the musical, Freddie related to Rocky's underlying condemnation of sexual puritanicalism and hypocrisy, something that makes the show still relevant to this day.

At the time of its release *The Rocky Horror Show* was a revelation. Gay men and women were experiencing a tiny degree of genuine sexual freedom for the first time. Finally, they could meet in public, could date (relatively) openly, and could see themselves represented positively in movies and books for the first time and represented as attractive, sexual, sexy people. *Cabaret* was one of the first films, along with *The Rocky Horror Show*, to portray gay men and women as handsome, alluring and visually stunning. With all of this sudden visibility, they were no longer required to conceal their sexual identity and live their lives in the closet, although many still did, or had to, as Freddie would for the rest of his life. But that aside, Freddie, like so many creatives, would be swept up by the newfound atmosphere of potential change and, dare anyone think so far ahead, perhaps even acceptance. Their reaction to this freedom was to, naturally, go crazy.

Over the coming decades *The Rocky Horror Show* would take on a new and different meaning, poignant and sad, but that still lay ahead. In 1973 who could possibly have known what was to come, what the price of sexual freedom would cost?

While all this was happening in the world of cinema and theatre, pop music, too, embraced androgyny through the appearance of glam rock. The first tentacles of glam rock touched culture in 1971 with T. Rex and their single 'Bang A Gong (Get It On)' but, in truth, it had been forming in the performances and personality of Mick Jagger through the second half of the 1960s in his video performances, dressed up as a nurse or Oscar Wilde, and in his song-writing ('Honky Tonk Women' has been commented on as being about a drag queen). Combining this with his unusual look, that he even carried into his acting in films such as Nicolas Roeg's *Performance* (1970), it's easy to see why Steven Simels wrote of Jagger: 'Hipless and emaciated, possessing lips of such astonishing lasciviousness, that when you put him on stage he resembles nothing so much as some weird mixture of both human sex organs'.[5]

Suddenly, at the beginning of the 1970s, thanks to cultural icons such as Mick Jagger, androgyny was not only accepted but was starting to become encouraged. Seventy-five years previously, in the late-1890s, the very term 'androgene' had meant a type of male homosexual who perhaps also referred to himself as a 'female impersonator'. Now it was back in fashion. As Marjorie Garber writes: 'The 1960s and 1970s, like the 1890s of Oscar Wilde and Aubrey Beardsley, demonstrated once again that androgyny – at least the "bad" androgyny, the bad-boy or bad-girl androgyny – could be sexy. It was exciting in part because it was a violation of one's parents' certainties about gender and gender roles and in part because reading – the interpretation of signs – is always exciting. It was exciting, in other words, because it was uncertain. It connoted risk.'[6]

This androgyny, combined with the philosophy of artist Andy Warhol that anyone could be a star if they looked like one, ushered in the new fashion of glam rock and this, in turn, would draw Freddie in. All the roads, across the shifting social and cultural decades, have led us here

Glam rock, in its very first classic incarnation in the UK, arose from a number of distinct musical trends: in particular the love for retro 1950s three-chord rock'n'roll, a general androgyny unleashed by the culture wars of that same time period, and the media and technology from the time itself and of the future. Colour television was introduced.

Pop in the 1960s was black and white, but burst into colour in British homes in the 1970s when you could hire a colour TV set for the new colour broadcasts. Suddenly pop was colourful, glittering and glamorous. Shining as a genre from 1972 to 1975, the typical UK glam rock song, therefore, was loud, stomping, simple and flamboyant, with big guitar riffs and repeated chants. The typical glam song of the time also featured heavy tribal beats (sometime two drummers would play on one track) and a lead vocal that blurred at least some gender distinctions. This fitted precisely with the ideas that Freddie had been forming throughout his adolescent years; all those lyrics and musical concepts he had scribbled down in his bedroom that his mother had been warned about discarding from under his pillow.

Then, in 1972, in the midst of the rise of glam rock, David Bowie created his persona Ziggy Stardust and instantly become the talk of the rock world. And no one seemed to mind, or see, the overtly homosexual overtones. Bowie was a defining cultural personality of the early 1970s, not merely because of his shifting sexuality, but because his emphasis on image, theatricality and pastiche, as well as the narcissism of his stage persona, seemed characteristic of the era. He set his own style with flamboyant colours and clothes, and it must have suddenly seemed to Freddie that anything was possible. Philip Auslander expands upon gender constructs and identity formations in his summation on the performative world of glam. He states: 'The demand for the freedom to explore and construct one's identity, in terms of gender, sexuality, or any other terms, is glam rock's most important legacy.'[7]

For Freddie, glam rock was a vehicle through which he could allude to his homosexuality without having to commit affirmatively or pronounce declaratively his preference towards men. He used Queen and then creative works as a window of opportunity to liberate himself publicly through sexual innuendo and allusion.

Freddie stated: 'I remember back in an interview where I said, "I play on the bisexual thing." Of course I play on it. It's simply a matter of wherever my mood takes me. If people ask me if I'm gay, I tell them it's up to them to find out.'[8]

Singer Marc Almond recalls well the era in the 1970s after Bowie and Marc Bolan of T. Rex embraced glam rock and hid behind androgyny to conceal or allude to sexual preferences: 'After Bowie and Bolan it was OK to flirt with androgyny. It didn't strike me then that Freddie was actually gay. When Bowie claimed that he was bi-sexual we really knew inside it was just play acting, all part of the shock value. Bowie had a wife and child, so did Marc Bolan. Bolan was incredibly camp too, and fey and pouting and preening, and had a breathy-lispy way of talking. I liked to imagine he was sleeping with his bongo player, Micky Finn, but we knew he wasn't really gay. So why should Freddie be gay?' says Almond.[9]

In some way one imagines Freddie must have been envious of Bowie, whose voracious heterosexual appetite enabled him to play gay with safety and surety. Bowie of course ceased all 'Gay Pretence' in 1983, coincidentally at the very advent of the AIDS crisis.

But, in the real world, the fans that followed Bowie's lead and cautiously came out of the closet often encountered hostility and violence.

'Looking back,' says Almond, 'it was easy for Bowie and Bolan to say they were bi-sexual because at the end of the day they could go back to their straight lives. Gay people couldn't. Claiming to be bi-sexual was a survival mechanism for gay men then.'[10]

In most places, wearing glitter and mascara was a sure way to get a beating. So was it any wonder that gay men and women, in their day-to-day lives and jobs, still felt compelled to conceal their homosexuality? It was too great a risk, not only to them personally and their families, but to their careers and their opportunities. Even superstars such as the ice skater and Olympic gold medalist John Curry, who had a long affair with the actor Alan Bates, stayed firmly in the closet. The only successful gays, though they never actually said the word 'gay' in showbiz, were on television: safe caricatures, grotesques and clowns. And there were no openly gay singers or musicians. It was still several years before Tom Robinson broke into mainstream culture and it was a decade or so away from Jimmy Somerville and the band Frankie Goes To Hollywood.

So, for now, Freddie had no intention of coming out as gay, even if in truth he had felt able to. And sadly he was likely right that it would have stalled any chance of a career before it began. He also found in his heterosexual band members in Queen a further and convenient smokescreen with which to confuse questions of sexuality.

A closeted gay man playing a straight man fronting a band called Queen. As they in turn adopted his images and attitudes, Freddie hid behind their normality and ordinariness.

And as Smile and Freddie began their journey, the audience suspected nothing.

9

In May 1970, Freddie Bulsara assumed his position as the lead singer of Smile, and his transformation began. It was the role he had been desperately wanting and waiting for, and he was supplanting the man, Tim Staffell, who had introduced him to the group in the first place. Although Freddie's ambition was insatiable, this was no *coup d'état* – Staffell had left of his own accord.

With their new singer, Smile began rehearsing earnestly in London. 'We played together for the first time in a lecture theatre at Imperial College, and Roger brought along an old friend of his, who played bass,' remembers Brian May. 'Freddie came armed with a few ideas for songs, and we had a couple of ideas, so we were immediately doing our own material and pretty much nothing else, with the exception of "Jailhouse Rock" and "Hey Big Spender", which were there to have fun with.'[1]

The band also had a new bass player, Mike Grose. 'I met them at West Cromwell Road,' he remembers. 'There was Roger and Brian, and Freddie Mercury, who was still Freddie Bulsara at the time, and we all shook hands and that was it. And I presumed we were still called Smile at the time, though nobody ever discussed it. They explained to me that Freddie was in the band – that they'd known him for ages, and in fact that he'd wanted to be in the band for ages. I liked Tim's voice more than Freddie's. Tim was good, bloody good. Freddie used to sing flat. When he got to high notes he would pull the microphone away from his mouth so you wouldn't quite hear him. But Brian used to talk to me about Freddie, and I think it was Brian who really believed in him at that stage.'[2]

Grose moved into Ferry Road in Barnes and when Smile weren't rehearsing at Imperial College, the four band members would all convene at the shared house to work on original compositions to extend their live repertoire. 'Obviously the dominant writers were Freddie and Brian,' recalls Grose. 'Freddie would just come along and sit in the garden and he would tell you what he wanted, and would, say, sing a tune, or he'd have the lyrics, and we used to piece it together. Simple as that. He might have come with chords or an arrangement on the odd occasion.'[3]

Although officially one of the newer members of Smile, even though he had been on the periphery of the group for a couple of years, Freddie was keen from the start to impose his vision on the band. 'His personality was so strong,' says Brian May. 'We didn't see a great singer or musician first of all: he was very wild and unsophisticated. We just saw someone who had incredible belief and charisma, and we liked him.'[4]

As rehearsals at Imperial College and informal songwriting sessions in the garden at Barnes continued, the very basic elements of what was to become the Queen repertoire in later years started to emerge. 'What would turn out to be their first single, "Keep Yourself Alive" and also "Seven Seas of Rhye", came out of sessions like that,' suggests Mike Grose. 'Even ones like "Killer Queen", which came a good bit later, were rumbling around in those days.'[5]

As well as having a major hand in the composition of original material, Freddie also used the weeks in the run-up to Smile's next concert in Truro to scoure the London fashion scene to create a 'look' for the band. He was still running his stall at Kensington Market with Roger, who was having a hiatus in his dental studies, and felt that it was his duty to fashion the band, as Mike Grose remembers: 'Freddie and I went shopping for stage gear – I think on the King's Road – and he got me into those black velvet trousers that were so tight I could hardly walk!'[6]

With rehearsals complete, and some semblance of stage attire assembled by Freddie, the four of them, together with roadies John Harris and Pete Edmunds, crammed their gear into Mike's Volkswagon van and headed down to Cornwall for their first ever gig as the new Smile line-up. This concert was held in Truro's City Hall, which could accommodate an audience of up to 800 people. However, barely 200 turned up on 27th June 1970 to listen to Smile play its first gig with new bassist Mike Grose and singer Freddie Bulsara.

Clad in their newly acquired attire of striking black silk stage costumes consisting of black crushed velvet trousers, black T-shirts and stack-heeled boots and adorned with silver rings, bangles and neck chains, Smile opened the concert with 'Stone Cold Crazy', a song that Freddie had already played with one of his previous bands, Wreckage. In a 1977 interview he recalls both the song and their stage attire: 'In the early days we just wore black on-stage. Very bold, my dear. Then we introduced white, for variety, and it simply grew and grew. "Stone Cold Crazy" was the first song Queen ever performed on-stage.'[7]

Although they had rehearsed, the gig was anything but polished as Mike Grose recalls: 'We were a bit rough at the edges that night. We had practised, but playing live is different to rehearsing in a college classroom. We also got a bit lost with one of us remembering a different arrangement on a song to the rest. We did our best to hide the gaffes but, let's put it this way, we didn't expect to be asked back.'[8]

It was a view shared by the one review of the concert printed in a local newspaper: 'Four very peculiar-looking young gentlemen clad in silk and too many jewels, making enough row to wake half the dead in Cornwall.'[9]

Roger Taylor, whose mother had organised the concert, remembers that it was for charity but that Smile still got paid for their efforts: 'We got fifty quid between us, which seemed huge. We thought we were rich! It was Freddie's first actual proper performance with us. My mother was quite shocked. And he didn't really have the technique that he developed later on. He sounded like a very powerful sheep!'[10]

Regardless of the reaction to Smile's first concert with the new line-up, Freddie was full of adrenaline travelling home to London and didn't shut up for the whole journey back. 'Freddie put a lot into that first concert,' recalls Mike Grose. 'I remember he jumped about all over the place, prancing about, a bit like Mick Jagger – but Freddie-style.'[11]

Smile's next gig was to be held at Imperial College in London. But before then two radical changes would take place. The first was a change in the band's name. Mike Grose remembers a discussion that took place in the garden of Ferry Road in Barnes. 'We were in the garden just learning a number and they came up with the name of Queen – which of course was Freddie's idea. They said to me, "What do you think?" I know it seems ridiculous today – but forty years ago if you called yourself Queen it was a bit risky really. I said, "Well, if we didn't get arrested or anything at least people will remember us!"'[12]

Freddie had been working on the name for a while and had mentioned it in passing to Sue and Pat Johnstone, two sisters from Cornwall, who had been visiting Ferry Road in 1970. 'We would hitch a lift back to Cornwall from the start of the M4, and on one of these occasions Freddie walked us to the bus stop and said, "What do you think of the name Queen?"' Sue recalls. 'We thought it was hilarious because he was always so camp. And we just laughed and thought of the gay connotation immediately, but he tried to make it more acceptable by persuading us that it was "regal". At that point he'd already started working on the crest and the logo. He'd thought about the whole concept from the start. He had a great marketing mind, and that's probably what swayed the others. And he usually got his way.'[13]

'It was Freddie's idea,' remembers Roger Taylor. 'I didn't like the name originally and neither did Brian, but we got used to it. We thought that once we'd got established the music would then become the identity more than the name.'[14]

'It's just a name, but it's very regal obviously, and it sounds splendid,' Freddie would say. 'It's a strong name, very universal and immediate. It had a lot of visual potential and was open to all sorts of interpretations. I was certainly aware of the gay connotations, but that was just one facet of it.'[15]

Smile was no more. From now on the band would be known as Queen.

The second change that took place before the band's next concert was that Freddie Bulsara would change his name, too. In the summer of 1970, Freddie Bulsara, the shy boy from Zanzibar, became Freddie Mercury, the flamboyant singer with Queen.

'He wrote a song for the first album called "My Fairy King" and in it there's a line that goes: "O Mother Mercury, what have you done to me?"' Brian May remembers. 'And it was after that that he said to me, "Well, I'm going to become Mercury because the mother in this song is my mercury and so I'm going to become Mercury." And we all went, is he mad, you know, but again he was serious and he changed his name to Freddie Mercury. I think changing his name was part of him assuming this different skin. I think it helped him be this person that he wanted to be, and the Bulsara person was still there, but for the public he was going to be this different character.'[16]

So how far removed was this new character from the teenager who had fled with his family from Zanzibar and landed at Heathrow in 1964? Six years had passed and Freddie had been exposed to a whole new lifestyle at the very pinnacle of a cultural revolution. He had followed his dreams of attending art school before breaking into music, thereby creating his own path rather than following the safer route his parents desired for him in accountancy or law. And the very confusion over his sexuality was at odds with his parents' Zoroastrian faith. By changing his name, was Freddie (in part) discarding his past, his Parsee roots, his colonial upbringing? His close friend, David Evans, has his own theory for the name change: 'Farrokh Bulsara was a name he had buried. He never wanted to talk about any period in his life before he became Freddie Mercury.'[17]

With new names assumed, Freddie Mercury and Queen set about their quest for musical domination with a small gig for close friends at Imperial College London on 18th July 1970. It was the very first time the four of them had taken the stage as Queen. 'I don't really remember a proper gig there. There might have been twenty or thirty of Brian's mates there, but that's all,'[18] recalls Mike Grose.

It would be a week later, on 25th July, that the band would make their full public debut as Queen, and it would be back on Roger Taylor's old stamping ground in Cornwall. Advertised as 'Queen (formerly Smile)' in local papers, the gig at PJ's in Truro might have been the first public show for Queen but it was the final one for Mike Grose, who left the band shortly afterwards to return to a day job in Cornwall.

With another concert booked for 23rd August, Queen urgently needed to find a bass player to replace Mike. A chance meeting in Cornwall led to Barry Mitchell becoming their new bass guitarist and he was welcomed into the band: 'They were great guys, really great guys,' Barry recalls. 'Brian, a particularly nice man. He's a wonderful, warm caring person. Freddie was a bit of a puzzle, he wasn't as flamboyant then as he became, he wasn't as confident as he became either, quite the opposite, he was pretty shy, I think, to my mind. Yes, they were good guys.'[19]

But at their first gig, at Imperial College on 23rd August, Mitchell discovered his role extended to more than simply playing the bass: 'It was a strange affair because we laid on refreshments which comprised of orange juice, well, squash in those days, and popcorn, you know real rock'n'roll stuff, and I cooked the popcorn.'[20]

With refreshments organised, Queen took to the stage wearing fancy stage costumes. Mitchell had already been somewhat shocked to find Freddie straightening his hair with tongs before the gig and then going on-stage with his fingernails painted black. He had also been teased in the run-up to the gig when Freddie suggested they all camp it up and wear women's clothes on-stage. 'He really wanted to play on it, but it just didn't happen, thank God!' says Barry.[21] But Freddie was keen to make an impression on-stage, regardless of what the other members of the band thought. He took to the stage in black shiny trousers, a velvet top, snake bracelet, boots and silver hair.

After a gig in September in Swiss Cottage, Queen's next performance was scheduled for 16th October, but before then, Freddie would suffer some devastating news. On 18th September it was announced that Jimi Hendrix had died from a suspected drugs overdose. The news shattered Freddie and Roger Taylor, both ardent fans of Hendrix. As a mark of respect, they closed down their Kensington Market stall for the day.

That evening, during Queen rehearsals, the band simply played a host of Hendrix hits rather than concentrate on their own material. It might have been a mistake, because their next gig, at the College of Estate Management in London, was a disaster. They were paid £20 for a 75-minute set and one of Freddie's fellow stallholders at Kensington Market, Alan Mair, was in the audience and remembers how bad it was: 'Roger and Brian were obviously already very accomplished but it was Freddie that was the problem. In the early days he had a bit of a habit of singing sharp. He would be too enthusiastic, and he would push his voice slightly sharp. And he was also quite awkward on stage. He would throw his head back and step forward but it would be slightly out of time. The hall was very echoey too, it wasn't packed and it would have had minimum advertising. The audience could have been three or four times bigger. I remember we all went to the pub, The Greyhound, after the gig, which is what we always did on a Saturday night. We were there saying, "What are we going to tell Freddie, guys? As he's so excited about it and it wasn't very good."'[22]

Queen played another six gigs in 1970, including one in the famous Cavern Club in Liverpool. Although Freddie had enormous drive and ambition, success and stardom seemed a long way away. Despite his occasional nervousness on-stage and any lack of progress in the music business off it, Freddie's belief that he would make it remained undimmed: 'When Queen first formed all of us were aiming for the top slot and we weren't going to be content with anything less. You have to have a lot of confidence to get on in this business. It's useless saying that you don't need that. If one starts saying, "Maybe I'm not good enough, maybe I'd better settle for second place," then forget it. We were full of confidence. You've got to have that. You have to have a kind of arrogance and lots of confidence and absolute determination, as well as all the other obvious skills, like music. Arrogance is a very good thing to have when you're starting, and that means saying to yourselves that you're going to be the number one group, not the number two group. We just had it inside us. We all had a very big ego as well.'[23]

One member of the group who didn't share this arrogance was Barry Mitchell. He had made up his mind in early 1971 to leave the band. Mitchell's final gig at Ewell could also have been Roger Taylor's final gig with Queen. Also on the bill was Genesis and afterwards Roger Taylor was approached by Peter Gabriel, wanting to know if Taylor would be interested in leaving Queen and joining Genesis instead. Taylor firmly declined the offer; he had invested a lot in Queen already and was certain the band had a future. It was not an opinion that Mitchell shared: 'I still didn't think they would make it because they weren't truly original or obviously commercial.'[24]

Determined to leave the band, he was asked to reconsider his decision by band members, but he was adamant: his Queen days were over. But Mitchell's decision coincided with the growing presence of a woman in the Queen entourage: Mary Austin.

10

Mary Austin was a beautiful blonde blue-eyed teenager from a poor family in Battersea, south London. Given their university educations and their cultural pretensions, she seemed an unlikely Queen cohort. Her father was a hand-trimmer for a wallpaper specialist and her mother worked as a domestic for a small company. Both her parents were deaf and she communicated with them through sign language and lip-reading.

At the age of 19, after her family had moved to a terraced house in Fulham, Mary began working in Kensington as customer public relations officer for the fashionable Biba store. Founded by Polish-born designer Barbara Hulanicki, Biba became the epitome of style and fashion in the late-1960s and early 1970s when everyone from Twiggy to Julie Christie to Sonny & Cher shopped there. Musicians such as Paul McCartney and Mick Jagger also frequented the store, seeking both fashion from the hat-stands and frolics from the beautiful store assistants.

The Biba store on Kensington Church Street was situated conveniently close to Freddie and Roger's market stall, and the two of them would often make a beeline for it. 'I was a Biba freak right from the beginning, way before it got turned into a big department store. When I used to go there it was just a small boutique,' recalled Freddie.[1]

The girls that worked in the store were also part of the attraction. However, unbeknown to Freddie and Roger, another member of Queen had already got there first. 'Part of the attraction of Biba was that the girls who worked in there were so beautiful and they were dressed just right, and they were well presented as well, and we used to just go in there to enjoy the scenery,' remembers Brian May. 'I know Freddie did as well. And one of those ladies was Mary Austin and I met Mary at a concert at Imperial College, my own college, and just got chatting to her because she was sitting behind me, and I was pretty shy but somehow I plucked up the courage to ask her out and we went out a few times.'[2]

It was 1970 and Freddie was in a sexual turmoil. His most recent girlfriend, Rosemary Pearson, had ended their relationship over his sexual confusion and his interest in exploring homosexuality. However, it appears he had not had any male lovers in the intervening period after Rosemary, certainly none of his bandmates or friends have ever suggested as much. But as he became an increasingly frequent visitor to Biba, Freddie started to become evermore attracted to the blonde PR girl working there and Mary Austin, in turn, became intrigued by him. 'Occasionally he was brave enough to come in on his own,' she remembers, 'but most of the time he'd come along with Roger or he'd come along with somebody and he would smile and say hello in passing, which became quite often and I think this went on for about five or six months.'[3]

She was, however, dating Brian May, although it became obvious pretty quickly to him that the relationship wasn't going anywhere: 'She was very wary of anyone, and so we'd generally just go out for a drink and say goodnight, and have a quick peck on the cheek, and that was it really. It really never got beyond that, but there came a point when Freddie started to talk to me about her and it became obvious that Freddie wanted to go out with her. So I said, "Look, we're really not going out as such, we're just good friends so I'll introduce you to her."'[4]

Brian kept his word and managed to get the two of them together. Initially, Mary was convinced that Freddie was interested in her friend rather than her, but she was fascinated by this man she found both intimidating and compelling. 'He was like no one I had met before,' she says. 'He was very confident – something I have never been.'[5]

Freddie finally asked her out on a date on 5th September 1970, his 24th birthday, but Mary declined, trying to play it cool. However he remained undeterred and continued to pester her to go out with him. Finally, after three weeks of Freddie asking her out, Mary could resist no longer and on 30th September 1970, he took her to The Marquee in London to see Mott The Hoople in concert.

At this time Freddie, despite his grand musical ambitions, was still eking out a living playing gigs with Queen at various London colleges and making whatever money he could from his stall on Kensington Market selling old clothes and his artwork, but Mary wasn't put off. Instead, she found herself slowly falling in love with him.

Five months later Freddie and Mary were sharing a £10-a-week bedsit at 2 Victoria Road, Kensington, together with their two cats,

Tom and Jerry. 'We could only afford one pair of curtains and so we hung them in the bedroom. We had to share the bathroom and kitchen with another couple,' Mary remembers.[6] 'Freddie didn't have much money then and so we just did normal things like any other young people. There were no fancy dinners – they came later when he hit the big time. It took about three years for me to really fall in love. But I had never felt that way about anyone.'[7]

Brian May remembers watching Freddie and Mary grow ever closer: 'Freddie was happy with Mary and they were very in love. I think it's fair to say she was the love of his life.'[8]

Having recently come out of his relationship with Rosemary Pearson and now well ensconced in another relationship with Mary Austin, any inkling that Freddie might be homosexual must have disappeared in the eyes of any onlookers. Barry Mitchell, who though he had left Queen, still bumped into Freddie occasionally on Kensington Market recalls: 'I'd often head off to the Market to see Freddie and Roger, just to knock about. Freddie was always full of wild gestures, hands flying around, and would be very demonstrative when he greeted you. Don't get me wrong, he was great fun, and we all got used to him, but all this limp wrist stuff – I was sure it was all part of the act. I already knew what he was up to with the band's image, and I assumed this caper was just an extension of that. I never wondered seriously about him being gay, because there was no sign of anything other than a heterosexual relationship with Mary.'[9]

Certainly, at the beginning of their relationship, Mary appears to have had no inkling about Freddie's homosexuality either and it wasn't long before she took him to Fulham to introduce him to her father: 'I hadn't warned my father how extraordinary-looking Freddie was and so I think my father handled the situation very well. My father opened the door and just stayed very calm and treated Freddie very warmly. There were a few glances and comments from the neighbours. Afterwards I realised bringing home this musician must have been quite a shock for him.'[10]

Freddie, however, wasn't quite so eager to introduce Mary to his own parents. Was this because of a fear that they would accept her all too readily as the perfect companion for their son and, consequently, put pressure on him to marry Mary and provide Bomi and Jer with the grandchildren they so desired? In fact, despite referring to her as his common-law wife, marriage was never going to be on Freddie's mind. 'I treat Mary as my common-law wife and we're getting on fine,' he would say. 'We're happy with each other and it doesn't matter what other people think. We believe in each other and that's enough for me. We believe in each other, so fuck everybody else. Nobody should tell us what to do. As far as I'm concerned we are married. It's a God given situation.'[11]

Freddie and Mary's love affair seems beyond question; those around them identified the love and passion they had for each other. At the beginning of their relationship, Freddie was all-consumed with Mary and their love for each other appeared to blossom, although Mary admits that the romance between them took time to develop: 'It took a long while for me to really fall in love with this man but once there I could never turn away from him. His pain became my pain, his joy became my joy.'[12]

So, was the length of time it took Mary to fall in love with Freddie a reflection on the nature of their initial friendship? A sought-after woman, she had many suitors but was fascinated by Freddie from the start, yet not immediately in love with him. As their friendship grew, and as she became intoxicated with his charisma, his personality, his flamboyance, she fell in love with him. Without knowing he was gay, it may be possible that Mary fell in love with Freddie precisely because he was gay and he offered everything that a straight woman gets from a homosexual man. As Seth Myers suggests in *Psychology Today*, 'Gay men usually learn to accept themselves and stop trying so hard to win the approval and acceptance of others. Similarly, the friendship of gay men offers something different than the companionship of straight men. Even when you remove the sexual element between a straight woman and straight man, the straight man is far more confined to embody a role as the strong, not overly emotional man. Meanwhile, gay men have the social licence to be as outrageous or emotional as they want to be because gay men don't have to fit into a tightly prescribed role.'[13] Only in this instance, Mary had no idea Freddie was gay; as far as she was concerned, she was falling in love with a heterosexual wannabe rock star.

As for Freddie, the relationship with Mary was perfect: she was a friend, a soulmate and a mother figure. He obviously loved her, and loved her deeply and passionately, but while Mary put her life on hold for Freddie, he had his career and his pursuit of men, certainly later in their relationship, to occupy his time. It was an unbalanced relationship that was doomed to fail as a romance, but it was destined to succeed as a friendship that would last until the day Freddie died.

While Freddie and Mary's relationship thrived, Queen were searching for a new bass player. A 17-year-old bassist from Weybridge in Surrey, Doug Bogie, answered their ad.

'I was an amateur musician, but I used to look for auditions in the *Melody Maker* music weekly paper. And one of the adverts in January 1971 was just for a "fabulous new band looking for a bassist",' remembers Doug. 'I rang the number and went along. I lived outside London, went on a bus and auditioned in a lecture theatre in Imperial College, Brian's university, just behind the Royal Albert Hall.'[1]

Doug was accepted into the band, and just in time as Queen's next booking was for a gig at Hornsey Town Hall on 19th February. Arriving at the venue, Freddie, Brian, Roger and Doug were dismayed when they entered the hall and found an audience consisting of just six people. 'It was a huge hall,' remembers Doug. 'Very dark, a few lights and some oil wheel projections on the wall. And what audience there was, seemed miles away. No seating, just a few folk wandering around.'[2]

The following night, 20th February, Queen supported Yes and Wishbone Ash at Kingston Polytechnic. Although Queen were supporting two acts who already had record deals, were releasing albums, and who both had devoted followings, they held their own on-stage that night, both musically and visually, as Tony Blackman, one of those in the audience, remembers: 'Really nobody knew Queen at this time and yet, quite amazingly, I thought, they didn't come over as in any way inferior to either Yes or Wishbone Ash. And the other thing was that they stood out. They were all dressed in very tight-fitting thin black costumes. There's no doubt that they were deliberately projecting – especially the singer – a very effeminate image. That wasn't the thing in those days, yet here were these guys going out of their way to flaunt it.'[3]

While it appears Queen went down well with some members of the audience, Freddie, Roger and Brian had already taken the decision that, after just two gigs, Doug wasn't the bass player they were looking for and, according to Doug, Freddie concocted a discussion to ease him out of the band without a confrontation.

'I thought we had played two excellent and exciting gigs,' reflects Doug. 'However, in the back of the borrowed van after the Yes gig at Kingston Polytechnic, there was one of those "taking everything apart" discussions: "so everything is terrible", "it's a waste of time", and Freddie announces he doesn't want to continue. So, as the new boy, who knows nothing of their past activities and relationships, I just accept that that is the end of the experiment! A shame, but not unusual with bands with creative members. I assumed a couple of years later, when the first album came out, that Freddie and the guys said all that simply to sack me without being nasty to my face.'⁴

It has been claimed that Doug was sacked from the band for stealing the limelight. 'He jumped up and down in a manner most incongruous,'⁵ says Brian May, and his antics, if they were indeed antics, were probably highlighted by the fact that Doug had enlisted his own friends to be impromptu spotlight operators at the gig. But, to this day, Doug protests that this should not have been the case: 'Absolute nonsense! I was quite an outgoing guy and, playing bass, well, it's quite easy to leap about a bit. So I was having great fun, standing beside Roger Taylor – who I admire greatly, drumming and singing. Must have just upset Freddie. It seems Brian was very unimpressed too. Why didn't they say so? I could happily have adapted. But I loved playing so much. Who wouldn't jump about? And perhaps they thought my playing was not good enough! It must be said that my experience of most "serious" guitarists is that they can be quite introspective and prone to moodiness. But, hey, I was young. They were, I think, four, five years ahead of me.'⁶

So, on 21st February 1971, Doug Bogie's Queen career was over and the band were, once again, looking for a bass player. Somewhat disenchanted, Brian and Roger took themselves off to a disco at the Maria Assumpta Teacher Training College in Kensington. That night, a mutual friend, Christine Farnell, introduced them to a young electronics student. His name was John Deacon. 'I'd heard they were looking for a bass guitarist so I chatted to them. They'd actually been auditioning for a few weeks before but couldn't find anybody who seemed to fit,' John recalls.⁷

Deacon had moved down to London in 1969 from his native Leicestershire to attend university. Born in Leicester in 1951, he was slightly younger than the other members of Queen but just as musical, playing guitar from an early age, after being bought one by his parents. 'I remember my first musical instrument,' he recalls. 'A little plastic Tommy Steele guitar when I must've been about seven. I had it around a lot but I didn't really play it much, nothing seemed to click, but a few years later some friends up the road started to practise on two bassed-up guitars. I only went along because I had a tape recorder which they could use as an amplifier but after a few weeks I got interested enough to get my mum to buy me a Spanish guitar and that's when it really started properly.'[8]

Deacon formed his first band, The Opposition, when he was 14 but saw little prospect of a career in music so he continued with his studies instead and, by the time he left school in June 1969, he had passed eight O-levels and three A-levels, which led to him being accepted onto a degree course in electronics at Chelsea College of Technology. He spent his first year focusing on his studies but it wasn't long before he realised he was missing music and he began attending gigs around the Queensgate area of London. One of the gigs he is known to have attended is the disastrous Queen show at the College of Estate Management in London on 16th October 1970 when Barry Mitchell was playing bass. 'They were all dressed in black, and the lights were very dim too, so all I could really see were four shadowy figures,' Deacon remembers. 'They didn't make a lasting impression on me at the time.'[9]

With his desire for making music returning, Deacon began scouring the music papers to seek out groups wanting bass players, but it was that initial meeting with Brian and Roger that led to him turning up at Imperial College with his bass guitar and homemade amplifier a couple of days later for his audition with Queen. In the regulation lecture theatre, he joined Freddie, Roger and Brian for the first time and played a few original numbers before Brian taught him the chords to 'Son and Daughter', which would go on to become the B-side to Queen's first single 'Keep Yourself Alive'. Finally, the four of them joined forces in a lengthy blues jam.

It was obvious early on that the final piece of the Queen jigsaw had been found as Roger Taylor remembers: 'We thought he was great. We were so used to each other, and so over the top we thought that, because he was quiet, he would fit in with us without too much upheaval. He was a great bass player, too, and the fact that he was a wizard with electronics was definitely a deciding factor.'[10]

A couple of days after the audition, Deacon was informed that he was the new bass guitarist with Queen and from that day in February 1971 until Freddie Mercury's death 20 years later, the line-up of Queen would remain exactly the same.

However, John Deacon's addition to the Queen line-up may have presented a problem to Freddie Mercury, one that might not have seemed apparent to outsiders but which potentially encroached upon Freddie's mind and may have caused him a serious crisis of confidence within the group in those early days. Though Freddie had left Ealing College of Art with a diploma in graphic art and design, he may have felt himself intellectually inferior to the other members of the band. Roger Taylor had given up his dental studies but was in the process of obtaining a BSc (Hons) in biology from North London Polytechnic. Brian May graduated from Imperial College London with a BSc (Hons) in physics and had been approached by Sir Bernard Lovell to join his research laboratory at Jodrell Bank, and now John Deacon was in the band, complete with his first class BSc (Hons) degree in electronics.

What's more, all three of them could play their instruments with some significant degree of skill, yet Freddie's singing was still developing and the band hadn't yet utilised his piano-playing skills. However, along with Brian he was one of the two songwriters of the group and he had also taken it upon himself to create the visual styling of the band as well as designing their logo. Perhaps the perception that he was inferior intellectually had something to do with Freddie trying to force his ideas on the band. He needed to justify his position; Brian and Roger had been together for a number of years now, and with the arrival of John Deacon, the instrumental unit of the band was formed. And they were good, *very* good. There was no shortage of other singers looking for bands to join, so Freddie had to vindicate his position. What he needed was for Queen to secure some form of recording deal to give his own position in the band a level of security.

But that was some way off. In the meantime the band rehearsed in anticipation of their next gig on 2nd July 1971, a somewhat low-key affair in front of 80 invited friends at a college in Surrey. Nine days later, Queen were booked to play at Imperial College London. They had played here, in various incarnations, many times before, but this time was different as, in the audience that evening, was John Anthony. He was one of the busiest producers of the progressive rock era and had come across Queen before, in August 1970, when Roger Taylor alerted him that they had a new singer in Freddie Mercury. Upon seeing Queen in 1970, Anthony commented that Freddie was 'gushing and camp' and that 'they more or less had their sound together, but they had a dodgy bass player.'[11] Now, almost a year later, as he was in the throes of setting up a new production company, Neptune Productions, Anthony was back to check out the new Queen line-up. As always, the band gave it their all that night, but when Anthony left the gig he simply told them, 'I'll call you soon...'[12]

Despite what might have been perceived as a knock-back by Anthony (given the band's confidence they had expected him to sign them on the spot), Queen were developing as a consistent and talented group of performers. All the years of Freddie's performance apprenticeship, when he had been prancing around college rooms singing into rulers, or using his half-a-mic stand posturing technique with Ibex, or had been strutting from one side of the stage to the other while throwing back his head with Wreckage, were beginning to bear fruit. Still supremely confident in his own ability, and that of Queen, Freddie was determined that he was going to make it – and he was going to do it on his terms and do it his way. Dressed-up, made-up, flamboyant, flouncy... he didn't care. It was the persona he had created; the boy Bulsara from Zanzibar had become Mercury the man, and he was destined for the top. Nothing was going to stop him now.

Returning to London in the autumn of 1971, after a brief Cornish tour, Brian and John resumed their studies while Roger decided he'd had enough of the market stall he shared with Freddie. He needed to return to his studies as well and so, having given up any idea of becoming a dentist, Roger enrolled instead at North London Polytechnic to complete a degree in biology.

Freddie, meanwhile, had no studies to return to and, consequently, nothing to fall back on. With his own market stall now no longer in existence, he accepted whatever few graphic design commissions came his way and also took a part-time job looking after Alan Mair's handcrafted boot shop in Kensington Market. But there was little future for Freddie at Alan's shop, certainly not the future he had planned for himself. He found himself in a precarious position; it appeared Queen were going nowhere fast and, once again, with the other members all studying at various universities and with the prospect of alternative careers ahead of them should the band fail, insecurities began to affect Freddie.

'I went to art school with the impression of getting my diploma, which I did, and then becoming an illustrator – hoping to earn my keep as a freelance,' Freddie said. 'Music was always a sideline, and that sort of grew. When I'd finished with the illustrating course, I was sick of it. I'd had it up to here. I thought, "I don't think I can make a career of this because my mind just wasn't on that kind of thing". So I thought I would just play around with the music side of it for a while. Everyone wants to be a star, so I just thought that if I could make a go of it, why not?'[13]

But, as he quickly realised, simply playing around with music wouldn't create the sort of career he wanted. In order to achieve the success and spoils he desired, Queen, and Freddie in particular because he had nothing to fall back on, would have to take it a whole lot more seriously.

'And then after a while there is a decision-making time, where you've got to take the plunge; you've either got to say, "I'm gonna go and do this, and just concentrate on this," or not. And we finally did that.'[14]

12

Brian May was also keen to take the plunge, desperate for something to happen with Queen. He had called an old acquaintance, Terry Yeadon, that autumn. Yeadon had worked with Smile a couple of years previously and was in the process of opening a new recording studio complex in Wembley, called De Lane Lea. He was looking for a rock band to test the facilities when Brian rang him. It was the perfect opportunity for Queen: they could be guinea pigs for the studio and, as recompense, would receive a professionally produced demo, recorded with some of the most state-of-the-art technology available. The studio's in-house producer/engineer, Louis Austin, oversaw the recording sessions and Queen, already exhibiting signs of the professionalism that they would eventually become known for, arrived in December 1971 with a complete set-list, determined to make the most of this opportunity.

With three different studios in the recording complex to test, the band found they were shunted from one studio to another. It was hardly the ideal circumstances in which to record, but the four members of Queen knew how important this studio time was to them and were fully committed to the process. 'They were very fussy,' Louis Austin recalls. 'Their songs were done one by one. They would carry on until they thought it was right. It sometimes took a very long time, but they put up with so much shit too, during that time.'[1]

Terry Yeardon recalls Queen at the studios during that period: 'They were a little rough at the edges, which was only to be expected, yet Queen were very much there and had already been there before Freddie joined them, with Brian's guitar playing and Roger's drumming being, to a large degree, responsible for the sound. But Freddie, unquestionably, put the cream on it. He was just larger than life, and with such a personality that he kind of instantly bowled you over. Even in the most sterile environment of a studio, Freddie was very much a showman. It was almost as if he literally couldn't sing a song if he didn't also do all the actions to go with it.'[2]

Queen managed to record five original songs at De Lane Lea and Freddie had composed three of them: 'Liar', 'Jesus' and 'Great King Rat'. It was during the recording of 'Liar' that a debate began over songwriting credits. 'Liar' had actually begun as a song from Freddie's Wreckage days called 'Lover' and was co-written with Mike Bersin. But following concerts, rehearsals and the recording process at De Lane Lea, the whole of Queen had provided some input and so they all wanted some ownership of it, as Brian May remembers: '"Liar" was one of the first songs that we worked on together, and there was a moment when we discussed if we should all be credited in such cases. Freddie said, "As far as I'm concerned the person who wrote the words has effectively written the song." It may not have been the most logical solution, but it was a workable rule which we used virtually unchanged right up to the last two albums, when we decided to share everything regardless of origin.'[3]

Freddie was already putting his stamp on Queen, not only as a songwriter, but also as a leader. He was the frontman on-stage, and his demand that the person who wrote the lyrics essentially wrote the song shows a man who wanted to be the frontman behind the scenes as well. Again, given his perceived intellectual inadequacy, these demands may have been an attempt to justify himself within the group; if he couldn't compete with Brian, Roger and John intellectually, then he could at least surpass them artistically. As Freddie said: 'I'm the only one in the band from the artistic field. The others are all scientists.'[4]

Queen left the sessions with a high-quality demo reel that they hoped would attract some attention from record companies. Financially, all four band members were getting increasingly desperate and Freddie was relying on any money he could earn working at Kensington Market supplemented only by whatever Mary earned. To make matters worse, the band had one solitary gig lined up for the first part of 1972, at Bedford College, which was organised by John Deacon and attended by only six people, and this lack of exposure threatened to undo all of the hard work Queen had done over the previous months slogging around the concert circuit gaining valuable exposure.

One of the producers passing through De Lea Lane as Queen were recording was Roy Thomas Baker. One of John Anthony's partners in the newly formed Neptune Productions, he was immediately impressed when he heard 'Keep Yourself Alive', so much so that he asked to take the demo away with him. Another figure keen on the sound of Queen was Ken Testi, the original Ibex manager, who was back on the scene in London, eager to carve out a career for himself in music management. Testi trudged around the A&R departments of major record companies on behalf of Queen and managed to get a few appointments for Freddie and Brian to accompany him to try to get a deal for the band.

Despite Freddie's confidence and the professional demo, no one they met would commit to Queen, including EMI who, years later, would sign them as part of a multi-million pound deal. That was until Charisma Records made them an offer of £25,000, the equivalent to roughly £230,000 at the time of writing, an astronomical sum to four struggling musicians in London. After sleeping on the offer, Queen stunned Charisma by turning it down citing reasons as diverse as not wanting to play second fiddle to Genesis (who were also on the label), needing a substantial investment to upgrade their equipment, which wouldn't be covered by this figure and, perhaps most tellingly and illustrative of their blind faith and confidence in themselves, they felt Charisma were not one of the major labels of the music industry.

'The moment we made a demo we were aware of the sharks,' said Freddie. 'We had such amazing offers from people saying, "We'll make you the next T-Rex," but we were very, very careful not to jump straight in. We went to probably every record company before we finally settled on one. We didn't want to be treated like an ordinary band. We approached it that way because we were not prepared to be out-of-work musicians, ever. We said, "Either take us on as a serious commodity or don't take us at all."'[5]

It was an astonishing show of confidence by Freddie and the band, and one that always had the potential to backfire. They had exhausted almost every record company and yet turned down the one major offer they had. All they could do in the short term was go back to gigging around London.

Meanwhile, Freddie spent his days working in Alan Mair's shop and any spare time was spent starting to experiment with the way he looked on stage. One of the people he worked with on Kensington Market was

Wendy Edmonds, and she recalls the lengths to which Freddie would go in early 1972 to stylise his on-stage appearance: 'Freddie knew how to sew. He was pretty good so, for example, he'd at least sew on sequins himself. Then I made him these wrap-around tops to wear on-stage. He was very specific about what he wanted and he'd ask me to copy things. So he had these little women's ballet tops, crossover things, and he'd give me the stretch velvet and say "Can you copy this?"'[6]

Behind the scenes, without Queen knowing, Roy Thomas Baker and John Anthony were becoming excited by the demo of 'Keep Yourself Alive' that they had in their possession. They took it to Norman and Barry Sheffield, two brothers who had opened Trident Studios in the heart of Soho and who also operated a management company. Norman Sheffield found the tape interesting but wasn't prepared to commit to signing them immediately. However, he was persuaded to go and watch them play live to see if that might sway his decision.

Accompanied by his brother, Norman travelled to the next Queen gig, which happened to be a hospital dance being held at Forest Hill Hospital. Unbeknown to the Sheffield brothers, Tony Stratton-Smith of Charisma Records had also turned up as well, convinced he could get Queen to change their mind and sign with Charisma, the band having previously rejected his £25,000 offer.

Aware of what might be riding on their performance, Queen performed their set perfectly and the Sheffield brothers were thrilled by what they saw, remembers John Anthony, who had joined them at the gig: 'We watched the gig and Barry couldn't believe it when they did Shirley Bassey's "Big Spender". Straight away, he was like, "Right, we have to sign them!"'[7]

A couple of weeks later, Queen walked into Norman Sheffield's office at Trident Studios in Soho to negotiate a deal, having totally dismissed Charisma. To Norman, the four band members were an intriguing mix: 'Roger Taylor was a really good-looking kid, with long blond hair and charm. Brian May was tall, with a mane of curls and a little introverted but clearly very intelligent. The bass player, John Deacon, was also quiet. I could tell right away that the fourth member was going to be high maintenance. He [Freddie] was charming, acted a bit shy and reserved at times and spoke in quite a posh, mannered voice. When he relaxed he had a very sharp sense of humour and spoke at a hundred miles an hour. Freddie apparently had a girlfriend but we were pretty certain he was gay. I agreed to offer the Queenies, as we christened them, a loose kind of arrangement. There were times when the studio was "dark", usually at 2am. So we said: "We'll give you this downtime in the studio to see what you can do."'[8]

But even at this early stage, despite a contract being on the table, Freddie and the rest of Queen were keen to have some control over the negotiations. They weren't simply prepared, as they had shown with Charisma, to agree to the first thing on offer and so negotiated three separate agreements to cover publishing rights, the recording deal, and the management contract. Trident agreed to their demands and even bought the band new instruments, a brand new PA system, and found them a manager, Jack Nelson. But for the time being the contract remained unsigned, and would do so for another seven months.

Freddie himself was keen for the agreement with Trident to be exactly what they wanted: 'It's not just a question of having a recording contract and that's it, it's not all going to be peaches and cream. You have to keep in check all of the things that are going on. Talent isn't just about being a good musician, these days. It's about being aware. It's vital to do the whole thing properly. Talent is not just writing good songs and performing them, it's having a business brain, because that's a major part of it – to get the music across properly and profit from it. You use all the tricks of the trade and if you believe in yourself, you'll go all the way.'[9]

Part of the Trident deal was that Queen were able to use the prestigious Trident Studios to record tracks for their debut album, for which Trident would secure recording and distribution deals with a major label. But the downside was that the band could only use the studios' facilities during what is known in the industry as 'Dark Time', that is when no other artists were working in the studio and, unfortunately for Queen, the studios were so popular that this generally meant they could only get in during slots starting at 11pm or 2am.

While Queen were recording at night, during the day Trident were trying to secure recording and distribution deals for the band, but nothing was forthcoming. Even in the US, Jack Nelson's attempts to get Queen a deal with EMI were scuppered when, about to make an offer, EMI backed off after they learned the band had to come as part of a Trident package with two other acts, Mark Ashton and Eugene Wallace. 'It took a long time, and it was a very frustrating time, because we made a load of demos and the record companies all went, "not bad, but come and see us in a couple of years,"' recalls Brian May. 'We felt like we were getting nowhere.'[10]

While the band recorded in the early hours and pored over the contracts during the day, their regular live gigs ground to a halt. Following their March concert at Forest Hill Hospital, Queen would not play again 'live' until November and would only play two more gigs in the whole of 1972. John Anthony wanted them to lay low and then come back with a sound that could enable them to play bigger venues.

'Why bother with tiny clubs?' he said.[11]

At the outset, John Anthony agreed to produce the recordings with Queen and Roy Thomas Baker, but Anthony was forced to leave the process when he was diagnosed with an illness, leaving Roy to cope with the eager – and stubbornly knowledgeable – musicians by himself. 'They turned out to be every bit as good – and demanding – as we'd anticipated,' Norman Sheffield, head of Trident, recalled. 'Things had to be one hundred per cent right, otherwise they wouldn't be happy. They'd spend days and nights working on the harmonies. Arguments would start about the tiniest little detail. They'd start screaming, shouting and chucking things. Sometimes it would blow over in a few minutes, but at other times they would stew on it, not talking to each other for a day or two. They'd always sort it out, however. It wasn't personal; it was about the work.'[12]

While Queen were infuriating everyone at the recording studios, Trident were still seeking a recording and distribution deal for the band. But the news coming back from Jack Nelson's discussions with record companies in the US wasn't encouraging: 'They all told me that Queen just weren't going to happen,' Jack said.[13]

Throughout the summer and autumn of 1972, Queen spent the early hours recording their debut album. All the tracks were written either by Brian or Freddie. While Brian's songs were more conventionally structured, Freddie's compositions were naturally eccentric, as Brian remembers: 'Freddie wrote in strange keys. Most guitar bands play in A or E, and probably D and G, but beyond that there's not much. Most of our stuff, particularly Freddie's songs, was in oddball keys that his fingers naturally seemed to go to: E-flat, F, A-flat. They're the last things you want to be playing on a guitar, so as a guitarist you're forced to find new chords. Freddie's songs were so rich in chord structures.'[14]

'I have no set rules for writing a song. It's haphazard,' Freddie would say. 'Some songs come faster than others. I never sit down at the piano and say, "Right, I've got to write a song now." No. I feel a few things out and get some ideas about them and then I begin. It's hard to explain but there are always various ideas going through my head.'[15]

Away from songwriting, another idea swirling through Freddie's head around this time was to create a logo for the band. He had already spent considerable time designing the look and style of the band on-stage, now Queen needed something identifiable, an emblem that was distinctly theirs. Convinced there was no one else in the band who could do this – he was the only artist in the group, after all – Freddie created an impressive crest based around the zodiac signs of the four band members. Atop the 'Q' was a Phoenix, the bird of classical Greek mythology. As well as the crest representing each member of the band, it also imparts a sense of royalty and a majestic bearing, resembling closely the British coat of arms, a fact presumably not lost on Freddie.

In September 1972, Queen finally signed the contract with Trident, which resulted in the company paying the four band members £20 each per week, about £240 at the time of writing, as well as trying to get them the best recording and distribution deal for their Trident recordings. Jack Nelson was continuing, without much success, to get an overseas label interested and, by now, Roger and John had finished their studies and Brian had abandoned, at least for the time being, his PhD thesis at Imperial College. Suddenly, they were all in the same boat as Freddie: depending upon Queen for their livelihoods. But Freddie was concerned that they might be old-fashioned and out of vogue before they had even begun: 'There was a long gap between actually forming Queen and having a recording contract. That's why we were so concerned about people saying, "Here comes Queen, glam rock is in, and they are following the tradition." We never copied anyone.

We were into glam rock before groups like Sweet and Bowie, and we worried that we might have come too late. Our way was to put together a different kind of theatrical music.'[16]

Despite the tracks for their debut album recorded and in the can, nothing seemed to be happening for Queen. All four bandmates were beginning to get increasingly frustrated. Brian May recalls, 'going on the number 9 bus up to town every day with Freddie to pummel the company into doing something because we felt that the album had gone cold. Groups like Nazareth were all over the radio and we couldn't get our foot in the door.'[17]

Trident set up two showcase gigs for the band, inviting executives and A&R reps from as many record companies as their contacts book allowed. The first gig, at The Pheasantry Pub on the King's Road, was plagued by problems with the PA equipment and no offers were forthcoming. The second gig, supporting Sparks at The Marquee in London on 20th December 1972, showcased their growing confidence and charismatic energy. Their set was well appreciated by the crowd, but despite an increasingly dynamic show, they remained unsigned.

However, 1973 would see the fortunes of Queen begin to turn.

13

While attending the MIDEM Festival at the beginning of 1973, a music networking event in Cannes, Roy Featherstone, a top executive at EMI (the label who had already turned down Queen in the US when they were offered as part of a package) happened to hear the demo tape of Queen. Liking what he heard, he got in touch with Trident immediately and requested a meeting with the band. In the meantime, Queen had accepted their first recording session with the BBC for their Radio 1 programme, *Sounds of the Seventies*. They wouldn't get paid for the session but the publicity and exposure were priceless.

Ten days later the sessions were broadcast on Radio 1 and such was the response from the listening public to the songs 'My Fairy King', 'Keep Yourself Alive', 'Liar' and 'Doing Alright' that EMI decided to speed up the process of signing the band. As a result, in March 1973, EMI, the company who had turned the band down once already, finally signed Queen to their label. A month later, Jack Nelson had persuaded Jack Holsten of Elektra in the US to sign Queen. Suddenly, the band had a recording deal that covered not only the UK and Europe, but the US too.

However, the first single released on EMI wasn't a Queen single, but a song Freddie had recorded during some downtime at Trident Studios while Queen were recording their album. Engineer Robin Geoffrey Cable had been working in an adjoining studio on his own version of The Beach Boys' 'I Can Hear Music'. Before long he had cajoled Freddie into providing the vocals and soon Roger and Brian were joining in on drums and guitar. The recording lay dormant for a few months before Cable persuaded EMI to release it. Unable to use the Queen name, EMI decided to spoof Gary Glitter, who was extremely popular during that period, and so named the 'artist' Larry Lurex. The single flopped, however, failing to chart in the UK and reaching 115 in the US.

Two weeks later, on 16th July 1973, Queen's first official single, 'Keep Yourself Alive', written by May, was released. However, with

Radio 1 turning down the song on five occasions and mixed reviews from the music press, the single was largely ignored and flopped on both sides of the Atlantic. In doing so it became the only Queen single never to chart in the UK. With such a disastrous debut single, it was vital that Queen's album was a success.

Released on 13th July 1973 the album, titled *Queen*, received varying reviews. *Rolling Stone* said: 'There's no doubt that this funky, energetic English quartet has all the tools they'll need to lay claim to the Zep's abdicated heavy-metal throne, and beyond that to become a truly influential force in the rock world. Their debut album is superb.'[1] *New Musical Express*, however, called it a 'bucket of urine'. To Queen's disappointment, initial sales were very slow, which only increased Freddie's anxiety as, unlike the others, he had no university education to fall back on. One of Freddie's old college mates, Chris Smith, still bumped into Freddie occasionally on the bus in London and recalls his concerns as the album limped along in the lower reaches of the charts: 'Fred was getting a bit desperate,' Chris remembers as Freddie would say, '"God! I hope this band takes off. I don't know what I'm going to do if it doesn't. I don't want to end up working in an art studio."'[2]

But, as had happened before and would happen again, the stars aligned for Queen. An unmarked white label copy of the album found its way onto the desk of the influential TV producer Mike Appleton. He was responsible for the BBC music programme *The Old Grey Whistle Test* – after *Top of the Pops* the highest-profile music show on BBC television. He put the record on and listened to the first track, 'Keep Yourself Alive', but with no identification on the vinyl and no accompanying press material he had no idea of the record's identity nor that of the band who had created it. Eager to showcase the song on *The Old Grey Whistle Test*, Mike commissioned Phil Jenkinson to edit some surreal compilations of old film footage to accompany the song and, consequently, a cartoon from F.D. Roosevelt's presidential campaign from the 1930s was shown as the song received its first television airplay on 24th July. The following day the BBC received many favourable phone calls about the track, as well as ones from irate Trident and EMI representatives. It was unexpected, but welcome, publicity for Queen.

By the end of summer 1973, Trident had invested £62,000 in Queen (almost three quarters of a million pounds in 2016), but hadn't much to show for their investment. Their only single had failed to chart and their debut album wouldn't even enter the charts for eight months, and then only peaking at number 37 on its first brief chart run. To address this and to give the band some more publicity, Trident hired the band a publicist, Tony Brainsby. He had seen them play live and was convinced they had talent. Upon meeting them, he quickly became accustomed to their personalities, especially Freddie's: 'Obviously Freddie stuck out the most. He was such a raving poofter, I couldn't believe my eyes at our first meeting. He was dressed in red velvet skin-tight trousers, had black varnish on his fingernails, long hair and of course all those teeth – he was extremely touchy about his teeth. He was strong-willed, nakedly ambitious but also very charming. In those days Freddie was an inwardly very aggressive and angry man in the sense that he knew he should be a star and wasn't yet. It's not a side of him that he allowed too many people to see, but it was definitely all the way through him. He felt that stardom was his by rights and he was extremely frustrated at the time it seemed to be taking for him to reach it. In my view, he was very much the fight in the band.'[3]

As Brainsby's relationship with the band grew, he became increasingly intrigued by Freddie: 'He had many stylish little quirks that would stick in your mind. He'd paint the fingernails of just his right or just his left hand with black nail polish. Or he'd just varnish one little finger. He'd say "Darling!" or "My dears!" every other sentence, and his camp delivery was highly amusing and very endearing. He was great to have around. Never a dull moment. The girls all loved it when he came into the office. At the time, of course, he was living with Mary. To start with, his sex life was a complete mystery to us all; we could never quite fathom it. He certainly never spoke about it.'[4]

By this point, August 1973, *Queen* were back in the studio recording their second album. Once more, Roy Thomas Baker would be the producer and he found a band still eager for perfection and desperate for a hit single: 'Singles are important to us and to have a hit now would help the band. We've more to offer than bands like The Sweet, we're not just pop, because our music covers a wide area,' Freddie said.[5]

Freddie composed six of the 11 songs on what was to become *Queen II*, including the entire second side of the album, which became known as 'The Black Side' (instead of having the standard 'Side 1' and 'Side 2', this album had a 'Side White' and a 'Side Black', with corresponding themes such as emotional songs on the white side and dark, fantasy themes on the black side – Freddie's side). The songs Freddie composed included 'Seven Seas of Rhye', which would eventually become Queen's first major hit single.

The recording process allowed them the chance to work on complex tracks utilising layered vocals (which would become a trademark), harmonies and instrumentations. '*Queen II*, by virtue of the band's incurably experimental tendencies, was a spectacle in the De Mille sense of the word,' wrote Daniel Ross. 'Everywhere your ears look, there's a sound you can't explain. It is myth, it is opera; it is a contest of bravado and a constant display of dashed-off genius.'[6]

Freddie's compositions on the album showcase his burgeoning writing range: from the heavy thrash sound of 'Ogre Battle' to the intricate medieval fantasy-based lyrics and harpsichord underscored 'The Fairy Feller's Master-Stroke'. The epic composition, 'The March of the Black Queen', proved to be a song too complicated to ever be performed live, a pre-'Bohemian Rhapsody' if ever there was one, and it hints at Mercury's operatic influences, gained initially through exposure to the records his parents would play during his childhood.

But for all Queen's intricacy and complexity in the studio, it hadn't escaped anybody's attention that the band had only played four gigs in the year up to that point. The previous year had seen them play just five gigs and the band were in danger of losing the devoted live following that they had built up over a number of years slogging around London, Cornwall and the north of England. Trident, too, were keen for Queen to re-establish their live presence, especially as they would soon have a second album to promote and so, following a BBC Radio 1 special recorded at the Golders Green Hippodrome on 13th September and two smaller gigs in Frankfurt and Luxembourg – Queen's first foreign concerts – the band embarked on a major UK tour supporting Mott The Hoople. Their support slot was paid for by EMI, the first time the company had paid for a band to have a support slot, and it didn't come cheap at a reputed £9,000 (£76,000 in 2016), but they knew that the audience on the tour was the perfect audience to be exposed to Queen's music and Freddie's flamboyant performances.

The 24-date tour began on 12th November at Leeds Town Hall following two sell-out warm-up gigs at Imperial College London. The second of these shows was reviewed under the title 'Queen's Loyal Subjects', and within the glowing review Freddie's own performance was highlighted: 'Their leader Freddie Mercury pranced about the small stage, waving his mic both violently and sensually as they performed numbers from their first album. The funniest moment was undoubtedly the first encore – Freddie's "Big Spender" was done à la Shirley Bassey, and thus was outrageously camp.' To conclude, the writer Rosemary Horide observed: 'If Queen are this good on the tour with Mott The Hoople (which they start next week) Mott had better watch out. Queen could turn out to be a bit more than just a support band.'[7]

On 21st November, Queen supported Mott The Hoople at Preston Guildhall and in the audience was a 16-year-old Marc Almond: 'I went on my own as none of my friends really liked or got Queen,' he remembers. 'I liked Mott The Hoople but Queen were much more exciting and Freddie was much more alluring. They were going through their Black & White phase. Freddie was a great showman and I was intrigued by the way he used half of his microphone stand like a sword or a phallus. He was skinny and pirouetted and posed a lot like a ballet dancer. As they were the support act they didn't seem to have a lot of extravagant lights and not even a great sound, just lots of smoke. Yet for all Freddie's performing skills and showing off, they were a definitive four-piece band: Brian's guitar with its distinctive sound, Roger's flamboyant drum playing and harmonies and John Deacon's solid bass. Freddie was a *star* but it wasn't the Freddie show.

'I was so exhilarated by Queen's show I didn't stay long for Mott – besides, I had to get the last bus back to Southport. Queen eclipsed Mott as something different and new. Freddie was the new "Star on the Block".'[8]

In December, Queen supported Mott The Hoople for two nights at London's Hammersmith Odeon. It was a concert attended by the DJ, author and broadcaster Paul Gambaccini who, after witnessing Queen's performance that night, would echo Rosemary Horide's comments: 'I went to the fabled Hammersmith Odeon gig,' recalls Gambaccini, 'where they were supporting Mott The Hoople and I thought these guys are not going to be second on the bill for long.'[9]

Despite all of this, Queen were not making any headway in the charts. 'We did a few gigs on our own, some small gigs,' recalls Brian May. 'Then went onto support Mott The Hoople and went around the whole country getting some really good reactions. Thinking, "Yeah, we're finally getting somewhere", and all the time watching the single and album and nothing appeared anywhere in the charts.'[10]

Following four smaller gigs to finish the year, Queen entered 1974 not knowing what to expect and wondering whether this would be the year they finally got their break. Their debut album hadn't set the charts on fire (in fact it wouldn't reach its chart high of number 24 until February 1976 on the back of the success of 'Bohemian Rhapsody') while their first single, 'Keep Yourself Alive', had failed to even chart. The significant backing from Trident demanded that Queen have success and there was only so long before Trident would switch their allegiance to another band. None of Queen had made any significant money from their efforts – their salary was just £30 per week and they needed a hit. And they needed it fast.

Booked to headline the Sunbury Festival in Melbourne, Australia, in February, Queen's beginning to the year started in disastrous fashion. Brian May suffered an infection in his arm following inoculations to visit Australia and became seriously ill, so much so that, for a while, it was feared that he would lose his arm as gangrene set in. With Brian barely recovered, Queen left the UK for Australia on 28th January, taking with them their own lighting rig and crew, but from the word go, the trip appeared jinxed. As well as Brian still recuperating, local Australian technicians were angered that Queen had brought their own crew. And local bands were mystified why a relatively unknown British band were headlining the festival instead of one of their own. In addition to Brian's illness, Freddie had also developed an ear infection that required medication and meant that he was drowsy and couldn't hear properly.

Being true professionals, Freddie and Brian took to the stage in Melbourne with Roger and John, but only after a significant delay –

they required night to fall in order for their extensive and expensive lighting rig to provide optimum lighting. Consequently, the Australian crowd, already annoyed at having a Pommie band headlining, grew increasingly angry at the delay. Queen were doomed the moment they walked on-stage, and matters only grew worse when their elaborate lighting rig failed halfway through the set.

The following day the Australian press slated the band, so Queen decided to cancel their next show and fly straight back to the UK at their own expense. Naturally, this retreat only provided the Australian press with more ammunition, but Freddie had already told the crowd that, 'When Queen come back to Australia we will be the biggest band in the world.' That moment seemed an awfully long way off in February 1974. The Australian tour had been an expensive fiasco and the release of the single 'Liar' in the US had also been an unmitigated disaster when it sank without a trace.

But the break Queen needed arrived on 18th February 1974, thanks indirectly to an artist they'd go on to share a number one single with in 1981 – David Bowie. Bowie was scheduled to appear on BBC TV's *Top of the Pops* on Thursday, 21st February 1974 to perform his single 'Rebel Rebel' but had to pull out at the last moment, prompting the show's producer, Robin Nash, to hastily seek a replacement. He called Ronnie Fowler, then head of promotions at EMI. Fowler had a particular fondness for Queen, especially their planned new release, 'Seven Seas of Rhye', and suggested they fill the gap. Nash was only too happy to have secured a band and two days later, on 20th February, Queen prepared to appear on the show.

In the mid-1970s *Top of the Pops* would regularly get audiences of 15m. For Queen, this exposure would be invaluable, an incomparable showcase for them and their new single. None of the bandmates had a television at this point and so, on the evening of Thursday, 21st February, Freddie, Brian, Roger and John all ventured out to a local electrical goods shop to peer through the window at one of the televisions on display and watch themselves perform on *Top of the Pops* for the very first time.

Keen to exploit this fortunate break, EMI rushed out a single release of 'Seven Seas of Rhye' two days later and within weeks the song had broken into the UK Top 10. With a running time of less than two minutes 50 seconds, this intricately woven song begins with a distinctive arpeggiated piano before the other instruments roar into the main body of the song. Composed by Freddie, he was asked in 1977 what the meaning of the lyrics were: 'Oh gosh! You should never ask me that. My lyrics are basically for people's interpretations really. I've forgotten what they were all about. It's really factitious, I know it's like bowing out or the easy way out, but that's what it is. It's just a figment of your imagination.'[11]

In the same interview, Freddie is asked whether he has a surrealistic approach to composition, but he preferred to call it 'imaginative': 'It all depends on what kind of song really. At that time I was learning about a lot of things. Like song structure and as far as lyrics go, they're very difficult as far as I'm concerned. I find them quite a task and my strongest point is actually melody content. I concentrate on that first; melody, then the song structure, then the lyrics come after actually.'

With 'Seven Seas of Rhye' becoming a hit and entering the UK Top 10 singles chart, Freddie finally felt confident enough to concentrate solely on music as a career. Despite being the composer of this Top 10 hit, royalties were not yet coming in, and it would be some time before they did so, but as far as Freddie was concerned, he had hit the big time.

14

In the early 1970s, Freddie and Queen were beginning to establish a reputation on the live scene and had gained a reasonable following. During this period Freddie was renting a flat with Mary Austin. Though to all their friends and colleagues – even Mary herself – theirs appeared a normal heterosexual relationship, when she accompanied Freddie to Queen gigs in those early years, Mary would have to witness him being mobbed by girls once he left the stage.

'Freddie was just so good on that stage, like I had never seen him before, as if it was something he'd stored up,' she recalls. 'For the first time I felt, "Here is a star in the making. He's on his way. I don't think he needs me anymore." I didn't feel tearful or upset. I was happy that it was at last happening for him because of his talent. When he came off the stage all the girls and his friends were crowding around him. He was so busy. I started to walk away and he came running after me. He said, "Where are you going?" I told him I was going home. But he wouldn't let me go. That night, I realised that I had to go along with this and be part of it. As everything took off, I was watching him flower. It was wonderful to observe. There was something about seeing that happen that was exciting. I was so happy that he wanted to be with me.'[1]

Within a couple of years of meeting and moving in together, Freddie and Mary had moved out of their bedsit in Victoria Road and found themselves a larger, self-contained flat in Holland Road, which cost them £19 a week in rent. By now, Freddie's determination and dedication were beginning to pay off: Queen had signed a record deal and had had their first hit single. As far as Mary was concerned, everything was going well: 'I felt very safe with him. The more I got to know him, the more I loved him for himself. He had quality as a person, which I think is rare in life these days. One thing, which was always constant, was the love. We knew we could trust each other and we were safe with each other. We knew that we would never hurt each other on purpose.'[2]

But it wasn't long before Freddie was secretly cheating on Mary. He had met David Minns, a 25-year-old openly gay record executive at

Elektra Records. One evening the two of them were drinking together at a club on the King's Road when Freddie shocked Minns with a display of public affection: 'Freddie grabbed me and kissed me, and I was so shocked because I don't kiss people I don't know. Not in those days, anyway. And I thought that was a very odd thing to do because I had no idea that he may have been gay, or was. Let's get this straight; he pursued me. Freddie was incredibly obsessive about people: he just wouldn't leave you alone. He was very sweet, you know, just a very nice guy and I thought why not?'[3]

Freddie and David began an affair during which Freddie consistently told Minns that he and Mary were simply just friends, but he was soon to be found out: 'Freddie had told me he shared a flat with Mary and that it wasn't a relationship. One night we went back with Mary to Holland Road. Suddenly it occurred to me there's one bedroom. I started to put two and two together that there was a little more to the Mary and Freddie relationship than he had been able to tell me. He was cheating on her.'[4]

Others around Freddie found the nature of his relationship with Mary strange. Tony Brainsby, Mercury's first publicist, says, 'When I first started working with Freddie, Mary was already with him. They seemed very close, but I always found it so odd because he was so gay.'[5] And Freddie's friend, Peter Straker, disapproved of Freddie's affair: 'Mary was his girlfriend, as such. I knew he was carrying on with David and I took no part in any of that because I didn't want to be involved. It was a very difficult situation and I didn't like it because he should have told her.'[6]

As Freddie's career took off, the distance grew between him and Mary. He started coming home late, if at all, and she became suspicious that he was having an affair but naturally, given their circumstances, assumed it was with another woman. 'Even if I didn't want to fully admit it, I had realised that something was going on,' she says. 'Although I didn't know what it was I decided to discuss it with Freddie. I told him, "Something is going on and I just feel like a noose around your neck. I think it's time for me to go." But he insisted nothing was wrong.'[7]

Freddie apparently needed the stability that Mary was providing for him. Even in his later life, as Lesley-Ann Jones suggests, Mary had become the 'matriarch of Freddie's "family", a largely gay entourage of employees who doubled as friends.'[8] Freddie was desperately unsure what effect admitting his homosexuality to Mary might have on their relationship. He began avoiding Mary, ensuring he was out when she was home and vice versa, and he withdrew from any form of confrontation.

'I felt something was going on and things cooled. The writing was on the wall. We just weren't as close as we had been,' she reflects.[9] The manner of their relationship couldn't go on much longer and then, one day, in the kitchen, Freddie said he had a confession to make. It was a revelation that would change their relationship forever. 'He said, "I think I'm bisexual." I told him, "I think you're gay." And nothing else was said. We just hugged. I thought he's been very brave. It had taken me a while to realise, being a bit naive.'[10]

The news signalled the end of their relationship, but not the end of their friendship. If anything, it grew even stronger. Mary moved out of the flat and found herself a small property nearby, as Freddie wanted her to remain close to him: 'I could see Freddie's own flat from my bathroom,' she recalls.[11] Eventually, Freddie's music publishing company purchased the property for her and they would continue to see each other frequently.

Reflecting on their relationship, Mary reveals the relief she felt when Freddie finally told her he was bisexual: 'It was a relief really, to actually hear it from him, to have surmised that that was really the problem of the last two years of the six years that we were together, to know that I had more or less guessed right. So it was a great relief for me. I felt a huge burden had been lifted so I enjoyed the fact that he was able to be honest and frank. But certainly, once that had been discussed, he was a different person again. He was like the person I had known in the early years. He was more at one with himself, more relaxed, more happy and I don't think he ever thought that I'd be supportive of him becoming a gay, but I was because it was a part of himself and it was nice to see Freddie at one with himself. It was more than nice; it was wonderful. He was such a happy person; you couldn't deny Freddie the right to be at one with himself.'[12]

The journalist David Wigg interviewed Freddie a number of times and witnessed first-hand the nature of the friendship between Freddie and Mary: 'It was an extraordinary relationship, which became like brother and sister but they had started off as lovers. The only person that he felt comfortable with, well and truly comfortable with, was Mary, who was, I think, the truest love of his life.'[13]

When Freddie would reflect on his relationship with Mary, he could only echo Wigg's sentiments: 'We were closer than anybody else, though we stopped living together after about seven years. Our love affair ended in tears, but a deep bond grew out of it, and that's something nobody can take away from us. It's unreachable. People always ask me about sexuality and all those things, right from the early days, but I couldn't fall in love with a man the same way as I have with Mary.'[14]

Combined with his confidence, a certain degree of fate and good luck seemed to be following Freddie's career. 'Seven Seas of Rhye' hit the Top 10 just as Queen were embarking on a major UK tour – a tour that had already been planned to promote the new album, *Queen II*.

The tour kicked off at Blackpool's Winter Gardens on 1st March 1974 and would feature Queen wearing stage costumes designed by Zandra Rhodes. 'Freddie had loved the tops I did for Marc Bolan,' she remembers, 'and what I was doing with a variety of fabrics right then, and he came to me knowing very much what he wanted.'[1] Freddie would later reveal that he needed a look on-stage to make him feel more secure. Again, it was his attempt to create a personality that distanced himself from the boy from Zanzibar. Freddie Bulsara was no more, and hadn't been for some time. He was now Freddie Mercury – and Freddie Mercury only – and the costumes, styling, look and performance helped him to cultivate this alter ego.

However, despite his change of name and the adoption of another character in the form of his stage persona, it seems deep down Freddie was still concerned about his sexual orientation and how the rise in the popularity of the band might be affected if his sexuality was revealed. During downtime at one of Queen's concerts on their UK tour, and basking in the glory of their newfound success with 'Seven Seas of Rhye', Freddie confided his fears to his friend Pat Johnstone, who helped to run Queen's fan club: 'He said, "Patti, I really need to talk to you. I really need to talk to you. I'm in love with David." I said, "What do you mean? You live with Mary." He said, "I'm gay and I can't tell anyone because it will destroy everything." And I just said, "Well, as long as it doesn't destroy you, that's all that matters." We sat there drinking cocktails and I didn't know what to say. Come out? Don't come out? What should I say? He loved Mary. He never stopped loving Mary. She was the loveliest, sweetest person. She loved Freddie and would have done anything for him – we all would have.'[2]

By the time the tour ended in Birmingham on 2nd April, 1974 Queen had cemented their reputation thanks, in part, to the prominence of 'Seven Seas of Rhye' in the charts, the notoriety Freddie was gaining from his live performances and the release of the second album, *Queen II*, which had climbed to number 5 in the UK album charts. But critical reaction to the album was mixed, with *Disc* saying *Queen II* was 'going to be a hit album', while *Rolling Stone* magazine declared it 'a floundering and sadly unoriginal affair.'[3] Meanwhile *Record Mirror* wrote, 'This is it, the dregs of glam rock. The band with the worst name have capped that dubious achievement by bringing out the worst album for some time.'

Despite such reviews Queen had had a single in the Top 10 and an album in the Top Five: they had arrived. But Freddie was keen to highlight the amount of work the band had done in getting to where they were now: 'To most people it must have seemed like an overnight success story, but really we'd been going for a while, doing the club circuits and all that, without having a recording contract. From the very start there were always business pressures of some sort or other. It was like a real obstacle race. I will always maintain the fact that for a major successful band, it's never plain sailing, otherwise there's something wrong about it. If it's too easy you hit your peak and then that's it.'[4]

But Queen hadn't hit their peak yet: far from it. In fact, they were still a support band when they flew to the US in April 1974 to undertake a 40-date tour with Mott The Hoople. The new album, *Queen II*, had only reached number 83 in the US album charts and the single 'Seven Seas of Rhye' had failed to chart altogether, but the band saw the tour as a potentially great experience after their shared UK tour. Yet once again, while on foreign soil, disaster struck. Brian May collapsed and was diagnosed with hepatitis. Queen's participation in the tour was over after just 20 of the 40 shows and the whole band flew back to England to be replaced by Kansas for the remainder of the tour.

Despite leaving the tour early, Queen had made a vivid impact on Mott The Hoople singer Ian Hunter: 'They planned the whole time,' he says. 'Like, if we haven't made it to such and such a level in two years, we're out of here, and they did exactly what they said they were going to do.'[5]

Back in the UK, with Brian May hospitalised for six weeks and writing material from his hospital bed, Freddie, Roger and John began work on the next album. Roy Thomas Baker would, once again, produce the album and it would be recorded at both Rockfield Studios in Wales and Trident Studios in Soho. Brian would only visit the studios in Wales occasionally with the plan to return to fill in the guitar and additional vocals at a later stage on the album, which was titled *Sheer Heart Attack*.

Freddie composed six of the 13 songs on the new album: 'Flick of the Wrist', 'Lily of the Valley', 'In The Lap of the Gods', 'Bring Back That Leroy Brown', 'In The Lap of the Gods...Revisited' and the biggest hit on the album, 'Killer Queen'. Together, they showed a remarkable ability to compose songs in different genres and styles. There's the heavy, dark and aggressive tone of 'Flick of the Wrist', the ukulele-based vaudeville tribute to the 1920s 'Bring Back That Leroy Brown' and finally, the eccentric melodic debonair 'Killer Queen', a single unlike any other at the time of its release, and the song that catapulted Queen to international fame.

'"Killer Queen" was one song which was really out of the format that I usually write in,' said Freddie in a 1974 interview. 'Usually the music comes first, but the words came to me, and the sophisticated style that I wanted to put across in the song came first. No, I'd never really met a woman like that. A lot of my songs are fantasy. I can dream up all kinds of things. That's the kind of world I live in. It's very sort of flamboyant, and that's the kind of way I write. I love it. "Killer Queen" I wrote in one night. I'm not being conceited or anything, but it just fell into place. I scribbled down the words in the dark one Saturday night and the next morning I got them all together and I worked all day Sunday and that was it. I'd got it. It gelled. It was great.'[6]

The *NME* said of the song: 'It's a turning point in that it sounds nothing like the noisy heavy metal sound to which we are accustomed from Queen, thus justifying their earlier claim of "versatility". It's more of a mixture of Beach Boys, early Beatles and 1920s music hall. Quite nice, actually.'[7]

Freddie would comment on it by saying, 'People are used to hard rock, energy music from Queen, yet with this single you almost expect

Noël Coward to sing it. It's one of those bowler hat, black suspender belt numbers – not that Coward would wear that.'[8]

Composer Mike Moran was another impressed by 'Killer Queen': 'I used to do all Kenny Everett's shows. Kenny was a good friend and I remember he used to go on and on about Queen in the Seventies. It took them a while to get established, but I remember having lunch with Everett and he said, "I'm going to play something on the radio, have a listen this afternoon" and I was driving through Regent's Park and he said, "Have a listen to this, it's the best record that's ever been made by anybody ever," and played "Killer Queen". Well, I actually stopped the car to listen to it; it's quite a remarkable record. And I said to myself, "What on earth is this?" It's just extraordinary; the production, the musicality, everything about it, the vocals, the lyrics, it was such a strange thing to hear at that time on the radio.'[9]

'Killer Queen' would earn Freddie his first Ivor Novello Award, but what was the song about? Who was the 'Killer Queen' of the title? And does it bear any connection to the sexual turmoil Freddie found himself in during that time? When asked, Freddie said, 'It's about a high-class call girl. I'm trying to say that classy people can be whores as well. That's what the song is about, though I'd prefer people to put their interpretation upon it – to read into it what they like.'[10]

But Queen's EMI plugger at the time, Eric Hall, has a different theory: 'He [Freddie] used to be infatuated with me, I don't know why. Was I his type? I assume I must have been. He told me that song ['Killer Queen'] was about me. He said to me, "I'm the queen, Eric, and you're killing me because I can't have you." Of course, every time I heard "Killer Queen" on the radio or saw him on *Top of the Pops* the first time, I knew what was in his mind when he wrote that song. The lyrics were, if I remember rightly, 'She keeps Moët Chandon in his fancy cabinet', I used to keep champagne in my little fancy cabinet. I had monster permed hair, like Marie Antoinette. But there was "Killer Queen" on *Top of the Pops*! I inspired that song because he fancied me.'[11]

'"Killer Queen" was the turning point,' Brian May recalls. 'It was the song that best summed up our kind of music, and a big hit, and we desperately needed it as a mark of something successful happening for us.'[12]

The song was released as a single on 21st October 1974 and became Queen's breakthrough hit, reaching number 2 in the UK singles chart and number 12 in the US Billboard Hot 100. The album, *Sheer Heart Attack*, hit the shops a couple of weeks later and peaked at number 2 in the UK album charts, selling over 300,000 copies. It also broke into the Top 10 in the US.

Rolling Stone magazine said of the album: '*Sheer Heart Attack* is still, like its two predecessors, a handsomely glossy construction. If it's hard to love, it's hard not to admire: This band is skilled, after all, and it dares,' [13] and the *NME* called the album, 'A feast, no duffers, and four songs that will run and run.'[14]

To promote the album, Queen spent the rest of the year headlining a British tour as well as venturing into Europe, playing sell-out venues in Sweden, Finland, Germany, Holland, Belgium and Spain.

Despite Eric Hall suggesting that 'Killer Queen' was written about him and that Freddie was gay, at the time Freddie was still living with Mary Austin in London and to all outsiders, it appeared he was involved in a normal heterosexual relationship. However, during the UK tour, John Anthony, who had accompanied the band to Sunderland, was exposed to the true nature of Freddie's sexual dilemma. After the gig Anthony had gone to bed in his hotel room and was woken in the middle of the night by a phone call from Freddie, who asked him to go to his room.

'And there was Fred sat in bed in his pyjamas and night cap,' Anthony remembers, 'and these two girls standing around in his room. Fred said, "Get rid of them, Johnnypoos." So I told them that Fred had a big day ahead of him tomorrow and was very tired and they'd best go." As soon as they were gone, Freddie told Anthony that he was gay and wanted him to tell Mary Austin on his behalf, but Anthony refused to do so before heading back to his own room.[15]

As 1974 ended, Freddie was clearly embroiled in his own personal turmoil about his sexuality and Eric Hall and John Anthony were both aware of it. Soon Freddie was to begin his relationship with David Minns, a relationship Mary Austin wouldn't find out about for some time.

The end of the year also saw Queen embroiled in a dispute about money. Despite their success of 1974, little money seemed to be rolling in to their own personal accounts. Trident had increased their salaries to £60 a week each (around £650 in 2016) but everyone assumed the band were millionaires.

As Norman Sheffield would recall: 'Freddie had found the acclaim he'd craved all his life. He felt like a god. Unfortunately, he soon started behaving like one too. Then Freddie demanded a grand piano. When I turned him down, he banged his fist on my desk. "I have to get a grand piano," he said. I wasn't being mean. We knew there was a huge amount of money due to come flooding our way from Queen's success. I explained that some of it was already coming in but the vast majority of it hadn't arrived yet. "But we're stars. We're selling millions of records," Freddie said. "And I'm still living in the same flat I've been in for the past three years."

'The amount of money we'd invested in the band was huge. We'd advanced them equipment and salaries right at the beginning and had continued to pour money into them for four years. The fact the band owed Trident close to £200,000 [the equivalent of over £2.1 million in 2016] didn't seem to register with Freddie. I can remember the conversation. "The money will come in December," I said. "So wait." Then came a phrase he would make famous around the world in years to come, although no one would have known where it was born. Freddie stamped his feet and raised his voice: "No, I am not prepared to wait any longer. I want it all. I want it now."'[16]

Freddie, and the rest of Queen, weren't satisfied and employed the services of a young lawyer, Jim Beach, to begin extricating them from their Trident contracts. These negotiations would go on for months and cost the band a small fortune, money that, at that stage, none of them had. However, that was soon to change: 1975 would prove to be the year Queen became global superstars and acquired all the trappings that came with such success, much of it due to Freddie Mercury. 'There are many things we want to do and I feel we have a great deal of room in which to achieve them,' he said in an interview at the beginning of 1975.[17]

But even Freddie couldn't have imagined the success that 1975 would bring, primarily as a result of the creation of his own *magnum opus*, 'Bohemian Rhapsody'.

16

By the mid-1970s, despite continued hostility and abuse, a gay subculture had emerged within the United Kingdom, and even the mainstream had adopted, up to a point, the integration of gay culture. This integration, however, was predominantly expressed by stereotypical representations of gay people in popular culture. Consistently, these gay stereotypes were used principally for the purposes of humour: characters mostly to be laughed at, not with, and willingly collusive in the mocking laughter of the TV audience. Comedian Dick Emery's character Clarence, Mr Humphries as played by John Inman in the BBC sitcom *Are You Being Served?*, any of Charles Hawtrey's *Carry On* characters and the stand-up television act by Larry Grayson all reinforced this gay stereotype.

These stereotypes could be sustained in the 1970s, according to writer Philip Hensher, because 'most people watching a sitcom or a drama were not at all likely to know what a gay person was like. That goes for both straight and gay viewers: many people who knew themselves to be gay also felt themselves solitary in their condition, or a member of a small and beleaguered community. The real-life gay people most Britons could recognise or identify would almost certainly be the ones conforming to the most predictable stereotypes. The stereotypes on-screen and off reinforced each other.'[1]

It was the 'campness' of these characters that portrayed gay people as literally different and inhuman and made it so much harder for gay men particularly to be treated with respect and as equals by their straight peers during the mid-1970s, and made it all but impossible to come out.

'What was wrong with these images of gay people,' continues Hensher, 'were not that they were insulting, nor that they were inaccurate, nor that they were unfunny. The trouble was that they were a portrayal of only a narrow reflection of gay people's experience and nature. Over and over again, talking to gay people who grew up in the 1970s, you hear the view that they knew they weren't like Mr Humphries [*Are You Being Served?*], but had no idea, from television or films, what sort of person they might grow up to be.'[2]

In 1975, however, with the production and broadcast of the bio-graphical television film, *The Naked Civil Servant*, a profound shift in the portrayal of gay men occurred. This landmark film, illustrating the extraordinary life of flamboyant homosexual Quentin Crisp, took Britain by storm and made Crisp an overnight celebrity. John Hurt gives an unforgettable performance as Crisp himself, for which he won a BAFTA.

Throughout his life Crisp had suffered constant abuse and hostility, but staunchly refused to compromise his lifestyle. The film was no shiny romantic period drama. It refused to glamorise events and is an episodic series of incidents charting Crisp's progression from self-discovery to his later life in New York. Unflinchingly honest, it certainly raised awareness of homosexuality and freedom of sexual choice. But still the mid-1970s remained a dangerous time to 'come out' to friends, family and acquaintances and, especially, employers or professional associates.

Gay subculture remained one that was mainly underground, ghetto-ised and hidden away. It led to communities, such as the South London Gay Community Centre in Brixton, being formed by people determined to come out with a public statement of gay identity. Occupying squats in Railton Road and Mayall Road, the community experimented with new communal living arrangements for gay people; people who were desperately fleeing oppressive situations in their lives or simply glad to find the company of unashamedly out gay people rather than remain confused and isolated.

However, communities such as these remained marginalised, occupying, as they did, deprived inner-city areas with high levels of unemployment and crime and a chronic shortage of housing amid dilapidated buildings and environmental decay. Similarly, at night, gay communities seeking entertainment were restricted to their own underground clubs and venues: either private members' clubs providing dinner, dance and cabaret for the gay establishment behind closed doors, or small dives tucked away with postage-sized dance floors for young gay men to dance the night away, concealed from the abuse they faced from the world outside. And it was in these clubs that the Americanisation of British gay culture began, thanks, in part, to the prominence of disco.

While some argue that the dance-club scene started in New York in the 1960s at clubs such as Regine's, Le Club and Ondine and others say it was in Paris in Chez Castel or Chez Rezine, arguably the true rise of the gay club happened in the early 1970s in New York. It was at this time when underground gay dance clubs such as the Loft, Tenth Floor and 12 West gave birth to a disco culture that saw sweating bodies gyrate, pulsating high-energy rhythms, flashing strobe lights and open drug-use, in-site sex and non-stop all-night dancing.

Opened on Valentine's Day in 1970 by David Mancuso, the Loft was at the forefront of this movement. Throwing informal house parties, Manusco's club would attract New York's gay community as they could dance together here without fear of police action (a New York bylaw criminalised two men dancing together). Before long, underground clubs in Philadelphia, Chicago and San Francisco were opening, playing music that came to be classified as 'disco'. Together with DJs such as Larry Levan and Frankie Knuckles, David Manusco helped to influence the sound of disco and soon acts such as The O'Jays, Isaac Hayes, Barry White and Gloria Gaynor were defining the music of the disco era. During this period Levan and Knuckles would begin playing at New York's infamous Continental Baths, a gay bathhouse known as the city's most hedonistic nightspot, as disco spread throughout the city and among the gay culture of the period before spreading out into the wider arena.

The Americanisation of the British gay culture scene began in London in 1975 when promoter Richard Scanes (usually known as Tricky Dicky) began to hold 'one-nighters' in venues as far afield as Croydon, Ilford and Euston to replicate the success of similar nights in New York. He would hire out a bar and put on gay nights under the name of 'Dick's Inn Gay Disco' and these attracted 100 or so gay boys and girls every time. But it was when he held a one-nighter underneath a hotel in Paddington at a venue called Fangs that he discovered he could attract larger crowds. Over 600 gay men turned up and lapped up every minute of the night, dancing away to songs such as Gloria Gaynor's 'Never Can Say Goodbye', which had been audaciously mixed into a 19-minute dance medley comprising all of the songs from one side of her album of the same name.

Extended dance mixes suddenly became the bedrock of the disco music scene and soon it had become a worldwide phenomenon. It was from this globalisation of disco that a record emerged in 1975 from the Munich studios of producer Giorgio Moroder and utilised an intense, repetitive beat, synthesizers, and minimal vocals to create one of the biggest hits of the era. 'Love To Love You Baby' was a 17-minute vinyl aphrodisiac performed by Boston singer Donna Summer that became a global Top 10 hit despite being banned by the BBC and radio stations in the US owing to its 'eye-watering 23 seconds of faked orgasm, which Donna Summer performed gyrating suggestively with her microphone stand.'[3]

But, in 1975, as the world of disco ruled the airwaves, how would a six-minute epic consisting of three distinct movements, with an operatic section at its core, fare?

Freddie Mercury had no doubt that his masterpiece would be a hit. However, few shared his optimism.

Part Two

17

Queen began 1975 with the release of the single 'Now I'm Here'. Written by Brian May, it was to become a concert standard for the band over the coming years and peaked at number 11 in the UK charts but wasn't even released in the US, which meant that of Queen's first four singles, it was only the two written by Freddie Mercury that had broken into the Top 10.

Meanwhile, the band prepared for their forthcoming tour of the US, Canada and Japan. Beginning on 5th February, this mammoth tour would continue until 1st May, but unlike their previous visit to the US when they were supporting Mott The Hoople, this time Queen would be the main event.

Before they left, however, John Deacon married his longtime and already pregnant girlfriend, trainee teacher Veronica Tetzlaff, in Kensington in January. Freddie turned up looking every inch the affluent rock star: he arrived in a stretch limo wearing a huge feather boa and with a woman on each arm. Despite appearances, the truth was the band were struggling financially and their debts were increasing. Deacon had already asked Norman Sheffield if he could borrow £10,000 to buy a house[1] yet Sheffield refused, just as he refused requests by Freddie for cash to buy a grand piano and Roger for cash to get a new car. With three reasonably successful albums, two Top 10 singles, and numerous sell-out shows behind them, Freddie and the rest of the band wanted to see some returns. To make matters worse, they grew increasingly suspicious when Trident bought their second Rolls-Royce for the management. In 1975 Queen hired the services of lawyer Jim Beach to secure their severance from Trident, and this would remain an ongoing saga while the band embarked on their US tour.

'We're just hoping to have a whale of a time,' said Freddie before they departed for North America. 'We're planning to go to Japan. Can't wait, actually. All those geisha girls. And boys.'[2]

As well as Japan Freddie was particularly looking forward to going back to New York, having only previously visited the city with Mott The

Hoople the year before. 'It had a very hectic pace,' he remembered. 'I enjoyed it basically from the reception we got. People were telling us how vicious the city can be, but I enjoyed it. There's so much to see, so it depends on how long you're there for. The record company took us to all the obvious places to go, to all the restaurants, clubs and things. When we come back again, we'll be looking for all the other places.'[3]

Less than a fortnight after playing two shows at the Avery Fisher Hall in New York, however, Queen's foreign jinx struck once again when Freddie began to suffer problems with his voice following two shows in one day in Philadelphia. After visiting a doctor, it was suspected he might be suffering from throat nodules and he was advised to rest immediately, speak as little as possible, and not sing for at least three months.

Travelling to Washington, D.C. for a show the following day, Freddie ignored the doctor's advice and took to the stage. It was an unwise decision. After the show at the John F. Kennedy Center, Freddie consulted another doctor, who was less forgiving and diagnosed him with severe laryngitis. As a result, the next seven shows were cancelled as he was forced to take 11 days off. Resuming in Wisconsin, Freddie quickly realised there were still problems with his voice but somehow he made it to the final gig of the tour in Portland, yet that was to prove one show too many and was also reluctantly cancelled.

On this US tour, according to writer David Bret, Freddie started frequenting the various gay scenes he found in some of North America's more liberal cities. Far away from the UK press, it was the ideal place for him to explore, undetected, and a world he really wanted to be a part of. However, as Bret explains, Freddie came very close to being 'outed' in Ohio: 'The US press (and for the time being their British counterpart) knew absolutely nothing about his discreet post-gig forays into the gay scene of each town or city on the tour circuit and that, unable to do so in Ohio, he had "bought in" from an agency specializing in such things. Thus, when he was interviewed by David Hancock of the fortunately obscure *Record Popswop Mirror*, he almost came unstuck when Hancock was shown into his hotel room thirty minutes early to find Freddie reclining on a pile of cushions, being waited on hand and foot by three scantily clad muscular young hunks. The reporter – in his feature he referred to Freddie as "The Quicksilver Girl" – was curious to know why he was apparently incapable of fixing himself a drink or lighting his own cigarettes. Freddie told Hancock, expecting to be believed, "They're servants, dear. I just love being pampered – it's just something that's grown with me. I mean, I can't even make myself a cup of tea. I'm useless at it, so I have someone else do it for me. That's the kind of environment I live in, dear."[4]

Still, Freddie had managed to keep his sexual preferences hidden from everyone, even the rest of Queen, as they left for a week's holiday in Hawaii before landing in Tokyo for their eight Japanese shows. Greeted by 3,000 screaming fans on arrival, Queen suddenly experienced something akin to Beatlemania. At their subsequent shows, they were greeted by crowds going berserk in their presence and the shows were hugely successful even without their trademark lighting and pyrotechnic elements, which had been banned by local authorities as a blackout was forbidden owing to the fact that all exits had to be clearly lit and visible.

By the time Queen left Japan, 'Killer Queen' and *Sheer Heart Attack* were topping the Japanese singles and album charts and their musical legacy was cemented there for years to come. The country also made quite an impression on Freddie. During the tour he, along with the rest of the band, had been showered with expensive gifts, leading him to begin buying silk kimonos. He also started a collection of Japanese art, a penchant he would indulge for the rest of his life. He was fascinated with Tokyo's *kagé-me-jaya*, the tea houses frequented by American GIs after World War II, where the delights of geisha boys could be sampled for an appropriate fee. Freddie, however, seemed content to be solely pampered by them and not engage in any sexual activity.

Queen arrived back in the UK at the beginning of May 1975, to find their struggles with Trident were still ongoing. These continued throughout the summer, while the band were working on their new album, and it wasn't until August that they reached an agreement that saw Queen separate from all their deals with Trident on the basis that they pay Trident £100,000[5] and forgo 1 per cent of royalties on Queen's next six albums.

'As far as Queen are concerned,' said Freddie, 'our old management is deceased. They cease to exist in any capacity with us whatsoever. One leaves them behind like one leaves excreta. We feel so relieved.'[6]

Having dispensed with Trident, Queen appointed a new manager, John Reid, who just happened to also be the manager of Elton John.

'There was a fellow at EMI named David Croker, and he rang me one day and said, "Are you interested in any groups?" as I didn't have a group at the time,' recalls Reid. Croker told him that, 'There's a group here called Queen who are having problems with their management and they're really quite good,' Reid was aware of Queen thanks to their two singles, 'Keep Yourself Alive' and 'Killer Queen' but needed to see for himself if the band could perform live.

'I knew that to crack America, which was very important, you had to be able to play live and play big, and he said, "Yeah, yeah, they're very good," so I told him I needed to see them and he rang back and told me "They're just about to go in the studio, but they'll set up a gig for you." So I went down to Bridge Farm and I went in and there's a full stage and a full lighting set-up – and me! And they did 40 minutes and I was blown away. I didn't find out until some time later that they'd invited three or four other managers and I was the only one who turned up. So I almost got the gig by default,' remembers Reid.[7]

'For a band that's starting off, guidance and good management is certainly vital,' said Freddie. 'But people like to think that artists don't have brains, and certainly a lot of them are very easily separated from their money. We were more cunning than that. After Trident, we approached a series of top-class managers to make sure we made the right choice. At the time John Reid happened to be the right choice. He flashed his eyes at me and I said, "Why not?" He was great, actually. It was the sort of combination we'd wanted for years. His approach and method of work was so right. He came in to negotiate the whole structure of recording, publishing and management.'[8]

'I was puzzled by Freddie at the beginning,' recalls Reid. 'I immediately said to Dave Croker, "Of course, he's gay, isn't he?" "Oh, no, no, no, he lives with a girl, Mary Austin." Well, that's not unusual but you know, he *is* gay! As individuals I was intrigued. John Deacon was kind of the quintessential bass player, mysterious. Roger was a great drummer and Brian was wearing clogs then and is still wearing them now and I was intrigued by their backgrounds, the fact they'd all been to university in diverse ways, so they were clearly intelligent. And I liked the melodies and I liked the songs. So I had a meeting with them altogether and we went through it and they were all feeling me out and I was feeling them out and then I took them out to dinner individually. Freddie had asked me to go around to his flat where he lived with Mary and I went round to pick him up, and when I went in he was playing the *Cabaret* soundtrack, blasting it out, and Mary was very nice, quite shy, but I didn't see the balance there.

'So we went to dinner in a restaurant in Fulham Road, just me and Freddie. We sat down and we were just talking. He was very funny, and he had a habit of touching his top lip and I said, "Maybe you should look at getting your teeth done," and he said, "I've had them fixed!" So we're having dinner, and in the middle of the conversation I said, "Look, Freddie, there's one thing I think you should know and I hope it doesn't make any difference to you or the rest of the band; you do know that I'm gay?" And he dropped his knife and fork and he said, "So am I, dear, we'll get on swimmingly."'[9]

Upon returning from Japan, Freddie was presented with an Ivor Novello Award for 'Killer Queen' and devoted some time to producing a song for an upcoming singer/songwriter, Ed Howell, whom he had met at the Thursday Club in Kensington. However, Freddie's efforts were in vain when the song 'The Man From Manhattan' was pulled from radio playlists after it was discovered the American bass player wasn't a member of the Musicians' Union and didn't even have a valid UK work permit. Consequently, Howell slowly slipped into obscurity as a performer and, at the same time, Queen themselves were facing an uncertain future. While they wouldn't have faded into obscurity, it was widely felt that a great deal hinged on the success of their next album and single. The band was significantly in debt and any perception of failure from their next record might mean they wouldn't survive.

So, with this pressure hanging over them, Queen assembled at a country house in Hertfordshire in August 1975 for three weeks of rehearsals prior to recording their new album, which would be called *A Night At The Opera* and would be produced, once again, by Roy Thomas Baker. Everyone in Queen was aware of how important this record was. 'Immediately prior to *A Night At The Opera* we were going through a really difficult period,' says Roger Taylor. 'We had a very successful album with *Sheer Heart Attack*, we thought it was a very good album and it had done very well, we had a major worldwide hit with "Killer Queen" and we were broke. We needed a big turning point, so we banked everything on the album.'[10]

The recording sessions, over three months, were long and rigorous and eventually took in six studios. The album's pre-publicity suggested it cost over £35,000 to produce[11], making it one of the most expensive albums ever and causing rifts, tensions and arguments among the band.

Aside from the traditional rendition of 'God Save The Queen', which would conclude the album, all four members of Queen wrote songs for *A Night At The Opera*, with Freddie composing five of the tracks on the album, which opened with 'Death On Two Legs (Dedicated To…)', an open hate letter to Normal Sheffield of Trident. '"Death On Two Legs" was the most vicious lyric I ever wrote,'[12] Freddie would say and the other band members were under no illusion at who the song was aimed. 'He was very aggrieved at our management at the time, who he felt didn't respect him, hadn't paid him, had stolen from him, you know, whatever, and he wanted to put it down on record,'[13] Roger Taylor recalls.

Norman Sheffield was aware of the record, too. 'By late 1975 I was hearing that they were making all sorts of derogatory comments about Trident. Then I heard a track from *A Night At The Opera* called "Death On Two Legs". The opening two lines summed up what was to come: "You suck my blood like a leech/you break the law and you breach," then "Do you feel like suicide?" it went on, "I think that you should." It was some kind of nasty hate mail from Freddie to me.'[14]

'No one would ever believe how much hate and venom went into the singing of that song, let alone the lyrics themselves,' Freddie would say in a 1977 interview. 'Just listen to the words carefully. It's a nasty little number, which brings out my evil streak. I don't usually like to explain what I was thinking when I wrote that song. It's about a nasty old man that I used to know. The words came very easy to me. I decided that if I wanted to stress something strongly, like that, I might as well go the whole hog and not compromise. I had a tough time trying to get the lyrics across. I wanted to make them as coarse as possible. My throat was bleeding – the whole bit. I was changing lyrics every day, trying to get it as vicious as possible. When the others first heard it they were in a state of shock. When I was describing it they said, "Oh yeah!" but then they saw the words and they were frightened by it. But for me the step had been taken and I was completely engrossed in it, swimming in it. I was a demon for a few days.'[15]

At the opposite end of the spectrum was Freddie's next composition on the album, 'Lazing on a Sunday Afternoon', a song that mixed the styles of Cole Porter with The Beatles' later work. Freddie's third composition, 'Seaside Rendezvous', harks back to the nostalgia of music hall while 'Love Of My Life' was his fourth track. Written originally on the piano but adapted for guitar by Brian May, it has often been considered a love song for Mary Austin but, during the writing of this book, Queen's manager of the time, John Reid, revealed who the song was really about: 'Freddie actually wrote "Love Of My Life" for David Minns. Freddie told me that. "Love Of My Life" was for Minns.'[16]

'Basically, I think if you put them all in one bag my songs are all under the label emotion, you know,' Freddie said. 'It's emotion and feeling, so I write songs that a lot of people have written before. It's all to do with love and emotion. I'm just a true romantic and I think everybody's written songs in that field, I just write it in my own way so they carry a different texture or whatever.'[17]

Freddie's final contribution to the album would be his greatest of all: a six-minute epic in three distinct movements that was the most expensive single ever recorded at the time of its release, contained no chorus, consisted of lyrics alluding to murder and nihilism and was ground-breaking in its use of an operatic middle section.

'"Bohemian Rhapsody" was a big risk and it worked. I mean, with a song like that, it was either going to be a huge success or a terrific flop,' Freddie revealed during a radio interview two years after recording the song.[18]

Nothing like it had been heard before, and nothing has been heard like it since.

Freddie began composing 'Bohemian Rhapsody' in his flat in Kensington long before the recording sessions took place, as John Reid remembers: 'Freddie invited me around to his flat in Holland Road. He showed me the flat and in the bedroom there was an upright piano with candle arms on it, which was his headboard, and he said that sometimes during the night he would think of something musical and flip it back and play it. He was double-jointed and his hands could bend back completely and I think that's where some of the passages from "Bohemian Rhapsody" started.'[19]

Another visitor to Freddie's Kensington flat was Roy Thomas Baker, the man who had produced all of Queen's albums so far, and would go on to produce *A Night At The Opera*. During one of his visits, Roy remembers that he was given a snippet of what was to become 'Bohemian Rhapsody': 'We were going out to dinner one night and I met Freddie at his apartment in Kensington. He sat down at his piano and said, "I'd like to play you a song that I'm working on at the moment." So he played the first part and said, "This is the chord sequence," followed by the interim part, and although he didn't have all the lyrics together yet, I could tell it was going to be a ballady number. He played a bit further through the song and then stopped suddenly, saying, "This is where the opera section comes in." We both just burst out laughing. I had worked with the D'Oyly Carte Opera Company at Decca, where I learned a lot about vocals and the way vocals are stressed, so I was probably one of the few people in the whole world who knew exactly what he was talking about.'[20]

'I'd always wanted to do something operatic,' Freddie explained. 'Something with a mood-setter at the start, going into a rock type of thing that completely breaks off into an opera section – a vicious twist – and then returns to the theme. I don't really know anything about opera myself, just certain pieces. I wanted to create what I thought Queen could do on that theme. I wasn't trying to say that it was authentic opera, certainly not – it's no pinch of *Magic Flute*. I wasn't saying I was an opera fanatic and I knew everything about it, I just wanted it to be opera in the rock'n'roll sense. Why not? It was as far as my limited capacity could take me.'[21]

When the band started recording *A Night At The Opera* in Wales, most of the songs were written within the studio or had been worked on in the three-week rehearsal period earlier in August from ideas band members had brought with them. But the whole concept for 'Bohemian Rhapsody' had been worked out by Freddie before they even got into the studio, and it was there that he first presented the idea to the rest of Queen. 'I remember the first time I heard the melody, the main melody, I loved the melody,' remembers Roger Taylor.[22]

Queen began recording the track in three sections in Wales. Later, they would move to studios in London to work on the complex vocal arrangements and guitar overdubs. 'The first half or ballad section was done with piano, drums and bass – the normal routine,' remembers Roy Thomas Baker. 'We never really started the opera section at that point. We just left a 30-second strip of tape on the reel for later use, not knowing that we would even overrun it. Then the end rock section was recorded as a separate song, in the way that we would normally record a loud rock number of that period. The thing that made it difficult was that even the end had lots of vocals on it (the "Ooh yeah, ooh yeah" part), so we had to record the basic backing track of drums, bass, guitar and piano, then do the background vocals without having the lead vocal on first. That wasn't the regular way of doing things, because the lead vocal would normally dictate the phrasing of the background vocals. But we wouldn't have had enough tracks left for the rich backing vocals if we hadn't gone down this route.'[23]

With the beginning and end sections of the song recorded, albeit still incomplete, the recording process switched to the complex operatic middle section. 'It was the first time that an opera section had been incorporated into a pop record, let alone a Number One,' says Roy Thomas Baker. 'It was obviously very unusual and we originally planned to have just a couple of "Galileos". But things often have a habit of evolving differently once you're inside the studio, and it did get longer and bigger. The beginning section was pretty spot-on and the end section was fairly similar, although we obviously embellished it with guitars and lots of overdubs. But the opera section ended up nothing like the original concept, because we kept changing it and adding things to it.'[24]

'Bohemian Rhapsody' took three weeks to record, as long as most bands took to record an entire album in the mid-1970s, and most of this was spent on the middle operatic section. Over a number of ten- to 12-hour days, the band laid down nearly 200 vocal overdubs in order to flesh out an entire choir. Roger provided the high vocals while

Brian took the lower end of the range and Freddie, with his incredibly powerful voice, contributed across the middle and lower end of the choir. John, meanwhile, volunteered to sit out the vocal recording as he had little confidence in his voice.

'The opera bit was getting longer, and so we kept splicing huge lengths of tape on to the reel,' recalls Roy Thomas Baker. 'Every time Freddie came up with another "Galileo", I would add another piece of tape to the reel, which was beginning to look like a zebra crossing whizzing by! This went on over a three- or four-day period, while we decided on the length of the section.'[25]

With all the vocals recorded, as well as the backing tracks of piano, bass and drums, Queen moved back to London to add the guitar elements and mix the complex vocals. They bedded down in SARM Studios with Roy Thomas Baker, alongside Mike Stone and Gary Langan, the studio engineers. SARM had a 24-track recording facility, extremely advanced for the time, and this was the ideal environment for Freddie to oversee the completion of his masterpiece.

'This was where technology and Fred went together,' says Langan, 'because here was a medium he could use to further his greatness. When 24-track came along it must have been like the sun coming out for him, the fact that he could use multi-tracking to do all these vocals.'[26]

With the song finally complete, it was ready for playback in the studio. The recording process had been such a technically complex affair that no one was entirely sure what to expect when they heard the finished result. Gary Langan remembers that occasion well: 'I stood at the back of the room and my jaw was on my chest. I just hadn't heard or felt or witnessed anything like this track. It was just amazing. You knew then it was destined for such greatness. It had this whole charisma about it.'[27]

Such was the reception of 'Bohemian Rhapsody' that most of the band felt it should be released as the first single from *A Night At The Opera*. But the nature of the time was that radio stations generally limited themselves to playing singles with the classic three-minute running length. 'Bohemian Rhapsody' was almost twice that and, without radio airplay, the chances of the song becoming a hit were minimal.

'We did have thoughts about, even in England, perhaps editing it down at all, but we listened to it over and over again and there was no way we could edit it,' remembers bass player John Deacon. 'We tried a few ideas, but if you edited it, you always lost some part of the song, so we had to leave it all in.'[28]

'There were lots of talks about cutting it down to a reasonable air-playing time, but we were adamant that it would be a hit in its entirety,' said Freddie. 'We have been forced to make compromises before, but cutting up a song will never be one of them. Why do that when it would be to the detriment of the song? They wanted to chop it down to three minutes but I said, "No way! Either it goes out in its entirety, or not at all. It either stays as it is or forget it!" It was either going to be a big flop or people were going to listen to it and buy it and it would be a big hit.'[29]

Others had their doubts about it as a single, as Queen's manager at the time, John Reid, recalls: 'I kept dipping into the studio and hearing things and I'd never been involved with a group at this stage of recording and I was fascinated by the way that they layered and layered and layered, and when they'd finished it they played it to me and I was astonished. So I took a copy of "Bohemian Rhapsody" to a couple of people, one of them being Elton [John], who said, "It'll never get played, dear, it's not going to happen."'[30]

Queen's record company, EMI, also thought the band were mad to think about releasing 'Bohemian Rhapsody' in its full form, even without listening to it. 'EMI said we had to edit it, but we stuck to our guns,' remembers Reid.[31]

EMI then tried to push Queen to release 'You're My Best Friend' as the album's first single instead, but once more the band put up a united front and refused. But the producer of the record, Roy Thomas Baker, had no concerns about releasing 'Bohemian Rhapsody' as a single: 'The way I rationalised it was that there had previously been Richard Harris' "MacArthur Park" and Barry Ryan's "Eloise", which were very long, and that justified to me that it was probably the right time to release a long song and get away with it.'[32]

When the album was complete, journalists and music critics were invited to hear a complete playback of *A Night At the Opera*. Among them was Paul Gambaccini and he, like John Reid and Freddie Mercury, was under no illusions about the stand-out track on the album after he had heard it: 'So they had the album playback,' recalls Gambaccini, 'and in those days everyone listened intently. It's not like in the 21st century where people talk over it. And when "You're My Best Friend" played, everybody thought, well, there's the hit single, it's all done, now let's just hear the rest of the album, and of course "Bohemian Rhapsody" was the last track on side two, so nobody thought there's going to be this nuclear bomb at the end of the record and it obviously stood out. But it took Kenny [Everett] to run away with it and make it a hit.'[33]

In 1975, 31-year-old Kenny Everett hosted a show on Capitol Radio that mixed inventive brilliance with unremitting disrespect and attracted a large and loyal audience. Sacked from Radio 1 five years earlier for an on-air gaffe about the then transport minister's wife, he was known as the *enfant terrible* of British pop radio. A friend of Freddie Mercury's, Everett was also struggling with his sexuality and, labelled as a tortured genius, he had married a spiritualist called Crystal Clear while keeping his homosexuality suppressed until coming out in 1985, divorcing his wife, and moving in with former Red Army soldier, Nikolai Grishanovich, and a Spanish waiter named Pepe Flores.

Everett had been a fan of Queen almost from the outset. In Freddie, he saw a kindred spirit – they were both gay, although neither had come out publicly, they were into the same kind of music and also shared an enthusiasm for production and studio techniques. As a result, their friendship blossomed and when, following a playback preview of *A Night At The Opera* to industry executives and DJs Freddie spoke with Everett, revealing all the negativity about releasing the record was forcing him to have doubts, the presenter attempted to convince him otherwise. 'It was like Mozart wondering if his next concerto was any good,' remembered Everett, 'when of course it was utter genius.'[34]

Armed with his copy of the record, and under strict instructions not to play it, Everett began teasing his audience by playing it in snippets on his radio show one weekend. Finally, he played the whole song, and, over the course of two days he would play the song in its entirety 14 times. Almost immediately, the switchboard at Capital Radio was inundated with people demanding to know where they could get hold of the record while the reception area was besieged by visitors arriving with cash and wanting to buy the record there and then. It was pandemonium. Yet the record hadn't even been pressed yet, let alone released.

'In the meantime, John Reid had got together with the MD at EMI Records and they just went ahead and started to press the single,' recalls Roy Thomas Baker. 'During the same weekend that Everett was playing the song, there was a guy called Paul Drew, who ran the RKO stations in the States. He happened to be in London and heard it on the radio. He managed to get a copy of the tape and started to play it in the States, which forced the hand of Queen's USA label, Elektra. It was a strange situation, where radio on both sides of the Atlantic was breaking a record that the record companies said would never get airplay!'[35]

'Bohemian Rhapsody' was finally released in the UK on 31st October 1975. It entered the UK charts at number 47. A week later, it was number 17 and the following week it had broken into the Top 10 at number 9.

With a potential date looming to appear on *Top of the Pops*, Queen were wondering how they could possibly perform such a song, with its operatic centrepiece, in the confines of the BBC's TV studios, not to mention the fact that they were about to embark on a major UK tour. They decided to make what would become a groundbreaking music video. The shoot for the video took just three hours but cost £4,500, a fortune at the time when music videos normally cost around £600.[36]

On 25th November 1975 'Bohemian Rhapsody' became the number one song in the UK. The video brought the song to life when broadcast on *Top of the Pops* and all opinions that a six-minute song would never be played on the radio were unequivocally destroyed. Despite a mixed critical reaction, it remained at number 1 for nine weeks and won Freddie another Ivor Novello Award as well as gaining Queen their first platinum disc. The same week that 'Bohemian Rhapsody' hit the top spot in the singles chart Queen released the album *A Night At The Opera*. It, too, reached number 1 for four weeks and would go on to sell over 12m copies worldwide, reaching number 4 in the US.

For many, *A Night At The Opera* is the definitive Queen album. 'It's the most important album for us and it had the strongest songs ever,' said Freddie. 'I knew it was going to be our best album. I was really pleased about the operatic thing. I wanted to be outrageous with vocals. At that moment we'd made an album which, let's face it, was too much to take for most people. But it was what we wanted to do. We wanted to experiment with sound, and sometimes we used three studios simultaneously. The actual album took four months to record. Brian's "The Prophet's Song" alone took two and a half to three weeks. There were just so many songs we wanted to do. And it makes a change to have short numbers as well. We had all the freedom we wanted and it was so varied that we were able to go to extremes.'[37]

With both single and album topping the charts, Queen's 26-date UK tour was a sell-out and on both sides of the Atlantic the band were enjoying enormous success. Things would never be the same again for any of the four members of Queen but life for Freddie, especially, would change beyond all recognition. In fact, it already had. His affair with David Minns had supplanted his sexual desire for Mary Austin. He still loved her emotionally, and he would do so until his dying day, but his homosexuality seemed liberated by the musical success he was having and it was giving him a freedom to explore this sexuality more deeply.

For decades there has been speculation as to the meaning of the lyrics of 'Bohemian Rhapsody'. Freddie himself would never give anything away in interviews: 'People still ask me what "Bohemian Rhapsody" is all about, and I say I don't know. I think it loses the myth and ruins a kind of mystique that people have built up. "Rhapsody" is one of those songs that has a fantasy feel about it. I think people should just listen to it, think about it, and then decide for themselves what it means to them,' he would say.[38]

Many listeners took the song's violent images at face value, thinking it was simply about a murderer confessing his crime. But others, such as critic Anthony DeCurtis, interpreted it differently. 'The song is about a secret transgression – "I'm being punished" – at the same time that there's this desire for freedom.'[39]

Freddie's personal assistant for the last 12 years of his life, Peter Freestone, was equally certain about the meaning of the song: 'If you look at the video and the way in which "Bohemian Rhapsody" is written, in its totally separate parts – not really a mixture of parts, its three parts – that would describe Freddie's life at that time. He was living with Mary, his coming to terms with his desire for men, and his actual sleeping with men.'[40] Authors Sheila Whiteley and Jennifer Rycenga suggest that 'Bohemian Rhapsody' provides 'a particular insight into the tensions surrounding gay identity in 1970's Britain, and Mercury's performance can be interpreted as challenging social, cultural, and musical structures in its invocation of gay male desire'[41] while the lyricist Sir Tim Rice says, 'It's fairly obvious to me that this was Freddie's "coming-out" song. I've even spoken to Roger about it. I heard the record very early on, and it struck me that there is a very clear message contained in it. This is Freddie saying, "I'm coming out. I'm admitting that I'm gay."'[42]

Scrutinising the song – even the word 'Bohemian' is defined as 'a socially unconventional person' – it is possible to create a homosexual subtext to virtually any phrase from it and, therefore, appear to confirm that it's about Freddie coming out to his mother and reconciling his own sexuality. It's possible to deduce that the images of murder, the gun, the trigger, the death are a metaphor for active homosexual engagement and the lyric, 'Mama, just killed a man', is not necessarily about the criminal act of murdering someone but more the metaphorical act of killing his old self; himself as a heterosexual 'man'.

The first two verses of the song, before we arrive at the operatic section, are a pure confessional which explores and reveals that this decision he has taken, the decision to embrace his homosexuality, is a matter of life and death to him and those around him. It also exhibits his struggle with himself and his coming to terms with his sexuality in the line: 'Sometimes wish I'd never been born at all'. The operatic section sees Freddie having to wrestle with his inner demons and it's interesting to note that the higher voices, perhaps the female voices, are beseeching him to 'go' while the deeper male voices are telling him 'we will not let you go' and these choral sections signal entrapments and the plea for his release.

In the operatic section Freddie calls out to Bismillah, the Islamic equivalent of 'In the name of the Father, the Son and the Holy Ghost', therefore asking the Almighty to 'spare him his life from this monstrosity', perhaps a life in denial, and finally, resigned to his fate – or celebrating it – he accepts and embraces his sexuality in the final section of the song, ending in a place of acceptance with the final line, 'anyway the wind blows'.

Freddie was already engaged in an affair with David Minns despite still living with Mary Austin and this affair would, undoubtedly, have influenced his writing. 'I think he was in love with David, absolutely, yes,' says Peter Straker, one of Freddie's closest friends, 'and I think David was in love with him.'[43] Authors Sheila Whiteley and Jennifer Rycenga explore this even further: 'The confessional of "Bohemian Rhapsody" and its intimate address to "Mama" provide an initial insight into Mercury's emotional state at the time: living with Mary ("Mama"), wanting to break away ("Mama Mia, let me go"). Bars 80–85, in particular, provide an emotional setting for the dialectic interplay. The heightened sense of urgency seems to resonate with Mercury's inner turmoil, leaving the security of Mary Austin, coming to terms with gay life ("easy come, easy go"), and living with a man ("So you think you can stone me and spit in my eye").'[44]

Freddie's bandmates were less forthcoming in dissecting the song: 'It's fairly self-explanatory,' drummer Roger Taylor told the BBC, 'there's just a bit of nonsense in the middle.'[45] While Brian May said of the song's meaning, 'I don't think we'll ever know, and if I knew, I probably wouldn't want to tell you anyway.'[46] And even John Reid says: 'There's been so much analysis of the song, but I subscribe to the theory, and I never discussed it with him, that it was his coming out song.'[47]

However it is interpreted, the song became Freddie Mercury's and Queen's biggest hit. By the end of January 1976 it had sold over a million copies in the UK, topped the charts in the UK, Australia, Canada, Netherlands, New Zealand and Belgium and reached number 9 in the US. At the time of writing it has sold over 6m copies worldwide and was voted number 166 in *Rolling Stone*'s '500 Greatest Songs of All Time',[48] while a *Rolling Stone* readers' poll voted Freddie's rendition of the song as 'The Best Vocal Performance in Rock History'.[49] 'Bohemian Rhapsody' changed the entire landscape for Queen: they were now global superstars.

As for Freddie, his life was going through massive changes too following the success of 'Bohemian Rhapsody', as his friend and Queen photographer, Mick Rock, reveals: 'Once "Bohemian Rhapsody" hit, that was what changed everything. That was when, I suppose, he threw all caution to the wind and became what he felt he was sexually.'[50]

Freddie considered 'Bohemian Rhapsody' to be his greatest accomplishment. He was right. We have discussed how Mercury's *magnum opus* was an autobiographical testimonial to his homosexuality, yet after his death the tragic narrative of the song's text would take on greater meaning.

But for now, life for Queen and Freddie Mercury would never be the same again.

18

We do not know how many people developed AIDS in the 1970s, or indeed in the years before, but 1976 seems a pivotal year in the spread of the virus.

On 4th January of that year, an eight-year-old girl died in the Norwegian village of Borre. Just over three months later, on 24th April, the girl's father also died of a mysterious illness. His name was Arne Vidar Røed and it would be a decade before Dr Stig Sophus Frøland of the Oslo National Hospital could confirm both father and daughter, as well as Røed's wife, had tested positive for HIV. This confirmation made the eight-year-old girl the first person documented to have died of AIDS outside the United States of America. In a grim forewarning of what was to come, it transpired Røed had infected his wife, who had then, unwittingly, passed on HIV to their daughter in childbirth. But what was especially frightening was the revelation of Røed's lifestyle: a lifestyle that indicated his unremitting, yet unknowing, transmission of HIV throughout Europe.

In 1961, Røed began work as a sailor on the merchant ship *Hoegh Aronde* when he was just 15 years old. One of his first trips was to the west coast of Africa. Here, the ship docked at Nigeria, Ghana, Côte d'Ivoire, Liberia, Guinea and Senegal over a ten-month period before returning to Norway. In Cameroon, Røed caught gonorrhea from a prostitute. He was treated for it and thought nothing more of the embarrassing illness as he sailed throughout Asia, Europe, Canada and the Caribbean. Little did he know that although medication had cleared up his gonorrhea, lying latent within him, possibly caught from the same woman in Cameroon, was HIV.

Four years later, 19-year-old Røed returned to Norway and married, but his time back in Norway found him feeling unwell. Although doctors could not classify his illness, Røed had aching muscles, a red rash over his body, and he found himself suffering frequent respiratory ailments. In 1967, his wife began to suffer similar maladies and in 1968 their youngest daughter would exhibit the same symptoms. Unable to return to sea, Røed gained new employment, this time as a long-distance lorry driver, with deliveries taking him to the Netherlands, France, Germany, Austria, Switzerland and Italy. Once again, according to co-workers, Røed sought comfort on the long and lonely lorry routes with many prostitutes as well as other women. Two cities he was known to have visited were Liège in Belgium and Lyons in France and investigators here would later find cases of HIV in individuals who had died in the late-1970s and early-1980s but had never visited Cameroon, where the strain that Røed was carrying, and those victims exhibited, came from.

Røed died in April 1976 at the age of 29, a few months after the death of his daughter. Soon, his wife would pass away too. When tissues taken from their bodies and saved by the original pathologist were re-examined by Dr Stig Sophus Frøland, a decade later, Røed and his wife and daughter were confirmed as the first recorded cluster of confirmed HIV/AIDS.[1]

What this tragedy confirmed, albeit too late, was the transient nature of HIV. It knew no boundaries and thrived upon transmission between hosts who would then venture across continents unknowingly passing it on.

We now know that 1976 was a critical year in the spread of HIV. The comfort of our present day allows us to see this because we have learnt that the average incubation period of HIV is approximately five years before it develops into full-blown AIDS, and the life expectancy thereafter between one and three years. Calculating backwards and then working forwards, it brings us round to 1983, which was when the tsunami of casualties began. Using this criteria, 1983 takes us back to 1976 as the launchpad for HIV spreading its tentacles of tragedy around the globe. The year 1976 is also of interest because three critical events took place in the US, which all come together to create the perfect breeding ground for an HIV epidemic.

Firstly, during the mid-1970s, gay tourism in the US was flourishing and the major destination for gay tourists was Haiti, the country that had already seen cases of HIV owing to the Haitian workers returning from West Africa around 1966. As evolutionary biologist Michael Worobey stated: 'There is strong evidence that HIV-1 subtype B arrived and began spreading in Haiti before it did elsewhere. Until AIDS was initially recognized in 1982[2] the virus was cryptically circulating in a sophisticated medical environment for the better part of twelve years.'[3]

In the late-1960s to early- to mid-1970s Haiti had become an important destination for gay North American men. They were attracted to the island not only because of its proximity and exotic appeal, but also because there was an abundance of sexually available men, whose services could be bought for little owing to the extreme poverty that many Haitians endured. Any one of these North American tourists could have, and probably did, bring HIV back to the US.

Secondly, 1976 was the year of the United States of America's Bicentenary, and Operation Sail was instigated as part of the celebrations of the adoption of the Declaration of Independence. Operation Sail saw 16 of the world's tall ships sail to New York to participate in the parade of ships on 4th July 1976. Joining them were over 50 naval ships from around the world, and author Randy Shilts suggests that 'the sailors from these sailing ships added to the sexual tenor of the times, and they brought their globally contracted infections with them.'[4]

That night New York City saw a party to end all parties. As fireworks burned brightly behind the Statue of Liberty ships from around the globe disgorged their crew, who flocked to the clubs, bars, hotel rooms, baths, sex clubs and peep shows of the city, ready to party hard. 'Deep into the morning, bars all over the city were crammed with sailors. New York City had hosted the greatest party ever known, everybody agreed later. The guests had come from all over the world. This was the part the epidemiologists would later note, when they stayed up late at night and the conversation drifted toward where it had started and when. They would remember that glorious night in New York Harbor, all those sailors, and recall: From all over the world they came to New York.'[5]

The five-day-long bicentennial celebration, culminating on 4th July 1976, saw 25,000 visiting naval officers and crews from around the world descend on New York from 94 maritime nations. Vessels from Belgium, France, the UK and Peru among others mixed with delegations from Ghana, Indonesia, Senegal and Thailand, to name but a few. The event was a vast mixing pot of pent-up testosterone and sexual frustration waiting to explode amid the hedonistic atmosphere of New York's liberal landscape. These sailors most likely enlisted the services of male and female prostitutes. They, in turn, may have become infected themselves if they weren't already and, in turn, infected some of their customers, at least some of whom would have had sex with a man. That man, or men, then had sex with several other men. And so it could have begun here. Likewise, if HIV didn't arrive with any of these sailors, it is very likely it left with them and so the march of what was to become known as AIDS was continued to nations new. Curiously, a cluster of perinatally[6] infected children was born in 1977 in New York City in the corresponding months after the 4th July celebrations. They were born to women with histories of introvenous drug use, but this indicates the growing prevalence of HIV in New York around the time of the 4th July 1976 celebrations.[7]

Thirdly, and finally, 1976 saw one more great party in New York City. It was New Year's Eve and revellers were seeing out a year that was to become notorious though no one yet knew that. Disco had left the gay clubs and become mainstream, but still the heyday of male sexual liberation continued underground in the dance bars and bathhouses that overflowed as meeting places for men who would share hundreds of sexual partners a year.

Suddenly, one of the most popular clubs in New York City was the Mineshaft, perhaps, as history suggests, the most notorious members-only gay club ever. Housed in a building constructed in 1927, it became the most incredible sex palace of the 1970s following its opening on 8th October 1976. Tucked away behind a nondescript doorway on Washington Street at Little West 12th Street, in the meatpacking district of West Greenwich Village, the entrance to the club was up a flight of stairs, where a doorman would only grant admittance if you passed muster. Denim and leather was allowed – positively encouraged – while designer clothes, sneakers and anyone wearing cologne were instantly rejected. A sign at the club stated the following:

> *The Mineshaft dress code*
> *Approved dress includes the following:*
> *Jocks, action-ready wear, uniforms,*
> *T-shirts, plaid shirts, just plain shirts,*

NO COLOGNES or PERFUMES
NO SUITS, TIES, DRESS PANTS
NO RUGBY SHIRTS, DESIGNER SWEATERS, or TUXEDOS
NO DISCO DRAG or DRESSES

'I was turned away from the Mineshaft in New York in the early 1980s,' recalls Marc Almond. 'Though I had a leather jacket and leather trousers on, I had traces of eyeliner and cologne, which of course was utterly unacceptable to the Mineshaft doorman. Years later, I wrote "Trials of Eyeliner", with the line "Eyeliner saved my life" – and likely it did.'[8]

Once inside, everything was fair game and the club existed for one reason only: pure hedonistic no-limits sex. A maze of small rooms was situated downstairs and a jail cell and dungeons existed within the club to enable gay men to recreate any sexual fantasy they desired. There was also the most notorious room in New York City within the club: a room with a bathtub in which men could let other men urinate on them. Almost all within the club would have been having unprotected sex, totally unaware of the virus that was, by now, lurking within New York and other parts of the US, such as Miami, Chicago and San Francisco. Film directors Vincente Minnelli and Rainer Werner Fassbinder were known visitors to Mineshaft and actor Rock Hudson too. Likewise singer-songwriter Patti Smith (one of the few female exceptions) and photographer Robert Mapplethorpe were seen there while Glenn Hughes, the original leather biker in the disco group Village People, was a frequent visitor.

While the building was safe, the sex definitely wasn't, but AIDS was still in the unforeseeable future, so everything went on that normally went on in Mineshaft during that great New Year's Eve party of 1976.

It wouldn't be until 1980 that Freddie Mercury visited the Mineshaft, but the US in 1976 would provide him with enough of a playground to enable him to indulge his newfound sexual freedom. It would be the year his attraction for New York City and the intensity of its underground gay scene would be cemented; also the year that Queen perfected post-gig excess in their partying. And it would be the year that Freddie, now finally famous and wealthy, and having come out to Mary Austin, could do whatever he wanted.

He wasn't to know – who possibly could? – that the backdrop of gay tourism to Haiti, the influx of sailors to New York for the bicentennial celebrations, and the anything-goes hedonism of clubs such as Mineshaft would be the beginning of a fatal journey that would end, for him, in 1991.

For now, it is 1976 and Freddie, on top of the world, is about to indulge himself in all the US has to offer as the Queen bandwagon rolls into North America for the next leg of their *A Night at the Opera* Tour.

19

The year 1976 started with Queen, and Freddie, riding high. 'Bohemian Rhapsody' was at number 1 in the UK singles chart and *A Night at the Opera* was sitting atop the album charts. The *NME* had awarded Queen Best British Stage Band, *Record Mirror* voted them Best British Group, *Sound* had given them the Best Band, Best Album and Best Single awards and 'Bohemian Rhapsody' had secured Freddie another Ivor Novello Award. It was the perfect position for the band to be in as they left the UK on 20th January for their world tour.

On 27th January the US leg of the tour kicked off in Connecticut and, with audiences in America now more familiar with Queen's material, it was a huge success. The band members were now true rock stars and were treated as such by adoring fans wherever they went. Naturally, given their newfound status, Queen's after-show parties began to grow in terms of scale and excess, and these would soon become legendary in the world of rock. During the 1976 tour, whenever the band rocked into town, local dignitaries, VIPs and celebrities would be invited backstage to meet and greet them. It was a necessary chore, but one that Freddie took a dislike to whenever representatives of Queen's record company would turn up. Author Mark Blake suggests a reason why: 'At his own parties, Freddie would happily play the attentive host. At parties thrown for him, he would become as shy and tongue-tied as the eighteen-year-old Farrokh Bulsara showing up for his first day at Isleworth Polytechnic. Unlike his teenage student self, Mercury could now throw a tantrum without fear of parental reprisal. He was the singer, the pop star, and he was indulged accordingly.'[1]

By the time Queen arrived in New York at the beginning of February for four shows at the Beacon Theatre, the band had grown accustomed to Freddie leaving them after a post-gig meal together whereupon, unbeknown to them, he would start to explore some of the seedier streets that the Big Apple had to offer. Shrouded in relative anonymity, and shielded from the British press, Mercury would prowl the city in his darkened limousine and expose himself to the underground gay scene.

'Freddie was quite well-behaved in London,' Paul Gambaccini recalls, 'compared to how he was in New York, or later, Munich. Those two cities were the capitals of anonymous, one-time-only sex – which never interested me in the least. Freddie undoubtedly enjoyed those places. It's a whole world, as rich in its magnitude as popular music is. I got the impression from him that his times in New York were always really wild, but the gay scene there at that time was much harder than anywhere.'[2]

It was during this brief stay in New York that Freddie's love affair with the city was sealed. He would eventually buy an apartment in the heart of the Big Apple, a base from which to indulge himself in the gay bars and nightclubs of New York. For now, though, he was just getting accustomed to what the place had to offer.

'When we went to America or Japan or Australia or wherever we were he was pretty outrageous,' recalls John Reid. 'He would walk into a bar, point at a man and say, "You." And that was it. He could pretty much get away with anything. Later, when he lived in New York, the hedonism really kicked in and that's where, I assumed, the illness took hold.'[3]

The US tour finished in March and the band headed to Japan and to another rapturous reception. 'I remember on that trip to Japan I kept discussing with him about the boys and whether he was going to be open with them,' says Reid, 'and he would say, "Let's keep it separate."'[4]

By this stage Freddie could see royalties from his songwriting starting to flow in and the relative riches he was now earning enabled him to indulge in his love of Japanese art. 'Money may be vulgar, but it's wonderful,' he once said. 'I cope with wealth very well, actually – I spend, spend, spend. Well, what's money for if not to spend? I spend it like it's nothing. I have lots of money, yes, but I honestly couldn't tell you what my bank balance is. I'm conditioned that way. I'll just go out and spend it. I'm not one of those who stuffs his money under the mattress and counts it every night. I'm not like some of those stars who are obsessed with counting their pennies. I know several people who do a show then rush home to count what they have, but not me. I don't give a damn about money. I just think it's for spending.'[5]

The money kept rolling in as Queen left Japan for Australia. It was the first time they had been back since their disastrous appearance at Sunbury

Music Festival in 1974. This time, they were welcomed with a virtually sold-out run of shows. At the end of April, with both their album and single topping the Australian charts and the reception much warmer than on their previous visit, the band flew back to the UK to begin work on their fifth album, which would be called *A Day at the Races*.

Shortly after arriving back in the UK, Brian May married his long-term girlfriend, Christine ('Chrissie') Mullen, who had been on the periphery of Queen ever since the days of Smile. John Deacon was happily ensconced in his marriage to Veronica and now had a son, Robert, and was living in Putney, while Roger Taylor, flush from his financial success, having written the B-side to 'Bohemian Rhapsody' and therefore sharing in the spoils of its success, had purchased a house in Fulham and was fully enjoying the bachelor lifestyle.

Freddie, however, was still living with Mary Austin, while continuing his affair with David Minns. He was also beginning to get a reputation as an outrageous international party animal, the legendary lord of excess, and a notable sex god. There were even rumours that he was using his newfound wealth to 'finance his growing use of cocaine and to indulge his fancies, whatever they were, in a private world that was changing at an unsettling rate'.[6] But beneath the exterior was a deeply romantic man, someone who constantly fell in love and was always looking for love. *The* love. He had thought, and those around him had thought, that he had found it with Mary Austin, and there was undoubtedly love there. But, for Freddie, it ultimately wasn't what he was looking for. And although he also seemed in love with David Minns, and Minns seemed in love with Freddie, Mercury was still battling with his feelings of being attracted to other men, all the while still living with Mary.

It was the success of 'Bohemian Rhapsody' that finally shifted the dynamic of the relationship between Freddie and Mary and, upon coming out to Mary and revealing his bisexuality to her, it may have appeared to Freddie that she gave him her blessing, enabling him to fully get into the swing of gay love. To keep his cover intact, Mary would agree to publicly attend events with him, posing as his girlfriend, and, in fact, she seemed to thoroughly enjoy these occasions. As far as Freddie was concerned, he loved to keep people guessing about his sexuality, and Mary was complicit in this by being by his side at various public functions. So successful was this deception, even Freddie's bandmates didn't appear to realise he was gay.

The Eurythmics singer, Annie Lennox, was studying at the Royal Academy of Music in London in the mid-1970s. Like many others, she was aware of Freddie's prowess as a performer but remained unaware of his true sexuality. 'Freddie Mercury's performance style was posturing, exhibitionistic and grandiose in a camp/machismo kind of way,' remembers Annie. 'So I guess only his close friends and associates would have known that he was actually gay and not "bisexual". He was publicly ambiguous about his sexuality for years. It wasn't public knowledge, as things were different back then and I'm sure he didn't want to risk alienating his broad fan base, so quite a few people might have been a bit surprised when the truth was finally revealed.'[7]

'Certainly within the music industry, as kind of tolerant and open as it was and supposedly is, it was not quite cool for a rock group to have an openly gay lead singer at that time,' suggests John Reid, 'so it was very much discouraged and Freddie dealt with it the way he dealt with it.'[8]

However, according to author David Bret, Freddie's sexuality was already beginning to gain unwanted attention from the British press during the summer of 1976: 'At around this time British newspapers began speculating over cracks which they said had begun appearing in Freddie's relationship with Mary Austin – according to the tabloids, because he had recently confessed his bisexuality to her. This, and further newspaper allegations that Mary was beginning to find Freddie an embarrassment, could only, of course, have been pure fabrication. During the summer of 1976, Freddie's antics were no more over-the-top that they had been years before when Mary had first met him – and even after their meticulously planned parting the pair still saw as much of each other as Queen's hectic touring and recording schedule permitted.'[9]

The difference was that now he was extremely famous. Throughout this period and, in fact, throughout the rest of his life, not once did Freddie give an interview to confirm or deny his sexuality.

'It was incredibly difficult for anyone in that period of time to come out,' says Paul Gambaccini. 'Anybody under the age of forty has no idea how homophobic society was before the Nineties.'[10]

Mercury once said that all the messages are in his songs, and close friends would say that Freddie didn't feel he had to answer the question of whether or not he was gay. 'Freddie was in his own prison, though a resolutely closeted Old School Outrageous Queen,' says Marc Almond. 'Though like many closeted Queens in showbiz, they spend their creative lives feeding us clues, sometimes screaming it out so loud, painting it so brightly, that it's just in too plain sight to be seen clearly in focus.'[11]

By the end of the year, Mary Austin had moved out of Freddie's flat and could only look on as he embraced a wild and ultimately destructive chapter of his life. 'I think Freddie reached a stage where he thought he was invincible,' she says. 'He convinced himself he was having a good time and maybe, in part, he was. But I think, in part, he wasn't. And then it was too late. The only person who could have made a difference was Freddie. But I think he'd stopped being honest with himself. Many of his so-called friends were there for the free tickets, the free booze, the free drugs, the free meal, the gossip and, of course, the expensive gifts.'[12]

Freddie would never admit to his homosexuality publicly and would constantly keep interviewers guessing. 'It's all in the songs,' he would say, and thereby lies the crux of the matter. It never needed to be said. As, years later, with AIDS, he felt it never needed to be said: it was there for all to see.

While all of this was going on in Freddie's private world, the Queen juggernaut rumbled on. Seeking a follow-up single to 'Bohemian Rhapsody', their record company settled on 'You're My Best Friend'. It was written by John Deacon for his wife and reached number 7 in the UK and number 16 in the US. On entering the UK Top 10, the song meant Deacon became the second member of Queen to write a Top 10 single.

The summer of 1976 saw Queen begin work in earnest on their next album. For the first time ever, they would self-produce the record, but they would be reunited with engineers Gary Langan and Mike Stone. Soon into the process, however, the band realised they were significantly behind schedule and any prospect of a major 1976 tour had to be shelved. As a result, Queen would only play four more shows

Freddie Mercury was born Farrokh Bulsara. Aged just one, little Farrokh experienced his first taste of fame when his baby picture won the local 'Most Beautiful Baby' Photo of the Year contest.

Freddie's childhood was comfortable as his parents had a high standard of living, enabling them to employ a nanny, Sabine, who looked after Freddie for three years.

Freddie's 4th birthday. Freddie rarely talked about his childhood on the island or his schooling in India. 'He didn't want to be considered Indian,' says close friend Peter Straker. 'He used to say he was Persian. He liked the idea of being Persian which I think is much more exotic.'

Freddie's first band, The Hectics, was formed at St. Peter's school in India in the early 60s, with Freddie playing piano. Standing in the center of the photo, Freddie looks toothily self-conscious and unmistakably Indian.

Ibex were a rough and ready band from Liverpool who had begun hanging out with Smile, and Freddie was Smile's chief 'hanger-on'. After seeing Ibex in an impromptu performance, Freddie suggested to one of the band members, 'What you guys need is a singer.'

In the summer of 1970, six years after he arrived in the UK, Freddie Bulsara became Freddie Mercury. According to close friend David Evans, '"Farrokh Bulsara" was a name he had buried.'

John Deacon joined Queen in February 1971, and the line-up remained the same until Freddie's death. 'We always argued. We fought on virtually the first day… We've all got our individual characteristics, but it's probably that that keeps us together.'

'I play on the bisexual thing,' said Freddie. 'It's simply a matter of wherever my mood takes me. If people ask me if I'm gay, I tell them it's up to them to find out.'

Freddie set about putting his stamp on the band from the start. He wrote songs, created the image of the band by designing a regal crest, and changed the name from Smile to Queen. He would also become Britain's first Indian pop star.

April 1975 saw Queen tour Japan for the first time. It was the beginning of a long love affair Freddie would have with the country, avidly collecting Japanese object d'art, attracted to its constant pursuit of perfection.

'I like people to go away from our shows feeling fully entertained, having had a good time,' said Freddie.

With the exception of one song, Freddie composed all of Queen's Top Ten singles during the 70s, including their first Number One, 'Bohemian Rhapsody'.

The success of Freddie's songwriting soon saw him receive fame and fortune he had dreamt of. 'I always knew I would be a star and now the rest of the world seems to agree with me.'

Gaëtan Dugas, the flight attendant labelled Patient Zero, and the man accused of sparking the AIDS epidemic in the US.

Freddie described Mary Austin as the love of his life. He would later say 'If I go first I'm going to leave everything to her. Nobody else gets a penny – except my cats. I'll love her until I draw my last breath. We'll probably grow old together.'

West End star Peter Straker became Freddie's closest friend. 'He'd turn up and see the shows and we'd drive back to London together and we just got on famously, really.'

Freddie often threw lavish and extravagant dinner parties for his closest friends at Garden Lodge, his Kensington home. He surrounded himself with people he could trust completely.

Peter Straker and Freddie at the mixing desk. 'We had the best of times, and then later the worst of them too. He was a kind, generous and sensitive person, and I adored him. We would talk several times a day on the phone, no matter where he was in the world.'

Freddie with John Reid, Elton John's manager, who would become Queen's manager in 1975.

in 1976, all in September: two at the Playhouse Theatre in Edinburgh, which would celebrate the reopening of the theatre after refurbishment, an open-air concert at Cardiff Castle in Wales, and finally, a huge open-air show in London's Hyde Park on 18th September. The Hyde Park show had been the brainchild of Richard Branson of Virgin Records and the significance of the date, although purely coincidental, was not lost on Freddie and the rest of Queen as it was six years to the day since the death of Jimi Hendrix, Freddie's idol.

Nearly 200,000 people flocked to Hyde Park to witness the concert. Taking the stage with smoke bombs and elaborate lighting, Roger, Brian and John could only look on from behind their instruments as Freddie rose from beneath the stage in a swirl of smoke and wearing a white leotard before greeting the crowd with his camp 'Darlings!' Then Queen launched into a blistering set that kept everyone entertained until a police curfew brought the show to a halt eighty minutes later without their usual encores. Despite Freddie wanting to continue and break the curfew, the thought of having to spend a night in the cells wearing a leotard with a glittering crotch-piece seemed enough to make him reconsider. Reviewing the show, *Record Mirror* said of Freddie: 'He's an overt poser, a slick precision-like and ultimately professional entertainer who has found his way into that small gang of people we call stars. His performance in Hyde Park on Saturday was proof that he could stand beside Jagger, Bowie and a handful of Americans.'[13]

The success of the show was not only a huge relief to the organiser, Richard Branson, but also to Queen, who, despite the massive success of 'Bohemian Rhapsody' and *A Night at the Opera*, had a feeling of uncertainty about how they were actually perceived within the UK, but the success of the Hyde Park gig and the reception they received from the crowd dispelled all that immediately. Buoyed by this, and the fact they had just been awarded a Don Kirshner/CBS Rock Award in the US for the Best-produced Album of the Year, *A Night at the Opera*, Queen hurried back into the studio to put the finishing touches to their new album.

A Day At The Races was, like *A Night at the Opera*, named after a Marx Brothers' film and the cover was adorned with a similar crest and typography to their previous album. Musically, *A Day at the Races* was an unapologetic sequel to *A Night at the Opera*. As the *Washington Post* said: 'For their next effort, they could either stick their necks out and try something new – or play it safe and deliver more of the same. It takes only a glance at the cover of "A Day at the Races" to determine the choice they made.'[14]

Recorded between July and November 1976, Freddie's contribution of four compositions to the album begins with 'You Take My Breath Away', a song on which, vocally and instrumentally, he provides everything and of which he would say, 'I multi-tracked myself. The others weren't used on that for the voices. I played piano and that was basically it. I don't know how we managed to keep it that simple, you know, with all our overdubs and things. People seem to think we're over complex, and it's not true. It depends on the individual track. If it needs it, we do it. So that track is pretty sparse, actually, by Queen standards.'[15]

His next track was 'The Millionaire Waltz', the album's would-be 'Bohemian Rhapsody' and a Strauss-inspired waltz about the band's then manager, John Reid. Freddie's next two songs were the most successful singles from the album: 'Somebody To Love' and 'Good Old-Fashioned Lover Boy'.

'Somebody To Love', with its complex melodies and deep layering of vocal tracks, was a song written with Aretha Franklin in mind. 'For "Somebody To Love", we had the same three people singing on the big choir section,' explained Freddie, 'but I think it had a different kind of technical approach because it was a gospel way of singing – which was different to us. That track was me going a bit mad. I just wanted to write something in the Aretha Franklin kind of mode. I was inspired by the gospel approach she had on her earlier albums. Although it might sound like the same approach on the harmonies, it is very different in the studio because it's a different range.'[16]

'I knew that I wanted a gospel choir feel to it,' he continued, 'and I knew we'd have to do it all ourselves. That song is something like 160-piece choir effect. You can imagine how long it took to do it – over and over and over again. We spent a week on that, but it was worth it. I never want to look back on one of our albums and think, "If only we'd spent longer, and done that it would have been better!" We are perfectionists about things and we think it's worth spending that time.

People probably think, "Oh, God, they're in the studio again for four and a half months," but we think it's necessary because it just has to be right, that's all.'[17]

Released as the first single from the forthcoming album on 12th November 1976, 'Somebody To Love' raced to number 2 in the UK singles charts and number 13 on the US Billboard Hot 100, going on to sell over 2m singles worldwide.

The fourth and final Mercury composition on the album was 'Good Old-Fashioned Lover Boy'. Describing the song, Freddie said it was 'another one of my vaudeville numbers. I always do a vaudeville track, though "Lover Boy" is more straightforward than "Seaside Rendezvous", for instance. It's quite simple piano/vocals with a catchy beat.'[18]

It would be released as the third single from the album in May 1977 as part of an EP, following Brian May's 'Tie Your Mother Down'. Both tracks failed to crack the UK Top 10, with 'Tie Your Mother Down' stalling at number 31 and the 'Good Old-Fashioned Lover Boy' EP reaching number 17. However, the album was a huge international success when released in December 1976 following a launch party at Kempton Races. It sold over 5m copies worldwide and topped the album charts in the UK, Japan and the Netherlands as well as reaching number 5 in the US. But, with the music scene shifting in the UK with the arrival of punk, the press were quick to run down the new album. *Rolling Stone* said, '*A Day at the Races* is probably meant to be the sequel to Queen's 1976 smash, *A Night at the Opera*, but nothing much has changed. Queen is the least experimental of such groups, probably because their commercial aspirations are the most brazen.'[19]

Nicholas Kent, writing in the *NME*, said, 'I hate this album. Adamantly so. If it wasn't going to be so obviously gargantuan, I would merely despise it, finding most of its contents daring to ply this sort of grand ultra-narcissistic self-indulgence. Almost everything bearing the composing moniker of one F. Mercury on this record seems to drip with that same cutesy-pie mirror preening essence or ultra-preciousness. All these songs with their *precious* pseudo-classical piano obligato bearings, their *precious* impotent Valentino kitsch mouthings on romance, their spotlight on a vocalist so giddily enamoured with his own *precious* image – they literally make my flesh creep.'[20]

At the heart of Kent's review is a deep-seated homophobia. His repeated use of the word 'precious' is indicative of the time, filled with derision and belittlement, disguising itself as a critical review while, at its core, inherently hate-filled. Earlier in his review, Kent had noted how the music scene was buzzing with the arrival of punk and how something was on the horizon that might topple the frazzled rock hierarchy. Queen were potentially seen as being one of the major culprits for what was now becoming perceived as overblown super rock and, in Britain of 1976 and 1977, a country heading for economic woes and dwindling opportunities, a young generation began to stir, eschewing the likes of Queen and embracing the world of punk.

Bizarrely, Queen had a byline in the emergence of punk, unwittingly bringing The Sex Pistols to national notoriety. As part of their promotional schedule for *A Day at the Races*, Queen had been booked to appear on the ITV show, *Today With Bill Grundy*, on 1st December 1976. Unable to fulfil their obligation, owing to the fact that Freddie Mercury had to make an unexpected visit to the dentist that day, Queen pulled out of the show, leaving Eric Hall to offer up another EMI band. Just as David Bowie had inadvertently given Queen their first break, so Queen did the same for another band when Hall presented The Sex Pistols as replacements to ITV. The rest is history as the punk outfit swore on live television, generally behaved badly and caused a national outcry. Grundy was suspended, The Sex Pistols' song 'Anarchy In The UK' climbed the charts, Britain's disaffected youth had a new soundtrack to their lives and, perhaps conveniently, Queen flew off to the US to begin a major 40-date tour.

Who knew what the musical landscape in the UK would be like upon their return and whether Queen would even be relevant?

'The whole punk thing was a tough phase for us and I thought that was going to be it,' Freddie would say. 'But if there's a challenge we embark on it and that's what keeps us going.'[21]

20

In January 1977, Queen flew to Boston to prepare for their forthcoming US tour leaving behind them the impending anarchy of punk, which was changing the very nature of the British music scene.

Released from his commitment to Mary Austin, and away from David Minns, who remained in the UK, Freddie was free to indulge himself in whatever he fancied and, out of sight of the British press, he had every intention of living life to the full in the US. It was the start of five years of promiscuity for Freddie as he pursued the gay life he had craved for so long yet kept secret from all.

Despite being in a relationship with Minns, he embraced this freedom. 'My sex drive is enormous,' he revealed. 'I sleep with men, women, cats – you name it. I'll go to bed with anything! My bed is so huge it can comfortably sleep six. I prefer my sex without any involvement.'[1] It was this lifestyle philosophy that enabled him to select whoever took his fancy and he would boast that he would bed hundreds. 'He wanted sex with no strings attached,' wrote Laura Jackson, 'and would leave for home around dawn with his conquest in tow. It appears that he wasn't fussy, and for someone whose artistic sensibilities were becoming increasingly refined, he could go extremely downmarket.'[2]

But Freddie wasn't the only one determined to enjoy himself. So too, it seems, were the rest of Queen. Their 1977 tour to the US was the one that set yet another new benchmark for excess, debauchery and post-gig notoriety that would pass into rock legend. The tour began in Milwaukee on 13th January and supporting Queen were the Irish rockers Thin Lizzy, led by Phil Lynott. They had just secured a breakthrough hit in the US with 'The Boys Are Back In Town' and were an exceptional live act.

The tour made its way across the US during January, but it was on 5th February 1977 that Queen knew they had well and truly arrived when they sold out the famous Madison Square Garden. The gig had sold out within minutes and almost 20,000 fans paid to watch Queen perform. A review of the concert stated: 'The show itself was far more free and creative than Queen shows of recent days. Each member of the group had just enough room to stretch out, but at no point was the soloing any kind of an imposition upon the audience.'[3]

Yet however much of a unit the band appeared on-stage, once off-stage they were spending more and more time doing their own thing. Brian May was spending his time with his wife while John Deacon had his wife and son accompanying him on tour. Roger Taylor would join Phil Lynott and Lizzy guitarist Scott Gorham in some club in whatever town they were in. Freddie, meanwhile, would often find himself alone, and loneliness was not something he could deal with well. As a result, he began trawling the gay bars of whatever city he was in, picking up men for sex knowing that, unable to deal with being alone but also unable to be restricted in a one-to-one relationship, he could discard them the next morning.

'By 1977, there was no question of him not being gay, but it certainly wasn't an issue,' says Brian Southall, EMI's head of promotion, who had joined the band in the US, 'but there was very much an attitude from the others of "We do what we do, and Fred does what he does."'[4]

'The subject of Freddie's sexuality never came up because it wasn't even mentioned,' recalls Brian May. 'None of us had any idea that he might be different from us. Is that saying it the right way? I mean, we shared lots of flats and stuff and I've seen Freddie disappear into rooms with girls and screams would emerge, so, you know, we assumed that everything was fairly much the same way as we knew it. It was only very much later that we realised there was anything else going on with Freddie. I mean, much, much later. We were on tour in the States and suddenly he's got boys following him into a hotel room instead of girls. We're thinking, "Hmmm..." And that's about the extent of it. I always had plenty of gay friends, I just didn't realise that Freddie was one of them until later.'[5]

On this tour Freddie had surrounded himself with his own coterie of assistants. Among them was Peter Brown, his personal assistant, as well as a 250lb bodyguard, a personal masseur and Dane Clark, 'a show-dancer that Mercury had picked up and who was now on the payroll as his hairdresser.'[6] Also accompanying Freddie was another personal assistant who had recently arrived on the scene, Paul Prenter.

'Paul Prenter was one of my first boyfriends, literally when I was about 17,' remembers John Reid, who was managing Queen at this time. 'I met him in Glasgow, I was still at home and he was from Belfast, his father was a bookie and he was at university, so when I came down to London I kind of kept in touch with him. And I was in California when, out of the blue, I get a phone call from Paul Prenter's father. This was at the height of the troubles in Belfast and he said, "We don't know each other but I know you know my son. Is there any way you can help him get out of Belfast?" Because things were so bad there and it was all a bit messy. So I spoke to Paul and I told him to go to London as I had a flat in South Audley Street. And when I got back, he was there, and I gave him a job as a runner. And in the course of that he got to know Freddie and that's how all of that took off.'[7]

Prenter managed to gain the confidence of Freddie by regaling him with stories of his apparently tragic life in Ireland and how robberies had left him penniless. Naturally, Freddie felt sorry for him, took him under his wing, and would provide Prenter with money and eventually employ him. But Freddie was complicit in their relationship; he was no fool, not some poor star taken advantage of. It was the beginning of a ten-year relationship that would, ultimately, end in betrayal.

'Paul Prenter wasn't my favourite person,' recalled Peter Straker, Freddie's close friend. 'Paul did everything that Freddie desired or wanted in terms of looking after him, and he could be quite a divisive person because he had Freddie's ear.'[8] 'He became a nightmare and he became divisive between Freddie and the band,' says John Reid.'[9] But, for now, Prenter was a valued member of Freddie's entourage, an entourage that astonished Thin Lizzy's manager Chris O'Donnell: 'He had this coterie of people around him, and it was all "Yes, Freddie", "No, Freddie". Dane Clark would prepare his clothes, take him to the car, put him onto a plane, and then into another car, and then onto the sound-check. Most people would sound-check at five o' clock, then have a meal from backstage catering with the road crew. But Queen would sit down after a gig and have a full meal with silver service. After a while, Brian and Roger got fed up with it and were asking to go with us to hang out at some clubs after the show. This left Freddie sat alone at this huge expensive meal, furious that his band had abandoned him.

He had this concept that you always had supper after a first night, so he decided you should do it every night. I had never encountered anything on that level.'[10]

Following their triumphant show at Madison Square Garden, the tour took Queen across the US until they arrived in Los Angeles in March. Here, they were due to play two nights at The Forum, a landmark venue where everyone from Elvis Presley to The Jackson 5 had played. But first they had another appointment. Having named two of their albums after films by the Marx Brothers, the band had been invited for afternoon tea at the home of Groucho Marx, then 86 years old and the sole surviving member of the Marx Brothers. The band presented Groucho with a gold disc in recognition of his inspiration and genius and also performed, at his request, an *a capella* version of '39' from *A Night at the Opera*.

From Los Angeles, the tour took in four more cities in the US as well as four shows in Canada before Queen flew back to the UK mid-March. But Freddie didn't return alone, much to the shock and surprise of his lover, David Minns. During the US tour, he had added another member of staff to his coterie, a 27-year-old chef named Joe Fanelli, and, before long, Freddie had fallen for him and persuaded him to return to Britain with him.

'Joe was a very, very sweet naïve kid from America,' remembers Freddie's friend, David Evans.[11] Another one of Freddie's friends, Peter Straker, had already been made aware that something was up in America: 'I got a couple of phone calls that he'd fallen in love with somebody else.'[12] Meanwhile David Minns, who had been Mercury's lover since 1975, was aware that Freddie was playing the field while on tour: 'Clearly he was having flings with other people. Well, obviously he was,' Minns would later say. But even he was surprised at the manner in which Freddie ended their relationship: 'Freddie came back from America after a long arduous tour, he came around to the flat and announced that he'd found somebody else, which was Joe. He actually said to me one day, "I have enough love for you all. Don't you understand that?" And I guess, in a way, he hoped that I'd respond in the same way that Mary had responded when he told her about me, and I think he got that wrong. He broke my heart.'[13]

In a bittersweet reminder of their relationship, Queen released 'Good Old-Fashioned Lover Boy' in the UK on 20th May 1977. Written by Mercury, it was a reminder of the early days of his courtship with Minns some two years earlier. 'Freddie, deep down, has very traditional values because he wrote that song, "Good Old-Fashioned Lover Boy", which was about our relationship,' reflected David Minns a few years later. 'He wrote that song about his, you know, dressing up, getting himself organised. He was courting. He was wooing me. That was all part and parcel of his performance.'[14]

Part of an EP, 'Good Old-Fashioned Lover Boy' reached number 17 in the UK singles charts in July 1977 while Queen were completing a European tour, taking in Sweden, Denmark, Germany, the Netherlands and Switzerland as well as 11 dates in England and Scotland. With the tour over, Freddie returned to his flat in Stafford Terrace to find David Minns had moved out. But before he left, Minns had taken an overdose: 'That was the day Jim Beach [Queen's lawyer at the time] rang me to tell me that my relationship with Freddie was over and could he please have a letter from me stating that I would not make any claims against Freddie, financial or otherwise, or go to the press,' Minns recalled. 'I asked my saviour, Sarah Forbes, to write it for me but I don't think I sent it to him. Freddie always had to have someone else do his dirty work. In my honour, he later wrote the song "Don't Try Suicide (Nobody Gives A Damn)". How sweet of him. The acid queen had finally shown his true colours and had not shown up when he was most needed. He was having his hair done in Knightsbridge no more than five minutes' drive away.'[15]

Over the next year, David Minns would see Freddie only occasionally, either in nightclubs such as Heaven, or when Freddie would rush over to Minns' Dovehouse Street flat seeking solace from his relationship with Joe Fanelli: 'Freddie confessed that Joe had flown back to New York and taken money and belongings from Stafford Terrace. He [Freddie] would arrive at the flat in Dovehouse Street whinging and sobbing about his loss and Joe's deceit on many occasions to follow.'[16]

Minns would eventually cut all ties with Freddie in May 1978 and would not see him again until 1986, but Joe Fanelli, despite his misdemeanours, would be welcomed back into Mercury's life. Their intimate relationship was destined not to last either but, in much the same way that Freddie kept Mary Austin close, so he kept Fanelli close to him, employing him as his live-in private chef until the day he died.

Queen embarked on the recording of their next album in London in July 1977. Punk rock was at its height and the press, particularly the *NME*, had taken to deriding Queen. Tony Stewart had written a critical review of Queen's 13th May concert in Hamburg for the *NME*. After being horrified when watching the full glory of the band's ostentation at the culmination of the Earl's Court show a couple of months later, when a crown weighing two tons and costing £50,000[17] rose spectacularly from the stage, Stewart interviewed Freddie in London in June. It was a prickly affair and one that Freddie was doomed to lose, a fact confirmed when the interview was published under the headline, 'Is This Man A Prat?'

In his earlier review of the Hamburg show, Stewart had referred to Freddie as a 'rock'n'roll spiv' who used the band 'as a vehicle for an elaborate exhibition of narcissism'. Stewart had suggested 'more importance was afforded their visual, than their musical presentation. And Mercury had led them over the top with his self-indulgence, to the detriment of the group performance.' Naturally, Freddie was aggrieved at such criticism and his demeanour at the June interview in London only served to antagonise Stewart further, as he described in his *NME* article. Upon Freddie arriving at the interview, Stewart writes how Freddie greeted him: '"I remember," [Freddie] opens, "speaking to you three or four years ago. That right? So you're still working as just a writer. Don't they have such a thing as... aha... promotion? Life is not treating you very well, is it? I would have thought," he adds lightly, "that since the last time I met you, if you had any go by now you should have become... aha... editor of *The Times* or something." Well, Fred, it was offered, but you know how it is. "Tart," he simpers quietly.'[18]

Stewart's article went on to criticise Queen, suggesting they were no longer 'majestic' and that their last album was 'mostly bland and insubstantial.' Worst of all, the band was guilty of 'believing their own myth'.[19] But Freddie had his own answer to Stewart's criticisms: 'I just don't think you know anything about style and artistry. Maybe they're beyond you, therefore you can't grasp them, therefore you dismiss 'em,' he fired back.[20]

Regardless of who was right and who was wrong, Queen needed to respond to such allegations and also create a record that would shatter the perception of them as being decadent and, possibly, 'past it' in a Britain undergoing an explosion of punk anarchy.

But before then, Freddie had another record to be part of. He had known Peter Straker, a Jamaican-born singer and actor, since the early 1970s. 'I met him in a restaurant called Provan's in the Fulham Road,' recalls Straker. 'He was with John Reid and I was with my then-manager called David Evans, who was also working with John Reid, and I was having dinner with David and we first met like that. And over the period of a few months we seemed to be going to the same restaurants, September's was another one, so we just kept bumping into each other, and then he formed a relationship with David Minns, who used to work for Paul McCartney, and we just kept crossing over and we just became mates. I then invited him to my birthday party and he didn't want to come as he was very shy, but he did turn up and had a good time and we really became good friends after that.

'We used to just hang out and I used to go to the theatre a lot so I remember one of our first meetings we went to the theatre together in Upper Regent Street, and it was one of those shows in those days when everybody was taking their clothes off after *Hair*, and what I remember is that we went out for a drink in the interval and, I'll never forget it, we went outside because the bar was very full and he wouldn't go back in to see the show. He said, "Once I've left somewhere I can't go back in." He didn't understand how the theatre worked. So we didn't go back in. He came to see lots of shows I was doing round the country in the 1970s. He'd turn up and see the shows and we'd drive back down to London together and we just got on famously, really.'[21]

As a result of their friendship, Freddie had agreed to produce an album for Straker, titled *This One's On Me*, for Mercury's own Goose Productions.

Freddie also had an album to record with Queen. The band had scheduled a US tour beginning on 11th November 1977, meaning all songwriting and recording for the new album had to be completed by then, although Freddie revealed to Tony Stewart that 'We haven't written a damned thing yet,' during the ill-fated *NME* interview in June.[22] However, ensconced in London's Basing Street Studios during the Silver Jubilee summer of 1977, Queen managed to create *News of the World*, their sixth studio album. Significantly different in musical tone from their two previous albums, *News of the World* benefited from a departure from flamboyance and focused more on experimentation in hard and soft rock, one that was more in step with the punk scene of the time than the output of most contemporary superstar acts. Using sparse production (Queen once again produced the album themselves), *News of the World* was recorded in just ten weeks, something of a sprint for Queen, and contained little of the overdubbing synonymous with the band's previous records.

Coincidentally, also recording at the studios at the same time as Queen were The Sex Pistols. With punk rock occupying the zeitgeist, Queen had every reason to be suspicious of the upstarts occupying the adjoining studio, but it appears the bands got on reasonably well and the fact that they were sharing the same facilities led to the story of Freddie encountering Sid Vicious and calling him 'Mr Ferocious' when the Pistols' bass player burst into Queen's studio and asked Freddie if he'd succeeded in bringing ballet to the masses. 'Dear,' replied Freddie, 'we're doing our best.'

Freddie only contributed three songs to the album but he did write the best-selling single from the album, and one of Queen's biggest-selling singles of all time, 'We Are The Champions'. 'I was thinking about football when I wrote it,' Mercury said. 'I wanted a participation song, something that the fans could latch on to. Of course, I've given it more theatrical subtlety than an ordinary football chant. I suppose it could also be construed as my version of "I Did It My Way". We have made it, and it certainly wasn't easy. No bed of roses, as the song says. And it's still not easy.'[23]

Blending florid theatricality with arena-rock thunder, 'We Are The Champions' is a power-ballad built around a cascading melody, multi-tracked vocals, Freddie's powerhouse main vocal, and Brian May's acrobatic guitar work. Thirty-four years later, scientists at Goldsmiths, University of London would declare 'We Are The Champions' the catchiest song of all time following a scientific study. 'Every musical hit is reliant on math, science, engineering and technology; from the physics and frequencies of sound that determine pitch and harmony to the hi-tech digital processors and synthesizers which can add effects to make a song more catchy,' revealed music psychologist Dr Daniel Müllensiefen. 'Over the course of the study, the researchers found that catchiness was most influenced by four factors: long and detailed musical phrases, multiple pitch changes in a song's hook, male vocalists, and higher male voices making a noticeable vocal effort.'[24] And 'We Are The Champions' had them all.

Released as a double-A side with Brian May's 'We Will Rock You' on 7th October 1977, 'We Are The Champions' reached number 2 in the UK charts, where it stayed for three weeks, kept off the top by ABBA's 'Name of the Game' and then leapfrogged by Wings' 'Mull of Kintyre'. In the US it reached number 4, their highest chart position to date, and it remained on the US charts for 27 weeks, selling over 2m copies. With none of their previous three singles cracking the Top 10 in the US, the performance of 'We Are The Champions' was a welcome fillip as the band flew to North America to begin rehearsals on 7th November for their forthcoming tour. Before leaving, however, Queen were presented with an award for the Best British Single of the Past 25 Years, for 'Bohemian Rhapsody', at the Britannia Awards on 17th October, an award shared with Procol Harum's 'A Whiter Shade of Pale'.

Eleven days later, the album *News Of The World* was released to mixed reviews and a disappointing chart position of number 4 in the UK. It was the lowest chart position for any Queen album since *Queen II* in 1974. However, it fared better in the US charts, reaching number 3 and gaining platinum status.

Once again criss-crossing the States to enormous acclaim and sell-out audiences, Freddie was afforded many opportunities to peruse and indulge in the US gay scene. Despite being a huge star, there was an anonymity in North America which he exploited to the full. He needed this anonymity; his homosexuality had to remain secret as far as he was concerned, and he didn't want his popularity and his success threatened in any way by being exposed or being forced to come out.

His heterosexuality was a façade he had to maintain. Queen, the band, were now a significant business in themselves, earning vast amounts and employing a host of people just to keep running. Queen had assumed a huge responsibility for the four members and those with vested interests in the successes – critical and commercial – of the band, and nothing could be allowed to rock the boat, least of all the lead singer coming out as gay. Somehow, Freddie managed it to such an extent that a year later, in an interview in Paris with *Daily Mail* journalist Tim Lott, it was noted, 'Although his outward make-up is coated with arrogance, he is certainly generous. He has treated his girlfriend, Mary Austin, to a luxury London apartment of her own, and he is known to toss the occasional gold watch to special friends. "After seven and a half years we have come to an understanding," he said. "I felt that as I'm on tour so much, Mary should have a life of her own."'[25]

The illusion of heterosexuality continued in the press and to the public, while Freddie embarked on a journey of one-night stands and unfulfilling acquaintances. 'The touring was Freddie on his sex safari in the nights following the little bit of work he had to do beforehand,' says his former PA, Peter Freestone. 'Usually with Freddie with touring it was the three "Fs": find them, fuck them, forget them.'[26]

Whatever Freddie was doing after the shows, his and Queen's professionalism on-stage could not be faulted. And off-stage, they were taking an increasing interest in the band's business, and this extended to their management. For a while it had become obvious to them that John Reid was not able to devote the necessary time to manage each of his two stadium acts, Queen and Elton John. Consequently, Queen were galvanised into making the decision to leave John Reid Enterprises.

'Jim Beach came to me,' recalls Reid, 'and said, "Thank you very much, the band really appreciate what you've done but they want to manage themselves." And we had a three-year contract and it had a bit to run and I said, "Well, okay," because when an artist tells you that, you're not going to fight it, so we made a deal and they paid me a lot of money and I kept my rights. I still get royalties from them, so I kept my commission from the records that were made under my tenure and after that individually, particularly with Freddie, we were able to spend more time together as friends.'[27]

Arriving back in the UK to spend Christmas and New Year with friends and family, Queen knew they had conquered the US. The press there had given them the respect they finally deserved, all shows bar one had been sell-outs, they had travelled by private jet, and even had an audience with the legendary actress and singer Liza Minnelli, much to Freddie's delight. Freddie, meanwhile, was throwing himself into the world of sex and drugs and rock'n'roll, seemingly wanting to make up for lost time.

'Even seeing a taxi driver on the way home and the limousine was turned around and it was "Follow that car,"' remembers his friend David Evans.[28] 'Eighty-five per cent of the time, Freddie would bring someone home for sex,' suggests former PA Peter Freestone.[29]

As well as sex Freddie had also developed a taste for taking more and more cocaine, spending a reported £4,000 a week on the drug.[30] 'I attended a dinner party once,' remembers the presenter Paul Gambaccini, 'and he actually served a drugs buffet and he passed around this tray. And I felt a little experimentally inadequate since I'd never done drugs and I'm looking at this tray of potions and powders and I only recognised one, which I thought looked like cocaine, but as to the others I was completely clueless. But the point being this was generosity, because while I had known people to offer friends a drug, I'd never known someone to offer a selection of drugs at a dinner party. That was an act of bizarre generosity.'[31]

'Freddie loved good times. He found cocaine helped him have a good time. But saying that, he didn't always have to have cocaine to have a good time,' says Peter Freestone.[32] The world of rock'n'roll – given his success, fame and wealth – meant that Mercury found he could have anything and everything, and he was now surrounded by a constant stream of 'yes' people attending to his every whim.

Back in England, Queen were now without a manager and had no management structure around them. What's more, they were facing the prospect of having to become tax exiles owing to the punitive tax laws of the time in the UK. As a consequence, Europe beckoned, and for Freddie this was to open up a whole new gay scene, one that would come to dominate his life for the next few years.

The year 1978 began with Queen and Freddie taking stock. 'We've all become businessmen,' admitted Freddie, 'even though it's against our better judgment. It's something that always happens if you get successful.'[1]

The band had decided that, having dispensed with the services of John Reid, they would set up their own management structure and manage themselves. Assisted by Thornton Baker accountants, tax specialist Peter Chant, and their lawyer Jim Beach, Queen set up a number of companies to look after their finances, their assets and their future. Included as part of the management team were Pete Brown and Paul Prenter. With income tax in the UK at punitive rates, Queen were advised to take a year out, meaning the band members had to spend, at least, 300 days out of the country to avoid paying UK tax. Freddie was known as not being very good with money, so he was more than eager to take professional advice. 'I've just been going on wild spending sprees,' he admitted. 'I've been told to cool down because the taxman will be coming to take a large sum away. I've spent in the region of £100,000[2] over the last three years.'[3]

The plan was to spend much of April and May touring Europe and then to go to the US towards the end of October and tour there until Christmas. The summer months would be spent recording their new album, *Jazz*, in the south of France and Switzerland. However, they would begin the year in Shepperton Studios in February, reconvening to rehearse for their forthcoming European tour. Also in February, Queen released a follow-up single to 'We Are The Champions'. John Deacon's 'Spread Your Wings' was a power ballad that crawled its way to a chart high of number 34, which only illustrated the dominance of Freddie Mercury's songwriting within Queen, particularly where hit singles were concerned. This would change in the 1980s, but the relative chart failure of 'Spread Your Wings' meant that of Queen's 11 singles released in the UK, only six had reached the Top 10 and five of these had been composed solely by Freddie Mercury (John Deacon's 'You're My Best Friend' being the exception).

If any member of Queen had the potential for a solo career, these statistics seemed to point towards Freddie as the only candidate. 'In the early days when Queen was formed a lot of people were asking, "When are you going to do your solo project?"' said Freddie. 'To be honest, I thought we would all be doing solo albums long before we did. I suppose when we made a Queen album they were like four solo projects within themselves. I had my bunch of songs and Brian had his, and Roger and John had theirs, so it was like four little solo projects working side by side, and then we put them together.'[4]

On 12th April, shortly after the beginning of the tax year, Queen began their self-imposed exile with the first concert of the European tour in Stockholm. By this point in their career, they had adopted a familiar routine, as Roger Taylor remembers: 'It was really album, tour, album, tour. It really was nonstop, pretty much. I guess it was hard. We got used to it. You know, in the very beginning, we would always assemble what material we had and then we would rehearse it. Then when we really got rolling, we would just turn up in the studio and try and write, see what came out then and we would come up with stuff. I'm sure some quality suffered at times; it must have – it's inevitable.'[5]

From Sweden, the *News of the World* Tour wound its way across Europe, before arriving in England for five shows in May. It was now costing £4,000 a day (over £22,000 in 2016) just to keep the Queen bandwagon on the road, but everywhere they went, sell-out crowds guaranteed the financial viability of the tour, even with tickets costing just £3.50 (the equivalent of £20 today).

'The regal quartet have style and swagger,' wrote one reviewer of the UK concerts, 'and the skill to accompany it, as they pulsate their way through their rhythmic hymnal. The show is ostentatious, exciting, and the only lull as they skip from heavy, to light and fantastic, is during indulgent guitar and vocal solos which are electronic exercises rather than music. Quicksilver Freddie Mercury in black plastic trousers and red braces makes "Bohemian Rhapsody" into something of a revelation.'[6]

This review is the first one to reveal to anyone who didn't attend the shows that Freddie's stage attire had changed considerably. Gone were the leotards, the Zandra Rhodes-designed angel-wing frocks, the all-white costumes. Now Freddie was taking the stage in a harsh shiny black PVC or leather look. Often he would simply wear black PVC trousers with black braces over his bare torso. Sometimes he would wear a leather-studded cap. In doing so he began to adopt the biker image popular in the gay nightclubs of the time. He had been particularly taken by the look of Glenn Hughes, the 'biker' in the Village People, whom he had seen dancing on the bar during one of his visits to The Anvil in New York, and began adopting the look for himself. Perhaps, as Laura Jackson writes, Freddie 'viewed his new look as a way in which he could fuse his two worlds.'[7]

With the European leg of the tour over, and to adhere to their new status as tax exiles, Queen began work on their next album at Mountain Studios in Montreux and then at Super Bear Studios in Berre les Alpes, 14 kilometres outside of Nice, France. Using two studios in different countries was yet another method to avoid paying tax in any one country – the benefits of employing their own tax advisor reaping instant dividends. Recorded over four months, Freddie contributed five songs to the 13-track album including the biggest-selling singles 'Bicycle Race' and 'Don't Stop Me Now'.

Recording an album in a foreign country meant the band often succumbed to temptation, focusing less on the music, as Roy Thomas Baker, back working with Queen, recalled: 'Every night we'd go to this club on the corner that had the most amazing stripper, so we had to stop the session at eleven o'clock, watch the stripper, and then go back to record again.'[8]

'It was the first time we'd done an album away from home,' reflects Brian May, 'the idea being that there would be no distractions. Just different kinds.'[9]

Roger Taylor's 29th birthday party on 26th July provided ample opportunity for the band to let their hair down and at the celebrations in a Montreux hotel Freddie was photographed swinging from a chandelier. 'I have always wanted to swing from a chandelier,' he explained. 'And when I saw this exquisite cut-crystal thing dangling there, I just could not resist it.'[10] However, this party was nothing compared to Freddie's 32nd birthday bash in Nice.

'Freddie's parties, of course, were some of the most famous parties in the world,' reveals dancer Wayne Sleep[11], and this birthday party was no exception. 'There was a limitless supply of exotic food, drink and cocaine and at the end of the evening everyone but Freddie, the voyeur, stripped off and dived into the hotel pool,' wrote David Bret.[12]

During his sojourn in Nice, Freddie had taken some time away from the recording process to watch the legendary Tour de France cycle race on 18th and 19th July as it passed through Montreux, where Queen were working, and the sight of all the male cyclists inspired him to write 'Bicycle Race'. David Bret suggests that Freddie spent the night with one of the cyclists, called Charles, who was suffering a hamstring injury and had to retire from the race.

'Watching the Tour de France go zipping by, Freddie observed how much more exciting the event would have been, had all those muscular young hunks been naked, or at least wearing jock-straps! He told me what a wonderful video that would have made,' said Charles.[13]

'Bicycle Race' was released as a single on 13th October 1978 and was part of a double-A side release, with Brian May's 'Fat Bottomed Girls'. The single was accompanied by video of 65 naked female models cycling around Wimbledon Stadium. Halfords had rented Queen the cycles for the day but, upon seeing the video, requested payment for replacement saddles. The single peaked at number 11 in the UK and number 24 in the US chart. 'It's cheeky,' admitted Freddie, 'naughty, but not lewd. Certain stores, you know, won't run our poster. I guess some people don't like to look at nude ladies.'[14]

The album *Jazz* was released on 10th November. It reached number 2 in the UK and number 6 in the US but was notable for receiving scathing reviews. Dave Marsh of *Rolling Stone* magazine wrote, 'There's no Jazz on Queen's new record, in case fans of either were worried about the defilement of an icon. Queen hasn't the imagination to play jazz — Queen hasn't the imagination, for that matter, to play rock & roll.'[15]

Marsh wasn't alone in his feelings: *Creem* said of the album, 'For me, their snappiest one-liner is on the inner sleeve: "Written, arranged and performed exclusively by *Queen*". As if anyone else would want to step forward and take credit.'[16] And Dave Marsh couldn't resist one final swipe at the band in *Rolling Stone*'s summary: 'Queen may be the first truly fascist rock band. The whole thing makes me wonder why anyone would indulge these creeps and their polluting ideas.'[17]

Despite the reviews, the US, for one, was still indulging its worship of Queen. The band had already started the North America tour before the release of *Jazz* and had 35 sell-out shows to complete before Christmas. And if they were at all concerned by the bad reviews of the album or accusations of ostentation, then it certainly didn't stop them living life on the road to the full. Their notorious after-show parties continued and one, in particular, passed into rock legend during this tour.

To celebrate the release of *Jazz*, Halloween night provided the backdrop for an evening of debauchery and hedonism that was both outrageous and expensive. That evening, Queen had played a show at the New Orleans Civic Auditorium. A review said that: 'Out of the soft blue and green lights and smoke, Freddie Mercury struts like a rooster, striking ballet poses, under an astral guitar blare that neatly skirts the sharp edges of rock & roll. The melodies are undistinguished, but the constant tempo changes of "Bohemian Rhapsody" and "We Will Rock You" keep an audience awake for nearly two hours of uninterrupted music. The lighting show is one of rock's most ambitious. Eerie purple lights shine out over the heads of the audience, making their hair seem cloudlike and inanimate. At the midpoint of the show, a smaller stage is lowered from the ceiling and 400 lamps meld into the sheer white plane of curtain light. Freddie is a whirling dervish, dominating every corner of the stage.'[18]

But in reality, the concert was merely a sideshow for what was to follow. Four hundred special guests had been invited to an after-show party at New Orleans' New Dreams Fairmount Hotel. Among the guests were 80 members of the press corps flown in especially from England, South America and Japan. Unaware of what was to come, these guests mingled in the hotel as a Dixieland band played and hors d'oeuvres were served. Then, shortly before midnight, Queen arrived, ushered in by the Olympia Brass Band. And that was the cue for the party to start, a party that would cost $200,000.[19] Bob Gibson, the LA-based publicist in charge of the evening's festivities says, 'Freddie decided that he wanted to bring in a lot of street people to liven things up. I was instructed to find anyone vaguely offbeat who might bring a little, ahem, colour to proceedings.'[20]

There are differing versions of what went on that night. Some accounts state that guests were 'greeted by a troupe of hermaphrodite dwarves serving cocaine from trays strapped to their heads'[21] while others recall, 'a twelve-hour orgy of excess which served up such exotica as a nude model hidden in a huge tray of slippery raw liver, half-naked girls dancing in bamboo cages that hung from the ceiling, topless waitresses and female mud wrestlers'.[22] Writing in *Playboy*, Merrill Shindler observed: 'On the tabletop in front of me is a painfully thin young woman whose sole item of dress is a G-string not much bigger than a 25-cent piece, and stuffed with twenty-dollar bills. There are drag queens in slingbacks and bouffants, and a bevy of 300-pound Samoan women, naked as jaybirds, one of whom has mastered the knack of puffing a cigarette with her vagina'.[23]

'It was deliberately excessive,' Brian May recalls. 'Partly for our own enjoyment, partly for our friends to enjoy, partly because it's exciting for record company people – and partly for the hell of it. There were all kinds of weird acts, including a guy who sat in a pile of liver, women who did unusual things with their anatomies! We made friends with all the strippers and transvestites, people who felt as misplaced as we did. On the face of it they were outrageous and promiscuous, but some of them were great souls. We had a hoot.'[24]

In keeping with such extravagance, while performing 'Fat Bottomed Girls' at Madison Square Garden, New York, 20 naked women cycled back and forth across the stage. While such debauchery might be accepted in the big cities of America, the reaction in other areas of the country, such as the mid-American Bible Belt, was less forgiving. To intensify the issue, in the US the album was released with a free foldout poster showing, in all its naked glory, an image from the nude bicycle race. Offence was taken in some parts of America and the album was banned as the poster was deemed pornographic. Queen were somewhat taken aback by all the fuss and furore, dismissing it as just a bit of fun, but as writer Lesley-Ann Jones states, 'the American backlash had started.'[25]

Despite its impressive chart performance, Freddie acknowledged the album didn't perform as well as they'd hoped: 'We've had albums that haven't been absolutely major, in the past, like *Jazz*, but we just moved on. That one was considered to have taken a slight dip, but that didn't stop us.'[26] The constant touring schedule, however, was beginning to take its toll on Freddie and his voice was suffering once more. Whether this was actually connected to his on-stage performances or his off-stage antics was open to debate and, in an interview with *Uncut* magazine in 2013, one of Queen's former road managers might have provided a clue: 'Around '78/'79, when Queen became huge, Freddie's appetites soared. He was non-stop sex and drugs. Before a show, after a show, even between songs. Before an encore, he'd nip backstage, have a few lines of coke, get a quick blow-job from some bloke he'd just met, then run back to the stage and finish the gig. The man had stamina.'[27]

For Freddie, and for the rest of Queen, there was to be no let-up in their hectic schedules. Following the completion of their North America tour with three sell-out nights at the Forum in Los Angeles, the band flew back to the UK for Christmas with their families. It would prove to be a brief stopover. On 17th January 1979 Freddie and Queen would be back on the road again, playing in Hamburg as they began a demanding 43-date tour of Europe and Japan. And following this tour, they would begin recording their eighth album, *The Game*.

This time, however, they would be recording it in Musicland Studios, right in the heart of Munich. And the city was to provide Freddie with his perfect playground.

Less than a month after ending the US tour, Queen were back on the road in January 1979. Instead of being the *Jazz* Tour, this leg, which took in Europe, was called the *Live Killers* Tour. All shows were to be recorded with the plan to release a 'live' album later in 1979 in an attempt to stem the number of 'bootleg' albums that were circulating among music fans.

Before that album was released, Queen put out another single from the *Jazz* album, once again a Freddie Mercury composition. 'Don't Stop Me Now' is a defiant up-tempo song with Queen's trademark multi-tracked harmonies over which Freddie proclaims he's 'having such a good time' that he's 'having a ball' and that he's 'a sex machine ready to reload'. Thirty-six years after the song's release, Dr Jacob Jolij, an expert in cognitive neuroscience and emotion, proclaimed it to be the number one feel-good song of all-time on account of its key, its feel-good lyrics and its beat.[1]

It was written at a time when Freddie was beginning to throw himself into every pleasure imaginable, the very lyrics pertaining to indulgence, and the meaning of the song is surely describing the highs of sex, drugs, and the gay scene that he was now an active part of. In the video for the song he is even wearing a T-shirt under his leather jacket emblazoned with the logo of the notorious New York gay club Mineshaft.

The meaning of the lyrics weren't lost on other members of Queen at the time. 'I thought it was a lot of fun but, yes, I did have an under-current feeling of are we talking about danger here because we were worried about Freddie at this point and I think that feeling lingers,' Brian May remembers.[2] Such was May's dislike of the meaning of this song, believing it to be celebrating the hedonistic and risky lifestyle that Freddie had taken up at the time, that he barely features as guitarist on the track except for a signature solo. One can only presume that May's referral to his fear of Freddie's 'risky lifestyle' meant Mercury's increasing drug usage at this time. With hindsight, he needn't have worried about the drugs.

Released on 10th February, ironically while the band were playing Munich, a location in which Freddie would revel in its gay scene, 'Don't Stop Me Now' was a UK Top 10 hit for Queen, their first since 1977. Again, it was a Mercury composition and the band was becoming increasingly reliant on his talents to write their hits. However, it appeared even Freddie couldn't crack the US charts any longer as 'Don't Stop Me Now' only reached number 86 in the Billboard Hot 100. Queen's four singles prior to 'Don't Stop Me Now' had reached numbers 49, 52, 74 and 24 respectively in the US charts and writing credits on these songs had been shared between Freddie and Brian May. But, it seemed, whoever wrote the songs, the US was falling out of love with Queen, and this was further proved when the next, and final, single released from *Jazz*, another Mercury composition called 'Jealousy', failed to even chart across the Atlantic.

Fortunately, there were no such issues in Japan, where Queen remained as popular as ever, and it was to Japan they headed in April for the next leg of their *Live Killers* Tour. This short tour allowed Freddie more time to indulge his passion in Japanese collectables, all of which had to be shipped back to London at even greater expense. 'I collect a lot,' Freddie said, 'and my whole house is filled with beautiful Japanese art and antiques. That's also why I want lots of fish, and lots of cats. I suppose it's a sort of shy outlook.'[3]

Prior to leaving for Japan, Queen had started work on editing and shaping the *Live Killers* album from the European recordings. It would be a live double-album that would depict their raw power and technical virtuosity on-stage. The tapes from their shows were shipped to Mountain Studios in Montreux and all four band members followed to oversee the mixing of the album. They had spent time at Mountain Studios the previous year recording *Jazz*, and were growing increasingly fond of the studio environment. Faced with a heavy tax demand from the UK based on previous earnings, Queen were advised to look at the possibility of purchasing Mountain Studios rather than paying off the Inland Revenue. Having been impressed with the studio while recording *Jazz*, they made an offer to the studio owners, who were unhappy with the way it was currently being run, and by October 1979 the negotiations had been finalised and Queen became owners of their very own recording studio in Switzerland.

The album, *Live Killers*, was released on 22nd June and went to number 3 in the UK album charts, meaning that of Queen's first eight albums, all bar one had made the Top 10. However, in the US, as if to emphasise the band's continued decline, *Live Killers* only peaked at number 16 and, in doing so, became Queen's first album since *Sheer Heart Attack* in 1975 to fail to crack the US Top 10. Bad reviews might not have helped: 'If *Live Killers* serves any purpose at all, it's to show that, stripped of their dazzling studio sound and Freddie Mercury's shimmering vocal harmonies, Queen is just another ersatz Led Zeppelin, combining cheap classical parody with heavy-metal bollocks,' wrote David Fricke in *Rolling Stone*.[4]

Despite buying their own studio, Queen's next album was recorded in Munich. Here, in the Musicland Studios founded by Giorgio Moroder, they would work with a new producer, Reinhold Mack (known simply as 'Mack'). Mack had arrived at exactly the right time for the band, who had seemingly become set in their ways.

'I was working in Los Angeles with Gary Moore at the time,' remembers Mack. 'One day I had lunch with Giorgio Moroder. He mentioned rumours that I was supposed to go to Munich to work with Queen. Which was news to me. After calling the studios in Munich, I was in a dilemma. Nobody knew anything about the sessions. So I figured [I would] take the trip. Worst case – a week and a ticket lost – no pain, no gain. Luckily it worked out pretty good. They were set in their ways like pensioners. Their credo was, "This is how we are used to doing things." I had the advantage of being a fast decision maker compared to the band. I could always try things while people were pondering delicate details.'[5]

Musicland Studios were housed in the basement of a 23-storey skyscraper in Arabellapark, towards the east of Munich. For many of the British bands recording in the city, Musicland appealed because of its proximity to the airport, the availability of good beer throughout the city, and having a hotel situated directly above the studios. For Freddie, though, the studios had a greater appeal: they gave him access to the cornucopia of forbidden pleasures that he so desired at that time in his life. And he would find those pleasures nearby within The Bermuda Triangle, an area of Munich notorious for its gay scene. Here, in the area formed by Sendlinger Tor, Gärtnerplatz and Fraunhoferstrasse, he could inhabit the gay bars and clubs and indulge in the gay scene without the prying eyes of the British press following him at every turn.

After recording sessions, Freddie would leave the studios and immerse himself in gay clubs such as Old Mrs. Henderson's, Frisco and Deutsche Eiche. In an article in *Rolling Stone* an indication of Mercury's priorities at the time are all too evident: 'In the late 1970s and through much of the 1980s, Queen considered Munich their home away from home, later to their regret. The city had an active and diverse sex culture, and the place seemed to prove both a heaven and hell for Mercury. [Brian] May later said that the singer [Freddie] could hardly bear being in the studio sometimes – "He'd want to do his bit and get out" – preferring to spend his evenings in Munich's discos and clubs.'[6]

'It's very safe there,' Freddie would say of Munich. 'And very beautiful… Munich is like a village. I was there so long that after a while the people didn't even consider that I was around. They didn't really pester me at all. I have a lot of friends over there and they know who I am, but they just treat me as another human being and they've accepted me that way. And that to me is a very good way of relaxing. I don't want to have to shut myself up and hide. That's not what I want. I'd go spare. I'd go mad… even quicker.'[7]

But it was while locked away, in Munich's Hilton Hotel, that Freddie wrote the first song to be recorded for the new album. He had just landed in the city after a delayed flight from Heathrow and was taking a bath before heading to the recording studios. As head of Queen's road crew, Peter Hince was also in the hotel at the time and heard Freddie shouting out chord structures from his bath. It wasn't long before Hince was summoned to Freddie's bathroom, where Mercury demanded that Hince get him a guitar urgently.

After a few more minutes of strumming, Mercury ordered Hince to get him to the studios as quickly as possible. Roger Taylor and John Deacon were already in Musicland Studios with Mack when Freddie came bursting in, proclaiming, 'My dears, I just wrote this in the bath!' and proceeded to play them the basic structure to what would become 'Crazy Little Thing Called Love'.

'"Crazy Little Thing Called Love" took me five or ten minutes,' recalled Freddie. 'I did that on the guitar, which I can't play for nuts, and in one way it was quite a good thing because I was restricted, knowing only a few chords. It's a good discipline because I simply had to write within a small framework. I couldn't work through too many chords and because of that restriction I wrote a good song, I think.'[8]

Freddie, Roger and John recorded their parts of the song in just half an hour, enjoying the spontaneity that Mack was encouraging them to embrace. The problem facing them now was how Brian would react when he arrived at the studios. Freddie's parting shot to Mack was: 'Brian's not going to like it.'[9]

Indeed when May arrived at Musicland, Freddie was proved right."Mack suggested that Brian ditch his trusted homemade guitar and record the solo for the song on one of Roger's Telecaster guitars. 'I got bludgeoned into playing it. That was Mack's idea,' recalls Brian. 'I said, "I don't want to play a Telecaster. It basically doesn't suit my style." But "Crazy Little Thing Called Love" was such a period piece; it seemed to need that period sound. So I said, "Okay, Mack, if you want to set it up, I'll play it." He put it through a Mesa-Boogie, which is an amplifier I don't get on with at all; it just doesn't suit me. I tried it, and it sounded okay.'[10]

Liking the song, EMI decided to rush the track out as a single and it was released in October 1979. An enormous hit worldwide, it became Queen's first US number 1, topping the Billboard Chart for four weeks and selling over 1m copies. It also topped the charts in Canada, Mexico, the Netherlands and Australia and reached number 2 in the UK. The video that accompanied the song had the whole band wearing black leather, with Freddie straddling a motorcycle while hands clapped beneath him from holes cut into a catwalk. It was a striking new look for the band, and one that Freddie embraced. The song would be one of the highlights of the forthcoming *Crazy* Tour, scheduled to begin in Dublin that November.

However, this tour wasn't the first occasion that 'Crazy Little Thing Called Love' had been performed publicly to an audience. That had happened earlier in October, two weeks before the single's release, and the setting had been, rather incongruously, London's Coliseum Theatre in St Martin's Lane. On Sunday, 7th October 1979, its stage was filled with dancers of The Royal Ballet, plus one – that one being Freddie Mercury, who had been invited to dance with them for a charity gala. 'I only really knew about ballet from watching it on television, but I always enjoyed what I saw,' said Freddie. 'Then I became very good friends with Sir Joseph Lockwood, at EMI, who was also chairman of the Royal Ballet board of governors. I began to meet people who were involved in ballet and I became more and more fascinated by them.'[11]

One of those Freddie got to know was Canadian-born Wayne Eagling, then a principal dancer at the Royal Ballet. He had originally asked Kate Bush to join them for the charity show but her manager had baulked at the idea and it was left to Sir Joseph Lockwood to suggest Freddie Mercury instead. 'I thought they were mad,'[12] said Freddie, and the Royal Ballet must have had second thoughts, too, when Freddie arrived for rehearsals, as Wayne Eagling recalls: 'Freddie turned up already wearing tights and ballet shoes, and we all took one look at him and nearly fainted. I think some of the group thought, My God! What have we got here? Because Freddie really made an entrance.'[13]

Throughout rehearsals at Barons Court, Freddie threw himself into his new role as a ballet dancer with energy and enthusiasm, as another principal dancer, Derek Deane, remembers: 'He would try absolutely anything. In fact, a lot of the time we had to hold him back in case he did himself an injury.'[14] Freddie would perform two numbers on-stage, 'Bohemian Rhapsody', while dressed in sequins, and 'Crazy Little Thing Called Love', which hadn't yet been released, dressed in leather. The London Symphony Orchestra would provide accompaniment, the first time any of Queen's songs had undergone a classical arrangement.

'I found it exceptionally difficult,' revealed Freddie. 'I said, "I just can't do it." I suppose because they'd seen me on stage they automatically assumed I was a worthwhile dancer.'[15]

'We never stopped laughing,' remembers Derek Deane. 'I saw right away that he liked to think of himself as a good dancer, but he wasn't really. He more than made up for that though by being terribly enthusiastic.'[16]

'They had me rehearsing all kinds of dance steps,' said Freddie, 'and there I was at the barre bending and stretching my legs. I was trying to do, in a few days, the kinds of things they had spent years perfecting, and let me tell you, it was murder. After two days I was in agony. I was aching in places I didn't even know I had. Then, when the night of the gala came, I was just amazed at the backstage scenes. When I had my entrances to do I had to fight my way through Merle Park and Anthony Dowell and all these people, and say, "Excuse me, I'm going on now." It was outrageous.'[17]

Despite his nerves, Freddie was in his element, being lifted, flipped and tipped by a host of bare-chested male dancers, a routine that concluded with him singing upside down in front of over 2,000 people. It brought the house down. 'In the main, ballet audiences tend to be quite stuffy,' says Derek Deane, 'and never in a million years did they expect a rock star to arrive on stage, but they loved Freddie.'[18] 'I'd like to see Mick Jagger or Rod Stewart trying something like that,' Freddie would later say of his adventure with the Royal Ballet.[19]

As well as giving him the chance to live one of his dreams, performing with the Royal Ballet also introduced Freddie to someone who would become a lifelong friend and an indispensable companion for the rest of his life. Peter Freestone had worked in the wardrobe department of the Royal Ballet since 1977 following a brief stint as a catering manager at Selfridges. Although born in Surrey, Freestone, like Freddie, had spent time at a boarding school in the tea plantations of the Nilgiri Hills in India while his parents ran a hotel in Calcutta. Perhaps it was this similarity to Freddie's childhood, the Indian boarding schools and the great periods away from parents and siblings, that helped the pair forge a formidable friendship. That friendship was formed when Freddie visited the wardrobe department at the Royal Ballet, accompanied by Paul Prenter, to see the costumes he would be wearing for his performance with the Ballet.

Following Freddie's successful on-stage performance on 7th October, a party was held for all concerned at Legends nightclub in London, and being part of the ballet company, Peter Freestone found himself invited along. It was during this party that he spoke with Freddie for the first time, although Peter describes it as a conversation lasting no more than five words. Freestone spent much longer talking with Paul Prenter, the Belfast-born chancer who had managed to inveigle his way into Freddie's close coterie and become Freddie's, and Queen's, personal manager at the time. Peter must have made a considerable impression on Freddie or Paul, or both, because two weeks later he was offered the role of wardrobe manager for the forthcoming *Crazy* Tour of the UK and Ireland, a job that he quickly accepted, having no inkling who Queen were and without any idea of their musical repertoire.

The *Crazy* Tour began in Dublin on 22nd November 1979 to mixed reviews, with Freddie being described as 'a mixture of Max Wall and Danny Kaye'[20] as he duck-walked back and forth across the stage. The extravagance and largesse of the show as a whole was also criticized: 'In terms of professionalism and musicianship, they rank amongst the best. But the technology that has always surrounded the band now threatens to swamp them'.[21]

As part of the tour, Queen played two nights at The Brighton Centre on England's south coast. Both shows were sell-outs, but it's not for the music that Freddie enjoyed these gigs. It was during these couple of days in Brighton that he met 28-year-old motorcycle courier Tony Bastin at a gay nightclub.

'Tony was about five foot eleven with fair hair,' remembers Peter Freestone. 'Of average build, he had a very winning smile. I have to say that, with hindsight, Freddie was not Tony's type at all, although he was to be the first person with whom Freddie had a long-term relationship while I was working for him.'[22]

Freddie took Tony back to his suite at The Grand Hotel in Brighton where, after a small party attended by Paul Prenter and Peter Freestone, he spent the night with Tony. This time, unlike his countless one-night stands that had become a regular part of his lifestyle, there was a connection between the two men. Something was different, and as Freddie left Brighton they exchanged telephone numbers and committed to keep in touch. It was the beginning of a two-year relationship between Freddie Mercury and Tony Bastin, a period in which Freddie would still remain promiscuous without his partner's knowledge.

Freddie and Queen ended the decade on top of the world. All four of them were now multi-millionaires, company directors, and professional musicians in charge of their own destiny as the 1980s dawned. As far as Freddie was concerned, he might have met someone new in Tony Bastin, but his lifestyle was still one of indulgence and hedonism, a bacchanalian world of sex, drugs and rock'n'roll. His bandmates remained concerned at the nature of his lifestyle, as Brian May had revealed with his dislike of 'Don't Stop Me Now', and the potential risks that Freddie was exposing himself to.

One of those risks, although no one knew it yet, was the deadly virus that was beginning to take hold in the US. HIV and AIDS were not words heard as the decade changed, the significance of them yet to be so brutally understood, but it would not be long before they were whispered with fear among the gay communities on both sides of the Pond and became indelibly linked with the story of Queen and Freddie Mercury.

23

New York in 1980 was a world apart from the safe, clean, cosmopolitan urban playground it is today. Its subway was the most dangerous mass transit system in the world. Graffiti stained Sixth Avenue and the Twin Towers cast their shadow over a city in which a crack cocaine epidemic was flooding the streets, bringing with it ethnic conflicts.

But against this backdrop New York in 1980 was a utopia for gay men, when it seemed the pleasures of dancing, casual sex and recreational drug abuse could go on forever. The focal points for such activities were the underground clubs that existed, predominantly in the West Greenwich area of the city, the old meatpacking district. Here, celebrities and shop boys, hookers and honchos would rub elbows – and more – pickpockets would work the rooms and muscled guys got to use the bodies they'd worked on all week while music pumped and testosterone-driven theatrics took place in dark backrooms. Clubs such as Rounds on East 53rd Street, Saint at 105 Second Avenue, and The Spike at 120 11th Avenue provided the perfect environment for gay men to enjoy everything they had to offer, be it dancing, voyeurism, drugs or sex. Among those making a pilgrimage to New York was a gay flight attendant from Canada named Gaëtan Dugas.

Dugas was born in Quebec, on 20th February 1953, to working-class parents. After leaving school, he worked as a hairdresser in Toronto but it was his dream to become a flight attendant. However, being raised in Quebec meant his native tongue was French so, at the age of 20, he took the decision to move to Vancouver on the west coast of Canada to learn English, one of the requirements of being employed as a flight attendant. Vancouver was *the* place for young gay men and women in Canada to congregate in the early-1970s and the residential West End of the city was rapidly emerging as the gay ghetto.

Gordon Price, one of the founders of the group, AIDS Vancouver, had, like Dugas, come to Vancouver in the 1970s and found it 'fragrant with the flowering of gay culture in a sympathetic, fertile way. It was a golden age within the West End. There was a new identity of what it meant to be a gay man. You had a sense of self, confidence, beauty, exuberance, health.'[1]

Gaëtan Dugas had settled among this community in 1973 and it wasn't long before his head-turning good looks and charm ensured he had found himself a lover, a local guy named Ray Redford. Over the next two years, now sexually active, Dugas remained in Vancouver while he continued to learn English, but he would often venture to San Francisco, 1,500 kilometres to the south of Vancouver, where he would partake in the annual Gay Pride ceremony and enjoy weekend-long sex-fuelled parties with like-minded men.

Eventually, Dugas achieved his dream and began work as a flight attendant with Air Canada in 1974. It was a job that took him across Canada, flying into cities such as Halifax, Toronto and Montreal, where he'd enjoy stopovers. Similarly, he'd regularly visit both New York and San Francisco. It provided the perfect opportunity for Dugas to engage in one-night stands after visiting the gay clubs and bars of the cities he was stopping over in. Throughout this period, he continued to live in Vancouver with Redford and they enjoyed a two-year relationship but, before long, the strain of Dugas' constant travelling took its toll and the affair ended, although Redford would remain a close friend, often writing to him with pictures of his new boyfriend for Dugas to pass comment on in his inimitable way.

Having left Vancouver and Ray Redford behind, Dugas began a sexual odyssey that took him across North America and saw him enjoy encounters with approximately 250 gay or bisexual partners every year. At some point, likely 1974, but perhaps a year earlier, he met someone who infected him with what would become known as HIV. Dugas was 21 years old. He was described as the man everyone wanted and Americans tumbled for his soft Québécois accent and his sensual magnetism. Using airline passes he travelled extensively for the next five years and picked up men wherever he went. And, given that he had been carrying HIV as early as 1974, he was a ticking time bomb. It was, as Randy Shilts wrote, the sexual equivalent of 'Typhoid Mary'.[2] [3]

In the ensuing time, Dugas had spent the six years before 1980 flying across Canada, the United States and the transatlantic route to Europe. He had regular sexual contacts in all his destinations and when they weren't available, he simply found someone new. One of his favourite destinations was San Francisco, and from 1978 he would make the pilgrimage to the city to take part in the annual Gay Pride ceremony. Held at the end of June each year, it's the largest gathering of lesbian, gay, bisexual and transgender people in the US and its reputation also means it is visited by revellers from around the world.

On 25th June 1978, 240,000 people had descended on San Francisco for Gay Freedom Day with the slogan 'Come out for joy, speak out for justice'. Dugas was making his first visit to the festival and he wasn't alone. Among those accompanying him was another flight attendant, 30-year-old John Murphy, a leather enthusiast from Los Angeles. Together, the two of them enjoyed the weekend of partying as, throughout San Francisco, thousands of gay men crowded into giant disco parties that had become a staple of the weekend-long celebrations. During this weekend, Gaëtan and John had sex with each other, as well as those around them as they partied non-stop in the bars and baths of Downtown San Francisco, neither of them aware of the virus Dugas was carrying.

By the spring of 1980, Gaëtan Dugas had started to feel unwell. He had swollen lymph nodes and purple lesions began appearing on his skin, including one larger-than-normal spot on his face, and he was diagnosed with skin cancer. Scared and upset, he frantically began seeking out all kinds of medication, whether standard or experimental. This led him to a specialist in New York and he would fly regularly to the city, where he would receive chemotherapy, weekly blood tests and a regime of VP-16 (etoposide) or interferon. Despite his illness, Dugas continued to have frequent sex and in October 1980 it is known that, while on one of his medical trips to New York, he made his first visit to the city's gay baths, where he would have unprotected sex with a variety of people. And why wouldn't he? No one knew anything about a virus, and besides he thought he had cancer, and 'everyone knew you couldn't *catch* cancer'.

By that point, Queen had just finished their 1980 tour of the US and Canada, a tour which had seen Freddie play hard and party harder in, among others, the city of Vancouver, the suburbs of San Francisco, and the metropolis of New York.

It wouldn't be until much later in the decade that the true havoc Dugas had unwittingly wreaked was revealed to the world and the tragic link it would have to Freddie. But, by then, it was too late.

24

The dawn of the 1980s appeared to find Freddie Mercury in a relatively stable period of his life. Not only had he embarked on a relationship with Tony Bastin, but he had also found a house in London that he could finally call home.

Freddie had been living alone in a Kensington flat since the end of his 'relationship' with Mary Austin a few years earlier, although they remained close friends. Now phenomenally wealthy, he had a desire for something sumptuous that would reflect his success. He was on the lookout for a luxury mansion in the capital and had tasked Austin with keeping an eye on London's property market for him while he was away touring, recording or partying. 'I wanted a country mansion in London, but it took me a long while,' said Freddie. 'I'd been living in the same little Kensington flat for ages, so I phoned Mary from America and asked her to find a place.'[1]

The place Mary found for Freddie was Garden Lodge in Logan Place, a small, residential road in west London, and just a stone's throw from Kensington High Street. It was an imposing property: a magnificent eight-bedroom Georgian mansion secluded behind high brick walls, with an extensive garden, something that Freddie would come to treasure over the coming years. The house had mahogany staircases, marble and wooden floors, and huge galleried sitting rooms that lent a palatial feel. It was ideal for Freddie and he fell in love with the property the moment he saw it, buying it for £500,000[2] within 30 minutes and paying in cash. 'I just wanted a beautiful house in reasonable-sized grounds. I'm a city person. I'm not into all the country air and cow dung,' he would say.[3]

The property needed extensive renovation before Freddie could move into it and, divided into two separate houses at the time of purchase, Mercury set about converting it back into one enormous dwelling. 'I call it my country house, in town,' he said. 'It's very secluded, with huge grounds, right in the middle of London. Once a month I would get inspired and go there with the architect. "Why don't we have this wall removed?" I asked once. Everybody groaned and the architect nearly died. I went in there sloshed one day, after a good lunch – there is a wonderful bedroom area at the top, I had three rooms knocked into one palatial suite – and in a sort of haze, I said, inspired, "What would be nice is a glass dome over the top of all this bedroom area." The architect flinched, but went rushing back to his pen and drawing pad.'⁴

Nothing but the best would do for Freddie, and the renovations at Garden Lodge would take a considerable amount of time. In the meantime Queen had reconvened in February 1980 to continue work on not one but two albums. While most of their efforts at this time would be focused on the upcoming release of their next album, *The Game*, the band were also devoting time to one of their most unusual projects to date.

While working at Mountain Studios in Montreux, Queen had been invited to compose and record the soundtrack for the forthcoming sci-fi film, *Flash Gordon*, which was being directed by Mike Hodges. *Flash Gordon* was being produced by the legendary Italian film producer Dino De Laurentiis and was planned to be a lavish, extremely kitsch and colourful affair. Hodges thought a rock soundtrack would complement this perfectly. 'In the late 60s,' recalls Hodges, 'I directed a children's six-part television serial, *The Tyrant King*. It was my first filmed drama. In those days you simply paid "needle time" and could use any recorded music. I plundered the current rock LPs of that wondrously creative period: using tracks from The Rolling Stones, Moody Blues, Nice, Cream and Pink Floyd. Their music gave the series a great sense of fun and a lot of energy. It was an experience I'd always wanted to repeat. *Flash Gordon* provided it.'⁵

But, contrary to popular belief, it wasn't Hodges' idea to have Queen compose the soundtrack. 'I played a lot of Pink Floyd's *Dark Side of the Moon* on the set while we shot certain scenes. This, I think, conditioned Dino [De Laurentiis] to the idea of using rock music. But Queen was actually his idea. I think he may have met Jim Beach, their manager, at a dinner party. Accident or not, it was a brilliant choice.

'The briefing was easy. I just showed them a rough cut of the movie and left the images to ferment in their own creative juices. Each member of the band then started providing musical motifs, which the editor, Malcolm Cooke, and I began to weave into the finished product. Once the music placings had been made we spent 21 consecutive days (starting at around two o'clock in the afternoon and ending in the early hours) laying down the final tracks. Although the band came in singly to record I had to be there for every session. Exhausting, hard on the eardrums, but boy, was it exciting!'[6]

Alongside composer Howard Blake, Queen worked on the sound-track at various intervals throughout 1980, delivering the finished work later in the year. 'The recording time was spread pretty evenly across the band with Brian May being the overall coordinator,' remembers director Mike Hodges. 'Interestingly, I found Freddie the antithesis of his stage persona: quiet, sensitive, almost shy. His musical talent was obviously prodigious and totally instinctual. It struck me that his surname has a certain ironic ring to it as he was, just that, mercurial. He liked to get things done and move on. One afternoon, he came into the recording studio having just bought a big expensive house in Kensington. While enthusiastically showing me the photos, he explained that he'd viewed it for the first time that very morning. Now it was his! Freddie didn't hang around.'[7]

As well as 'Flash', Queen were working on their eighth studio album, and the band spent four months in Munich at the beginning of 1980 completing *The Game*. It was the first time they'd spent so long working in one place and, naturally, their minds – and bodies – wandered. Freddie, in particular, would rather indulge himself in the gay bars than spend hours grinding out tracks in Musicland Studios and, for the rest of the band, a daily routine of cocktails, dinner and nightclubs with a bit of recording thrown in wasn't conducive to making hit records and soon tensions began to rise, as Brian May recalls: 'We went through a bad period in Munich. We struggled bitterly with each other. I remember John saying I didn't play the kind of guitar he wanted on his songs. We all tried to leave the band more than once. But then we'd come back to the idea that the band was greater than any of us. It was more enduring than most of our marriages.'[8]

'In retrospect, it's probably true to say that our efficiency in Munich was not very good,' adds May. 'Our social habits made us generally start work late in the day, feeling tired, and (for me especially, and perhaps for Freddie) the emotional distractions became destructive.'[9]

Freddie escaped briefly from Munich's combination of hedonism and routine to fly back to London to make a cameo non-speaking appearance on his friend, Kenny Everett's, TV show. This rare and odd appearance, and generosity of spirit, reflected how much he valued their friendship. Returning to Munich, he slipped back into his routine of periods recording in the studio followed by trawling the gay bars for one-night stands. When not doing either of these, Freddie could be found playing his favourite game, Scrabble, or spending time at the home of the album's producer, Mack. There, in the comfort of a family home, Freddie became friends with Mack's family, so much so that he was made godfather to one of their children. Perhaps, in this domestic setting, he found something that was missing in his life, a bliss that had evaded him because of his sexuality, and for the fact that he had no family life as a child.

'One day I overheard a conversation between Freddie and my second son, Felix,' Mack remembers. 'Freddie was telling him, "I never had any of this. When I was young, I spent a lot of time away from my parents because I was at boarding school. Sometimes I would hardly ever see them."'[10]

For Freddie Mercury, this early displacement appears to have shaped his life. He seems to have consistently found authenticity and intimate relationships beyond him and his suffering went unacknowledged as those around him, or observing him from a distance, perceived that, as Freddie Mercury the fabulously famous and wealthy rock star, he had everything he wanted. As we can see upon reflection, the things he really wanted appeared to elude him, as the exchange with Mack's son illustrated.

In an article for *Therapy Today*, the acclaimed author Nick Duffell explores this issue more deeply: 'The dissociative, defensively organised personality structure typical of the ex-boarder, which I have named the "strategic survival personality", is developed as a protective mantle, under duress, often in the very first moments of the child having to survive alone at boarding school. Over time it tends to crystallise into masochism, pathological rebellion or grandiosity – or a combination of all three – as well as intimacy avoidance. It is very hard to shed.' Duffell continues: 'Many boarders grow up feeling their parents are strangers, unable to rely on anyone but themselves. They want desperately to be loved but cannot surrender to trust and perversely end up embodying the self-reliance that the public schools promote above all things. Game, set and match to the boarding habit, and hence why it seems so indestructible. But bad news for relationships and families. Even those who know they were hurt by it may unconsciously become players of a game of one, threatened rather than made safe by the beckoning of intimacy – safe only in the arms of the strategic survival personality.'[11]

For the time being, the other three members of Queen were Freddie's family, and back in Musicland Studios recording for the new album was completed in May 1980. Of the ten songs on the album, Freddie had composed just three. As well as 'Crazy Little Thing Called Love', he had also written 'Don't Try Suicide', allegedly for his ex-lover David Minns, and 'Play The Game', supposedly about his relationship with Tony Bastin. 'Play The Game' was chosen as the third single from the album and it was the first Queen single to use synthesizers. The video for the song was also the first time the public had been exposed to Freddie's new moustache. However, the look didn't go down well, with angry fans sending razors to Queen's fan club. The song didn't fare well either, only reaching number 14 in the UK and number 42 in the US charts.

On 30th June 1980, Queen began *The Game* world tour in Vancouver, Canada. The first leg of this tour would see the band play 45 sell-out shows across North America. On the same day, EMI released *The Game* and, once again, reviews were mixed; while *Record Mirror* wrote that, 'This album is a straight kick into the goal (Christ, what a pun). It's like winning the men's singles at Wimbledon.'[12] *Rolling Stone* said of the album, 'Certainly, "The Game" is less obnoxious than Queen's last few outings, simply because it's harder to get annoyed with a group that's plugging away at bad rockabilly than with one blasting out crypto-Nazi marching tunes.'[13]

The reviews didn't seem to have any effect on the record-buying public though as, helped by the inclusion of 'Crazy Little Thing Called Love', *The Game* went to number 1 in the UK album charts and also reached the top of the US Billboard 200 charts, their first, and at the time of writing, only album to top the charts in the US, where it would go on to sell over 4m copies. The success of the album was undoubtedly helped by the release of their next single, the fourth release from the album, and one with a markedly different style than anything Queen had released before.

'Another One Bites The Dust' was put out as a single while Queen were performing in Philadelphia. Written by John Deacon, it became a colossal hit, staying at number 1 in the US for five weeks and selling over 3m copies there. It was also number 1 in Argentina, Mexico and Spain and was another Top 10 hit in the UK.

'Freddie got deeply into it,' recalls Brian May. 'Freddie sort of sang it until he bled, because he was so committed to making it sound the way John wanted it, which was like hardcore, kind of more towards black music than white music.'[14]

'The song got picked up off our album and some of the black radio stations in the US started playing it, which we've never had before,' said the song's composer, John Deacon.[15] One of those radio stations was WBLS-FM in New York and, according to Brian May, 'It's kind of hearsay from my point of view, but apparently most of those black DJs who were playing it thought we were a black group and thought that Freddie was black.'[16]

With the huge chart success of 'Another One Bites The Dust', as well as *The Game* topping the charts, Queen was, once again, the biggest band on the planet. As a result, their shows in North America were sell-outs wherever they went and critically acclaimed by the press. It was Queen's time, and Freddie was determined to make the most of it.

While the band's legendary after-show parties continued, Freddie would prowl the gay bars and clubs of each city he visited using the *Spartacus Guide* to places of gay interest. There was one *Spartacus Guide* to the world and a separate publication for the US. 'If truth be known, I think these were the only two books he ever read from cover to cover in all the time I knew him,' says Peter Freestone.[17]

During a short break in the tour in August, and having recently broken up with Tony Bastin, Freddie decamped to New York for a couple of nights. The tour was going well, but he needed some refuge. Despite his own infidelity during their relationship, he had become increasingly suspicious of Tony's behaviour. Rumours had filtered through from Freddie's coterie that, while the band was in the US, Tony had been seen enjoying himself with a young blond guy in England.

'Although Tony had been showered with expensive presents, including an amazing camera complete with case and special lenses,' remembers Peter Freestone, 'he had not really appreciated anything; rather, he had taken all Freddie's generosity for granted.'[18]

Freddie felt used and, across the Atlantic, he plotted his revenge. While in Charleston, South Carolina, he called Tony and asked him to fly out to the States to see him. Freddie said he would pay for the flight and that there would be a chauffeur waiting for Bastin at the airport to whisk him to the hotel where, Bastin assumed, his lover would be waiting for him. But as soon as Tony arrived at the hotel Freddie told him face-to-face that the relationship was over and that another ticket was waiting for him to make an immediate return to London on the next available flight. Freddie wanted Tony to move out of his Stafford Terrace flat at once. There was one demand: Tony was ordered to leave his cat, Oscar, behind, as Freddie was besotted with the animal.

With another relationship over, Freddie freely threw caution to the wind in the gay clubs of New York. It was during the couple of days in New York, following the end of his relationship with Tony Bastin, that Freddie met Thor Arnold. A male nurse, Thor was of Scandinavian descent and 'blond and big and beautiful' according to Peter Freestone.[19] Arnold lived in Manhattan and was a familiar figure around the gay clubs of New York. Freddie met him at one of the familiar haunts he frequented and the two of them spent the night together in New York. Although their affair was brief, they remained friends and, whenever he was in America, Thor would often fly to meet Freddie for sex, if Freddie asked, and always at his own expense.

Unlike Tony Bastin, Thor was not going to exploit Freddie and it was for this reason that their friendship would remain intact. Thor, as it happened, was also a friend of air steward John Murphy, whom Freddie had already met on a transatlantic flight, and during another break in the tour, between 1st and 9th September, Freddie once again travelled to New York to visit the clubs and bars of the city's gay scene.

At some point during this tour, possibly in this break, he had a one-night stand with John Murphy. Murphy had also been a friend and lover of Gaëtan Dugas, who, by now, was in Canada and beginning to exhibit signs of Kaposi's sarcoma. As far as Dugas was concerned, this was a symptom of skin cancer and it's highly likely that Murphy wouldn't have mentioned anything to Freddie about Dugas or his illness while they were together.

Three weeks later, at the end of September, Queen played three sell-out shows at Madison Square Garden to conclude their hugely successful North American tour before flying back to the UK. There would only be a short break before the European leg of the tour would begin in Switzerland. This leg would consist of another 17 shows before the band could take Christmas off, and they also had to finish work on the soundtrack for *Flash Gordon*. Any concerns about this schedule impacting on their creativity were dismissed by *Flash Gordon*'s director Mike Hodges, who was delighted with their contribution: 'Over the moon,' he said. 'The film and Queen's score are as entwined as a DNA double helix.'[20]

The day after the European leg of *The Game* tour began, Queen released the single 'Flash'. Written by Brian May, it proved to be his first Top 10 composition, meaning he became the third member of Queen to pen a Top 10 hit. Meanwhile, the European tour, now containing a synthesizer on-stage for the first time, continued to roll across the continent. But reviews there weren't always encouraging and a review of the Paris show suggested that Queen had become more concerned with making money than making music: 'Queen came over as a cross between a third-rate Judas Priest and a tenth-rate Quo, peddling sterile, stale HM [heavy metal] without any of the endearing idiosyncrasies of either of those bands. It's annoying when a band of their potential devote their talent to making the fastest buck but it's their game and they can play it how they want. Another one bites the dust? Sure, but why should they care?'[21]

On 8th December, Queen played the first of three nights at Wembley Arena in London. It was the day that their soundtrack to the *Flash Gordon* movie was released as an album: it would break into the Top 10 in the UK album charts and peak at number 23 in the US.

The album, although not typically Queen, received rave reviews, with *Record Mirror* calling it 'An album of truly epic proportions,'[22] and *The Guardian* saying that if the album's 'instrumentals weren't covered in dialogue, it's tempting to think they would be afforded the same hipster reverence as Giorgio Moroder and Vangelis.'[23]

The film had been released three days previously but, despite its success and that of the soundtrack, Queen's mood was darkened on 8th December with the news of the murder of John Lennon. Freddie admired Lennon greatly and was deeply affected by his death, subsequently writing a song for him, 'Life Is Real', which would feature on their next album. 'To be honest, I would never like to put myself on a par with John Lennon at all because he was the greatest as far as I was concerned,' Freddie would say. 'When I heard that Lennon was dead, I was shocked and dumbfounded. What do you do? Words fail me, to be honest. It was something that you think could always happen, to somebody else, or to you, or whatever, and then it did happen to somebody, and it was John Lennon. There was shock and disbelief.'[24]

After two more shows in London, Queen flew to Belgium and then ended the tour in Munich on 18th December. Despite his love for the city, especially its nightlife, Freddie flew home to the UK the following day to spend Christmas in London, celebrating with friends, overseeing the renovation of his new house at Garden Lodge and planning, with the rest of the band, their schedule for 1981, which included world domination.

25

The year 1981: the tenth anniversary of Queen. In the previous decade they had become one of the biggest bands in the world, selling over 45m albums and 25m singles worldwide. 'We had a lot of belief to start with,' admitted Freddie, 'but I thought it would be over after five years and I would be doing something else.'[1]

Being so successful had also meant that Freddie Mercury, Brian May, Roger Taylor and John Deacon had become extremely wealthy, and they had recently been classified in *The Guinness Book of Records* as the highest-paid directors of a company, receiving a reported £700,000 each.[2] But there was no sign of them stopping yet. 'I'm driven by my work and will go on for as long as my system will allow me,' Freddie would say. 'The things that I admire the most are the things that require total dedication, twelve hours of work a day, and sleepless nights.'[3]

Queen began their tenth anniversary year with a trip to Japan. They combined the Japanese premiere of the movie, *Flash Gordon*, with a lucrative mini-tour, playing five nights in Tokyo's Nippon Budokan Arena. The mini-tour was a huge success; Queen were constantly lauded in Japan and it gave Freddie another chance to spend some of his wealth accumulating more Japanese art and objects. Following Japan, the band would fly, via New York, to their next continent for a series of seven concerts. It was a continent they were visiting for the first time: South America. 'We went to South America originally because we were invited down. They wanted four wholesome lads to play some nice music,' said Freddie. 'The idea to do a big South American tour had been in our minds for a long time. But Queen on the road is not just the band, it involves a vast number of people and costs a lot of money for us to tour. In the end we said, "Fuck the cost, darlings, let's live a little!"'[4] The plan was to play five concerts in Argentina and then two dates in Brazil.

En route to South America, Freddie stopped off in New York, where he started negotiations to purchase an apartment in the city. The Big Apple's gay scene had been a constant lure to him since his first visit there in the 1970s and it was a natural home for him given his tireless pursuit of true love and great sex. Tired of constantly spending time in hotels, Freddie wanted to put down some roots in the city, and Sylvia Stickells, the wife of close friend and Queen tour manager Gerry Stickells, had volunteered to scout various properties in New York for him. Sylvia found approximately 100 flats, houses and apartments for Freddie or Peter Freestone to look at and finally, Freddie plumped for a stunning apartment with virtually panoramic views of New York City, with a balcony that overlooked the 59th Street Bridge. It would take a few months for the negotiations to be concluded but Freddie was confident he had made the right decision in purchasing the property at 425 East 58th Street.

With the purchase of his new home underway, Freddie joined the rest of Queen on the journey to South America and on 26th February 1981, they landed in Buenos Aires, the first Western rock band to visit the Argentine capital. The country Queen was landing in was one in turmoil and in the midst of what was known as the 'Dirty War', an infamous campaign waged from 1976 to 1983 by Argentina's military dictatorship against suspected left-wing military opponents. With civil rights violations rife, it was estimated that 30,000 citizens had been killed by a junta led by Jorge Rafael Videla.

A government delegation was at the airport to meet the band and, accompanied by flanks of armed guards, Freddie and his bandmates were ushered through security and sped to the Sheraton Hotel in Buenos Aires, where they would be staying and where, most probably, the Argentine secret police could keep an eye on them.

At this point in his life, Freddie was involved in a tempestuous affair with bodybuilder Peter Morgan, who had flown out to Buenos Aires to be with him. Morgan was a bouncer at the London club Heaven and his arrival meant that Mercury's coterie in Argentina, apart from Morgan, included Paul Prenter, Peter Freestone, Jim Beach, and his former lover Joe Fanelli (who was acting as his personal chef). With the exception of Beach, all of them were gay and, consequently, this tour apparently created a divide between Freddie's gang and the remainder of the band. But, whether there was a divide or not, on-stage Queen were the consummate professionals and on the first night in Argentina over 50,000 turned out to watch them play a 29-song set. A Canal 9 television audience of over 30m witnessed the following night's performance at the same venue, a concert that saw Freddie joined on-stage by Argentina's footballing superstar, Diego Maradona.

The next concert in Argentina would be held in Mar del Plata, a coastal city 400 kilometres south of Buenos Aires. Before that concert, however, and given the political nature of Argentina at the time, the junta saw enormous political PR to be gained from exploiting the visit of Queen, particularly with impending elections, and the band were subsequently invited to dinner with the country's ruler, General Viola. While Freddie, Brian and John accepted the invitation and dined with Viola ('How nice for them to have a president named after a pansy!' said Freddie[5]). Roger Taylor declined, saying he was in Argentina to play for the people and not the politicians.

Arriving in Mar del Plata for their upcoming concert, Freddie discovered his hotel suite overlooked the promenade. His new lover, Peter Morgan, was accompanying Freddie on this trip but, while in Mar del Plata, Morgan was eager to go for a walk alone. This suited Freddie, given the security risks, and he was more than happy to let Morgan go for a wander. But when Freddie stepped out onto his balcony to gaze at the view, he got more than he bargained for. Beneath him on the promenade, Freddie spotted Morgan with another man, someone quite a few years younger than Freddie, and it was obvious from their body language, according to Peter Freestone, that Morgan and this man were more than mere friends. Back at the hotel, Morgan protested that nothing was going on but this only infuriated Freddie further. So, like Tony Bastin before him, Morgan was put on the first plane back to London, and Freddie was alone once again.

Following the concert in Mar del Plata, Queen played another show in Rosario before returning for a final performance in Buenos Aires. From Argentina, the band flew to Brazil. They harboured dreams of playing the fabled Maracanã Stadium in Rio de Janeiro but a recent law change by the Governor of Rio meant the stadium could only be used for 'football matches and cultural or religious events and Queen didn't qualify'.[6] So, instead of the biggest stadium in Brazil, Queen set their sights on the second biggest, the Estádio do Morumbi in São Paolo. This stadium had an attendance record of 138,032 for a football match, but no rock group had ever played there.

When negotiations for the concert had been completed, tickets were put on sale and sold out so quickly that a second show was added. So it was that on 20th March 1981, Queen played to 131,000, which, at that point in time, was the largest paying audience for one band anywhere in the world. Queen would return to South America later in the year, playing six shows in Venezuela and Mexico, but in the meantime they headed back to Europe to begin work on their tenth studio album; an album which, despite generating a number 1 hit single, would see the band take a different musical direction, alienate their fans and come up with a work that the music magazine, Q, later listed as one of the Top 15 Albums Where Great Rock Acts Lost the Plot.[7]

Queen began work on the new album, Hot Space, in June 1981, in Munich. Once again they were working with the producer Mack and studio engineer David Richards. Both had worked with Queen on The Game and the success of the sparse groove track 'Another One Bites The Dust' had made them determined to replicate the formula. One of the first songs Queen worked on in Munich was Freddie's tribute to John Lennon, 'Life Is Real (Song For Lennon)'. Another track that Freddie wrote for the album, and one that was recorded early in the sessions, was 'Cool Cat'. This was the first song Queen recorded that was a co-composition, written by Freddie and John Deacon. During the recording process, Deacon played all of the instruments including drums, guitar and synths, and Freddie provided the vocals, with backing vocals by David Bowie planned.

It would be later in the summer when Bowie arrived at Mountain Studios to record them. While in the studio, Bowie and Queen began an impromptu jam session that would result in the hit single 'Under Pressure'. The recording session lasted around 24 hours, fuelled by copious amounts of alcohol and cocaine – 'There was so much blow,' revealed Mack.[8]

'"Under Pressure" came about by pure chance, my dears,' said Freddie. 'David [Bowie] came in to see us one day in the recording studios we owned at the time, in Montreux, where we were working. We began to dabble on something together, and it happened very spontaneously and very quickly indeed.'[9]

'We all brought stuff to the table,' recalls Brian May, 'and my contribution was a heavy riff in D, which was lurking in my head. But what we got excited about was a riff which Deacy began playing, six notes the same, then one note a fourth down. Ding-Ding-Ding Diddle Ing-Ding, you might say. But suddenly hunger took over and we repaired to a local restaurant for food and a fair amount of drink. (Local Vaux wine as drunk in Montreux is a well-kept secret.) A couple or three hours later, we're back in the studio. "What was that riff, you had, Deacy?" says David Bowie. "It was like this," says John Deacon. "No, it wasn't," says Bowie – "it was like this." This was a funny moment because I can just see DB going over and putting his hand on John's fretting hand and stopping him. It was also a tense moment because it could have gone either way. Deacy did not take kindly to being told what to do, especially by physical interferences while he was playing! But he was good-natured, and it all went ahead. Then we began playing around – using the riff as a starting point.'[10]

'We felt our way through a backing track all together as an ensemble,' May continues, 'and then David brought up an unusual idea for creating the vocal. He was kind of famous for writing lyrics by collecting different bits of paper with quotes on them. And we did a corresponding thing as regards writing the top line for the song. When the backing track was done, David said, "Okay, let's each of us go in the vocal booth and sing how we think the melody should go – just off the tops of our heads – and we'll compile a vocal out of that." And that's what we did. Some of the original bits even made it onto the record. Freddie going "b-b-b-boom-ba," that scat singing stuff, was part of the initial track he went in and did off the top of his head. Odd, isn't it? That's why the words are so curious, some of them, anyway. There was a point where somebody had to take control, and I think it's fair to say that David took the reins and decided that he wanted to rationalize the lyrics and then say what he felt they should say.'[11]

'The song was written from the ground up on the night I visited their studio,' Bowie revealed on his website in 2004. 'I believe the riff had already been written by Freddie and the others so then we jointly put together the different chord sections to make it a cohesive piece of music. Then Freddie and I came up with our individual top line melodies. So when you hear Freddie sing, that's what he wrote and when you hear me sing, that was mine. Then we worked on the lyrics together. I still cannot believe that we had the whole thing written and recorded in one evening flat. Quite a feat for what is actually a fairly complicated song.'

Such was the spontaneity of the recording session that Queen's record label was totally unaware of the existence of the song (which was originally called 'People On Streets'). When they learned, however, that Queen and Bowie had contributed to a song together they were determined to release it as soon as possible and the song was finished off at the Power Station in New York, where it was mixed with both Bowie and Mercury present, alongside Roger Taylor, who was to become peacemaker during the mixing sessions.

The 18-hour mixing session was extremely fraught with Bowie and Mercury at loggerheads to such an extent that Bowie is reported to have threatened to block the release of 'Under Pressure' as a single. 'It was hard,' Brian May remembers, 'because you had four very precocious boys and David, who was precocious enough for all of us. David took over the song lyrically. Looking back, it's a great song but it should have been mixed differently. Freddie and David had a fierce battle over that.'[12]

In fact, despite the precociousness and the battles between the talents working on 'Under Pressure', David Bowie was the consummate collaborator. Following his death in January 2016, numerous commentators wrote how he 'used his considerable fame to help popularize artists who would have had less of a chance without him'.[13] Queen were already hugely successful but 'Under Pressure' showcased Bowie's unique generosity towards his peers. Hilton Als wrote, 'Rock stars are not generally known for their generosity to other artists; it takes a lot to get up there and be such a huge presence. Early on, Bowie realized he was more himself – had more of himself – when he built bridges between different worlds.'[14]

Credited as being written by Queen and David Bowie, 'Under Pressure' was released at the end of October 1981. It became the band's second number 1 single in the UK, almost six years after their previous number 1, 'Bohemian Rhapsody'. 'Under Pressure' was also a chart-topper in Argentina and the Netherlands and a Top 10 hit in another nine countries. However, in the United States it only reached number 29 in the charts despite *Slant Magazine* saying it was 'the finest standalone single either act [Queen and David Bowie] released during the 80s'.

January of 1981 was a bitterly cold month in New York City. On 5th January the temperature had dropped to minus 23 degrees Celsius, but inside the city's St. Luke's-Roosevelt Hospital, at 1111 Amsterdam Avenue, doctors weren't so worried about the weather; they were more concerned about a young patient, called Nick, whose life was ebbing away from him. Nick had been brought into the hospital by his boyfriend the previous November suffering a seizure. Not knowing what they were seeing, doctors diagnosed the young gay man with toxoplasmosis, a disease usually found in cats. He also exhibited the signs of Kaposi's sarcoma, something doctors in the city had become increasingly puzzled by as that month had already seen an outbreak of 20 similar cases of the skin lesions in New York. 'All used poppers, amyl nitrate. We suspected it could be that,' reflected Dr Alvin Friedman-Kien.[1]

Sadly, there was nothing that could be done for Nick, who died on 15th January 1981. Just a month earlier – and, at first, there seemed to be no connection – a German patient had died in Mount Sinai Beth Israel Hospital on First Avenue, New York. The 33-year-old German had been admitted in June 1980 with bloody diarrhoea and a low white blood count. He had worked as a chef in Haiti for three months, but no one thought there was anything suspicious about that. Despite treatment, the patient became cognitively impaired[2] over the coming months and developed *cytomegalovirus* in his eye.

Cytomegalovirus (CMV) is a common virus that belongs to the herpes family of viruses and is spread through bodily fluids. It is generally only reactivated in people who have a weakened immune system, such as those with untreated HIV. The German patient died in December 1980 and, just a month later, another patient, a male nurse, was also admitted to Mount Sinai Beth Israel Hospital suffering *pneumocystis carinii pneumonia* (PCP). He died soon after and the autopsy showed that, he too, was infected with cytomegalovirus.

Donna Mildvan, the chief of infectious disease at the hospital, had been studying sexually transmitted intestinal infections in gay men for a number of years and there was no question in her mind that she was seeing signs of a new disease. She went to see a colleague, Dan William, at New York's Department of Health to explain to him her concerns. Openly gay himself, Dan was working on cases of sexually transmitted diseases in the city. To accomplish this he had gathered together a group of gay men and was studying them closely to provide case studies and detailed data. During the course of his studies he had noticed that a number of them had swollen lymph glands. Three of them also had developed Kaposi's sarcoma, another disease of immunocompromise. When he told Mildvan of this, they began to fear the worse: 'We really saw the whole thing written out before us,' she recalls. 'We couldn't have dreamt that it would be of these proportions. But we knew we were scared. We were really scared.'[3]

Across the city, Dr Alvin Friedman-Kien at New York University's Medical Center examined a gay man whose symptoms had totally perplexed other physicians. When he examined him he found purple-lavender spots on his feet that no one else had looked at. Performing a biopsy, Friedman-Kien was surprised when the results came back as Kaposi's sarcoma. Two weeks later, Friedman-Kien saw another man, an actor, who had similar markings on his face and who was struggling to conceal his Kaposi's sarcoma with make-up. The only connecting factor between all of these cases was that every single one of the patients was gay. Friedman-Kien hastily formed a group of gay doctors who specialised in treating homosexual men and within four weeks they had found 20 cases of Kaposi's sarcoma in New York alone.

Friedman-Kien called Marcus Conant, a medical colleague in San Francisco. Conant was a dermatologist and was able to make Friedman-Kien aware of a further six cases of Kaposi's sarcoma in San Francisco. And all of them were gay men, too. When Conant went to discuss this with Marion Salzberger, the Dean of American Dermatology at the University of California in San Francisco, Salzberger said: 'This is not some new manifestation of an old disease. Homosexuality has been here for at least as long as Alexander the Great, and we haven't seen this before. What you're seeing is a new disease.'[4] Soon doctors were calling in saying they had a similar case in their practice but still, at this early stage, no one realised the gravity of the situation.

In Los Angeles, the first case that exhibited similar symptoms to those seen in New York and San Francisco presented itself: '[He] was known as Queenie, because he called himself Queenie,' says Dr Jerome Groopman. 'He was a very sad person, probably 18 years old. He was a street prostitute with bleached blond hair. He was found to have pneumocystis. He then developed a severe invasive perianal herpes simplex, which was so aggressive and so hard to control that it required surgical intervention. It was really gruesome. And ultimately he died.'[5]

Back in New York, rumours of a gay disease were circulating among the city's homosexual community. Dr Lawrence Mass, one of the early New York physicians to recognise a problem, contacted the Centers for Disease Control (CDC) in Atlanta in April 1981 to enquire if the rumours were true. The rumours were denied but it didn't stop Mass writing an article for *The New York Native*, a gay newspaper under the headline 'Disease Rumours Largely Unfounded'. Published on 18th May 1981, it began: 'Last week there were rumours that an exotic new disease had hit the gay community in New York. Here are the facts. From the New York City Department of Health, Dr Steve Phillips explained that the rumours are for the most part unfounded. Each year, approximately 12 to 24 cases of infection with a protozoa-like organism, *pneumocystis carinii*, are reported in the New York City area. The organism is not exotic; in fact, it's ubiquitous. But most of us have a natural or easily acquired immunity'. In the article Dr Mass concluded, using the evidence presented to him, that there was insufficient evidence, at that time, to make a clear connection between the new disease and the gay community.

'At the time, we had no idea of the scope of what we were dealing with,' Dr Mass would later say. 'Nor did we know what it was. It wasn't clearly infectious. It was an epidemic by definition because it was an outbreak of new disease cases and associated deaths. The epidemiology was inadequate to identify it as an STD. At that time, there were no civil liberties protections for LGBT people. And public tensions around gay issues and gay rights struggles were explosive.'[6]

On the west coast in Los Angeles, a 33-year-old immunologist at UCLA, Michael Gottlieb, had been studying five cases of gay men who had all exhibited similar conditions: chronic fevers, swollen lymph nodes, diarrhoea, thrush and rashes. Ultimately, all the cases developed *pneumocystis carinii pneumonia* (PCP). These five cases led Gottlieb, and the Center for Disease Control (CDC) Epidemic Intelligence Officer in Los Angeles to write the *Morbidity and Mortality Weekly Report*, which was published on 5th June 1981.

Two of the five men Gottlieb had studied in LA had already died by the time the report came out. It was a landmark report, but largely went unnoticed by both press and other physicians, and it wasn't until a second *Morbidity and Mortality Weekly Report* article appeared, written by Dr Alvin Friedman-Kien and describing the discovery of Kaposi's sarcoma in 26 gay men in New York and California, eight of whom had died within 24 months after Kaposi's sarcoma was diagnosed, that the nation's press began to sit up and take notice. In his report Friedman-Kien described how, of these 26 men, 'six patients had pneumonia (due to *pneumocystis carinii*), and one had necrotizing toxoplasmosis of the central nervous system. One of the patients with pneumonia also experienced severe, recurrent, herpes simplex infection; extensive candidiasis; and cryptococcal meningitis'. The article also revealed that, in the four weeks since the previous report of 5th June 1981 detailing five cases of '*Pneumocystis pneumonia* in homosexual men from Los Angeles, 10 additional cases have been identified in the state. [This] suggests that the 5 previously reported cases were not an isolated phenomenon.' In a grim forewarning it suggested that, 'Physicians should be alert'.

The New York Times had received an advance copy of the report and, under the dramatic headline 'Rare Cancer Seen in 41 Homosexuals' revealed how doctors in New York and California had diagnosed 41 cases of a rare and often rapidly fatal form of cancer among homosexual men. 'The cause of the outbreak is unknown, and there is as yet no evidence of contagion. But the doctors who have made the diagnoses, mostly in New York City and the San Francisco Bay area, are alerting other physicians who treat large numbers of homosexual men to the problem in an effort to help identify more cases and to reduce the delay in offering chemotherapy treatment,' the newspaper reported, before ending with, 'Dr. Curran said there was no apparent danger to non-homosexuals from contagion. "The best evidence against contagion," he said, "is that no cases have been reported to date outside the homo-sexual community or in women.""[7]

At this point in time, the new disease was being called GRID – Gay Related Immune Deficiency – a name that forever embodied the association between homosexual men and AIDS and only heightened fear among the wider community of this being a 'gay plague'. Such was the fear and disgust at the disease among the straight population at the time that a collection for gay cancer, organised by novelist Larry Kramer in New York City, raised just $124.

One of those in New York at this time was Gaëtan Dugas, who was being treated for what he thought was a form of skin cancer. Dugas continued his prolific sex life in the city and in other cities on the west coast and back in Canada when he wasn't undergoing chemotherapy. He saw no reason to change his ways as he viewed the medical claims and advice with some scepticism. And even if those claims of a gay disease were true, as far as he was concerned he was being treated for cancer and there couldn't possibly be any association with his illness and the cases of pneumonia and other infections afflicting gay men throughout the US. He continued to believe this even when, in 1981, his skin cancer was officially diagnosed as Kaposi's sarcoma. And, continuing to believe, he continued to have sex in the gay bathhouses of New York.

Meanwhile, across the US, cases of Kaposi's sarcoma began to rise and there was a connection: all the men were gay. There was another connection too, although no one would discover it until the following year: one of those with Kaposi's sarcoma, a man in Orange County, and another in Los Angeles, had both slept with a Canadian flight attendant in 1980. Another four of the first 19 cases discovered in LA had also slept with the same Canadian flight attendant. What's more, four more of the first 19 cases had slept with people who had gone to bed with the *same* Canadian flight attendant. That Canadian flight attendant was none other than Gaëtan Dugas.

Despite knowledge of the disease, despite doctors' orders, and despite health warnings among the gay community, Dugas was continuing with his prolific sexual exploits, sleeping with around 250 men every year, and had done so for almost ten years. They, in turn, had slept with other men and, in so doing, the boundaries of the virus grew ever-wider and affected more and more people. Doctors and epidemiologists, frantically searching for clues to see how any infection or disease is spread, created maps of contact, which they could then link to identify clusters or patterns of the disease. And it was this method that enabled them to identify clusters in San Francisco and New York, all of which connected to Gaëtan Dugas.

Only a few years earlier, while in San Francisco, Dugas first met and had slept with his friend, John Murphy. While on a transatlantic flight from London, on his way to North America for a sell-out tour with his band, Freddie Mercury met the same airline steward John Murphy and during another break in that same tour, between 1st and 9th September 1980, Freddie once again travelled to New York to visit the clubs and bars of the city's gay scene. At some point during this tour, likely in this break, he had a one-night stand with John Murphy. Freddie was now almost certainly being exposed to the virus, though he had not yet been infected.

The dangerous ripples moved ever closer.

After the summer of 1981 recording in Montreux, Queen were scheduled to tour Venezuela and Mexico. Before then, Freddie would take another trip to New York. There was a good reason for this: he was approaching his 35th birthday and wanted to celebrate in style. With the purchase of his apartment in the city still ongoing, Freddie stayed, as he generally did, in the Presidential Suite at the Berkshire Place Hotel. The party he had organised for his birthday was a five-day extravaganza and, ever the generous host, Freddie flew 100 of his friends over on Concorde for the celebration, telling them not to worry about the expense and, ironically, promising them that the only thing they would have to pay for was the condoms.

'I went to his birthday party in New York,' recalls Peter Straker. 'I'd just finished a play at the Bristol Old Vic and I nearly couldn't go, but I arrived on the morning of his birthday and the first thing he showed me was this huge fridge of Cristal champagne and it was downhill from then on. I came for three days and stayed for three weeks.'[1]

Just a week before Freddie landed in New York, the Associated Press had released a story revealing a rare disease had struck more than 100 homosexual men in the United States in recent months, killing almost half of them. However, the partygoers flying in from the UK were oblivious to this report and, although there were whispers in New York City among the gay community, no one seemed willing to alter their lifestyle, least of all Freddie. Consequently, the five-day party was one of non-stop hedonism and debauchery, with over £30,000 worth of champagne being consumed (over £116,000 in 2016). 'I remember the absolute mess our suite got into. And I remember Freddie sprawled out on a huge heap of gladioli,' recalls Peter Freestone.[2]

Before rehearsals for the short Venezuela and Mexico tour began in New Orleans, Freddie decided to fly back to the UK for a few days after his birthday party. Leaving the Berkshire Place suite, he took a limousine to JFK International Airport. As the car dropped down off the Williamsburg Bridge out of the city, Freddie's mind was preoccupied, according to the driver Larry Stoke: 'Freddie gazed out of the window. He was half listening to the radio that I had switched on, but his mind was elsewhere. Something was bothering him. I remember the voice on the radio was saying something about "a cancer that homosexual men were getting". I remember when he heard it, Freddie leaned forward and asked me to turn off the radio. I remember that so clearly. I mean, it's not often you get to drive someone that famous.'3

Likely Freddie had heard enough of such talk from his friends during his brief sojourn in New York. He didn't want to hear anymore. Several days later he flew to New Orleans to join the rest of the band in preparation for their South American tour.

Queen's first three shows in Venezuela went off without a hitch, the final show being televised, but after that, the Venezuela leg of the tour turned into a farce. On a scheduled day off, Queen were invited to appear on a live TV show. They would merely be guests and wouldn't be expected to perform. Freddie refused to entertain the idea and stayed in his hotel room while Brian, Roger and John dutifully made an appearance.

The band had arrived in Venezuela at a time when the country's former president and national hero, 73-year-old Romulo Betancourt, lay dying in hospital in New York. The country feared the worst and a period of mourning would be expected once he had passed away. News of his death reached the country as Taylor, May and Deacon were appearing live on TV and, totally unaware of what was going on, they could only watch and observe a two-minute silence when the music show was interrupted with the announcement of Betancourt's death. But it turned out, minutes later, the news had been premature and Betancourt was still alive. It was a false alarm and the music show with the three bemused English guests carried on. Later that night, however, the inevitable happened and Betancourt passed away, meaning a two-week period of mourning in Venezuela and the cancellation of Queen's remaining two shows in the country. With a ten-day break, the crew concentrated on transporting the stage equipment to Mexico while Freddie and the rest of Queen flew to Miami for a break.

By this time medical centres in Miami, along with similar centres in San Francisco, New York, Los Angeles, Philadelphia and Chicago were admitting several homosexual men daily with PCP (*pneumocystis carinii pneumonia*). Most of these men were in their twenties and thirties, some had been ill for months, but others had been healthy until a few weeks prior to their presentation. But all of them were gay. Still little was known about the causes of this influx of a disease, which was seemingly only related to gay men. While some medical practitioners thought it was a disease in which the patient's immune system became overloaded as a result of contracting many communicable diseases through a high number of sexual encounters with other men, which in turn led them to be more susceptible to opportunistic agents such as PCP, others doctors thought the illness was as a result of using recreational drugs, particularly amyl nitrate, which was thought to be partially carcinogenic. But in truth no one knew what it was.

Nor was any link made to the legacy of cheap frozen blood plasma imports into the US from Haiti, a lucrative trade for the importers, who paid impoverished Haitians to donate blood from which plasma could be harvested. With the plasma removed, the blood cells could be returned to the donor but poor hygiene, such as failing to change needles between donors, and unregulated operators, meant blood-borne diseases had the perfect opportunity to thrive. With HIV already prevalent in Haiti, this meant the rapid spread of the condition, and with untreated plasma cells being frozen and shipped to the US, it also meant that HIV travelled across international borders quickly and efficiently.

'Once the virus had been introduced in this way it quickly spread in a population with no natural resistance to the virus and with a proclivity for promiscuity,' says Dr Peter Jones of the Newcastle Haemophilia Centre.[4] And Miami was a centre of Haitian immigration in the US in the 1970s and 1980s, as well as a popular gay destination.

In 1981, Miami was a city in demise. But despite the fact it had become too unruly and too dangerous for many, for others it was *the* place to be. With clubs closing down throughout the rest of the US, there were nightclubs popping up all over South Florida, especially on Miami's South Beach.

'The name of the music was no longer disco, that became a bad word across the country,' DJ Alex Gutierrez said. 'In the 1980s it was called Italo-disco, high energy and freestyle, but to all of us who had grown up listening and dancing in Miami, we recognized it for what it was – disco.'[5]

And with disco came a vibrant gay scene; the perfect environment for Freddie Mercury to inhabit during late nights and early mornings as he visited the bars and clubs looking for gay men seeking, like himself, uninhibited one-night stands.

'The music [disco] was also the backbeat to the growth of South Beach,' Louis Canales, one of South Beach's creators, explained. 'Disco was popular in the gay community as well as with the Northeast transplants and, of course, the Cubans. Disco club life is what South Beach was built on.'[6]

Given his desire to explore the gay scene in the cities he visited on tour, Miami was a dangerous place for Freddie to be, just as New York and San Francisco were. As early as 1979, Dr Arthur Pitchenik from the University of Mexico had seen Haitian immigrants in Miami with a mystery illness that later turned out to be AIDS, and Dr Margaret Fischl in Miami had a practice that was overwhelmed with dying women and children, all Haitians.

'When we were beginning to investigate the initial cases, we picked up the MMWR [CDC's *Morbidity & Mortality Weekly Report*], and there were cases described in California, and eventually New York,' recalls Fischl. 'And I'm reading it and saying, "This is exactly what we're seeing." We immediately called the Center for Disease Control and said, "We think we're seeing the exact same thing in south Florida," and described the population that we were seeing. Their first comment back to me was they didn't believe me. They began looking at all different types of aspects. Did they have unusual rituals in Haiti, Voodoo rituals? Did they inadvertently have homosexual contacts? They were convinced something else was going on.'[7]

In late 1981, while Freddie was cruising the gay bars of Miami, no one really knew what was going on – yet. And Freddie, despite the whispers on the radio, in the press, and among the gay community, continued on his promiscuous way. 'Excess is part of my nature,' he would say. 'To me dullness is a disease. I really need danger and excitement. I was not made for staying indoors and watching television.

I am definitely a sexual person. I like to [have sexual intercourse] all the time.'[8]

Freddie saw little risk in his lifestyle when, in October 1981, Queen flew to Mexico for a concert at Monterray's Estadio Universitario, where they played in front of 50,000 fans. However, a second concert at the venue was cancelled when a structure outside the stadium collapsed following the first concert, with no fatalities but a number of injuries.

Problems followed the band as they made their next appearance in Puebla. First of all their promoter was arrested and thrown into jail, with Queen having to pay $25,000[9] to release him. Then, stepping on stage in Puebla's Estadio de Beisbol Ignacio Zaragoza, they were pelted by shoes, stones and batteries from recorders the audience had been using to record the gig. While none of the band were struck by anything, Paul Prenter was hit, which caused a great deal of delight among the road crew. At the end of the show, Freddie said to the crowd, '*Muchas gracias*, Mexico, take your shoes, *adios amigos*, you motherfuckers!'

The following night Queen played one more show at the same venue and then flew out of Mexico immediately afterwards, making a promise never to return to the country. The band had lost a considerable amount of money during the tour of Mexico, a seven-figure sum was suggested, but it had also hit the group's pride: Queen weren't a band used to being second best or failing. It was time to lick their wounds back in Europe and to head, once again, for Munich. But before arriving back in Germany to continue recording their next album, Freddie headed for New York to conclude the purchase of his new apartment on East 58th Street.

Freddie fitted perfectly into New York, where he could be the rock star when he wanted and indulge in anonymity when it suited him. He could walk down the street and not be bothered; he could tirelessly pursue great sex in the gay clubs and bars of the city too. At this point he developed a routine so formulaic that we can pick any given night to get an insight. A not untypical evening for Freddie might begin with dinner at nine o'clock in one of his favourite New York restaurants, such as Clyde's in the Village, before he'd be picked up by car (always parked a discreet distance away) and then driven to one of the many clubs in the area.

Freddie hated being dropped off directly outside the club – he thought it flashy – and so he would always be dropped off again a short distance away to enable him to walk to the door of the club. On any given night the bars or clubs he would frequent might be Uncle Charlie's (also in the Village), or perhaps the Eagle or the Spike. Or the Anvil, the infamous club situated in the meatpacking district. Then again the Mineshaft. In fact anywhere that took his fancy, and anywhere that promised sex. On this particular night, Freddie headed for The Saint and, strolling the last few yards to the door, he insisted on joining the queue.

The Saint is a private men's club situated at 2nd Avenue and 6th on the Lower East Side of Manhattan. It was formerly an old Yiddish theatre, which had been converted into a state-of-the-art nightclub for gay New York. Obtaining membership was relatively easy, but to get the all-important locker, one had to join an ever-growing waiting list. The locker was necessary so you could change from street clothes into fetish clothing or dancing gear but, more importantly, it was the place to stash a night's supply of drugs, which would consist of, and in any combination, acid, MDA, cocaine, Quaaludes, Placidyl, Seconal and Black Beauties. But the most popular of all was the new drug, ecstasy, which was still legal and sold as a 'happy pill' across the bar for $10. Freddie might have all or any, but on this night he had ecstasy, a bump of cocaine, poppers and ethyl chloride, which was soaked into a hankie or rag and then bitten down on.

It was here, in The Saint, that Freddie met Charles from Montreal, Canada. Freddie, his confidence lifted from the drugs, wasn't afraid to make the first move, or speak up. Soon, the two of them were making plans to leave and head back to Freddie's apartment. As they left together, stopping to get their jackets, a pretty blond man with a thin moustache seemed to recognise Charles and came and kissed him. The man drew him close and whispered in his ear, something Freddie couldn't quite hear. The accent seemed French, but more extreme. He was from Quebec.

Earlier that week Charles had met this blond Canadian and, as was the way, had casual sex. Why not? It suited both of them and besides Charles actually liked this man: he was warm and funny. The young man looked at Freddie quizzically, suddenly recognising him, and reached out his hand and introduced himself. Freddie couldn't make out his name – it was unusual, one that he hadn't heard before. That was the first time Freddie met Gaëtan Dugas, the air steward from Canada. But it was a fleeting moment and before he knew it, he and Charles were both outside and looking for the car. Also outside was Nikolai Grishanovich, a handsome Russian ex-soldier, known to Freddie through his friends Kenny Everett and Robert Lang, a London barman who was visiting New York for his own long weekend of hedonism.

During the mid-1980s, Freddie began frequenting gay nightspots in London, especially the famous nightclub Heaven with the adjoining leather bar – The Cellar Bar – where Robert Lang worked, and which at the time had a 'dark room' where anything went. Freddie would come to this club and Robert remembers him well. They would often chat before it got too busy.

'I remember he told me about New York, and that was why I went. We never spoke that often, maybe once every couple of months, but when we did it was for an hour at a time before the bar got busy. Not specifically about anything, though, never about his fame or celebrity. It's odd what stays in our minds. One night whilst we were talking, he told me about a dream he had, in which everyone dies.'[10]

With the car waiting a block down the street, Freddie, Charles, Robert and Nikolai embraced and chatted briefly while walking, and then the four of them got in the car and headed back to Freddie's place, where they spent the night together.

'I had sex a couple of times with Freddie, once in New York, and in London. Everyone was having sex with everyone. It was not big deal,' Robert recalled.

According to his friends, Mercury went to bed with hundreds of men. Many who knew him said he had a great fear of spending time alone, especially at night. Freddie often admitted that his promiscuity was an attempt to cure the loneliness he felt, or to heal over the scars left by a number of his relationships. While there may have been more than a grain of truth to this, he felt he had to defend what to many might seem unpalatable: his liking for straightforward sex without any kind of emotional involvement. Mercury enjoyed sex for sex's sake and there was no real need for him to explain it away, but he also liked the comfort and security that a steady relationship brings and tried to juggle those conflicting needs.

'I want to have my cake and eat it, too,' he admitted. 'I want my security but I also want my freedom.' Most of those he picked up were taken back to Freddie's apartment for one-night flings, but in one club, Freddie happened to meet Bill Reid, a 'stocky homosexual from New Jersey' according to writer Lesley-Ann Jones,[11] and the two of them embarked on a relationship that proved to be one of the most tempestuous that Freddie would ever have. Freddie flew Reid over to Europe with him – he had to return to the studio to complete work on *Hot Space*, which would be released in 1982. Pretty soon the rest of the Queen entourage took a dislike to Reid, but being Freddie's beau at the time, they had no option but to sit and watch as the relationship began to crash and burn almost immediately.

While recording the new album towards the end of 1981, the band were in good spirits. They had recently had a number 1 single with 'Under Pressure' and 26th October had seen the release of their *Greatest Hits* album. An instant success, the compilation went to number 1 in the UK album charts and would go on to sell 25m copies worldwide, becoming one of the most successful albums ever. In the UK alone, the album, at the time of writing, is the best-selling UK album of all time. In the US, it would go on to sell over 8m copies, but it was the last Queen album to break into the US Top 20 in Freddie's lifetime. Queen's appeal in the US, despite constant touring, had declined. Worse was to come with the release of their next album: an album the fans would hate, an album Brian and Roger would come to loathe, and an album that *Rolling Stone* would describe as 'downright offensive'.[12]

Yet, in the grand scheme of things, chart positions and reviews counted for little as Freddie was becoming increasingly aware of other numbers emanating from the US: statistics revealing that, at the end of 1981, there had been a cumulative total of 270 reported cases of severe immune deficiency in the US among gay men and of those 121 individuals had already died. The Centers for Disease Control in the US, suspecting something strange and suspicious was afoot, had declared the new disease an epidemic in October 1981. Within a year, the virus was reported by 14 nations as it graduated from a seemingly local phenomenon to a global killer.

Despite these developments Freddie's lifestyle remained unrestricted and hedonistic. 'Life is for living,' he would say. 'Believe me, I would be doing those things and having that philosophy even if I wasn't successful.'[13] And Freddie was by no means alone. Writing in 1995 Dr Thomas Schmidt claimed: 'To begin with, there is an almost compulsive promiscuity associated with homosexual behaviour. 75% of homosexual men have more than 100 sexual partners during their lifetime. More than half of these partners are strangers. Only 8% of homosexual men and 7% of homosexual women ever have relationships lasting more than three years. Nobody knows the reason for this strange, obsessive promiscuity. It may be that homosexuals are trying to satisfy a deep psychological need by sexual encounters, and it just is not fulfilling. Male homosexuals average over 20 partners a year.'[14]

It was this attitude to life and love that meant the following year, 1982, would mark the beginning of the end for Freddie Mercury.

28

God's Judgement

The week before Christmas 1981, *Time Out* magazine in London printed a story that struck fear into the hearts of gay men in the UK: 'A rare and dangerous disease whose victims are almost exclusively homosexual and bisexual men has hit Britain. Doctors released the worst possible news for gay men last week with a report on the first death in Britain from one of the extraordinary "gay syndrome" diseases, which have stunned the US gay community during 1981. A 49-year-old gay man died from *pneumocystis carinii pneumonia* (PCP) ten days after being admitted to the Brompton Hospital. He had lost weight over three months and suffered three weeks' general malaise and progressive breathlessness. His case is identical to a series of puzzling US reports collated by the federal Centers for Disease Control (CDC) in Atlanta. Brompton Hospital doctors believe it may be significant that their patient regularly visited the States.' The article concluded with a quote from a London doctor, who said: 'We have to be careful not to be alarmist. The numbers we are talking about are very small. But I think this problem is going to become a large one.'[1]

Despite his warning still no one knew what this disease was, what was causing it, how it could be acquired or how it could be cured, if indeed it *could* be cured. Mystery and ignorance was fuelling fear and stigma on both sides of the Atlantic but especially in the US, where there had already been many more cases and many more deaths (San Francisco cops had started wearing masks and gloves to shield them from gay men). By May 1982, GRID (Gay Related Immune Deficiency) had afflicted at least 335 people in the US and killed 136 of them. It had been reported in 20 states but the overwhelming majority of cases were seen in New York State (10 cases), New Jersey (14) and California (71), but they were most frequent in New York City (158).

The *New York Times* reported that 'Federal health officials are concerned that tens of thousands more homosexual men may be silently affected and therefore vulnerable to potentially grave ailments'.[2] The immunological time bomb was ticking in the US and medical professionals were doing all they could to understand it, but there was still no solid proof of what was causing these lethal symptoms. There was certainly no proof that it was a virus of any sort. It was only a guess – this was completely unmapped terrain.

But while the syndrome flummoxed expert medical brains in the US, connections about how it might be transmitted slowly began to fall into place. In early 1982, Dr David Auerbach was approached by a member of the gay community in Los Angeles, about a possible sexual link between the rare cases of the syndrome in Southern California. Joining forces with Dr William Darrow, they investigated 13 of the first 19 cases of GRID in Los Angeles, and found that nine of the men had reported sexual contact with one particular person. They then extended their investigation nationwide to 90 patients, which was roughly 75 per cent of reported cases of the virus among gay men alive at the time, and they discovered that 40 of the 90 patients in ten cities were linked by sexual contact with the same particular man.[3] According to Randy Shilts, the one man linking all the cases was dubbed 'Patient Zero'.[4]

And Patient Zero was none other than Gaëtan Dugas.

Dugas was still visiting New York regularly in 1982 to undergo chemotherapy for Kaposi's sarcoma. In letters to his former lover, Ray Redford, he would tell him how he was one of a group of gay men in New York being treated for 'gay cancer'. Despite his diagnosis, Dugas continued to be promiscuous in New York, a fact which angered Dr Friedman-Kienm, who was one of the team treating him: 'While he was in New York, he would go to the gay bathhouses and have unprotected sex with a variety of people despite the fact that we warned him against it. I once caught him coming out of a gay bathhouse and I stopped the car and said, "What are you doing there?" And he said, "In the dark nobody sees my spots." He was a real sociopath. I stopped seeing him. I refused to see him, I was just so angry.'[5]

On 17th June, NBC transmitted their first report on the new form of 'cancer' that seemed to be only affecting homosexual men and, a day later, the New York Times reported how federal epidemiologists had found new evidence to suggest that no specific infectious agent had been identified, but they were intensifying laboratory efforts in an attempt to identify a virus, bacteria or other micro-organism as a possible cause for the serious disorder of the body's immune system that was affecting male homosexuals. Speaking to the newspaper, Dr Harold W. Jaffe said, 'We think the findings are important but they don't solve the problem. They do show pretty convincingly that this is not occurring as a random event among homosexual men.'[6]

Increasingly worried and frightened, the New York playwright Larry Kramer had decided to set up a group to raise money and distribute material on the streets of New York to the gay community, suggesting caution might be something to consider in their sexual practices given that something might be afoot. Already, however, despite their message, and the growing evidence coming out of the medical authorities, a lot of the gay community was up in arms at Kramer's efforts, accusing him of being alarmist.

In 1982, Kramer decided he needed to form a more official organisation and escalate activity in order to bring the message of caution to as wide an audience as possible. 'So I called a meeting with six of us: Larry Mass; Paul Popham, who had already lost several close friends; Paul Rapoport, a rich real estate man who had lost his lover; Nathan Fain, who was a journalist and a friend of mine; and Edmund White, the writer, because I thought his name would help us get attention,' recalled Kramer. 'At some point, Paul Rapoport said something like, "Gay men certainly have a health crisis," and I said, "Let's use that for our name, Gay Men's Health Crisis." And awkward as it was, that's what it became. It was useful because it announced the problem and it also showed that this was an attempt at community empowerment; that gay men were actually trying to help themselves.'[7]

One of the first people to volunteer to help the Gay Men's Health Crisis in New York was Rodger McFarlane. Walking into the makeshift office one day, this 6ft 7in former American football college star offered to start an AIDS hotline on his home phone before the disease even had that name. By the end of the first day, he had fielded 125 calls: 'One-hundred twenty-five scared people. And fucked-up people,' McFarlane recalled of the first night that he opened the GMHC hotline out of his own apartment. 'I mean, they were sitting in shit in Mount Sinai and

NYU. We had a patient set on fire. This stuff was surreal. We had people literally beaten up with bats and thrown out of their apartments. You can't make this shit up.'[8]

While most members of the gay scene in the US were starting to become frightened by this potential threat, fear was also beginning to consume some elements of the heterosexual population. The illness had made the gay community more visible, and the uncertainty about the condition they were dying from (it was still referred to as GRID, Gay Related Immunodeficiency), heightened the prospect of gay men becoming targets of aggression and violence. A 1978 study of 1,600 gay men living in Chicago found that 27 per cent of those living in a gay neighbourhood had been assaulted because of their homosexuality.[9] With the perceived threat of a gay-related disease, these hostile acts only increased, so much so that in a 1982 study, when the condition was beginning to make headlines in the US, 289 gay men were interviewed and it was found that 72 per cent had experienced verbal abuse as a result of being gay and in a 1988 study, that figure had risen to 92 per cent. In the same 1988 study, 73 per cent of gay men had experienced criminal violence because of their sexual orientation.[10]

Given that GRID was still associated with being connected to homosexual men in 1982, and the term 'gay plague' was routinely being used in dramatic newspaper headlines, the gay communities in the US not only began to feel threatened, but also isolated. 'We were forced to take care of ourselves,' Rodger McFarlane told the *Times*, 'because we learned that if you have certain diseases, certain lifestyles, you can't expect the same services as other parts of society.'[11]

As well as setting up their own support groups and helplines, in 1982 two gay men in New York City, Michael Callen and Richard Berkowitz, published *How to Have Sex in an Epidemic*, which helped spread the idea that safe sex could be used as protection against spreading the epidemic – an idea that hadn't yet become prevalent in the medical community. The pamphlet was one of the first places that proposed that men should use condoms when having sex with other men as a protection against GRID.

But the perception that GRID was a disease solely affecting homosexuals was to be challenged in the summer of 1982 when an elderly man with severe haemophilia A was reported to have died from PCP. Within weeks, two more PCP cases were reported in different states, both young men with severe haemophilia. Upon closer inspection, these young men had accompanying unexplained immunosuppression and neither had any history of homosexual contact. Within the next few weeks and months, cases were also reported among infants, female sex partners of men with, or at high risk from GRID, and an infant and adults who had received blood transfusions. The conclusion reached was that, 'Taken together, these cases provided strong evidence that AIDS was caused by an infectious agent that could be transmitted by blood and from mother to child, as well as through homosexual and heterosexual contact'.[12]

Suddenly, health authorities were realising that non-homosexuals were being diagnosed with the symptoms of GRID, and there was the possibility that the case of a haemophiliac with GRID symptoms suggested donated blood and blood products within the US were contaminated with the syndrome. When 32 Haitian migrants to the US were reported with opportunistic infections, Kaposi's sarcoma and a high mortality rate, and none of them were homosexual, it was clear that GRID was not simply a 'gay plague' and that others were at risk from the disease. What had been complacency turned into serious concern, even panic. As a result of these new observations, it was on 24th September 1982 that the US Centers for Disease Control and Prevention (CDC) renamed GRID, and the name AIDS was officially used for the first time.

In the three months leading up to the renaming of GRID to AIDS, CDC had received reports of 593 cases of AIDS and death had occurred in 243 of them, a staggering 41 per cent. The same report concluded that the incidence of AIDS by date of diagnosis was doubling every six months, and the cities where it was most prevalent were San Francisco and New York.

AIDS had also reached Europe, with five cases being found in Spain, France and Switzerland, and in the UK, a letter written by American tourist Pete Ossinger and published as the main front-page article in *Capital Gay* served as a warning to gay British men: 'On recent travels through Europe I have noticed how terribly unaware most European gay men are of the recent AIDS (Acquired Immune Deficiency Syndrome) epidemic outbreak in the USA. There are now some 525 reported cases, out of which approximately 25 have recently been reported from Europe (two in England). The case fatality rate is over 40%. Approximately two new cases are reported every day. Latest research does indicate that AIDS could very possibly be spread through a virus, which makes it a sexually transmitted disease. Perhaps gay men in Europe can learn from the terrible news we are hearing here in the US and possibly prevent a serious spreading of the disease into the European communities. Please do whatever you can to inform and alert your readers'.[13]

The British authorities had already started to take notice of what was happening in the US and the Communicable Diseases Surveillance Centre at Colindale, north London, had begun a national investigation to determine whether Kaposi's sarcoma was spreading to, and within, the UK. By this time, however, four British men had already died of AIDS-related illnesses including Terry Higgins, a barman at the popular gay club in London, Heaven. The terror of AIDS in Britain had struck home but actually, it had been in the UK for some time, as the *Guardian* reported: 'In 1981, Dr Tony Pinching, a 33-year-old specialist in the workings of the immune system, helped to conduct a study at St Mary's Praed Street Clinic in London. One hundred sexually active gay men were asked intimate questions about their lives and took a battery of blood tests. The men displayed none of the Aids marker illnesses that had been evident in the United States, but their blood samples showed many immune cell abnormalities and a decreased ability to fight off disease. Within weeks, Pinching was seeing his first Aids patients'.[14]

For months, people in the UK had thought of AIDS as a 'media import, like *Hill Street Blues*'[15] and thought the one seriously advocated method of prevention was simply not to have sex with Americans. But the death of Higgins started to change attitudes, particularly when the Terrence Higgins Trust was set up later in 1982 to organise fundraisers, hold public meetings and produce an AIDS information leaflet, which outlined the symptoms to look out for. However, it didn't mention anything about using condoms or the risks of anal sex. 'Have as much sex as you want,' it stated, 'but with fewer people and with HEALTHY

PEOPLE'. It ended by saying, 'Help yourself!' The subtext was: because nobody else will.[16]

Meanwhile, in the United States, Gaëtan Dugas was pleased that his Kaposi's sarcoma didn't seem to be spreading and, despite the news beginning to filter out that AIDS was transmitted sexually, he continued to have sex with many men in New York and San Francisco as well as Vancouver and Toronto. However, when Dr William Darrow had appeared to establish sexual links between Dugas and at least 40 of the 248 gay men diagnosed with AIDS in the US, it seemed imperative that he must be stopped.

According to author Randy Shilts, Dugas was approached in San Francisco by Dr Selma Dritz, an official at the city's public health department.[17] Recalling the encounter, Dritz says, 'I knew that Gaëtan Dugas was still in town. I couldn't get to him, but I put word out, "If you see Gaëtan Dugas, let him know I want to see him." He came up. I told him, "Look, we've got proof now." I didn't tell him how scientifically accurate the information was. It wasn't inaccurate, but it wasn't actually scientifically proven. I said, "We've got proof that you've been infecting these other people. You've got AIDS, you know. We know it's transmissible now, because you're transmitting it."'[18]

According to Dritz, Dugas didn't believe her and suggested that she should mind her own business before saying he could do what he wanted with his body. When she told him he was infecting others, he apparently said, 'I got it. Let them get it,' before walking out.[19] Dugas, suggests Randy Shilts, then moved to San Francisco, where he would inhabit the gay bathhouses and soon rumours began circulating on Castro Street, the centre of San Francisco's gay scene, about a blond with a French accent who would have sex in the bathhouses before turning up the lights, pointing out his Kaposi's sarcoma lesions and saying, 'I've got gay cancer. I'm going to die, and so are you.'[20]

Gaëtan Dugas was described as having a lot of energy and full of life as well as great at interacting with people, which made him an excellent flight attendant, laughing and joking with customers. 'He was very, very gay,' says Richard McKay, 'and wouldn't put up with any crap, certainly would not put up with any sort of discrimination he was receiving.'[21] But in truth Gaëtan Dugas (Patient Zero) was only an actual early case. He was representing all the people who refused to stop having unprotected sex even after they became ill. Those who knew Dugas found it difficult to believe what he was being accused of. 'His sandy hair fell boyishly over his forehead. His mouth easily curled into an inviting smile, and his laugh could flood colour into a room of black and white'[22] – wasn't that the description of him?

Since the early days of the AIDS epidemic, researchers have reasoned that a handful of people – maybe even a single individual – bore the unknowing responsibility for having introduced the disease to North America and its first large group of victims, the homosexual community. As a French-Canadian flight attendant, with almost cost-free privileges to travel, Gaëtan Dugas flew often between major cities in North America. Dugas was likely the one on whom blame would be cast. He would become one of the most talked-about figures in the early days of the epidemic. Contrary to accusations, it seemed, in truth he was not making people sick on purpose. These were different times: no one knew anything about this disease.

But Gaëtan Dugas was not really Patient Zero, as claimed by Shilts, and it is impossible to know who was, but the effect of those around him in cities such as San Francisco and New York towards contracting AIDS was terrifying. 'I remember laying in the front room one night and discovering that there were lymph glands under my armpit that hadn't been there before. And it just triggered something and I started crying. I was afraid,' recalled Bobby Reynolds. 'When you're diagnosed with AIDS, very often, you lose your support system, you lose your families, you lose your job. I've lost the majority of friends that I had before my diagnosis.'[23]

And sufferers of AIDS in the US weren't helped by the Ronald Reagan administration. Reagan's press secretary, Larry Speakes, joked about the disease during a White House briefing in October 1982, laughing at the term 'gay plague' and jokingly asking whether reporters had AIDS because, 'I don't have it', which was followed by his own laughter. And, as so often happens, the question of who would meet the cost for paying for the treatment of AIDS caused much debate but little action. 'The question of what to do about it became very controversial,' remembered Dr Edward N. Brandt, 'as most things do when sex is involved, over the issue of these gay men who were bringing it on themselves, and why should my tax dollars go to help them? These are people who are socially unacceptable in most people's minds – IV drug users, particularly those that share needles, homosexual men. And especially if you added those who engage in anal intercourse, of course, that really makes it worse in much of the public's mind.'[24]

Bumper stickers on vehicles in California confirmed the continued hostility towards AIDS sufferers when they were seen during a Republican Party convention saying, 'AIDS: It's killing all the right people', and the Reverend Jerry Falwell proclaimed, 'I believe that when one breaks the laws of nature and the laws of moral decency – and I do believe homosexuality is moral perversion – when we go against nature – and God, of course, is the creator of nature – we therefore pay the prices for that. We do reap it in our flesh when we violate the laws of God.'[25]

By the end of 1982, AIDS was not solely associated with homosexuality: it was known that haemophiliacs could become affected with AIDS through tainted blood transfusions, that IV drug users could transmit the disease through shared needles, and that heterosexual women could become infected by their partners who were either bisexual or had used prostitutes who had contracted AIDS from clients or drug use.

In the United States, as 1982 drew to a close, 1,614 people had been diagnosed with AIDS and, of those, 619 had died. It had also been recognised that AIDS was not a disease that occurred solely in the US. In Europe, the number of newly reported HIV diagnoses would rise 21-fold throughout the 1980s.[26]

And one of the most famous of those would be Freddie Mercury.

29

At the start of 1982 Freddie flew to Munich with Brian May to join Roger Taylor and John Deacon to continue work on Queen's forthcoming album, *Hot Space*. All four of them would remain in Munich until the end of February 1982.

For its centrality, Queen and their crew lodged at the Hilton Munich Park Hotel, some 1.5 miles from Musicland Studios and approximately two miles from the entertainment district, an ideal locality because the musicians evenly divided their time between work and extra-curricular activities.

While at the Munich Hilton their suites were split into the HH, the Hetero Hangout, and the PPP, the Presidential Poofter Parlour. No prizes for guessing which one Freddie inhabited. And the evenings would see the band, especially Freddie, inhabiting the clubs and bars of the city. Consumed by partying, the recording process appeared to take second place. Brian May recalls Munich as being a time when outside influences encroached on the recording process as well as their private lives: 'The latter days in Munich were lost in a haze of vodka. There were no drugs in my case, but there were so many drugs around.'[1]

Freddie was taking advantage of the availability of cocaine in Munich, but although he used it recreationally, he never became an addict. He controlled cocaine, it never controlled him, and he would often work furiously on songs in a studio under the influence of cocaine, songs that he would consider fantastic at the time, but on hearing them the next morning, clear and free of drugs, he would discard them instantly. Even without drugs, the attractions of Munich were plentiful for Freddie, as Brian May remembers: 'We all got ourselves into deep trouble emotionally in Munich. Freddie was no exception. He got himself deep into emotional waters, which he couldn't really handle and was very unhappy for some of the time. He was being sucked into places which, probably, weren't good for him, and we all felt that and realised he was in some kind of danger.'[2]

When Queen were in the studio, away from all the physical, emotional and chemical attractions of Munich, they found themselves embarking on a whole new sound. Driven predominantly by Freddie and John, the album *Hot Space* mined a disco/funk sound that was unlike anything the band had come up with before. It was a curious decision, given that the US was in the middle of a disco backlash. Drum machines and synthesizers were used, as well as a brass section, and it seemed that everything Queen was known for was either taken away or subverted during the recording of this album. Brian May's guitar was relegated to the background, Roger Taylor's powerhouse drumming was hidden behind click-tracks, electro-percussion and synthesized handclaps, and there was no sign of Queen's trademark multi-tracked harmonies.

One influence on the direction of *Hot Space* was Paul Prenter, who was gaining an increasingly influential presence in Freddie's life. He had become Mercury's personal assistant, and wasn't shy of giving his input on the direction Queen should take. Unfortunately for Brian, Roger and John, Freddie tended to listen to Prenter.

'He was a very, very bad influence on Freddie, hence on the band, really,' says Roger Taylor. 'He very much wanted our music to sound like you'd just walked in a gay club. And I didn't.'[3]

Prenter hated the guitar sound and so encouraged Freddie to have a sparser sound for this album, one that concentrated on bass lines and synthesizers rather than the driven rock sound which had been the familiar domain of Brian May and Roger Taylor. 'He became very ambitious and undermined and tried to peel Freddie off,' says John Reid. 'I don't know whether they had a sexual relationship or not but it's symbiotic. Both were heavily into drugs, so he became Freddie's fixer across the board. Freddie needed support. Look at his household. It was a kind of revolving door, so he had to have somebody he could call upon and Paul was good at that, and had it not been Paul, it would have been somebody else.

'But being Paul, I recognised that somebody in his position should always have Freddie's best interests at heart, but he didn't; he only had his own interests at heart. He used to describe himself as Freddie's manager but the position of strength that Paul Prenter got to was all with Freddie's permission. Freddie knew what he was letting him do. He [Paul] wasn't a nice man. He was a nice boy but turned into a real nightmare.'[4]

Apart from 'Under Pressure', which had been co-credited to Queen and David Bowie, and 'Cool Cat', a joint composition between Freddie and John Deacon, there were three other Freddie tracks on *Hot Space*: 'Life Is Real (Song for Lennon)', Freddie's tribute to the murdered Beatle, 'Staying Power' and 'Body Language'.

'Body Language' was the first Queen single not to feature guitars (except on the fade-out) and was accompanied by a notorious video directed by Mike Hodges featuring a scantily-clad model writhing around: 'This was an even closer collaboration [with Freddie],' recalls Hodges, 'because I had to interpret his visual ideas as well as his music. It was very funky, sexy, slinky. Too much so for some. I think it was the first video to be banned by MTV.'[5]

Described in *Rolling Stone* as 'a piece of funk that isn't fun', 'Body Language' was released in April 1982 and stalled at number 25 in the UK charts. Perhaps riding on the back of the success of 'Another One Bites The Dust', the single reached number 11 in the US, but the song's lack of success would be a foreboding of what was to come, with the poor reception of the album on both sides of the Atlantic.

With the album recorded, and Queen having signed a new six-album deal with EMI, the band took to the road once more, beginning a UK and European tour that would conclude with a show at the Milton Keynes Bowl in front of a 65,000 crowd in June. But by the time Queen arrived in Milton Keynes, they would have been aware of the less than enthusiastic reaction to *Hot Space*.

Paul Loasby was the promoter of the *Hot Space* Tour in the UK and, having already paid a considerable amount to secure Queen and the venues, was aware that their stock was diminishing rapidly as a result of their 'new' sound although, to begin with, poor album sales was the least of his problems: 'The original aim was to do Arsenal when it was at the old Highbury Stadium and Old Trafford and I did all the usual work, and it took ages and ages and cost a fortune in legal fees, and I didn't get a licence for either of them,' recalls Loasby. 'So then I had to go to Milton Keynes and Elland Road, and even Elland Road was a real struggle to get the licence, including not even allowing me to sell tickets on the day.'[6]

Unable to use the artwork from the new album to promote the tour, Loasby was about to use the image from the cover of Queen's massively successful *Greatest Hits* album when he spotted a slight problem: 'At the time we were about to go to war with Argentina over the Falkland Islands and we used the *Greatest Hits* cover photo of the band to promote the tour,' remembers Loasby. 'On that photo, Roger Taylor, if you look closely, is wearing a badge on his jacket of the Argentine flag. I remember, at the time, thinking, "What are we going to do?" So we airbrushed that out – without asking!'[7]

If problems with licensing and promo material wasn't enough, worse was to come on a tour that was beginning to appear jinxed: 'We managed to get the tickets on sale and it started to go very well, as you'd expect,' Loasby says. 'And then "Body Language" came out, and at the same time The Rolling Stones announced their open-air shows, which included numerous nights at Wembley, and, a little later, they announced Roundhay Park in Leeds, and they were 50p cheaper, so the ticket sales went to nothing. Obviously when you get Queen you think, fantastic, this is a licence to print money, and suddenly I had *Hot Space*, The Rolling Stones, licensing difficulties and a rock band that had seemingly gone to a disco band and we were in trouble. And we *were* in trouble. I went bankrupt as I lost my financial backers.

'We did two nights in Edinburgh between Leeds and Milton Keynes, with Heart supporting, and even they didn't sell out. That's two nights of an 8,000-capacity venue, and that gives you some indication of the impact of that album on their core audience which, from my observations, they didn't get back until Live Aid.'[8]

Although *Hot Space* reached number 4 in the UK, it only climbed to number 22 in the US. The singles released from the album all fared poorly, with only 'Las Palabras De Amor' breaking into the Top 20 in the UK, while in the US, 'Calling All Girls', the first Queen single written solely by Roger Taylor, could only reach number 60. Worse was to come with the reviews. *Rolling Stone* called it 'routinely competent and, at times, downright offensive'[9] and 12 years after its release, *Q* magazine voted *Hot Space* One of the Top 15 Albums Where Great Rock Acts Lost the Plot.[10]

'Because they were such a unique band, they had their own sound, they were a rock band although they could do some interesting variations on the theme, but I don't think anybody would have expected a *Hot Space* in a million years,' says Paul Loasby.[11]

Such was the fans' disapproval of the album that, performing at Milton Keynes on the final show of the UK and European leg of the *Hot Space* Tour, Freddie was forced to acknowledge the poor reception with a certain amount of angry stubbornness. 'Now most of you know we've got some new sounds out, and for what it's worth, we're going to do some songs in the funk black category, whatever you call it,' he told the crowd, before continuing, 'People get so excited about these things, it's only a *bloody* record!'

But the fans weren't the only people not enamoured by Queen's new sound: 'I can remember having a go at Freddie because some of the stuff he was writing was very definitely on the gay side,' says Brian May. 'I remember saying, "It would be nice if this stuff could be universally applicable, because we have friends out there of every persuasion." It's nice to involve people. What it's not nice to do is rope people out. And I felt kind of roped out by something ['Body Language'] that was very overtly a gay anthem.'[12] Even Roger Taylor said 'I thought it [*Hot Space*] was going to be great, and it was absolute shit.'[13]

Freddie was unrepentant, however. 'I think *Hot Space* was one of the biggest risks we've taken, but people can't relate to something that's outside the norm. I'd hate it if every time we came up with an album, it was just the norm. It's not to say that we're always right, because we're not. This whole dance/funk mode was basically my idea and it obviously didn't do that well. I think it was way ahead of its time, but we did what we felt like doing at that time and at that time we felt it was right.'[14]

Hot Space is full of mixed messages: the rock fusion with disco and funk, not to mention Freddie Mercury's gender politics, which inadvertently coincided with the emergence of AIDS. In the 1970s he was all flowing shirts, long hair and painted nails, a look that in the context of Glam wasn't that outrageous. In 1980, influenced by the gay leather scene in New York and Munich, his style changed accordingly. He cropped his hair, grew a moustache and was often photographed in a Muir cap and Mineshaft or Heaven T-shirt or vest. Peter Freestone explains Freddie's new look: 'It gave Freddie an excuse to get rid of the long hair and it made him easier to blend in at bars, so he didn't stand out like a sore thumb.' By which Freestone means Freddie adopted the 'clone' look popular in the early 1980s in the underground gay sex scene. [15]

The 'clone' was, in many ways, the manliest of men. He had a gym-defined body; after hours of rigorous bodybuilding, his physique rippled with bulging muscles, looking more like a competitive body builder than a hairdresser or florist. He kept his hair short and had a thick moustache or closely cropped beard. There was nothing New Age or hippie about this reformed gay liberationist. And the clone lived the fast life. He 'partied hard', taking recreational drugs, dancing in discos until dawn, having hot sex with strangers.

Arguably this clone look (synonymous with the macho look) was introduced to the general public by the Village People, a pop-disco group formed in 1977 by French music producer Jacques Morali. In its inception the Village People targeted a homosexual demographic by projecting personae associated with gay fantasy. Of the six differing personae in the Village People's original line-up, it was the construction worker David Hodo, Freddie's friend, whose physical appearance resembled that of Mercury's around the time of *Hot Space*'s release, and introduced the gay clone/macho image to the mainstream.

'I never liked Freddie's "Clone" beefed-up image,' says Marc Almond, 'and it was by then obvious to me that Freddie was gay. It was, however, on reflection, incredibly subversive; the gayest image ever at the time, if you were in the know.'[16]

Richard Dyer discusses the gay clone/macho image's appropriation by homosexual minorities. He states: 'Although many members of the general public would have been familiar with David Hodo [from the Village People] and his cartoonish portrayal of the macho gay construction worker, I argue that Freddie Mercury, who along with his thick moustache, slicked hair and a lean and muscular physique sported tight blue jeans, muscle shirts and various athletic outfits, was not regarded outwardly as a gay rock celebrity. Because the gay clone signified a type of homosexual, many Queen fans were not able to decode the inferred levels of signification. Conversely, for those advocates whose intuition persuaded them of Mercury's rather clandestine sexual orientation, they may have opted towards wilful blindness, for during the 1980s, a time steeped in homophobia and AIDS, no place existed within the rock domain for an openly gay icon.'[17]

'This attitude towards androgynous and effeminate artists – read as "gay" – continued into the 80s with the onset of Thatcherism, to the point of offensive homophobia being rife,' says Marc Almond. 'As an artist of that time I was informed by my press department, Colin Bell (outrageously, gay himself) and Mariella Frostrup (my PR woman then) that they had come up with "girlfriends" for me – Cindy Ecstasy, Mari Wilson and even American Bebe Buell (who had a reputation as a "Rock Girlfriend") was mooted. When Siouxsie Sioux wanted to meet me it was a joy to my press people and an opportunity for another imaginary and implausible relationship to be leaked.'[18]

The UK and European tour ended at Milton Keynes but, just prior to that concert, Freddie found himself involved in some off-stage contretemps. He was still seeing Bill Reid and the relationship was causing raised eyebrows among the Queen entourage, as the two of them seemed to be constantly arguing. It was well known that the relationship between Mercury and Reid was tempestuous – it had been since day one – but the friction seemed to be intensified on the road.

Author Mark Blake reveals how the relationship was unfolding in front of every crewmember: 'Morgan Fisher (the keyboard player) still recalls hearing the same argument at every post-gig dinner. "Every night, sat in the restaurant, Fred's boyfriend would tell him, 'Freddie, you have got to stop smoking,' and every night Freddie would snap, 'Oh, shut up!' and light another cigarette. And so it went on."'[19]

At the Milton Keynes show, however, Reid snapped and following a tumultuous row just before Freddie went on stage, he sank his teeth deep into Freddie's left hand. Hastily patched-up, Freddie took the stage and Reid joined a long line of lovers who had been cast off, banished into the darkness, never to be seen again, while Freddie held court with 65,000 of his other admirers.

After a short break, which included a rare appearance on *Top of the Pops* miming 'Las Palabras De Amor' and the filming of two promo videos for 'Back Chat' and 'Calling All Girls', Queen set off for Canada, where they would prepare for their forthcoming world tour, the North

American leg of which would be a defining period for the band. It kicked off in Montreal on 21st July and, from there, the band travelled to Boston where, on 23rd July, mayor Kevin White declared the day 'Queen Day' and presented them with the keys to the city. From Boston, the band criss-crossed the US and, as always, they did it in style, this time using Elvis Presley's private jet, the *Lisa Marie*, as their mode of transport.

For Freddie it was a personal thrill to get so close to Elvis, someone he admired greatly, and later during the tour, Elvis' daughter, Lisa Marie, would present him with one of the King's personal scarves. It was something Freddie treasured for the rest of his life.

Days were set aside throughout the tour for the band to relax and recharge their batteries and, whenever he got the chance, Freddie would fly back to his New York apartment. Once again, following Bill Reid's banishment, Freddie was alone, and his days off in New York City allowed him to continue his predilection of scouring the gay scene for no-strings sex.

When Queen were performing two sell-out nights in Madison Square Garden on 27th and 28th July, Freddie had five nights in New York between 26th and 31st July and later, after their Cincinnati show on 7th August, Freddie spent another five nights in New York, leaving on 13th August.

Six weeks later, Freddie and Queen were back in New York City to record a performance for *Saturday Night Live* in the Rockefeller Plaza with Chevy Chase. In the meantime they had completed their North America tour on 15th September, flown back to the UK and then returned to New York to play two songs live, 'Under Pressure' and 'Crazy Little Thing Called Love', on *Saturday Night Live*. This performance, although no one knew it at the time, would be Queen's final performance in the US.

But, performing both songs, Freddie was clearly not himself. Wearing jeans, a white T-shirt with a red lightning motif, and a leather jacket for 'Under Pressure', and changing into a red singlet for 'Crazy Little Thing Called Love' with no jacket, while playing acoustic guitar, Freddie appeared unwell – looking pale and drawn. His voice came in short breaths, and his vocals were shot with Roger having to back him up. As it happens, Freddie was in recovery from a serious bout of flu (described by him as 'the worse flu ever') and shingles, combined with an upset stomach. He was also suffering from severe headaches that had left him extremely sick in mid-August, when he was last in New York. During that visit he had seen a doctor on Fifth Avenue as he was concerned about a white lesion that had developed on his tongue.

Throughout his time in New York City, Freddie was actively engaged in casual and promiscuous sex. There was a density of infected men in New York City, and Freddie's lifestyle while in the city made him a high-risk participant. It is highly likely therefore that sometime in the summer of 1982, while Queen were on the North American leg of the *Hot Space* Tour, Freddie was exposed to HIV and became infected. It is possible (though unlikely, given two years had passed) that infection had happened earlier, when Freddie had had a one-night stand with John Murphy who, himself, had had sex with Gaëtan Dugas, but given the symptoms that Mercury was exhibiting prior to and during the *Saturday Night Live* show on 25th September, it is likely he had contracted HIV between two to six weeks earlier, when he spent five nights in New York City. Certainly, his appearance on *Saturday Night Live* would suggest the symptoms of a person who has recently become infected with HIV.

Within the first few weeks of contracting HIV, 70 per cent of people will experience flu-like symptoms – fever, headache, upset stomach, and muscle soreness among the most common initial signs of an HIV infection, just as Freddie had in the lead-up to the *Saturday Night Live* recording. This can lead to opportunistic infections or infections that are more rampant than normal and these infections may involve the skin. Within two to six weeks after HIV infection, many develop flu-like symptoms, often severe. Symptoms can include fever, swollen glands, sore throat, rashes, mouth infections, muscle and joint aches and pains, fatigue and headaches. This is called Acute Retroviral Syndrome (ARS) or primary HIV infection, and it's the body's natural and immediate response to the HIV infection.

During this early period of initial infection large amounts of virus are produced in your body. The virus uses CD4 cells to replicate and destroys them in the process. Because of this, your CD4 count can fall rapidly. Eventually your immune response will begin to bring the level of virus in your body back down to a level called a viral set point, which is a relatively stable level of virus in the body. At this point, your CD4 count begins to increase, but it may not return to pre-infection levels.

Of course, Freddie had already been feeling unwell in New York in mid-August, which means it is also possible that he became infected with HIV during the 26th to 31st July visit, although this is right on the early limits of infection. And then there's the white lesion on his tongue. It is extremely likely that this was hairy leukoplakia, also known as oral hairy leukoplakia or HIV-associated hairy leukoplakia. It manifests itself as a white patch on the side of the tongue with a corrugated or, as its name suggests, a hairy appearance. It occurs in people with HIV and is one of the first signs of the virus infection. Robert Lang remembered Freddie had had this checked out by a doctor on Fifth Avenue in New York in mid-August, which also makes it highly likely that, at some point between 26th July and 13th August 1982, Mercury contracted HIV in New York City – but from whom? That's anybody's guess.

But that certainly doesn't mean Freddie knew he was infected. Many of the symptoms of early infection can also be attributed to numerous other causes, but there are several that we now know specifically suggest infection of HIV, especially when combined over the same period. Of course, none of this was known at the time. Like so many others, Freddie simply thought he was poorly, and carried on living life to the full. After all, he was exhibiting no signs of Kaposi's sarcoma, so it may well have been that in his mind there was no way he had the 'gay cancer'.

On 19th October, Queen began a short tour of Japan to round off their *Hot Space* Tour. There, the band were still as popular as ever, but the year had been a sobering one. In the UK, *Hot Space* had not performed well, but it had done even worse in the US. Only a year earlier Queen was the biggest band in the world on the back of 'Another One Bites The Dust'. Now, 12 months down the road, other British bands such as The Human League and Soft Cell, with their hits 'Don't You Want Me' and 'Tainted Love' were riding high in the end-of-year Billboard Top 100, while Queen were nowhere to be seen.

The Police had been voted Best British Band at The Brits, new British bands such as Duran Duran and Culture Club were beginning their domination of the UK charts, and three weeks after Queen returned from Japan, Michael Jackson released *Thriller*, an album that swept all before it. Bizarrely, Freddie had become friends with Jackson during 1981 and had written a song called 'There Must Be More To Life Than This' for them to duet while Queen were recording *Hot Space*. Queen had even recorded a backing track for the song, but the track was never completed. While *Hot Space* ended up selling around 4m records worldwide, at the time of writing *Thriller* had sold over 65m.

After the Japan tour, the four members of Queen were beginning to get on each other's nerves. It seemed a break might suit all parties and there was the potential for solo recordings: Roger Taylor had dipped his toes in the water and Freddie had his own solo aspirations. But there was likely something else on his mind too; how could there not be with the news emanating from New York and San Francisco revealing the disease that was beginning to decimate the gay scene there? His lifestyle, particularly his time in New York, meant there was every chance he might already be infected. With every one-night stand, with every new lover, with every casual fling, his chances of becoming infected with HIV increased.

'I pray I'll never get AIDS,' said Mercury. 'So many friends have it. Some have died, others won't last much longer. I'm terrified that I'll be next. Immediately after each time I have sex I think, "Suppose that was the *one*? Suppose the virus is now in my body?" I jump in the shower and scrub myself clean, although I know it's useless.'[20]

But the reality was, by the end of 1982, Freddie *had* been infected with HIV, most probably in New York City earlier that summer, and his fate was sealed. He had no signs yet of Kaposi's sarcoma, so he probably thought – or hoped – he was not infected, but regardless he continued to do everything with everybody in Munich and New York City, and wherever they went on tour. He felt fine – he had been ill but now he felt good, though not always 100 per cent. There were constant minor infections, throat and ear infections, styes... but nothing serious. The world wasn't *officially* aware of AIDS yet, safe sex wasn't being promoted to the extent it would be, and many people just lived for the moment. It was a different time, a different scene, and a different world.

And against that backdrop Freddie would throw himself into solo work, partying, lovers and, eventually, towards the end of that year, he was to meet the man who would stay with him until the very end.

Towards the end of 1982, Queen were growing increasingly unhappy about their record deal with Elektra, the label that looked after their interests in Australia, New Zealand, Japan and most importantly the US.

Disappointed with their handling of *Hot Space*, which although it had been a Top 10 album everywhere except Australia and the US, had been perceived as a flop, Freddie was adamant he would no longer make records for Elektra. Consequently, it was left to Jim Beach to negotiate Queen's way out of these contracts, which he eventually did in October 1983 at a cost of $1m to the band[1]. Beach then managed to get the band signed to Capital in the US, and, as part of the negotiations, also secured a solo deal for Freddie Mercury.

A solo project had long been on the cards for Freddie: 'I always wanted to do a solo album,' he said. 'I just wanted it to be the right time and the right place so that I could actually work properly on the songs that I wanted to do before I got too old.'[2]

Knowing he now had a solo record deal, Freddie booked some studio time in Montreux at his own expense to begin work on what would eventually become his debut solo album, *Mr. Bad Guy*. It was while recording these early sessions that Freddie met producer Giorgio Moroder. Born in Italy as Giovanni Giorgio, Moroder was a trailblazer producer who came to prominence in the 1970s with the seminal hit singles 'Love To Love You Baby' and 'I Feel Love', which he wrote and produced for Donna Summer.

In 1983, Moroder was working on a soundtrack to accompany a restored version of Fritz Lang's 1927 silent film, *Metropolis*. His plan was to colorise the film, add special effects, explanatory subtitles, and accompany the whole film with a synth-rock soundtrack to reboot a relic of the silent screen for the MTV generation. One of the artists that Moroder thought would be suitable to record a song for the soundtrack was Freddie Mercury and, thrilled to be invited, Freddie began work with Moroder on a track titled 'Love Kills'.

Moroder wasn't Freddie's only collaborator in 1983. After a short break relaxing at his apartment in New York, Freddie flew to Michael Jackson's mock Tudor mansion in Encino, California, to begin one of the most unusual working relationships in pop history. He and Jackson had known and respected each other for some time. In fact, it was Michael who suggested 'Another One Bites The Dust' was released as a single. 'He [Jackson] has been a friend of ours for a long while,' remarked Freddie. 'He used to come and see our shows all the time and that is how the friendship grew. We were always interested in each other's styles. I would regularly play him the new Queen album when it was cut and he would play me his stuff. We kept saying, "Why don't we do something together?"'[3]

So it was that Freddie accepted Jackson's invitation to his Californian home. After passing through strict security, Michael took Freddie and Peter Freestone on a tour of the house, which included the recording studio housed within the grounds where Jackson had laid the foundations for *Off The Wall* and *Thriller*. Entering the studio, Freddie found the recording complex complete with state-of-the-art equipment and scores of instruments. Here, he and Jackson began work on three different songs: 'Victory', 'State of Shock' and Freddie's own composition, 'There Must Be More To Life Than This'. They would have only a few hours together and with no session musicians booked, Freddie played the piano while Michael made use of whatever was around to add a beat.

Departing at around six in the evening, Freddie seemed happy with the way the collaboration had gone and the two artists parted with the promise to get in touch with each other in the near future. On the journey back to their hotel, Freddie couldn't resist commenting on Jackson's house and said to Peter, 'All that money and no taste, dear. What a waste.'[4]

But any plans for Freddie and Jackson to reconvene never materialised. The reasons for this have never been confirmed, although Freddie would later say: 'We had three tracks in the can, but unfortunately they were never finished. They were great songs but the problem was time – as we were both very busy at that period. We never seemed to be in the same country long enough to actually finish everything completely.'⁵ However, two other possible explanations have come to light. Journalist David Wigg, a close friend of Mercury's, suggests that the fall-out between the pair was due to Jackson's insistence on bringing his pet chimpanzee, Bubbles, into the recording studio and asking for the ape's views on how the recordings were going. According to Wigg, 'Freddie got very angry because Michael made Bubbles sit between them and would turn to the chimp between takes and ask, "Don't you think that was lovely?" or, "Do you think we should do that again?" After a few days of this, Freddie just exploded. He phoned his manager and told him to "get me out of this zoo"⁶.'

However, the presence of Bubbles is never mentioned by Peter Freestone, who was actually there. A more sinister (and plausible) reason for Freddie and Michael never recording again is referred to by *The Hollywood Reporter*, who wrote: 'Jackson was also reportedly less than thrilled with Mercury's behaviour during the recording session. Mercury subsequently fell out with Jackson because the U.S. star objected to Mercury taking too much cocaine in his living room'.⁷

These stories, while both potentially being true, are more likely to have been constructed or exaggerated from imagination or hearsay to generate newspaper headlines. What is more probable is a combination of comments made by Brian May and Freddie Mercury later. Brian would say, 'There's a bit of history there. But I do know that Fred came out of it all a little upset because some of the stuff he did with Michael got taken over by the Jacksons, and he lost out,'⁸ while Freddie himself would comment, 'Michael and I grew apart a bit after his massive success with *Thriller*. He simply retreated into a world of his own. We used to have great fun going to the clubs together but now he won't come out of his fortress and it's very sad. He's so worried someone will do him in that he's paranoid about absolutely everything. I get worried myself, but I'll never let it take over my life like that.'⁹

Although any prospect of further recording with Jackson had evaporated, Freddie decided to stay on in Los Angeles for a while. Despite the growing fear of the illness spreading through the gay community, he would still take the opportunity to indulge himself in the local gay scene of Boystown, frequenting bars such as the Spike, the Motherlode and the Eagle.

It was in Spike, on Santa Monica Boulevard, that Freddie became enamoured by a barman called Vince. He was a biker, tall and chunky, and, straightaway, the two of them got on well together.

'I was in a club playing pool and I had seen Freddie in a video and I said to my friend, "God, that guy's really hot," and then three weeks later, here I am in bed with him,' recalls Vince. 'I just couldn't believe it. I was a biker-man at that time. It was macho and we didn't wear shirts behind the bar; we were bare-chested and kind of buff. I was attracted to Freddie, the dark hair and the beautiful eyes. We were physically attracted to each other.'[10]

Vince wasn't overly influenced by Freddie's fame and refused to alter his own lifestyle to be at the beck and call of a rock star. It may have been this attitude, so unlike the ungracious yet fawning behaviour of most of Freddie's former lovers, that made the barman so attractive. It seemed Vince was taking Freddie for who he was as a person, not simply because he was a famous, and wealthy, music star.

'We all liked Vince a lot,' says Peter Freestone[11] and for the remainder of the time Freddie was in the US that year, he and Vince appeared to be a great couple. But Freddie had a habit of encouraging his lovers to give up their normal life, whereupon he would transport them either to London or take them on tour with him, where they would be like rabbits caught in the headlights, unable to cope in an unreal environment or culture they had previously had no experience of.

'That was always the problem with these hot, heavy romances Freddie had,' suggests John Reid. 'I saw lots of them, these rushed romances, plucking people out of their environment, give them the watch, give them the car and then on to the next. Freddie was looking for a soulmate, a lover and an intellectual equal. How the hell are you going to find that for Freddie with all his interests? Freddie's interests were so extensive outside of his day job, so how was he going to find somebody to intellectually match him?'[12]

Vince was determined it wasn't going to happen to him. 'We were sitting and he came from behind and put his hands on my shoulders and asked me to go on tour with him,' remembers Vince. 'I couldn't do that. That wasn't what I wanted. Where would that have led me? I never became Mr Mercury. Or Mrs Mercury.'[13]

Freddie wasn't accustomed to being rejected and it hurt him badly. Within the Queen fraternity, Vince became known as 'the one that got away'.

Freddie returned to England for a brief visit in August to begin work on the next Queen album. Bruised by Vince's rejection, he needed to escape from California and the trip back to England allowed him the opportunity to oversee the conclusion of the renovation of his luxury Kensington mansion. It was while in London that he was encouraged, at the behest of Peter Freestone, to accompany him to a night out at the Royal Opera House in Covent Garden. That evening Freddie's operatic idol, Luciano Pavarotti, was performing and it turned out to be a night that would change Freddie's life.

Given the operatic tone of some of his compositions, many people assume Freddie to be a connoisseur of opera, with a detailed knowledge of its history, its musical nuances, and its techniques. In fact, he knew scarcely anything about opera and even less about opera singers and stars. Peter Freestone thought it an opportune moment to expose him to the live voice of an internationally renowned tenor. So, in May 1983, they sat down to watch Verdi's *Un Ballo In Maschera* in the heart of Covent Garden. As the opera progressed Pavarotti lived up to every expectation that Freddie had of him but it was the appearance of a soprano in a later scene that truly captivated Mercury. He was spellbound as her voice soared throughout the Opera House, literally captivating him. As she finished singing, Freddie applauded enthusiastically and immediately wanted to know who this stunning singer was. It was none other than Montserrat Caballé. Freddie's love affair with the great soprano had begun.

His immediate future saw Freddie fly back to North America to begin the recording of a new Queen studio album in 1984, which would be called *The Works*. Once again, the co-producer would be Mack, and recording in the US would continue on and off until the end of the year. While recording in California, with the other members of Queen having bought houses for their families, Freddie rented out a five-bedroom house at 649 Stone Canyon Road built in 1935. He believed that Elizabeth Taylor had stayed there as well as the actor George Hamilton.

It was at this rented house that Freddie celebrated his 37th birthday with 100 guests: 'The house was smothered with Stargazer lilies, those huge trumpet-like pink blooms with red-striped inner petals whose pollen indelibly stains anything and anyone touching it. But the upside is that the aroma is heavenly. No entertainment had been planned. This was a basic eat and drink and be merry party. The food Joe [Fanelli] prepared included Freddie's favourites. Prawn Creole, Coronation Chicken – that British Empire staple favourite – Potato Salad, Rice Salad and a huge array of cold cuts. The party was a welcome high point partway through the recording schedule and all the band and their wives came,' recalls Peter Freestone.[14]

For three months Queen had been sporadically recording material for *The Works* in California and a stand-out candidate for the first single to be released from the album had already emerged. Written by Roger Taylor, the title of the song, 'Radio Ga Ga', was inspired by his young son, Felix. With the single chosen ('It was commercial, very strong and different, and very current,' remarked Freddie)[15] the band returned to the UK in late-November to shoot the video. For the futuristic look of the video, Queen used a cast of 500 extras to create a crowd at a rally, all of whom handclapped in unison during the song's chorus. The hand clapping would be a motif that would be copied by Queen fans around the world whenever the band performed 'Radio Ga Ga' and would become one of the most striking images from their performance at Live Aid in 1985.

With the video wrapped and the finishing touches to the album scheduled for Munich in January 1984, Queen were able to take the last week of November and most of December off. Freddie divided his time between his New York apartment and London. While the finishing touches were being put to Garden Lodge in Kensington, he would stay at his flat in Stafford Terrace. His insatiable desire for sex would continue to lead him around the gay clubs of whichever city he was in and, in late 1983, he found himself in the Copacabana, a gay club in a basement on the Earl's Court Road, less than 100 metres from Garden Lodge.

It was here that Freddie set eyes upon Jim Hutton, an Irish-born hairdresser who was working at The Savoy Hotel and who, on this particular night, was out with his lover, John Alexander. But that didn't stop Freddie, who found himself instantly attracted. Waiting for the right moment, Freddie pounced when Hutton's companion disappeared to the bathroom. Dressed in jeans and a white vest, Freddie offered to buy Hutton a drink to which he politely declined. Freddie then asked him what he was doing that night. 'Fuck off,' Hutton replied. 'You'd better ask my boyfriend about that.'[16]

Freddie retreated, unaccustomed to being rebuffed, and went back to his friends. Hutton appeared to have no idea who the man who had just chatted him up was, but when he told his boyfriend about it and pointed him out he was told it was Freddie Mercury.

Over the coming months Jim Hutton was to bump into Freddie Mercury a number of times and within two years they would become lovers. But before then there would be a lot of water to pass under the bridge.

There would also be many more lovers, two of whom would make their indelible mark on Freddie in Munich in the next few years.

31

In April 1983, the same year that Apple launched Macintosh, Michael Jackson performed the moonwalk for the first time, and Margaret Thatcher was elected Prime Minister for the second time, *Newsweek* in the US published its first AIDS cover story under the headline, 'EPIDEMIC: The Mysterious and Deadly Disease Called AIDS May Be the Public Health Threat of the Century'.

Featuring a number of mini-profiles of those who had contracted AIDS, the article began: 'A new and deadly disease is coursing through the country, wasting bodies of victims, incubating in an untold number of others who have yet to show symptoms and triggering one of the most intensive investigations in medical history'. Earlier in the year, the CDC held a summit in an attempt to find any means for halting the spread of AIDS. But this gathering of some of the top doctors, scientists and representatives from the pharmacological industry and bleeding disorders community was unable to arrive at a conclusion – they simply had no idea. Among them was Dr Donald Francis. He was an epidemiologist at the CDC and during the meeting he grew frustrated and reacted angrily at the lack of progress by standing up and shouting, 'How many people have to die before we do something?' But even he couldn't comprehend how many would die in the next few years.

In New York's gay community, the initial feeling of fear that had pervaded for many months now was turning to one of anger. 'We feel like a disenfranchised community,' said playwright and co-founder of the Gay Men's Health Crisis, Larry Kramer. 'We can't seem to get the Government, the National Institute of Health, to accelerate the research that's going on. We can't even get the mayor of New York to tell us.'[1] Kramer, and the gay community of New York and across the US in general, had every cause to feel disenfranchised and isolated. There was little support from the Reagan government, who limited funds needed for AIDS research and inhibited the necessary health programmes required.

Dr Donald Francis, one of those at CDC desperate to find a cure or treatment for AIDS, was under no illusion about the neglect of the Reagan administration in the response to AIDS: 'I don't know their reasons behind this, but they could not be convinced, despite our great attempts to go to high levels and convince them, that there was something going on that needed major government involvement to intervene.'[2]

In the early years of AIDS, the period when research into HIV was needed most, the Reagan administration was keen to cut back on spending, and despite the urgency required to investigate this disease, a disease perceived as being new but that was, in fact, already well established within the US given its incubation period, the Reagan administration provided no appropriate response fiscally and, in fact, cut spending and limited grants to HIV research. It was a devastating and tragic approach to a disease that affected those that the Reagan administration was all too willing to cut adrift: homosexuals, drug users and immigrants.

One Republican, Bill Dannemeyer of California, even delivered a speech on the House floor, where he read graphic descriptions of sexual acts carried out by homosexuals into the Congressional Record and also pushed to create a government register of AIDS patients, quarantines, and deportation protocols.

'The rest of the world often turns to the United States, and specifically CDC, for guidance in dealing with epidemics. The lack of American response was a guidepost for the rest of the world, and so the ramifications to the lack of U.S. response really echoed around the world,' says Dr Don Francis.[3]

Larry Kramer described the early days of the disease as 'like living in London during the Blitz, when you didn't know when the next bomb would strike.'[4] Kramer's words were well-chosen because, in London in 1983, despite the first attempts to spread information on AIDS and how to avoid it, the most intense period for the incidence of HIV transmission between homosexual men was recorded in the UK that year, with over 6,000 transmissions occurring, the highest annual number between 1979 and 1999.[5]

The increasing number of casualties of the epidemic and the lack of definitive research into AIDS was creating an environment of fear and mystery, not only among the homosexual population, but among the straight population, too. In the US, health workers were hesitant to touch AIDS patients, members of the public feared they might get the disease by riding the subway or dining out and in New York State in 1983, funeral homes stopped embalming AIDS victims for a two-month period for fear of AIDS being transmitted to them when touching cadavers. In the UK, pathologists refused to conduct autopsies, firemen banned the kiss of life, and even Communion wine was thought too risky to take.

As always in these situations, it's those affected who are left to do most in the first instance and look after themselves. The gay community of New York was no exception and in May 1983, two gay authors from the city wrote the pamphlet 'How to Have Sex in an Epidemic', which was published in an initial run of 5,000 copies. It began with lyrics from the Burt Bacharach/Hal David song, 'I'll Never Fall In Love Again': *What do you get when you kiss a guy? / You get enough germs to catch pneumonia...* [6]

Since the first appearance of the disease, even before it had the name AIDS, public misconceptions and a general lack of awareness and education meant all sorts of myths surrounded the disease, and even in 1983, many people thought that AIDS could be caught from kissing, from sitting on toilet seats, and even from travelling on public transport. It was also still considered to be a gay disease and in the UK, just as in the US, gay groups were feeling vulnerable, alone and very scared.

Tony Whitehead, a London teacher, a member of Gay Switchboard and a volunteer with the Terrence Higgins Trust, remembers that, at the time, their support work was 'essentially a crucial survivalist policy formulated by a community that believed it was being left to slowly die.' [7] But 1983 in the UK saw a change in the perception of AIDS away from solely being a gay disease when two haemophiliacs were diagnosed with the disease. In the US, ten haemophiliacs had already been affected in the previous year, five of whom had died, including a seven-year-old girl, but that hadn't stopped the British Government's Health Minister, Kenneth Clarke, from declaring that 'There is no conclusive evidence that AIDS is transmitted by blood products.' As a consequence, no checks were put in place nor any ban implemented on US blood being imported into Britain and, in 1983, some 60 per cent of the UK's blood-clotting concentrate, Factor VIII, was coming directly from the US. It was unscreened. If the US Government was being negligent by failing to fund research, the British Government was just as culpable for failing to stop the import of potentially infected blood.

On 9th May 1983, Dr Galbraith sent a paper entitled 'Action on AIDS' to Dr Ian Field of the Department of Health & Social Security in the UK, saying that, 'I have reviewed the literature and come to the conclusion that all products from blood donated in the USA after 1978 should be withdrawn from use until the risk of transmission by these products has been clarified'. This paper was considered at a meeting of the biological sub-committee of the Committee on the Safety of Medicines in July 1983 and rejected. It wasn't until two years later that the true folly of their lack of action was exposed when Dr Peter Jones of the Newcastle Haemophilia Reference Centre tested 99 of his patients with severe haemophilia A. Ninety-eight of them had received commercial Factor VIII from the US and he found that 76 now tested positive for HIV.

Meanwhile, in the US, despite the apparent connection between infected blood and the transmission of HIV, the Reagan administration refused to bring in legislation to ban the use of commercial Factor VIII or even to screen blood donors.

'This was a time when IV drug users were already transmitting the disease. It was well known that it was in blood on the end of needles shared by IV drug users; it would be logical, therefore, that it would be transmitted through therapeutic blood product used with haemophiliacs or blood transfusions,' says Dr Donald Francis of the CDC. 'For us as epidemiologists, this was not a great leap, and we waited until we had a couple of cases, at least or three or four or five cases, before we held big meetings. But then we held big meetings and turned to those responsible for protecting the recipients of those materials to do something about it, and that was another public health disaster.'[8]

Through a combination of laziness, profit motive and incredible inertia, no one within the US commercial blood agencies wanted to acknowledge there was a risk, despite the evidence put forward by people such as Dr Francis. Their profits were at risk and they saw (or refused to see) no conclusive link to AIDS. The non-profit organisations didn't want to change their methods to eliminate donors with risk of transmitting HIV/AIDS, and blood bankers in the US were simply trained to do things by the book and felt it a violation of privacy to ask donors if they were gay. Consequently, HIV continued to be spread throughout the haemophiliac population of the US and, by default, the UK, too.

And even though it was now known that AIDS affected all of society, it was still a disease predominantly associated with the gay community.

'Although it looked like a disease of gay men, it was not, it was a disease of sexual transmission,' says Dr Anthony S. Fauci, M.D. of the National Institutes of Health in the US. 'And it just so happened that at the time of the evolving of the permissiveness of sexuality among the gay community back in that period of time, after they had just essentially been able to win their freedom to express themselves sexually as they wanted to do in society – unfortunately, it came at a time when a virus was introduced. And the bathhouse culture was a perfect breeding ground for a sexually-transmitted disease.'[9]

By 1983, increasingly ill and frail, Gaëtan Dugas had left New York and had moved back to Vancouver. He had already defied all the odds by surviving this long. Dugas had been diagnosed with Kaposi's sarcoma back in June 1980, but now he confided in friends he had grown tired of fighting the disease. One of his friends travelled from Toronto to visit him and, during a discussion, Dugas finally acknowledged that he should abstain from sex. But, by then, the damage had already been done.

With deaths rising rapidly there was still no solid proof of what was causing these lethal symptoms. Certainly no proof it was a virus of any sort. But in France, a physician named Willy Rozenbaum speculated that a retrovirus might be responsible for the disease. A retrovirus inserts its genome into the host's genome and, in this way, the retrovirus becomes part of the host's cells. Seeking help to prove his theory, Rozenbaum turned to Luc Montagnier, an expert on retroviruses, and through a process of elimination at the Institut Pasteur in Paris, Montagnier and his team confirmed that the underlying cause of HIV was a retrovirus. They had found it in the samples of white blood cells extracted from the lymph nodes of Frederic Brugiere, a French fashion designer who had AIDS. Montagnier's discovery was published in the *Science* journal on 20th May 1983 and discovering what it was at least gave experts the beginnings of clues as to how to deal with it – but that was over a decade away.

Too late for so many. And too late for Freddie Mercury.

Of course, in 1983, Freddie was unaware that he was infected with HIV and that he would get AIDS.

'I first really learned about the spread of HIV when I made a trip to New York in 1983,' remembers Paul Gambaccini. 'I came back, of course, horrified beyond words and I ran into Freddie at The Star Bar in Heaven. I said to Freddie, "Have you altered your behaviour in light of the new disease?", because, remember, it didn't have a name yet and that's when he swept his arms and said, "Darling, fuck it, I'm doing everything with everybody." And at that moment I had this sinking feeling.'[10] But doing so had already put him on a path to self-destruction. His bandmates, especially Brian May and Roger Taylor, had already acknowledged their concerns at his reckless lifestyle (likely referring to his increased drug usage). However, Freddie didn't stop. As he said in his song: 'Don't stop me now, I'm having such a good time, I'm having a ball.'

'I met Freddie myself for the first time in 1983 in the nightclub Heaven,' remembers Marc Almond. 'I was drinking at the downstairs bar when a strong arm grabbed me from behind and a voice in my ear whispered, "Hello Marcia", and I came face-to-face with Freddie. He was with the singer and performer Peter Straker. I was surprised that Freddie seemed so small, bearing in mind I'm quite short too. He had that unmistakable moustache and the teeth. "Stop looking so serious, Marcia, it's all that bloody miserable music you make and all that ghastly black you wear, dear. Cheer up, girl, come on and have a dance," he said, and with that he threw me over his shoulder, and took me onto the dance floor where we danced. It did the trick because he soon had me laughing. He was a rascal, full of life, effervescent and mischievous. He was the good time that was had by all.'[11]

But while some continued the good times, in other parts of the gay communities of New York and London, men were closing their doors, shutting themselves in, staying with one partner and rejecting the hedonistic club scene of the past couple of years. As Dr Joseph A. Sonnabend M.D. wrote in the foreword to *How to Have Sex in an Epidemic*, 'In some ways, the tragedy of AIDS is bringing gay men closer together, and many are looking for more enduring and loving relationships. Perhaps the most important message contained in this pamphlet is the authors' premise that when affection informs a sexual relationship, the motivation exists to find ways to protect each other from the disease'.

Freddie too, despite his promiscuity, had indicated that he was desperate to have an enduring and loving relationship. He had the money, the fame, the success, the huge house, the number-one singles, but there was one thing he didn't have: 'I would have loved to have found a really beautiful relationship with somebody, a long-lasting one-to-one, but I don't feel I'm going to get that in my life now, and I don't think my life can actually cater for it. It never seemed to work out. This is what I think my life is going to be, and I have to come to terms with it,' he said.[12]

But that was all to change and, despite the horrific backdrop of AIDS, he was to find the man that would alter his outlook on life.

It was the happiness Freddie had searched so long for.

Yet it would touch him only fleetingly.

By the end of 1984, there had been 7,699 AIDS cases in the US with 3,665 AIDS deaths recorded. In Europe, 762 cases had been reported. But this was just the tip of the iceberg, borne out by the fact that in the next 12 months these figures would double.[1] The statistics were starting to become extremely frightening and so overwhelming, with no idea what lay ahead, that officials in San Francisco ordered gay bathhouses to close due to high-risk sexual activity occurring in these venues. Before the end of the year bathhouses in New York and Los Angeles would close as well.

But it was known that the virus was no longer solely affecting the gay community – heterosexuals, haemophiliacs and intravenous drug users were all being stricken with AIDS. In 1984, the median survival time for those diagnosed with AIDS was 9.4 months.[2] The picture was bleak, and without a cure or treatment the future was even bleaker. In the UK, cases of HIV were rising dramatically. A study by the Virus Reference Laboratory in London estimated that in July 1984, there were at least 2,600 homosexual men in the capital infected with the HIV/AIDS virus.[3] In 1984 the US Secretary of Health and Human Services, Margaret Heckler, made an historic announcement by confidently declaring that a vaccine (note: not a cure) would be available within two years. If ever there was a statement of hope over science, then this was it. As far as virologists were concerned, the end of the epidemic seemed an eternity away.

Meanwhile, for those living with HIV the stigma associated with it was almost as debilitating as the virus itself. Suddenly emergency services refused to take care of people with HIV and those with AIDS, suffering the physical manifestations of the disease such as sunken cheeks (facial wastage) and the purple lesions associated with Kaposi's sarcoma, found themselves isolated and forgotten as friends, neighbours and even family distanced themselves. In addition, as *The Los Angeles Times* commented: 'The virus brought the ugliness of homophobia to light. Insidiously, it even invaded our science. Some researchers refrained from working on the disease because of its association with gay men. Others found themselves having to defend their work on a disease perceived by critics as a lifestyle choice'[4].

The health services in both the US and the UK were ill-informed and ill-equipped to deal with AIDS. Patients were isolated in hospitals and faced the inhumane experience of 'barrier' nursing, where everyone who came into contact with them had to wear hats, gloves, masks, gowns and aprons. Swiss-American psychiatrist Elisabeth Kübler-Ross said, 'They had to endure the worst kind of discrimination. Many of them had to suffer in isolation. With such enormous prejudice against AIDS patients, and fear of them, people lose sight of the fact that most – if not almost all – die an early death at a time when their lives have just begun. Not only do people with AIDS have to go through the "stages of dying", they are faced with issues the world never had to deal with to such an extent, in such massive numbers and from every direction. AIDS has become our largest sociopolitical issue, a dividing line of religious groups, a battleground for ambitious medical researchers, and the biggest demonstration of man's inhumanity to man.'[5]

'The first time I realised that AIDS needed to be taken very seriously was in rather incongruous circumstances,' recalls singer-songwriter Annie Lennox. 'Eurythmics were on an Australian tour in 1984 and we were having a somewhat rare day off, sailing around Sydney Harbour on a boat trip, relaxing and drinking glasses of champagne. Someone was reading a newspaper and had come across an article outlining the sobering facts about a sinister public health threat called AIDS. They were so shocked by the contents of the piece that they felt compelled to read it out aloud to everyone. People had never considered that having unprotected sex could expose you to a potential death sentence.'[6]

Throughout the AIDS crisis in the West, it would remain for a long time that the largest group of AIDS patients were homosexual men, such as Freddie Mercury, who carried the virus, and saw friends and acquaintances die from the disease itself. During that time, many AIDS patients allowed doctors and pharmaceutical companies to experiment on them, suffering debilitating and incredible side effects from untested drugs in the process, but determined to participate in anything that promised a cure, or at least progressed towards a cure for others. But with the agent at the heart of HIV identified, medical experts assumed that science would come up with a vaccine for the disease quickly. However, it soon became apparent that the problems were more extensive than previously thought.

'It became clear that HIV could infect, but doesn't cause problems until some years later,' said Dr David Ho of the Aaraon Diamond AIDS Research Center. 'And there is a period where one is symptom-free but HIV-positive, and potentially infectious to others.'[7]

What made HIV even harder to comprehend was that after the acute stage of HIV infection the disease moves into a stage called 'clinical latency'. 'Latency' means a period where a virus is living or developing in a person without producing symptoms. During this stage, people who are infected with HIV experience no HIV-related symptoms, or only mild ones, but HIV continues to reproduce at very low levels, although it is still active. As a result, those with HIV brush off their symptoms. This was the stage of infection that Freddie Mercury had entered into almost two years earlier, just after becoming infected.

'So we had a skewed appreciation of what this disease was all about,' comments Dr Anthony Fauci, 'because we thought that you get HIV infected and you were deathly ill, and that was it, not fully realizing the vast numbers of people who were incubating this illness for years and years. As we described back in the '80s, it was like an iceberg. And what we were seeing was the tip of the iceberg.'[8]

Across the globe, AIDS was beginning to invade communities and countries in the same way that it invaded the human body. A stark reminder came when it was revealed that by the time the first cases of AIDS were diagnosed in the US, 250,000 Americans were probably already infected, and most of them were showing no symptoms, and with no symptoms they were free to unwittingly spread the virus to more people. The march of AIDS seemed unstoppable.

'It seems like it was just an avalanche,' recalls Cleve Jones, founder of *The Names Project* in Atlanta. 'It was like one week, we'd never heard of it, and then the next week, everybody started to die. People began to vanish. I was having coffee in the café, the Café Flore, and I looked up and saw what I thought was an old man leaning against the telephone pole. And I thought, "Oh, look at that old man. He needs help." And he fell down. And we went over and he was dead. And he wasn't an old man, he was my age [in his mid-30s].'[9]

Dr Margaret Fischl of the AIDS Clinical Trials Group was also finding the burden of seeing so many with AIDS depressing and devastating: 'After I got to about 15,000 patients that died, I stopped counting numbers. One of my patients that I had followed for a long period of time just asked me, "Should I just stop?" I said, "I can just give you the same medicines, but you're not going to get much better than that." So he said, "No, then I want to stop," you know. And then he said, "Well, I guess this is then goodbye." And I will never forget the expression on his face – I mean, just the total loss of life, you know, that his young life was over. I mean, that expression is something I will take with me forever.'[10]

On 30th March 1984, Gaëtan Dugas died in Quebec, Canada. Ironically, his death was caused by kidney failure exacerbated, but not caused, by AIDS. Dugas was 31 years old and had somehow survived four bouts of pneumocystis. The constant illness he had suffered in the last few months of his life – causing him to waste away and suffer a constant fever – had forced him back to Quebec, where his family cared for him. Before he returned home though, Dugas had been living in Vancouver with a male model, whom he managed to persuade to come and visit him in Quebec. By the time he arrived, however, Dugas had died. It had been nearly four years since Dugas had visited his doctor in Toronto to have a purple lesion near his ear examined. Much has been written about Gaëtan Dugas, his sexual exploits, and his alleged controversial refusal to obey the recommendations of public health officials in the early 1980s. Part of that written about him is that he slept with over 2,500 men during his indiscriminate and promiscuous sex life and, as far as many are concerned, Dugas was the gay Air Canada flight attendant at the centre of the 'Patient Zero' myth: the man who supposedly introduced AIDS to the United States. However, although in truth he was originally Patient 'O' in the medical papers, it was author Randy Shilts who branded him Patient Zero for his book *And the Band Played On*. 'Zero' felt so much more dramatic than the letter 'O'.

But Dugas wasn't Patient Zero, and that was what the media and Shilts chose not to acknowledge. Gaëtan Dugas didn't conceive the AIDS virus himself. Everything comes from somewhere, and he got it from someone else. Dugas *was* infected by some other person, almost certainly in a sexual encounter, but he never took HIV to North America, because, in reality, when he was a child it had already arrived there. As an adult he undoubtedly played a role as a transmitter during the late 1970s and early 1980s, though.

Although Dugas was proactive about health check-ups after his diagnosis, he maintained a firmly obstinate view on his sexual lifestyle despite his doctor's recommendations. Randy Shilts illustrates Dugas' frustration with AIDS with the following quote: "'Of course, I'm going to have sex," [Dugas] told his doctor. "Nobody's proven to me that you can spread cancer."'[11] Dugas' initial decision to continue his sexual practices indicates his assertion of the individual rights of his own body. His initial decision significantly highlights the gaping holes of the American health system, because his situation had never been encountered before. In addition, Dugas did not have a comprehensive understanding of the transmission of HIV, and we can also identify this as a strong critique of the American health system. His adamant response indicated his misunderstanding of the transmission of HIV. By examining Dugas' wavering perspective on the disease, we can show empathy for his challenging life. His gay identity and open personality were arguably his most attractive traits. As Shilts wrote: 'At one time, Dugas had been what every man wanted from gay life; by the time he died, he was what every man feared.'[12]

It is known that Freddie Mercury met Gaëtan Dugas twice. Once outside The Saint, which we already know was a brief moment. The second time was in the nightclub Heaven in London, where they spent time together chatting. That was all. Or perhaps there were other times, but it is highly unlikely. However, what is known is that Freddie did have a one-night stand with John Murphy, and John Murphy was one of Dugas' countless lovers.

In the early and mid-1980s a lot less was known about HIV than we know today. In 1984 there were no definitive tests available to determine whether or not someone had the virus. People simply didn't know they had the virus until they were becoming ill and showing serious opportunistic infections. It was virtually impossible for doctors to tell if someone had HIV or not and rudimentary tests were only introduced in 1985. Even those weren't that accurate.

Did Freddie know he had HIV in 1984? Again, probably not, or at least not for certain, but he knew he was in one of the highest-risk categories. He could not have been able to ignore what was happening around him, people getting infected and dying, people he knew. Based on the fact that Freddie was still healthy and hadn't changed any of his behaviour before or during 1984, it's likely he had no real inkling that he was infected. As far as he was concerned, he didn't want to think about AIDS. It was something that would affect others, not him.

Any mild HIV symptoms would be nothing unusual for someone like Freddie and would be dismissed as the result of excessive drinking, drug taking or the pressures of work. Even any recurring illness could be explained away. Yet still, he couldn't have helped but wonder. There are varying accounts about how Mercury coped with the risk of contracting AIDS. Some thought it was why he was never anxious for Queen to tour America again after 1982, but we will never know for sure.

On 21st November 1984, an article in *The Times* in the UK demonstrated that AIDS was still largely synonymous with homosexuality and promiscuity in the eyes of the public: 'AIDS horrifies not only because of the prognosis for its victims. The infection's origins and means of propagation excites repugnance, moral and physical, at promiscuous male homosexuality – conduct which, tolerable in private circumstances, has with the advent of "gay liberation" become advertised, even glorified as acceptable public conduct, even a proud badge for public men to wear'.

For Freddie Mercury, this article must have been deeply disturbing on many levels – just as it was for so many gay men looking for answers and support. Homophobia was rife. But as Queen and Freddie headed to Munich, he still didn't do anything to change his ways.

33

In 1984 in Munich, the city they were beginning to call their home away from home, the band were putting the finishing touches to their new album, *The Works*, at Musicland Studios while Freddie was using any spare time at the same studios to record 'Love Kills', his song for Giorgio Moroder's *Metropolis*, as well as also taking the opportunity to work on additional solo material.

During these sessions, Freddie was staying at the Arabellahaus Hotel, a monstrous concrete rectangular building. In fact, the aura of greyness only increased with the knowledge that the hotel was a notorious suicide spot with people jumping to their deaths from its rooftop. Not that Freddie appeared depressed at this point. Even though the dark shadow of AIDS was continuing to make its way across the world, he continued to throw himself into the active and diverse sex scene of Munich. But it wasn't only sex that was consuming him: Freddie had also increased his drinking, smoking and drug taking by this point, and even though he was recording during the days, he was partying harder every night. This was the first real indication that there was something troubling him. To outsiders, it appeared Freddie had hit the self-destruct button. Perhaps this was because he was accepting the inevitable; maybe he thought it inconceivable that he hadn't already contracted HIV and that his time left was marked out. He was already aware of so many who had died in North America and Europe and with no cure or treatment in sight, possibly assumed *he* could be facing the onset of AIDS at any moment. He was being totally reckless, a recklessness that could only lead to destruction. And he didn't seem to care.

It was in Munich that Freddie met two people who were to have a significant impact on his life. The first person was a restaurateur called Winnie Kirchberger, a big, burly German with a bristly moustache. 'Winnie was a bit like a tank,' recalls Freddie's friend Trevor Clarke,[1] while Peter Straker says of him, 'Winnie was alright; he was very jolly. Large and jolly, and they liked each other.'[2]

Just as his relationship had been with Bill Reid, Freddie's time with Winnie was tempestuous and rocky. Neither was faithful to the other during their relationship and it always appeared to those around Freddie that the affair was likely to implode at any moment. But it seemed to sustain itself, perhaps because their ability to converse was limited. 'Winnie didn't speak a word of English,' explained Peter Freestone. 'Freddie didn't speak a word of German. There's only so much you can do with sign language. Winnie provided Freddie with good sex and he provided him with the fight. They had huge arguments. I mean Munich *is* about their arguments.'[3]

The second person that Freddie met in Munich was the busty blonde Austrian actress Barbara Valentin. She had been born in Vienna and was six years older than Freddie when they met in a gay bar in Munich called New York. Valentin was a reasonably well-known figure within Germany, especially Munich, where she had a considerable gay following owing to her frequent collaborations with the famed German film director Rainer Werner Fassbinder. Often dubbed 'the German Jayne Mansfield', she appeared in seven of Fassbinder's movies as well as a number of other low-budget German horror films, and she and Freddie fast became inseparable. According to author Rick Sky, their 'first meeting resulted in Mercury accompanying the buxom actress into the ladies' toilet, where they chattered away without being disturbed by the noise of the bar or the din of the disco. As Valentin sat on the toilet seat, Mercury crouched beside her on the floor, a glass of his favourite Russian vodka in his hand. Here they talked about their lives like a couple of long-lost friends.'[4]

'Freddie and I would speak to each other on the phone nearly every day, even when he was abroad,' says Peter Straker, 'but all of a sudden these new friends turned up, like when he went to Munich and Barbara turned up as his new best friend, and he'd say, "She's wonderful and fun", and she is, but there was always this constant fight with Barbara, and a lot of people in England didn't like Barbara. I mean, she was alright to me, she was nothing to worry about. He just liked her because she was well known in Munich and she was an actress and she was quite outrageous and she introduced him to a lot of people and things, and that's quite good if you're coming into a city and you have two or three bright people to open doors.'[5]

Freddie and Barbara soon embarked on an intense and passionate romance. Since the end of his relationship with Mary Austin in 1976, he had not had a meaningful relationship with a woman, but Barbara captivated him, although he would joke about the nature of her allure: 'Barbara Valentine fascinated me because she's got such great tits,'[6] while Barbara would comment, 'I adored him. We fitted together absolutely instantly and we never separated for three whole days. He stayed at my house, I went to the studio with him, and we went out to the clubs together. We talked all the time, and Freddie told me, "My God! Finally I can talk to someone who understands the real me and what I want to do with my life." That was something he needed badly.'[7]

While with Barbara in Munich, Freddie would continue to see Winnie Kirchberger for sex, and occasionally, Freddie, Winnie and Barbara would take part in threesomes and sometimes find someone else to join in, too.[8] While Winnie was jealous of the other men who would be attracted to Freddie, Barbara would say she didn't feel any jealousy towards the men – and women – who seemed to throw themselves at him. 'I was never jealous of his affairs as such,' she once told the German magazine *Bunte*, 'I always spent much longer with him than anyone else.'[9]

While Freddie's relationship with Barbara was blossoming, and while Queen continued to put the finishing touches to *The Works* album, the first single from the album was released in the UK. 'Radio Ga Ga' quickly became a massive chart success, peaking at number 2. It even reached number 16 in the US, the last time Queen would have a Top 20 single in the US Billboard Hot 100 while Freddie was still alive. The song was a triumph for composer Roger Taylor. By achieving its success in the charts, it now meant that all four members of Queen had written a Top 10 track, a unique achievement in UK pop chart history.

With the album ready for release, and with strong sales predicted following the success of 'Radio Ga Ga', Queen travelled to the San Remo Festival in Italy, where they would mime the song to a television audience. Heading back to Munich after the two-day festival, Freddie continued his fractious affair with Winnie Kirchberger alongside his passionate relationship with Barbara Valentin. It was a roller-coaster period of drink, drugs, sex, rows, fights and clubbing before the whole cycle would begin again. Allied to this hedonistic lifestyle in Munich, Freddie still had to record material for his new solo album whenever he was fit to do so. But the nature of this lifestyle couldn't possibly continue without incident and on a couple of occasions Peter Freestone was called to attend to Freddie, who had blacked out and was having mysterious attacks of serious tremors. Unsurprisingly, doctors diagnosed excessive use of drink and drugs as the cause of these sudden attacks of illness, but still he continued with his debauched lifestyle in Munich, where one of his favourite games apparently involved groups of young men being invited to his room, where they were made to strip naked and parade in front of him wearing nothing but women's hats. Freddie would then choose which of the men would be his companion, or companions, for the night.

At the end of February 1984, Queen's eleventh studio album, *The Works*, was released. It was an immediate success in the UK, reaching number 2 in the UK album charts. Throughout their entire career, the release of a new Queen album seemed to generate mixed reviews and *The Works* was no exception. *Sounds* commented that, 'This time around, Queen have played it safe(r)' and suggested the album is 'little more than a reworked pile of cuttings from Queen's greatest tricks'.[10] *Rolling Stone* magazine, whose reviewers had given Queen's albums a tougher time than most over the years, wrote that the album was 'perhaps the first record to refute the maxim that the words *Queen* and listenable are, of necessity, mutually exclusive'.[11]

Freddie's thoughts about the album were revealed in an interview with Mary Turner: 'To be honest, it's just a bunch of songs that four people have written and they happen to be on an album and people have to try and make a concept out of it, and if there's a thread running through it, or if there's some sort of meaning. There's love ballads and there's happy songs, there's just about every kind of song that you can get from Queen and so we just threw them on the disc and that's why we called it "The Works" because it is the works, we just tried every possible attack on every song there was and I think "The Works" is a good title for it.'[12]

Freddie spent much of February and March 1984 back in Munich recording more material for his solo album while also enjoying his life with both Winnie Kirchberger and, more enthusiastically, Barbara Valentin. He and Barbara threw themselves into a relationship that was both intense yet full of careless abandon. While they undoubtedly loved each other, neither was totally faithful.

'He and I were lovers in the truest sense,' Barbara Valentin told author Lesley-Ann Jones. 'We did have sex together regularly. Yes. Yes. It took a while. When it happened, it was beautiful and innocent. I was completely in love with him by this time, and he had told me that he loved me. We even talked of getting married. Of course, he'd still pick up dozens of gay guys and bring them back night after night, but I didn't mind. Sounds insane, doesn't it, but that's the life we were living, and I couldn't stop him even if I wanted to.'[13]

While Freddie was living it up in Munich, *The Works* was released in the US. Disappointingly for the band, it actually performed worse than *Hot Space*, reaching only number 23 in the Billboard 200 album charts. It was their most poorly performing album in the US since *Queen II* in 1974. But worse was to come in the US with the release of their next single, 'I Want To Break Free'. Written by John Deacon, the song was a huge hit across most of the world, reaching number 3 in the UK, but it died a death in the US, thanks mainly to its video, which featured the four band members dressed in drag, in part as a homage to the British soap opera, *Coronation Street*, with Freddie stealing the show as a Bet Lynch-type housewife complete with moustache.

Freddie had planned to shave off his moustache for the shoot but the director managed to persuade him not to: 'I said, "No, the one thing you mustn't do, the funny thing is that your moustache is there and you're in drag!" To this day, when he comes around the corner with that hoover, I laugh,' says David Mallett.[14]

'I was dying to dress up in drag,' said Freddie. 'Doesn't everybody? It was just one of those things. I'm sure everybody thought it was my idea, but in fact it wasn't my idea at all. It came from Roger, and actually the other three *ran* into their frocks quicker than anything.'[15]

However, wearing a wig and fake breasts was just too much for the US. While audiences in the UK understood the *Coronation Street* cross-dressing references, and fans in Europe and across the world took the song to their hearts as a statement of the fight against oppression, the US audience rejected the song wholeheartedly as a result of the video. As EMI's Brian Southall says, 'You could be terribly arty in New York or Los Angeles, but don't try it in Kansas.'[16]

While Middle America was outraged, at last having some sort of confirmation that Freddie might be gay and perceiving this as his coming-out statement, MTV dropped the video altogether and refused to play it. 'I think it's one of our best videos to date,' Freddie would say. 'In fact, it still makes me chuckle every time I see it, and I've seen it a lot of times. I'm glad we did it. People were quite amazed by the fact we could fool around and drag up and still be good musicians. In America it wasn't accepted at all well because they still regarded us as the heavy rockers there – the macho thing. They reacted with, "What are my idols doing dressing up in frocks?" There's a big risk element involved with most things we do, and I think our staunchest fans will know that we can come up with all sorts of ridiculous things. Some of them will work, and some don't, but I think the rest of the group will take my view on this… that we don't give a damn. We do what we want to do, and it's either accepted or not.'[17]

But the video for 'I Want To Break Free' wasn't the only reason Queen were having issues in the US. The increasing power and influence Paul Prenter was having on Freddie was beginning to have a detrimental effect, at the precise time they required as much good publicity as possible there. 'We had this guy who looked after Freddie, who was called Paul Prenter, and he got a little too big for his boots, I think,' says Brian May. 'This guy in the course of one tour told every radio station to fuck off, but not just fuck off, but "Freddie says fuck off, Freddie says he doesn't care about you" and so we sort of lost our relationship with the media at a stroke.'[18]

With the US furore continuing, Freddie returned to Munich to work on his solo album, but also to indulge himself (once more) in the partying that the city offered him. It was during one trip back that he seriously damaged ligaments in his leg during an incident at the New York nightclub in Munich. He refused to elaborate on precisely how he received the injury, explaining only that, 'This cunt kicked me. I'm hoping my knee will be ready in time for the tour, but it's still giving me a lot of trouble. It might mean I will have to cut down on some of my more elaborate gorgeous stage moves.'[19]

He was in plaster for three weeks and the injury affected him during the filming of the video for Queen's next single, 'It's a Hard Life'. Penned by Freddie, the song was highly thought of by both Brian May and Roger Taylor and considered by them one of Freddie's finest compositions. Barbara Valentin was roped in to appear in the video, which featured operatic-style costumes and the band at a masquerade ball. Even though the song was a favourite of some of the band, the video most definitely wasn't, with Roger Taylor calling it 'the most stupid music video ever made.'[20]

'It's a Hard Life' was yet another Top 10 hit in the UK for Queen, but only reached number 72 in the US Billboard Hot 100, their worst single performance since 1979. It continued a bleak run that hadn't seen the band have a Top 10 hit in the US since 'Another One Bites the Dust' reached number 1 in 1980. Given the issues around the 'I Want To Break Free' video, the stranglehold Paul Prenter was having on Freddie's availability to the US media, and their diminishing returns in both album and singles charts, it seemed the doors were quickly closing on Queen's US career. As a result, *The Works* Tour of 1984 and 1985 wouldn't contain any North American performances.

On 28th August 1984, Queen began the first leg of their new tour in Brussels, which included four nights at London's Wembley Arena, scheduled around Freddie's 38th birthday party. However, he hardly had cause to celebrate as *The Sun* printed a story, spread over several editions, in which a former employee of Freddie revealed that the singer was spending £1,000 a week on vodka and cocaine[21] and that he had confessed to being gay. Freddie ignored this, continued with the tour and only referred to it during a subsequent interview with *Melody Maker*, later in the year:

Melody Maker: Freddie, I understand you were upset about a story in *The Sun* that claimed you had 'confessed' to being homosexual.

Freddie: I was completely misquoted. But from the beginning, the press have always written whatever they wanted about Queen, and they can get away with it. The woman who wrote that story wanted a total scoop from me and didn't get anything. I said: 'What do you want to hear? That I deal cocaine?' But for God's sake, if I want to make big confessions about my sex life, would I go to *The Sun*, of all papers, to do it? There's no fucking way I'd do that. I'm too intelligent.

Melody Maker: But this is a good time to be gay. It's good for business, isn't it?

Freddie: But it's wrong for me to be gay now because I've been in the business for 12 years. It's good to be gay or anything outrageous if you're new. But even if I tried that, people would start yawning, 'Oh God, here's Freddie Mercury saying he's gay because it's trendy to be gay.'[22]

Freddie escaped the British press and their constant pursuit of his sexuality as Queen continued their tour in Europe, but he found himself at the centre of controversy once again in October 1984 when Queen flew to South Africa to play a series of concerts at Sun City in Bophuthatswana.

Sun City was a luxury resort and casino situated in the North West Province of South Africa. Opened in December 1979, the venue, dubbed 'Sin City' by the whites who travelled there, took advantage of Bophuthatswana being declared an independent state by South Africa's apartheid government, which meant it could provide entertainment such as gambling, golf and topless revue shows banned elsewhere in South Africa. Consequently, Sun City became a symbol of the opulence that whites enjoyed at the expense of South Africa's black natives.

'The position taken by most of the rock community was that if you went to South Africa you were supporting apartheid,' says Paul Gambaccini.[23] Nevertheless, Queen thought it appropriate to flout the cultural boycotts, the attitudes of their peers and the consensus of most of the world and play Sun City. They had had assurances from their manager Jim Beach that they wouldn't be playing to segregated or whites-only audiences and protested they were giving some of their South African royalties to a school for black deaf and blind children near Sun City. But the decision was still a massive faux pas.

'They used to say, "We're doing it for our fans, we're not politicians" but the truth is, they didn't care. They were being paid millions to perform there,' says South African art critic Peter Feldman[24], and Jim Beach is equally blunt: 'The principle reason Queen went there undoubtedly was because they offered a very large amount of money.'[25]

While controversy swirled around them, Queen were also licking their wounds at the disappointing performance of their latest single release. 'Hammer to Fall' had failed to break into the Top 10 in the UK and barely graced the Top 40 in the US. Meanwhile, Freddie had finally released his own solo single, 'Love Kills', the song he had co-written and co-produced with Giorgio Moroder. It outperformed Queen's latest single by reaching number 10 in the UK.

This success began to generate rumours that Queen were on the verge of breaking up. Chart success was eluding them, the reaction to their South Africa tour was extremely critical, and tensions within the group were starting to run high. What's more, back in the UK, Queen had been blacklisted by the British Musicians' Union because of their Sun City performances. The band were, most likely, desperate to put the whole South Africa controversy behind them when they landed back in Britain (Brian May even visited the Musicians' Union to make an impassioned plea against their boycott, to no avail).

But Queen weren't making the headlines anymore in the UK, even *with* their shows in South Africa. Instead, the UK news was dominated by the ongoing Ethiopian crisis, a widespread famine that was the worst in a century and one that, because of the Ethiopian Government's inability or unwillingness to deal with it, was causing widespread condemnation and concern. With close to 8m people affected by the famine and daily images being broadcast on British news channels and on the front pages of newspapers, something had to be done.

Watching the news reports was the Irish-born singer of post-punk band, The Boomtown Rats, Bob Geldof, who was determined to help and to raise whatever money he could from his contacts within the music industry. He and Midge Ure, from the band Ultravox, set about creating a charity record. On 25th November 1984, with the song 'Do They Know It's Christmas?' written, the great and the good of British pop music arrived at SARM Studios in Notting Hill to record the single. Conspicuous by their absence, however, were Queen: they hadn't been invited to take part. Whether it was as a result of their trip to South Africa, no one ever knew, but Freddie appeared genuinely hurt: 'I would have loved to have been on the Band Aid record, but I only heard about it when I was in Germany,' he said later. 'I don't know if they would have had me on the record anyway, because I'm a bit old. I'm just an old slag who gets up every morning, scratches his head and wonders what he wants to fuck.'[26]

The day after Band Aid had recorded 'Do They Know It's Christmas?', Queen released their one and only Christmas single. Written by Brian May and Roger Taylor, 'Thank God It's Christmas' had no promo video, which meant the song couldn't be broadcast on television, thereby hindering any prospect of success. But, in December 1984, even if Queen had made the greatest video ever, the song would not have stood a chance against the charity juggernaut of Band Aid, which became the fastest-selling single in UK chart history and, by the end of the year, had sold over 3m copies.

Ensconced in Munich, Freddie could only look on and ponder his future: Queen had been snubbed by Band Aid and ridiculed for their South Africa shows, the band's chart performances had started to dwindle rapidly and they looked to be distinctly unfashionable. And in the background, as it had constantly been for the past couple of years, the inky shadow of AIDS grew shorter.

The end of 1984 saw Queen and Freddie at a crossroads, and no one knew whether they were finished or not. The future was extremely uncertain.

Surely, even in his wildest dreams, Freddie couldn't have thought that within six months, he would bring an audience of more than a billion to a standstill. And in doing so, reinstate Queen as rock royalty.

34

At the beginning of 1985, Queen seemed at a crossroads. They were on a United Nations blacklist after appearing in South Africa and their reputation in North America appeared to be in tatters. However, they were still, possibly, the biggest act in South America and on 6th January, they headed to Brazil to headline two nights at the enormous Rock In Rio Festival.

Billed as the world's biggest rock festival, Rock In Rio was an eight-day festival in Rio de Janeiro that saw some of the world's top acts play to audiences approaching 3m over the course of the festival. AC/DC, Def Leppard, Iron Maiden, Yes and Rod Stewart were all on the bill, but it was Queen who would headline the festival with two shows, a week apart, to open and close the event.

Freddie flew in separately from the rest of Queen, making his own way from Munich via Paris accompanied by an entourage including Barbara Valentin, Mary Austin, Peter Freestone, Paul Prenter and a minder. Such was Freddie's fame in South America, he found himself, out of necessity and safety, holed up in his Copacabana Beach Hotel's Presidential Suite, overlooking the expanse of beach below, for virtually his entire stay in Brazil

Queen played their first concert on 12th January, coming on-stage at 2am to the biggest audience they would ever play to. The temperature during the day had been in the mid-30s and the humidity was peaking at 90 per cent by the time the band began. While 250,000 had paid to watch Queen that night, some sources suggest another 220,000 had got in without paying, meaning the band could potentially have played to 470,000 in one show.

This first show was going well until Freddie emerged on stage to perform 'I Want to Break Free' dressed up, as in the video, in his Bet Lynch-style clothing. It was a look not appreciated by the local audiences as *Record Mirror* explained: 'Some outraged Brazilians decide this just isn't on and got very nasty. Instead of throwing beer cans at the stage in time-honoured tradition, they decide that pebbles and bits of concrete are far more effective.'[1] *The People* elaborated on the fracas: 'Pop star

Freddie Mercury, of the outrageous British rock group Queen, received a royal pelting when he appeared on stage in Rio de Janeiro wearing women's clothes, huge plastic falsies and a black wig'.[2]

The following night, Freddie briefly attended a party that EMI had put on for them at the nearby Copacabana Palace Hotel. As well as other rock stars and music journalists in attendance, beautiful Brazilians paraded around the pool and throughout the bar and draped themselves over Freddie as he held court. One of the journalists, Robin Smith, asked Freddie about the crowd's reaction to 'I Want to Break Free': 'They're a wonderful audience and I love their displays of emotion,' Freddie replied. 'They get overexcited sometimes but I can bring the whip down and show them who's in control. I don't know why they got so excited about me dressing as a woman. There are lots of transvestites here. It seems second nature to a lot of people. Just go and look on any street corner and you'll find them.'[3] But perhaps the most plausible answer for the crowd's reaction to the song is provided by Maria Caetano, who worked as an interpreter at the concert: 'The song is sacred in South America because we consider it a political message about the evils of dictatorship.'[4]

With a week between shows, Mercury and his entourage would explore the local gay club scene, accompanied by security guards, but the general hysteria that accompanied any public appearance – even those discreet ones – made it apparent that it was easier to take the party to Freddie in his hotel suite. Drink, drugs and sex alleviated the boredom, with Rio's 'taxi' boys, the young male prostitutes of the city, being ushered into the singer's suite, plied with cocaine, and then having sex with Freddie or, alternatively, with his assistant, Paul Prenter.

Prenter would organise everything Freddie wanted, but more often than not, for his own benefits. One of his tasks was to select young male prostitutes – 'taxi boys' – that he felt were Freddie's type. Few resisted the invitation 'to join Freddie Mercury at his hotel suite', where they were offered alcohol and cocaine. One of the 'taxi' boys invited to Freddie's room was a blond blue-eyed young man called Patricio. 'Having travelled from Buenos Aires to Rio to try his hand at acting, Patricio had fallen into prostitution through destitution and despair'.[5]

Patricio revealed to author Lesley-Ann Jones what went on in Freddie's suite: 'First we drank and then snorted some cocaine. Next, we'd shed our clothes and enter Freddie's room, where he would greet us, wearing just his dressing gown. Throughout proceedings, Paul [Prenter] remained fully clothed. Freddie engaged in sexual activity with each in turn, in front of the others. When he was tired, Prenter paid the boys and asked us to leave. Freddie was always passive.'[6]

Freddie, it seemed, had developed an addiction to casual sex. But, according to Patricio, 'He did not even seem to be enjoying himself. Just going through the motions.'[7] Patricio had a number of sexual encounters with Freddie during his time in Brazil before travelling to Israel, where he would become yet another victim of AIDS.[8] Writer Mark Blake describes Freddie's behaviour at this time: 'The impression given was of a soulless encounter with a moneyed rock star, who had grown bored of having everything and anything on offer, and was merely going through the motions, though Prenter was cast as "the instigator". He [Mark Malden] later said about Prenter, "Paul led things. Paul controlled things. Freddie was very strong when it came to his music, but not as strong in his personal life."'[9]

A week later, when they closed the festival, Freddie decided, wisely perhaps, not to wear drag during Queen's rendition of 'I Want to Break Free' and, despite the pouring rain and Freddie's voice not being in as good shape as it was for the previous concert, the show passed without a hitch.

Freddie Mercury would never perform in South America again. Without doubt, he had made his mark on the continent but, as he remarked in an interview, Freddie saw South America for what it was: 'It's a tremendous market. If you crack it here the amount of money you make is tremendous. We've opened South America to the rest of the world. We came to South America originally because we were invited down. They wanted four wholesome lads to play some nice music. Now I'd like to buy up the entire continent and install myself as President.'[10]

With their Rio sojourn over, Queen flew back to Europe, where the four members of the band would all go their separate ways until they flew to New Zealand at the beginning of April 1985 for the culmination of *The Works* Tour with shows in New Zealand, Australia and Japan.

Freddie, meanwhile, returned to Munich to have some fun and to put the finishing touches to his solo album, *Mr. Bad Guy*.

Part Three

The year is 1985. In the UK, plans were being made for one of the biggest charity concerts of all time following Boy George performing an impromptu version of 'Do They Know It's Christmas?' with a gathering of his fellow pop stars at the end of Culture Club's 1984 tour in Wembley Arena on 22nd December.

Taking up the baton, Bob Geldof told *Melody Maker* in January 1985 that: 'If George is organizing it, you can tell him he can call me at any time and I'll do it. It's a logical progression from the record, but the point is you don't just talk about it, you go ahead and do it!' Geldof added: 'The show should be as big as is humanly possible. There's no point just 5,000 fans turning up at Wembley, we need to have Wembley linked with Madison Square Garden and the whole show to be televised worldwide. It would be great for Duran [Duran] to play three or four numbers at Wembley and then flick to Madison Square Square where [Bruce] Springsteen would be playing. While he's on, the Wembley stage could be made ready for the next British act like the Thompsons [Twins] or whoever. In that way lots of acts could be featured and the television rights, tickets and so on could raise a phenomenal amount of money. It's not an impossible idea, and certainly one worth exploiting.'[1]

By March, Geldof had met Harvey Goldsmith, the top promoter in the UK, to discuss his idea. 'Bob said this should be the definitive statement for the music business,' said Goldsmith. 'He said we ought to do a show in England and one in America as well. The idea was to do a worldwide television hookup and raise money with a telethon. We just talked about it, and he asked, "Is it possible?"' Goldsmith paused a moment, then added with typical British understatement, 'And that's when the nightmare started.'[2]

It was in March, while Geldof and Goldsmith were beginning to formulate plans for their charity concert, when Freddie returned to London. In fact, Freddie was beginning to spend most weekends back in London, where he was starting to prefer the gay scene of the UK's capital to that of Munich. One of his favourite haunts was the nightclub

Heaven, where he would head straight to the Cellar Bar, which would be quieter and less intrusive. There he would chat to Robert or Richie the barmen, who had come to know him over the years. He preferred it to the main club unless there was a group of friends with him.

It was on Saturday, 23rd March that Freddie, together with Joe Fannelli and Peter Straker, frequented their usual positions at Heaven. Later that night, Freddie offered to buy a drink for someone he recognised at the bar. It was Jim Hutton, who Freddie had met two years earlier, and who had recently split up with his long-term boyfriend. Freddie still had Winnie Kirchberger and Barbara Valentin back in Munich, but that didn't stop him giving Jim one of his typically forthright opening gambits: 'How big's your dick?' Jim still claimed he wasn't aware who Freddie Mercury was, but at 4am, he accompanied Freddie back to his Stafford Terrace flat.

'Eventually Freddie and I fell into his bed, too drunk to do anything more than fumble about with each other to little effect,' Hutton recalled. 'Freddie cuddled up to me affectionately. We both nattered away until we finally flaked out. Next morning we lay entwined, carrying on talking where we'd left off. When we got around to discussing what each of us did for a living, I told him I was a hairdresser. He said, "I'm a singer." Then he offered to go and make me a cup of tea.'[3]

Despite exchanging telephone numbers, it would be another three months before Freddie would reach out to Jim.

In the meantime Freddie shot the video for his forthcoming solo single, 'I Was Born To Love You' at Limehouse Studios in London. Freddie, in case anyone had any doubts, plays a role in the video that he was struggling with in real life, that of a heterosexual. Unconvincingly he cavorts, comedically, with a scantily clad blonde woman and then proceeds to chase her through a series of rooms, falling onto beds and embracing her with a less than passionate kiss. Once the video was complete, Freddie flew out with the rest of Queen to New Zealand to begin the final leg of their tour. Just before their first show in Auckland, 'I Was Born To Love You' was released as a single and rose to number 11 in the UK and made the Top 10 in both Germany and South Africa.

A few weeks later, as Queen were playing their final show in Australia, Freddie's solo album, *Mr. Bad Guy*, was released, reaching number 6 in the UK album charts, and although *People Weekly* said the album 'sounds like an uninspired cabaret review,'[4] and *Rolling Stone* wrote that, '"Mr. Bad Guy" is unlikely to win Freddie many new converts, but Queen fans will eat it up,'[5] Freddie himself was proud of the album: 'I put my heart and soul into "Mr. Bad Guy" and I think it's a very natural album. It had some very moving ballads – things to do with sadness and pain, but at the same time they were frivolous and tongue-in-cheek, because that's my nature. I think the songs on that album reflect the state of my life, a diverse selection of moods and a whole spectrum of what my life was.'[6]

While his album was performing very respectably in the UK charts, Freddie was on the other side of the world for Queen's show in New Zealand. Eight shows in Australia and five shows in Japan followed, but before they left New Zealand, the cogs that would finally see Queen perform at Live Aid had begun to turn. Queen's 'fifth' member on *The Works* Tour was Spike Edney. A keyboard player and rhythm guitarist, Edney had worked with a number of bands such as Duran Duran, Dexys Midnight Runners and The Rolling Stones before beginning his collaboration with Queen in 1984, where he would play guitar, synth and piano during Queen's live performances.

Another band that Edney was familiar with was Bob Geldof's The Boomtown Rats, and Geldof exploited this connection as he attempted to contact Queen. 'Bob asked me to ask the band if they'd be up for it, which I had the opportunity to do when Queen were on tour in New Zealand,' says Edney. 'To which they replied: "Why doesn't he ask us himself?" I explained that he was afraid they would turn him down. They didn't sound that convinced, but said they might be prepared to consider it. I told Bob, and he approached [Queen's manager] Jim Beach officially.'[7]

Bob Geldof managed to track Beach down to the small seaside resort where he was staying and phoned him. Geldof recalls clearly how the conversation went: '"Look, for Christ's sake," Geldof said, "what's *wrong* with them?" Jim replied, "Oh, you know, Freddie's very sensitive." So I said, "Tell the old faggot it's gonna be the biggest thing that ever happened – this huge mega thing."'[8]

Geldof then went directly to Freddie. 'I just had to find Freddie's G-spot,' recalls Geldof, 'Roger Taylor was saying he'd do it but he didn't think Fred would. The band was exhausted and they were really questioning their future as well. When I eventually got to speak to him I literally said to him, "Fred, why wouldn't you do it? The entire stage was built for you practically. Darling, the world." That's literally what I said. I said that. He laughed and he said, "Oh, you have a point, Mr. Geldof.""[9]

With their world tour over, and the Live Aid negotiations taking place, Freddie headed off to Munich. But before he left, he finally called Jim Hutton, who he had spent the night with three months earlier, and invited him over to his London flat for dinner. When Hutton arrived at Stafford Terrace, armed with two bunches of £1.99 freesias, he found Freddie with a group of friends and high on cocaine. Following supper, the group all went off to Heaven before Freddie and Jim returned to the flat and embarked on a relationship that would last until Freddie's death, six years later.

A few days after, Hutton was whisked away to join Freddie in Munich, the chauffeur-driven car and first-class flight being a new experience for the £70-a-week hairdresser. But it soon became clear to Hutton, on his second trip to Munich, that Freddie was playing games: 'I'm not sure why, but I had the distinct impression that Freddie had another boyfriend in the city somewhere. I thought back to my arrival a fortnight earlier and realized why Freddie probably wanted me there so desperately. I was just part of a game between lovers. He wanted to flaunt me so that his boyfriend would see or hear of me and be jealous. Freddie had managed it all very successfully.'[10]

It certainly did the trick; when Winnie Kirchenberger discovered Freddie had a new beau, and a Burt Reynolds' lookalike to boot, he had a fit of rage, even selling the car that Freddie had given to him as a present. It was the last straw for Freddie in his relationship with Winnie and Freddie cut him out of his life.

Hutton's time in Munich was either spent in Freddie's apartment drinking tea and watching old black and white films such as *Some Like It Hot* and *The Women*, two of Freddie's particular favourites, cruising the gay bars together or having sex – 'His drive was amazing,' said Hutton.[11]

The following weekend was spent in London. Hutton had already been introduced to Mary Austin and following breakfast on a Sunday, Freddie announced he had something he wanted to reveal to everyone present: Hutton, Mary Austin, her new boyfriend, Joe Bert, and a couple of other friends. Ordering them all to follow him, Freddie took them on a 20-minute walk in the spring sunshine to a property in Logan Place, where he introduced them all to his new home, Garden Lodge, which, by now, had been totally renovated and into which he was about to move.

With the property ready to move into, Freddie's thoughts turned to the upcoming Live Aid shows, which were scheduled for 13th July. Both shows in London and Philadelphia were sold-out, TV rights had been snapped up around the world, and it was estimated audiences could approach 2bn viewers. It was vital Queen got it right.

But before then, Freddie had agreed to give a rare interview to Simon Bates on BBC Radio 1. Following six weeks of negotiations with the Queen office, a date was fixed, but with everything all set up, it was suddenly cancelled when Queen's office told the BBC that Freddie was ill and unable to undertake the scheduled appointment. A few days later, with Freddie apparently better and with the caveat that the interview had to take place in Queen's offices and that no questions about his parents were permitted, the interview finally took place. It was 22nd June.

There was speculation on the BBC's part that, perhaps, Freddie wasn't ill at all, but upon arriving at the offices, presenter Simon Bates dispelled all doubts when he revealed to his listeners what he saw when Freddie walked in: 'He looks amazingly fit and amazingly well. Until he opens his mouth and sticks his tongue out at you, and then you see a tongue which has got a duffle-coat on it, probably the most unhealthy sight I've ever seen in my life, and I suddenly realized he had been quite ill, and still wasn't well by any means.[12] So we settled down, and I got the tape machine out, got it working, which is a miracle, and I asked him if the whole illness syndrome had anything to do with the fact that he's hard-working, that he's energetic, and possibly, and I was careful how I said this, because he's a fitness freak, if he'd been over-doing things.'[13]

Freddie responded with: 'That's what I'm all about, I guess. But I think the way people get news is whenever something goes wrong, and that's newsworthy, isn't it? So I mean, over the past six months or whatever, it's either I've broken my leg, I lost my voice in South Africa or something's happened and it does take its toll. I mean I have been working very hard. I have been doing my solo project and I was also working with Queen, so basically I was undertaking two very heavy projects simultaneously. And that does take its toll.'

As we have seen earlier, Freddie had already consulted a doctor in New York in 1982 with a white lesion on his tongue and now, less than three years later, he was again exhibiting another symptom associated with HIV: oral thrush. He may not have started to realise that he was showing some of the symptoms of HIV (indeed, if he was aware, why would he risk showing his tongue to Simon Bates?), but these small ailments were pointing to something more significant and more sinister. However, at this point, he'd refused to take an AIDS test, and he hadn't given up sex, either.

'The thing about safe sex is all very worthwhile, but you can still have fun,' Freddie would say. 'You can't expect people to just give up sex. People get freaked, they think they have AIDS and they shoot themselves, and then people find out they didn't have it at all. People should be careful but not get paranoid.'[14]

The interview with Simon Bates was broadcast on Radio 1 at the end of June and spread over a number of days. While this was happening, the pop world was consumed by the forthcoming Live Aid concerts. Nothing like this had been attempted on such a scale before and a veritable 'who's who' of rock and pop were scheduled to appear, and that meant the biggest collection of egos possibly ever gathered together. 'Everyone will be trying to outdo each other, which will cause a bit of friction,' said Freddie. 'It makes me personally proud to be a part of it.'[15]

A formidable list of artists had been lined up, each given a maximum of 20 minutes stage time, and Queen appeared to have their work cut out to make their mark on the day. But, cleverly, Queen made four decisions before their performance that ensured they would steal the show. Firstly, the band suggested they shouldn't open or close the show. Instead they cannily requested a time slot between 6pm and 7pm. This was primetime in the UK, guaranteeing a huge TV audience as people sat down for tea, while in the US, who were five hours behind, it ensured that the audience there wouldn't be jaded by the time Queen appeared. Secondly, Queen chose to play a medley of however many of their hits they could squeeze into the 20-minute slot, rather than trying to use the performance as a window to promote new material. Thirdly, Queen would rehearse for the three solid days in the run-up to Live Aid, honing their act precisely, almost to the second, maximising every moment. And finally, on the day of the concert, just before they were due to perform, their sound engineer, Trip Khalaf, would sneakily set the limiters to ensure Queen were louder than anyone else. It was an old trick, but yet another element that set the band apart from the rest that day.

On 10th July, Freddie, Roger, John, Brian and their team of crew and technicians all convened at London's Shaw Theatre on Euston Road. For three days they rehearsed their running order, which consisted of a medley of six of their biggest hits. By the day of Live Aid, Queen were note perfect, their timing spot-on. On the eve of the show Freddie described how much Queen were looking forward to it, while also revealing a hint of hurt that they hadn't been invited to perform on the single 'Do They Know It's Christmas?' Freddie told BBC *Breakfast Time*, 'It is a very good cause, and initially we would have liked to have taken part in the Band Aid single, but I think we were in separate parts of the globe and so the second bash at it was this thing and also the fact that some of the biggest and best known groups around the world are taking part, so why not us? It makes me personally proud to be part of it actually.'[16]

At noon on Saturday, 13th July, Live Aid, the brainchild of Bob Geldof, kicked off at Wembley Stadium. 'I was shitting myself,' said Geldof. 'If the bands didn't show up, 17 hours of The Boomtown Rats would have been a little too much for anybody.'[17] Status Quo started proceedings with 'Rockin' All Over The World' while Brian May and Roger Taylor took their seats in the Royal Box. Meanwhile, back at Freddie's flat, a group of friends were watching Live Aid on television amid a party atmosphere when, at about 4 in the afternoon, Mercury, who had yet to leave for Wembley, revealed he had a surprise for Jim Hutton.

Hutton had only just got back from work at The Savoy (earlier in the week, he had cut David Bowie's hair) when Freddie asked him when he was going to get ready. When Jim asked what he needed to get ready for, Freddie screamed that he was taking Jim to Live Aid. Hutton had never been to a concert before, something Freddie had no knowledge of. Within minutes Freddie and Jim cut through the traffic in a fleet of black limousines and arrived at Wembley with about an hour to spare.

Queen were due on stage at 6:44pm. Before them it was U2 at 5:20pm and Dire Straits at 6pm, with The Beach Boys and George Thorogood playing in the intervals from Philadelphia.

It was U2 who were the first band to really make the Live Aid audience sit up and take notice. The Irish band had yet to become a household name despite the success of their most recent single, 'Pride (In The Name of Love)'. Live Aid was a career-defining performance for U2, thanks mainly to a moment of personal interaction by their lead singer, Bono, who, during the band's rendition of 'Bad', appeared to rescue a girl being crushed at the front of the crowd. As he grew increasingly frantic at the apparent suffering of this girl, Kal Khalique, Bono urged security guards to help her before he jumped off the stage himself and went to her aid, pulling her out of the crowd and dancing with her.

As a result of Bono's antics, 'Bad' lasted 14 minutes, swallowing up most of U2's set, and meant they couldn't perform their hit single. For most of those in the stadium, and those watching on TV around the world, the feeling was that U2 had blown the rest of the acts away with their performance, and Bono's antics threatened to be the defining moment of Live Aid. But no one had reckoned on Queen, who were waiting in the wings.

At 6:44pm Queen took to the stage.

Before that, however, in the corridors behind Wembley, where stars were brushing shoulders with each other, where egos were colliding, and where drink and drugs appeared on tap ('If there had been a Lance Armstrong-style blood test, then there wouldn't have been many who would have passed,' said PR Gary Farrow), Bono had an encounter with Freddie Mercury, who had finally arrived at the stadium.

Recalling the meeting, Bono said, 'Freddie pulled me aside and said, "Oh, Bono, is it Bo-No, or Bon-O?" I told him, "It's Bon-O." I was up against a wall and he put his hand on the wall and was talking to me like he was chatting up a chick. I thought, "Wow, this guy's really camp." I was telling somebody later and he said, "You're surprised? They're called Queen!" But I was really amazed. It hadn't dawned on me.'[18]

Jim Hutton, Freddie's new boyfriend, was observing everything going on backstage with a sense of bewilderment and wonder, at the very epicentre of the biggest show the world had ever seen, and he walked with Freddie to the edge of the stage as Queen prepared to entertain the masses.

But Queen's participation was actually in doubt right up until the last moment. Freddie was still suffering from a severe throat infection. Backstage, a doctor was called to examine him and it was decided he was simply too ill to perform. However, Freddie wasn't going to be stopped. He literally had the world waiting for him and, given Queen's recent fortunes, this was an unmissable opportunity.

'He wasn't well enough at all,' recalls a member of the BBC Live Aid team, 'but he absolutely insisted.'[19]

Queen strode on stage as though they owned it. Beginning with the opening of 'Bohemian Rhapsody', what followed was a 20-minute eruption of supreme stagecraft that captivated not only the 72,000 crowd inside Wembley, but the estimated 2bn watching around the globe.

'I remember a huge rush of adrenalin as I went on stage and a massive roar from the crowd, and then all of us just pitching in,' recalls Brian May. 'Freddie was our secret weapon. He was able to reach out to everybody in that stadium effortlessly, and I think it was really his night.'[20]

As Nick DeRiso wrote in *Classic Rock*: 'Mercury was everywhere: at the piano for the beginning of "Bohemian Rhapsody," marching around with his sawed-off mic stand during "Radio Ga Ga" as the Wembley crowd clapped in unison, singing with a striking reserve of emotion, owning the fans and the moment. It was a turn as virtuosic as it was surprising. Where others might have shied away from the moment, or even made smaller by it, Queen rose to the occasion.'[21]

In 20 minutes, Queen had covered the breadth of their catalogue and given a performance of passion and bravado that blew away all before them.

'Queen were absolutely the best band of the day,' says Bob Geldof. 'They played the best, had the best sound, used their time to the full. They understood the idea exactly – that it was a global jukebox. They just went and smashed one hit after another. It was the perfect stage for

Freddie: the whole world. And he could ponce about on stage doing "We Are The Champions." How perfect could it get?'[22]

From the moment Freddie ran out on stage, he looked fit and energetic. Having likely been almost three years HIV positive, the result had left him lithe and pale, but still looking every inch like a more-than-healthy man in his late-thirties. Even his dyed hair, the outline of the dye still visible on close-up, the light make-up and simple jeans and vest betrayed nothing of what was to come. In fact he arguably never looked better than this again. There were outwardly no signs of his HIV status except, perhaps, when he lifted his arm in the rendition of 'Radio Ga Ga'. Several inches below the leather armband was a purplish bruise that might have been Kaposi's sarcoma. Surprisingly though, KS of the skin can also occur at any point across HIV in infection, even early on prior to AIDS developing.

'I was always amazed that nobody connected the dots at Live Aid,' says Paul Gambaccini. 'Freddie performed against doctors' advice because he had a throat condition, but he knew that this was the showcase of his life and he gave the performance of his life and Queen were the stars of the show, but nobody ever said, "Wait a minute… why is he ill?" But I always thought, I bet this is one of those opportunistic infections.'[23]

It must have been a surreal experience for Jim Hutton, standing in the wings, allowing him a close-up view of the greatest music show in history. He had only known Freddie for a short while and knew little about the performer, but now he was witnessing him steal the show in front of billions on television and tens of thousands in Wembley.

'At last I had seen the real Freddie at work, whipping seventy thousand people into a frenzy,' recalled Hutton. 'He gave everything to his performance; nothing else mattered to him. When he came off, he rushed to his trailer and I tottered behind like a puppy. His first words were, "Thank God that's over!" Joe ripped his wet clothes from him and dressed him. Adrenalin still overflowing, Freddie knocked back a large vodka to calm himself. Then his face lit up. The expression said: "Yes, we've done it!"'[24]

Queen *had* done it. And although Freddie would later return to the stage with Brian May for an acoustic rendition of 'Is This The World We Created?' it is their blistering set earlier in the evening that is remembered, a set that revitalised Queen's fortunes and gave the band a new lease of life.

After this acoustic performance, Freddie returned with Jim to his Stafford Terrace flat, eschewing the parties that were in full swing backstage. He spent the rest of the night watching other acts perform on both sides of the Atlantic.

Yet none of them could touch Queen.

Once again, the band and Freddie were on top of the world. In 2005, their Live Aid performance was named the greatest live rock performance of all time by a BBC poll, ahead of Jimi Hendrix at Woodstock and The Rolling Stones' free gig in Hyde Park. It's been described as '20 minutes that changed music' and there was a tacit understanding among the other musicians performing at Live Aid that Queen had, indeed, stolen the show.

Queen had set off on their quest to conquer the world in 1973 with the release of their eponymous debut album. It was this appearance at Live Aid that completed that journey.

In November of 1985, some months after the success of Live Aid and the hysteria surrounding Queen's performance, 4,000 miles away from Wembley a group of friends and volunteers assembled beneath the pouring rain on an exposed patch of land near Stanley Park in Vancouver, Canada. They had come together in the early morning to remember three friends who had died of AIDS in the past 18 months: Cedar Debley, Ray Scott and Gaëtan Dugas. The gathering was quiet, sombre and reflective, only the dull roar of the nearby highway accompanying their silent vigil.

Leading the gathering was Bob Tivey. He was the first executive director of AIDS Vancouver and he had come up with the idea that three cherry trees should be planted to remember three of the first men to die of AIDS in Canada, one tree for each man. This was not long before Dugas would become the subject of lurid front-page headlines and indignant condemnation on talk shows across North America for being Patient Zero – the Plague Rat of AIDS – as he was cast in the melodramatic bestseller *And the Band Played On: People, Politics and the AIDS Epidemic*, written by *San Francisco Chronicle* reporter Randy Shilts.

There were no television cameras at the planting that day, no reporters nor bible thumpers. As the last soil was patted down over their roots, Tivey hoped, one day, people would admire the cherry trees and remember Gaëtan Dugas with respect. But if there was a light on the horizon to those gathered to bid farewell to their friends on that bleak November day, then it was that the world had finally woken up to the disease owing to the highly publicised revelation of one of Hollywood's leading men just a few months earlier.

On 2nd October 1985, legendary actor Rock Hudson died of AIDS-related complications at his home in Beverly Hills, just six weeks shy of his 60th birthday. It was news that shocked the world. Hudson was Hollywood royalty, a strikingly handsome leading man, who had the pick of the world's most glamorous and gorgeous leading ladies throughout his life. He was the personification of the American masculine embodiment, a close friend of President Reagan, and was perceived globally as all a heterosexual movie star should be.

Hudson had been diagnosed with HIV/AIDS in 1984, but had kept this secret from all but his closest friends. It had begun with a minor irritation on his neck, which he continually scratched and picked at. When he went to see his doctor, he learned that this wasn't a minor skin problem; it was a lesion that he had developed into Kaposi's sarcoma. The actor had a track record in keeping secrets – he had somehow managed to hide his homosexuality within Hollywood for decades, living a double-life under the constant glare of the movie industry's star system.

'It was career suicide to reveal you were gay,' recalls his boyfriend, Lee Garlington, who dated him in the early 1960s. 'We all pretended to be straight.'[1] Now he needed to keep the biggest secret of all.

However, in 1985, rumours started to circulate about Hudson when he joined his old friend and star, Doris Day, to publicise a new television series she was appearing in. Day and Hudson had known each other since the 1950s when the two of them were paired up in the hit movie, *Pillow Talk*, a film in which Hudson pretends to be gay in order to get closer to Day. Now Doris Day had emerged from semi-retirement to host a TV show on pets for the Christian Broadcasting Network. Hudson was due to appear as her first guest and on 15th July 1985, a press conference was held where Day and Hudson would appear to promote the series. But from the start it was apparent all was not well with the Hollywood heart-throb. To begin with, Hudson arrived late, and when he finally turned up, onlookers were shocked by his appearance. The once-handsome film star now looked ravaged and gaunt. He was frighteningly thin, moved with an unsteady slowness and acted and appeared much older than his 59 years.

'He promised her [Doris] he would be there so he went,' remembers his business manager Wallace Sheft.[2]

'I hardly knew him,' said Doris Day, recalling Hudson arriving on set that day. 'He was very sick. But I just brushed that off and I came out and put my arms around him and said "Am I glad to see you."'[3]

The gossip columns went into overdrive with speculation regarding Hudson's gaunt appearance but there was no gossip about HIV or

AIDS. How could there be? This was Rock Hudson. Instead, reporters simply spoke of a 'mysterious' illness and that was that. Less than a week later, on 21st July, Hudson collapsed in an airport lounge in Paris. He had flown undercover to the French capital in a desperate last bid to get further medical treatment with the antiviral HPA-23 drug from the pioneering French military doctor, Dr. Dominique Dormant, at the Percy Military Hospital. HPA-23, at that time, wasn't available in the US.

If he had collapsed in Los Angeles, he would have died with all of his secrets still intact and no one, except those closest to him, would have been any the wiser. He was aware of the limited time he had left, and had already made elaborate arrangements to undergo treatment in his final days in a manner that would enable him to die without the stigma of AIDS. Hudson and his closest friends, those he could trust, had planned a scenario in which he would be taken to an apartment out of town and away from the glare of publicity, where a hospice-like environment would be created. Male nurses, sworn to secrecy, would care for him and when he died, the cause of death would be given as a heart attack or cirrhosis of the liver. There would have been no mention of AIDS, no revelation that Hudson was gay, and none of his personal details would have been revealed.

Rumour has it that it had been done successfully for other stars, and, if true, then no one had found out. He would simply have passed away from what most people consider a routine illness and his legacy as the great heterosexual heart-throb would have remained. Hudson had spent 35 years carefully constructing his image and he thought of AIDS as the plague.

His escape route was well planned – except he couldn't have foreseen his collapse in Paris. It was the worst place for him to collapse at the time and the officials at the Hospital Americain at Neuilly-sur-Seine in the suburbs of the city, where Hudson was taken, were furious. They recognised his symptoms and refused to accept AIDS cases, their official line being they were not licensed to treat infectious diseases. The Percy Military Hospital also refused to admit Hudson as he wasn't a French citizen and so the only option open to him was to be allowed to remain in the Hospital Americain. But in order to do so, they stipulated he must announce to the world that he had AIDS: if he didn't, *they* would. It was a frightening and no-win ultimatum for the movie star.

Faced with no other choice, his spokeswoman in Paris, Yanou Collart, helped to draft a press release but before she did so, the doctor that Hudson had travelled to Paris to see, Dr. Dormont, had an idea that might get him transferred to Percy Military Hospital. He thought they should reach out to President Reagan, a close friend of Hudson's, and immediately, Dale Olsen, Hudson's American publicist, sent a telegram to the White House. 'Only one hospital in the world can offer necessary medical treatment to save the life of Rock Hudson or at least alleviate his illness,' he wrote, suggesting that, 'a request from the White House or a high American official would change [the head of the hospital's] mind.'[4]

But the response they received back from the White House was not what they wanted, or expected. A telegram bounced back from a young White House staffer, Mark Weinberg, saying, 'I spoke with Mrs. Reagan about the attached telegram. She did not feel this was something the White House should get into and agreed to my suggestion that we refer the writer to the US embassy, Paris.'[5]

Speaking years later, Weinberg stated that, 'The Reagans were very conscious of not making exceptions for people just because they were friends of theirs or celebrities or things of that kind. They weren't about that.'[6] But, Peter Staley, a member of Act Up and founder of the Treatment Action Group, is dismissive of the argument that the Reagans did not wish to be seen to be giving preferential treatment to a friend: 'Seems strange that the Reagans used that excuse, since they often did favours for their Hollywood friends during their White House years. I'm sure if it had been Bob Hope in that hospital with some rare, incurable cancer, Air Force One would have been dispatched to help save him. There's no getting around the fact that they left Rock Hudson out to dry. As soon as he had that frightening homosexual disease, he became as unwanted and ignored as the rest of us.'[7]

It was left to French Defence Minister, Charles Hernu, to speed Hudson's passage into Percy Military Hospital but, once there, Dr. Dormont's diagnosis was less than positive, telling Hudson that the disease had progressed too far for even HPA-23 to have any effect. There was no alternative but to acknowledge publicly that he was suffering from AIDS and a press release was composed, his only stipulation being that they said he collapsed in the Paris Ritz Hotel, rather than an airport lounge – he felt it more befitting a Hollywood movie star.

Publicist Yanou Collart is adamant that the decision to release a press statement was Hudson's alone: 'The hardest thing I ever had to do in my life was to walk into his room and read him the press release. I'll never forget the look on his face. How can I explain it? Very few people knew he was gay. In his eyes was the realization that he was destroying his own image. After I read it, he said simply, "That's it, it has to be done."'[8]

On 25th July 1985, thanks to his press release, the world knew that Rock Hudson had AIDS.

'Freddie Mercury took an incredibly keen interest in the whole Rock Hudson revelation,' said Paul Prenter.

Knowing there was no hope in the treatment afforded in Paris, Hudson wanted nothing more than to return to the US to die in what relative dignity could be mustered from the sensational accounts of his life and last days which were filling gossip columns in newspapers worldwide, much as they would do in Freddie Mercury's final days. But getting back home was easier said than done as airlines refused to fly him, fearing his disease was infectious. The only option available to Hudson was to charter his own aircraft to fly him and ten medical practitioners back across the Atlantic. 'The airline wanted $250,000 to charter a 747 to fly him back home, an enormous amount,' recalls Wallace Sheft, Hudson's former manager. 'They called me from the tarmac. They wanted me to make sure the funds were wired before they took off.'[9]

The amount Hudson paid to fly him home didn't go unnoticed by Dr. Dormont: 'That's my research budget for four years,' he said.[10]

'He had the disease for a long time before it was diagnosed,' said biographer Sara Davidson. 'Perhaps as long as three to five years. He may have been one of the earlier cases. When he learned that he had it, he said, "Why me? I don't know anyone who has AIDS." It was thought that perhaps Marc Christian, his last lover, was the source, but Christian tested negative.'[11]

By the time Hudson had made his announcement, thousands of people across the US, many in Europe and countless in Africa, had already died of AIDS-related illnesses, but their deaths had gone unnoticed. Suddenly Rock Hudson's revelation – and he *was* movie royalty – made people aware of 'children with AIDS who wanted to go to school, laborers with AIDS who wanted to work, and researchers who wanted funding,' suggested author Randy Shilts.[12]

Hudson himself lived out his final days aware of the difference his announcement had made as Dr. Michael Gottleib, who visited him regularly in Beverly Hills during the end of his life, remembers: 'He was well aware of the publicity. He had a sense it was worthwhile. He expressed he was glad he had gone public. Maybe he knew it was doing some good, that his disclosure was making a difference.'[13]

On 2nd October 1985, just a week after he had set up a foundation to battle AIDS and donated $250,000 of his own money[14] to the cause, Rock Hudson died in his sleep at his Beverly Hills home, his once robust 6ft 4in body reduced to just 91 pounds. He was pronounced dead at 9am after being found by a member of the household staff. Three hours later, his body was placed in a cardboard coffin and cremated at the Glenview Crematory in suburban Glendale. For the former Hollywood legend there would be no funeral.

When Hudson died in October 1985, it is not known whether or not Freddie Mercury knew he had HIV himself, though 1985 would have been the first year that alarm bells began ringing for him. It was highly unlikely he would have known in 1984 as the only test for HIV – the ELISA Test – was in the early stages of development. So, based on the fact that Freddie was still relatively healthy and hadn't changed his behaviour by the end of 1984, it's very probable that he didn't have any real inkling that he was infected that year.

However, in 1985, the ELISA test had become more accessible, and available for doctors in the UK and Germany, as well as the rest of Western Europe, to test their patients for the possibility of antibodies to viral proteins. The drawback of this test, though, was that it only informed you if someone had been exposed to the virus – not whether they actually had the virus. And even though this test was now more reliable Freddie was still healthy at this time, or at least not showing serious opportunistic infections. However, he did seem to be exhibiting some of the telltale signs of HIV infection that doctors in the mid-1980s began to recognise as precursors for a person who had the virus, but who had not yet developed full-blown AIDS. Some of these initial symptoms were swollen lymph nodes throughout the body, night sweats and a mild to moderate general malaise.

Freddie may have mentioned something to his doctor at one of his checkups – or his doctor may have had his blood tested for HIV along with other possible sexually transmitted diseases that were routine checks for sexually active gay men. If an ELISA HIV test came back positive in 1985, Freddie's doctor would have told him, but would also have told him of the high possibility that, although he had been exposed to the virus, there was no definitive sign that he had been infected.

In fact, it was in late-1985 that Freddie first had an AIDS test. The results, as far as he claimed, were negative. However, in reality it is likely that it merely showed he had developed the antibodies, which confirm exposure but do not establish viral infection success (this can occur up to a year after infection, especially with the early generation tests). Such a result enabled Freddie to claim, with uncertainty, that he did not have AIDS. It is almost certain that he was told by the doctor that the results indicated he was positive, but with the caveat of the high possibility of a 'false positive'. For someone who might be in denial, it was a satisfactory result.

It certainly didn't stop Freddie partying. In September, he was back in Munich to celebrate his 39th birthday. He hired the club Henderson's for the night and put on an elaborate party featuring a black-and-white drag ball for 300 guests, many of whom he had flown in and put up at the Munich Hilton at his own expense. It cost him £50,000[15] and the following day, despite the party finishing at 6am, Freddie was back in Henderson's to film the video for his new single, 'Living On My Own'.

'"Living on My Own" is very me,' said Freddie. 'I have to go round the world living in hotels. You can have a whole shoal of people you know looking after you but in the end they all go away. But I'm not complaining. I'm living on my own and having a boogie time.'

In the same interview he touched on his enduring search for love and how he felt he had been used in the past: 'When you're a celebrity, it's hard to approach somebody and say: "Look, I'm normal underneath." Then what happens is they tread all over me because by trying to be normal to somebody, suddenly I've come out of my shell and become far more vulnerable than most people. Because I'm successful and have a lot of money, a lot of greedy people prey on me. But that's something I've learned to deal with. I'm riddled with scars and I just don't want any more.'[16]

In another interview in 1985, Freddie reveals a deeper scar: 'You can have everything in the world and still be the loneliest man. And that is the most bitter type of loneliness. Success has brought me world idolization and millions of pounds, but it's prevented me from having the one thing we all need, a loving ongoing relationship. It's like the old Hollywood stories where all those wonderful actresses just couldn't carry on a relationship because their careers came first. That's the way it is with me. I can't stop the wheel for a while and devote myself to a love affair because all sorts of business problems would pile up. The wheel has to keep turning and that makes it very hard for anyone to live with me and be happy. I'm driven by my work and will go on for as long as my system will allow me – until I go insane. There's a voice inside me saying, "Slow down, Freddie. You're going to burn yourself out." But I just can't stop.'[17]

Freddie's comments appear to be from a man resigned to his lot and yet they are strange remarks considering one of the things he so desperately craved, that of a solid relationship, he had now found, thanks to his partnership with Jim Hutton. It is possible that the rumours starting to circulate about his health were beginning to get him down. John Deacon was certainly aware of Fleet Street's predilection for gossip and their focus on Freddie Mercury: 'Well, I heard that someone asked, I think it was *The Sun* or something, because AIDS is so much in the press at the moment, so they ring up and they want to know, is it true? And if you say no, then it becomes, "So and so denies etc. etc." I mean, they can twist it any way they want.'[18]

The disappointing sales of his solo work could also have had something to do with Freddie's malaise. His single, 'Made In Heaven', had flopped in the UK earlier in 1985, reaching number 57, and 'Living On My Own' barely did any better, peaking at number 50. Freddie had been asked by Dave Clark to record a song for his new London musical, *Time*, and Roger and John had devoted some time to their own solo projects but, given their success at Live Aid, it was obvious to all in Queen that they were better as a unit rather than solo performers.

Their performance at Live Aid meant that Queen were once again the name on everyone's lips. Back issues of their albums had re-entered the charts, and the band's career was seemingly revitalised. So, in September 1985, all four members of Queen, together with producer Mack, were back in Munich and ready to record. Accompanied by a documentary crew, who captured Freddie drinking vodka constantly and chain-smoking incessantly, the initial song Queen recorded was 'One Vision', the first Queen song ever to have the whole band sharing the writing credit.

'One Vision' was released as a single in November 1985 and the song became a Top 10 hit in the UK, peaking at number 7, although it made only number 61 in the US, where the band were still distinctly unpopular and unfashionable. There was also an element of backlash in the UK towards 'One Vision' with some sections of the British press seeing the record as an example of the band blatantly cashing in on their success at Live Aid a few months earlier.

Meanwhile, Freddie went into the world-famous Abbey Road Studios in London, where he recorded a concept-album version of 'In My Defence', a power ballad written by Dave Clark, for his musical. Freddie also found time in November to do a stint on the catwalk, accompanying actress Jane Seymour, dressed in an Elizabeth and David Emanuel wedding gown, across the stage at the Royal Albert Hall in aid of Fashion Week.

Throughout this period, he was shuttling between London and Munich with his partner, Jim Hutton, who was flying out to Germany to be with him every other weekend. But if Jim had hoped their time together in Munich would be relaxing, he was to be disappointed as Freddie had thrown himself into the next Queen project and Jim found himself, more often than not, left to his own devices: 'In the studio Freddie had a one-track mind – work, work and more work,' he recalls. 'I watched him through the glass, but he rarely glanced my way because he was so totally absorbed in his work. He chain-smoked, or rather, chain-lit Silk Cuts, and to boost his energy and adrenalin he slipped down slugs of Russian vodka. He only drank Stolichnaya.'[1]

Evenings, too, were often spent in the recording studio, after which the whole group would go to a restaurant together and then Freddie and Jim would slip away to one of the clubs in the Bermuda Triangle. But either Munich's appeal was seemingly beginning to fade for Freddie, or the risks on offer within the city were starting to frighten him. He began spending more time in London, living in his newly renovated luxury mansion, Garden Lodge. Going out to nightclubs seemed to have less appeal to Freddie, whatever city he was in, and the gay scene was becoming increasingly distant to him.

Back in the UK, Freddie's record company, CBS, released another one of his solo singles, 'Love Me Like There's No Tomorrow'. Though his two previous releases had performed badly, this song was the biggest flop of all, scraping into the charts at number 76. Perhaps its dismal performance took place at an appropriate time given that he wrote the song for Barbara Valentin, his Munich friend, lover and cohort. Now, at the tail end of 1985, Freddie was growing tired and wary of Munich and the lifestyle he had followed there for a number of years. He had already given up sexual relations with Barbara and the distance between them had started to grow. Something had happened to Freddie to make him change his ways, but no one could put a finger on it. Barbara claimed to recall an incident, although no date was forthcoming, when he cut himself and she told author Lesley-Ann Jones about how, when she was trying to help him when he had blood all over his hands, he screamed at her, yelling 'NO! Don't touch me! Don't touch me!' Valentin continued by telling Jones, 'It was then that I realized. He never told me, but after that I knew.'[2]

Freddie's new mindset was compounded when, towards the end of 1985, he abruptly and without warning abandoned the Munich club scene, as well as his affair with Valentin, whom he had still been seeing occasionally. He left the German city, leaving behind him a life that he had created and revelled in for several years, without any explanation for his sudden decision, and it was a shock to Valentin.

'One minute we were inseparable, doing literally everything together. The next, he was gone. He just disappeared out of my life,' she recalled.[3]

Freddie was not one to take his decisions lightly and once made, rarely backed down. It seems that something monumental affected this decision.

'Maybe he wasn't well, because he was very secretive about his not being well,' suggests Peter Straker.[4] Freddie had already discussed with Jim the possibility of moving back to London, so abandoning Munich must have been on his mind for a number of weeks – possibly since he took an AIDS test in the autumn of 1985. Most likely, it was because he knew in all probability he was HIV positive. Various writers have suggested that his fear of contracting HIV in the gay scene of Munich was linked to the decision, but it was perhaps more complex than that. To those close to him back in London he seemed different somehow.

His move back to London, unexpected and sudden as it was, was life altering for Freddie: a possible acknowledgement of the folly of his ways and the dangers that he had exposed himself to and for which he was now paying a price. He was 39 years old, wealthy and famous, and in a steady relationship for the first time properly since 1976 and Mary Austin. What's more, his band was undergoing a resurgence. Life should really not have been any better for Freddie Mercury. But he had been hit badly by the news of the death of Rock Hudson and the manner in which the movie star's legacy had been picked apart by the tabloids and gossip columnists.

'The whole Rock Hudson exposé and then the actor's death really disturbed him. If it came on the news he would watch it intently, and then not speak afterwards,' said Peter Straker.[5]

Would Freddie's legacy go the same way if it were discovered he had HIV? Would his band be cast into the musical wilderness because he had to come out as gay and admit he was infected with HIV? Freddie could only mull over these consequences in his mind, and Munich was not the place to do so. His reaction was to surround himself with stability and those he loved, understandable considering the news he likely believed to be the right diagnosis. His deeds, age, personality, his fame and his wealth, they must all have seemed meaningless in the face of death.

Returning to London, and the sanctuary of Garden Lodge with Jim, who had by now moved in, Freddie had not only cut off his friends in Munich, many of whom would die of AIDS-related illnesses in the coming months and years, but he also cut out the one-night stands, the cocaine use and the nightclubbing.

'I used to live for sex but now I've changed,' Freddie said. 'I've stopped going out, stopped the nights of wild partying. I've almost become a nun. It's amazing, I thought sex was a very important thing to me but now I realize I've just gone completely the other way. Once, I was extremely promiscuous, it was excess in every direction, but now I'm totally different. I have stopped all that and I don't miss that kind of life. Everything is fine.'[6]

But everything *wasn't* fine. It's clear that something happened in late-1985 that made him ditch Barbara Valentin, the party boys at the nightclubs in Munich, the drugs, the one-night stands, and retreat so suddenly and so abruptly to Garden Lodge in London. It could only have been that after repeated HIV tests that the latest test, and the most reliable test to date, taken by his doctor in Munich had confirmed that he was certainly HIV positive, and a reality he could not longer deny. Freddie knew it was not only going to kill him but also threatened to destroy his band and his musical and artistic legacy.

And like Rock Hudson's worries about his movie-star heart-throb status, it may have been this that Freddie feared the most.

Freddie spent the Christmas of 1985 in his Garden Lodge mansion with Jim Hutton, who had moved in with the singer in November 1985. Part of the deal was that Jim would contribute to the housekeeping budget, despite the fact he was only earning £100 a week at The Savoy and Freddie was a multi-millionaire. It hardly seemed a fair arrangement but, between them, Freddie and Jim agreed that Jim should pay a £50-per-week contribution to the household bills and Freddie would take care of the rest.

'It represented over half my weekly wage although Freddie never knew that,' said Hutton. 'But I paid it willingly; it went some way to keeping our relationship on a fair footing but later he dropped the idea.'[1]

The New Year saw Queen and Freddie working on a new movie project. Directed by Russell Mulcahy, *Highlander* was a big-budget and lavish adventure fantasy starring Christopher Lambert and Sean Connery. The band were invited to view a 20-minute rough cut of parts of the film to decide whether it was something that might appeal to them and they were instantly hooked. Queen weren't creating a complete soundtrack for the movie – that would be created by the American composer, Michael Kamen – but they would contribute nine songs. Freddie wrote just one of them, a track titled 'Princes of the Universe', which was used over the film's title sequence. Queen's next album, *A Kind of Magic*, became the unofficial soundtrack release to *Highlander* and comprised five of the songs used within the movie and another four songs written specifically for the album, including 'Pain Is So Close To Pleasure' and 'Friends Will Be Friends', both songs co-written by Mercury and Deacon, as well as the band's previous single release, 'One Vision'.

At the time of the imminent release of *A Kind of Magic*, Queen had been together for 15 years and questions had been asked about how much more could they give. In a 1985 interview John Deacon had given an indication about how disparate the band had become: 'We're not so much a group anymore. We're four individuals that work together as Queen but our working together as Queen is now actually taking up less and less of our time.'[2]

There were always rumours about Queen breaking up, but now those rumours seemed to have some substance about them. A meeting – some would say a *crisis* meeting – was held in Switzerland and there the four band members said they would give it one more try. The result was *A Kind of Magic*, the songs for *Highlander* and the spectacular tour that would follow. As Peter Freestone would say: 'When it came down to it, Freddie knew that he could create what he wanted on his own, but his life, his music, revolved around Queen.'[3]

The album *A Kind of Magic* was crucial for Queen in keeping the group unified, but Paul Prenter remained a negative influence. Freddie was constantly being told by Prenter he was bigger than the rest of the band and that he would be better off on his own. 'He [Prenter] became a nightmare and he became divisive between Freddie and the band,' recalls John Reid,[4] while Peter Straker says, 'Paul was very difficult and a lot of people around Freddie weren't mad about him but they had to put up with him. I just used to be wary of him, that's the best thing I can say about Paul.'[5]

With work complete on their new album and the music for *Highlander* done, Freddie turned his attentions to recording the track 'Time' for Dave Clark's musical of the same name. Clark was keen for Freddie to take a role in the stage production of *Time*, even inviting him to dine with him and Lord and Lady Olivier one evening. Lord Olivier had a part in the stage production, appearing as a hologram in every performance, and Freddie, an admirer of Olivier's, jumped at the opportunity to have dinner with the great man. It was the only occasion that the two of them met, with Freddie recalling how Lord Olivier told him to 'Fuck the critics' when told how the music press often derided Queen and their music.[6] But even so, Freddie declined Dave Clark's offer of a role. 'For one thing, my darling, I don't get up until 3 p.m so I can't do matinees. For another, when I do a show, I sing my butt off for three hours and then I drop dead. So it would be impossible to do eight shows a week,' he told him.[7]

While this was going on 'A Kind of Magic' was released as single and reached number 3 in the UK. It was also a Top 10 hit across Europe. Less than a month later, Freddie attended the celebrity opening night of *Time* at London's Dominion Theatre. He took his partner, Jim Hutton, to the show and although their relationship appeared to be going well, Freddie made sure Jim was under no illusions that his music came first.

'I wouldn't sacrifice my career if a partner wanted me to,' Freddie said. 'It's my career that keeps me going. What else would I do? Dig weeds, get fat and be beautifully in love? No, I'd like to remain as successful as I am, write beautiful songs *and* be in love – not that it's worked up 'til now. My private life will always be erratic. I'll keep on trying.'[8]

Certainly, Freddie showed no signs of slowing down during the spring of 1986. The single 'Time', performed and co-produced by Mercury, was released and reached number 32 in the charts; he went into the studio with the American rock singer Billy Squier to collaborate on two songs, 'Love is The Hero', on which Freddie provided backing vocals and played piano, and 'Lady With A Tenor Sax', which Mercury co-wrote; and he devoted some time to writing a song, 'Hold On', for a German movie, *Zabou*, directed by Hajo Gies.

As well as all Freddie's solo work, and that of the other members of the band, Queen were gearing up for a major UK and European tour, the biggest they would ever undertake, and, as it turned out, the final tour with the original Queen line-up. The *Magic* Tour was scheduled to begin on 7th June in Stockholm and would take in 26 shows across Europe before ending on 9th August at Knebworth Park in England. Tickets for every show sold out in a matter of hours, confirming Queen's status as one of the top live draws in music. And fans wouldn't be disappointed: as well as picking the largest venues, the band hired the biggest stage and lighting rig ever assembled. It would be the show to end all shows.

Five days before the tour began, Queen released their 12th studio album, *A Kind of Magic*. It went straight into the UK album charts at number 1 and, in doing so, became their first album of new material to top the UK charts since *The Game* in 1980, selling over 600,000 copies. While the fans lapped it up, the music press were less than enthusiastic, among them *Rolling Stone* commenting: 'The album, which might have been Queen's crowning moment, is absolutely bankrupt of gauche imagination'.[9]

The bad reviews didn't harm record sales, or stop people buying tickets to Queen shows, and outwardly didn't seem to bother Freddie Mercury at all: 'I don't give a damn about critics, to be honest. The backing of the press is important only at the beginning of a career as a rock musician. When success arrives, it's the fans who decide on whether it's to be, or not to be. They can write what they want.'[10]

With the album riding high in charts throughout Europe, Freddie and Queen embarked on the *Magic* Tour, which steamrollered its way across the continent before arriving in England on 9th July when Queen played at St James' Park in Newcastle and donated all the proceeds from the show to Save The Children. On 11th and 12th July Queen returned to Wembley Stadium, scene of their Live Aid triumph, and played to two sell-out crowds.

Once again Freddie was having problems with his throat, constantly prone to infection. He suffered recurring problems with nodules on his vocal chords and, when on tour, always travelled with a steam inhaler and would suck throat lozenges prior to going on stage. But nothing was going to stop this triumphant homecoming. The concerts blended classics from their back catalogue with some of the new material from *A Kind of Magic* as well as a rock'n'roll medley in the middle of the set. To conclude the show, Freddie would emerge from off-stage draped in an ermine gown and wearing a crown fit for a king as Brian May's rendition of 'God Save The Queen' filled the stadium.

The first show at Wembley was followed by a raucous party for the road crew that featured the usual rock'n'roll debauchery while the second show at the Stadium was followed by a more refined party for the band at London's Roof Gardens Restaurant. While this might have been a more sedate affair, it still followed in the grand tradition of Queen's after-show parties, with female lift attendants wearing nothing more than body paint and dwarfs, topless waitresses and bathroom attendants wearing only G-strings, while looking after the 500 guests.

Freddie attended the party, which cost over £80,000[11], with Jim Hutton, but because of the press gathered there, he had to be seen to attend with Mary Austin and be photographed only with her on his arm. Even now, in 1986, the façade had to remain – Freddie couldn't risk coming out.

But while the guests indulged themselves at the party, Freddie was not his usual self. In fact, his unusually reserved after-show behaviour throughout the tour had started to be noticed by other members of the entourage. Spike Edney, who played keyboards on stage with Queen during the tour, recalled how Freddie had quietened down on the road: 'Fred was much more settled. He didn't have the taste for going out clubbing and staying up all night, the way he used to. Also, he was really looking after his voice. We'd often end up back in his suite, drinking champagne and playing Scrabble or Trivial Pursuit. I can remember several occasions still being up at 9 a.m., just me and Fred, finishing off a game.'[12]

Roger Taylor also noticed a difference in Freddie. 'Freddie's different this year. What have you done to him?' he asked Jim Hutton before going on to describe how he was a decidedly changed man, no longer prowling the gay scene in the cities they visited. Yet paradoxically, others commented that he could hardly sit still: constantly worrying, fidgeting, crossing one leg and then the other. It felt like he could throw off sparks. He appeared to be filled with an anxiety that does not come from thinking about the future, but from wanting to control it.

Perhaps the absence of Paul Prenter had something to do with this. Queen had collectively got rid of him in 1985 ('He got a little too big for his boots, I think,' said Brian May[13]) but Freddie, in an act of typical generosity, had immediately employed Prenter himself. Paul was out and then back in – closer to Freddie, it seemed. However, just before the *Magic* Tour a year later, something changed. Prenter upset Freddie by holding an impromptu party in Freddie's Stafford Terrace flat. Freddie had let him have the keys to his flat, as well as some money to keep himself afloat, but Prenter abused that misguided loyalty by hosting the party at Stafford Terrace without Freddie's knowledge and trashing the place.

Livid, Freddie sacked him on the spot. Prenter, though, was equally volatile, threatening to 'do this and that', although no one, including Freddie, had any idea exactly what the 'this and that' he was threatening was. They were to discover just what Prenter meant by his threats a few months later.

After the two shows at Wembley, Queen played one show in Manchester and then travelled to Germany and Austria before playing an historic concert in Budapest on 27th July, which remains the largest show ever by a Western rock band in what was then Communist Europe. During the acoustic part of the Budapest concert, Freddie and Brian May attempted a rendition of a traditional Hungarian song, with Freddie reading the lyrics from notes he had written on the palm of his hand. The rendition was greatly appreciated by the sell-out Hungarian crowd. However, it is clear from footage of the performance that Freddie looks fatigued. He is utterly professional and goes through the motions, but not much more. Coming off-stage at the end of the show, Freddie was briefly accosted by a Hungarian reporter who asked him if this concert was the beginning of a long friendship with Hungary. Freddie's response was brief, but full of portent: 'If I'm alive, I'll come back,' he says.

Following one show in France the band headed to Barcelona for the first of three shows in Spain. It was while in Barcelona, at the end of July, that Freddie gave a rare interview on Spanish television. During the course of the interview Freddie was asked which singers he admired the most. Expecting him to answer with the name of some soul legend, such as Aretha Franklin, he surprised everyone by saying that the singer he most admired at that time was the Spanish opera singer, Montserrat Caballé. He had been first exposed to her voice when Peter Freestone had taken him to watch Luciano Pavarotti at the Royal Opera House in 1981, where she had blown him away with the power and beauty of her voice. Whether it was intentional or not, in his interview Freddie chose the right place to state his passion for Caballé as the opera star was born in Barcelona and she was proud of her Catalan heritage.

After his television interview Queen took to the stage at Barcelona's Mini Estadi on 1st August and it was a few days later when Jim Beach came to him and told him that he had received a phone call from Carlos Caballé, who was Montserrat's brother and manager, and also Pino Sagliocco, who was Queen's promoter in Spain. Montserrat Caballé, as it turned out, was away touring at the time but word had got back to her about Freddie's comments and the idea was mooted that, perhaps, he might like to meet to consider writing a song for her.

It was a prospect that was both daunting and exciting and, at first, Freddie was reluctant to entertain the challenge. But following persuasion from Jim Beach and Peter Freestone, he eventually agreed to discuss it further and it was arranged for him to meet Montserrat in Spain in the spring of 1987 to discuss a potential project.

From Barcelona, the tour took Queen to Madrid and then Marbella before they arrived back in the UK for the biggest show of the tour, the grand finale, and the last show they would ever do together. Over 120,000 fans paid to watch Queen perform at Knebworth Park on 9th August 1986. Bursting onto the stage with 'One Vision', Knebworth saw Queen at the peak of their live powers as they entertained the crowd with a 26-song set that included virtually all of their hits before concluding with Freddie taking his bow, dressed in his regal ermine robe and crown, which he held up to salute the audience. If they had any inkling that this would be their last show ever, then Queen certainly went out in style.

Perhaps Freddie sensed an inevitability during that show, one that might have started to manifest itself throughout the tour, that he was approaching the end of the road, particularly where touring was concerned. He had spent much of the tour uncharacteristically reserved. And while it had been observed and commented on, no one in the band or in Queen's entourage suspected anything, certainly not regarding his health. But the signs were there. After a row in Spain with John Deacon, Mercury had let slip the comment that 'I'm not going to be doing this forever. This is probably the last time.'[14] And walking off-stage after the Knebworth show, Freddie muttered some prophetic words to Brian May: 'Freddie said something like, "Oh, I can't fucking do this anymore, my whole body's wracked with pain!" But he normally said things like that at the end of a tour, so I don't think we took it seriously, really,' recalls May.[15]

Photographs of Freddie performing at Knebworth seem to show markings on his left cheek that, to some people, suggests he has facial Kaposi's sarcoma. Closer inspection seems to show a collection of small raised lumps on his cheek, rather than a lesion – a possible sign of shingles, another symptom common with people infected with HIV.

Following the show, Freddie rushed off, not wanting to be involved in any post-gig party. As *Rolling Stone* commented: 'At the show's end, Mercury left the concert site hurriedly. It was apparent something was on his mind. He would no longer want to be seen by the audiences that had loved him.'[16]

'We played our last shows with Fred in 1986,' remembers Roger Taylor, 'though at the time I never expected them to be our last shows – none of us did. None of us could foresee that he was going to get ill and die so soon.'[17]

Only Freddie knew. He had played his last show in front of 120,000 fans. It was the perfect way to bring the curtain down on Queen's reign as the best live act of recent times. Perhaps ever.

Conspicuous by their absence on the *Magic* Tour were any shows outside the UK and the rest of Europe. Granted, Queen weren't setting the charts alight in the US, but they still had a faithful following there, even if they had incurred the wrath of Middle America, thanks to their video for 'I Want To Break Free'. Surely a tour of arenas in the US would only serve to promote their latest album, *A Kind of Magic*, which had stalled at number 46 in the Billboard Top 200, Queen's lowest album position in the US since 1974. And, as Live Aid had been shown simultaneously in the UK and the US, where the band had bagged a prime time slot on US television, there were millions of viewers across the Atlantic who had watched Queen steal the show and who, perhaps, wanted to see them live.

So why were so many territories left off the touring schedule, specifically North America? Dwindling popularity in the US is a possible answer, or excuse, but much more likely is the effect AIDS was having on the entertainment insurance industry. It was in the mid-1980s that the major domestic insurance companies began to sit up and take a specific interest in HIV. In 1985, the Los Angeles-based Transamerica Occidental Life Insurance Company discovered it had paid over $2.5 million in death benefits in about 20 AIDS cases, and other insurance companies, reflecting concern that AIDS would cost the insurance industry billions of dollars in death benefits, were beginning to screen policy applicants to weed out likely victims of the deadly virus.

Specific questions about AIDS were becoming routine in 1986 with physical examinations, especially in the US, demanded before policies were issued and a memorandum had been issued the previous summer by US financial group Lincoln National recommending that 'life styles and habits of life insurance applicants be considered by the nearly 700 insurance companies that it presently reinsures [that is, assumes part of their insured risk]'. The memo went on to advise that, 'if an applicant's life style fits the AIDS-prone profile, it should not constitute grounds for rejection but rather should trigger further inquiry'.[1]

'Our worst fears are materializing,' said Nancy Langer, a spokes-person for the Lambda Legal Defense and Education Fund, a homo-sexual rights group in New York. 'It's no surprise that insurance agencies would seek to minimize their liability on clients who come down with the disease.'[2]

Entertainment insurers began to take similar views with regards to insuring their clients. Given the perception of the lifestyle that those in the film and music industry led, with copious amounts of drink, drugs and sex, the possibility of a major talent being infected with HIV was a huge concern for the entertainment insurance industry. They simply couldn't afford actors, singers and performers failing to fulfil contractual commitments owing to AIDS-related illness. The cost of a movie star pulling out of a major production or a band having to cancel a tour because one of its members was ill thanks to HIV was potentially huge and the insurance industry decided to address this urgently. And Freddie Mercury, given his sexuality and lifestyle (although, to all intents and purposes, his sexuality was still a secret), was a prime candidate.

Freddie claimed he had taken an AIDS test in 1985, though it's likely two separate tests were taken (the first in London and the second in Munich), which he further claimed were negative but, by 1986, US insurers, particularly within the entertainment industry, were insisting on carrying out their own AIDS tests before issuing policies. In the UK and Europe, it wasn't so stringent, and insurance companies simply relied upon clients providing their own medical histories where appropriate and signing to confirm that all information provided was correct to the best of their knowledge.

Freddie knew that the US insurers would have insisted upon another AIDS test, which he would have failed. Due to the tabloids in Britain he was already on the insurers' radar. If he failed an AIDS test in the US (which he likely knew he would), it would be difficult to keep the news out of the public domain, the Queen tour would have to be cancelled and he would be forced to tell his bandmates, his parents and the world that he had HIV, which in turn was tantamount to coming out too. It was simply something Freddie was unwilling to contemplate. Far better not to entertain any thoughts of touring the US and the rest of the world in the first place and, instead, bow out in Europe and the UK.

But how did he explain his reluctance to tour the US or other territories to the rest of Queen?

'He just told us that he wasn't up to doing tours, and that's as far as it went,' remembers Brian May.[3]

Nevertheless, even undertaking a tour in the UK and Europe represented a major gamble for Freddie. He must have suspected it would be the last tour he did, and for such a born performer, it is likely he wanted one last swansong, but if he suddenly developed an illness or lost his voice during the tour, then the financial ramifications could be enormous, potentially ruinous if he was subsequently to test HIV positive and the virus was seen to be a cause of his illness.

Given the fact that, in all likelihood, he had already tested positive in 1985, there was never any chance of Queen performing in North America in 1986 or after, or anywhere that had strict AIDS testing guidelines in order to fulfil insurance terms and conditions. Freddie may have taken out his own insurance policy for the UK and European shows, a policy that covered him if he lost his voice due to a health issue, but given the liability risk he posed to his bandmates and fans in the US, such a policy was useless there. With potentially millions of pounds at stake without insurance, in all probability Freddie simply told the insurers covering the UK and European shows that he hadn't failed an HIV test and signed the documents accordingly. He just needed to remain fit and well enough to get through to Knebworth and then bow out in front of the biggest crowd of all. It was a perfect farewell if he *had* planned it – and it looks as though he had.

Following Knebworth, Freddie was determined to stay out of the spotlight for a while. He didn't do any promotional work when Queen's next single, 'Who Wants to Live Forever', was released in September (it only reached number 24 in the UK charts) and he didn't appear at a ceremony when the group won the Best Live Performance Video for *Live In Rio* at the 1986 British Video Awards, leaving it up to Brian May and Roger Taylor to collect the award. Instead, Freddie spent the rest of August and early September planning his 40th birthday. By now fully ensconced in Garden Lodge, he decided to hold a 'Mad Hat' party for his closest friends on Sunday 7th September, but first, on Friday 5th, the actual date of his birthday, he celebrated with Jim Hutton, who gave him a gold wedding ring as a present. However, while Freddie would wear the ring around the house, he always took it off in public.

A few days later, he and Jim Hutton took off on the holiday of a lifetime, an extended trip to Japan that cost over £1m.[4] Travelling first class all the way, they began in Tokyo, where Freddie delighted in outlandish shopping sprees and by the time they left the city, he had spent £250,000.[5] The two of them then travelled to the ancient city of Kyoto to visit the Golden Palace and then on to Osaka, where Freddie was determined to visit a department store that had a large collection of koi (he was transforming his garden at Garden Lodge into a Japanese garden complete with a pool for koi carp). As they continued their tour of Japan, so Freddie continued his spending: over £½m[6] was spent in one visit to a store specialising in lacquerwork. Over the course of the next few months all of these items would be carefully shipped back to Freddie's London home at additional expense to take pride of place in Garden Lodge.

Despite the flight back being delayed and re-routed via Alaska and Munich, the holiday had been an incredible experience for both Freddie and Jim, and Jim recalled it being full of romance. But when Freddie stepped off the plane at Heathrow, his mood darkened as he discovered that *The News of the World* had run a story under the headline of 'Queen Star Freddie in AIDS Shock' a few days previously. *The Sun*'s Hugh Whittow was at Heathrow when Freddie's plane landed and tried to question the singer about the allegations in *The News of the World* story that Freddie, registered under his real name of Farrokh Bulsara, had had his blood examined at an AIDS clinic in London's Harley Street under an alias.

'Do I look as though I am dying?' Freddie snapped back, 'I'm perfectly fit and healthy, thank you. I don't know what anybody has said. It's all so silly. Of course I'm concerned about my health, isn't everybody? I've had a wonderful time in Japan but now I've got to put up with this rubbish. It makes me feel sick. Now go away and leave me alone.'[7]

When they got home, Jim couldn't help but notice that the allegations had touched a nerve within Freddie, but the singer told him categorically that he hadn't been tested. Nevertheless, Jim already had concerns about the health of his boyfriend as 'before we met he'd done more than his fair share of living the fast-lane life of a successful rock star: all sex, drugs and rock and roll, with a string of one-night-stand strangers.'[8]

Hiding behind the walls of Garden Lodge, Freddie barely ventured out for the rest of the year. But if he thought by doing so he could weather the storm, he was badly mistaken. On 11th November 1986, Freddie discovered that John Murphy, the airline steward he had had a one-night stand with in the US a few years before, had died of an AIDS-related illness, soon followed by the death of Murphy's lover, James Wynethorpe, also from an AIDS-related illness. And if that wasn't bad enough, a few weeks later, Freddie received a phone call to inform him that his ex-boyfriend, with whom he'd had a two-year relationship, Tony Bastin, had also passed away from the disease, aged only 35.

Freddie must have been truly devastated and frightened. One by one, those he had loved and those he hadn't but with whom he had had sex were dying of this terrifying disease. He couldn't ignore the fact that the circle of friends around him was getting smaller and smaller, and he spent the last weeks of 1986 holed up and helpless in his London mansion with the oblivious Jim Hutton, surrounded by his beloved cats and countless framed photographs of those important in his life.

Freddie, allegedly, had a further ten HIV tests in 1986 after his initial test in 1985, the one that, in all likelihood, was positive. With doctors obliged to tell him that the reliability of the test was not 100 per cent, Freddie continued to have them, desperately, in the hope that one would be negative. He continued showing signs of being exposed to the virus, and these tests were indicating as much, but as yet no test fully confirmed without doubt that he had the virus. Any result that showed him not to be HIV+ would be the one he accepted. He had these continual tests clinging to the vain hope that one would give him the negative result he was so desperate for. But every single one of them came back positive that he had been exposed to the virus. And each time they came back positive, they reduced the likelihood of a future negative result. Sooner or later, he would have to accept one of these tests as true. Freddie knew what that meant, and he knew what the outcome was going to be, but still he told no one.

'We talked about other people dying but not about us,' remembers Peter Straker. 'He never talked about those things.'[9]

The one thing Freddie didn't know was how much time he was likely to have left. Somewhere and sometime in the early 1980s he had crossed some kind of invisible line: he had been exposed to the virus and was HIV positive. The certainty then was that it would lead to AIDS. He had so much he wanted to do, so much creativity to express, but it may well have been dawning on him that his days were numbered, unless he could find a treatment.

Freddie was luckier than most. His financial clout meant that he could seek out treatments anywhere in the world, whether they were tested or experimental. And there suddenly seemed to be hope. Across the Atlantic in the US, the drug AZT appeared to be having remarkable effects. Wellcome announced at a press conference towards the end of 1986 that they had been conducting tests that had been so successful that the 24-week trial they had planned had been halted after 16 weeks for 'ethical' reasons. During the tests, a group of patients already ill with AIDS or ARC (AIDS-related complex) were given either AZT or a placebo. Mortality rates among those taking AZT were staggeringly lower than those taking the placebo: 19 people from the 137 taking the placebo had died but there had only been one death among the 145 taking AZT. In addition, those on AZT also had a decreased number of opportunistic infections and showed improvement in weight gain and T4 cell counts. Wellcome agreed, in response to pressure from some sectors of the gay community, that if AZT was effective, then dying people should be taken off the placebo at once.[10]

Such an undertaking, to be a guinea pig, is not without risks. Drug trial participants affectionately know it as 'the court of last chances'. A breakthrough appeared to have been made and the results were exciting, although no one claimed AZT was a cure. For tens of thousands of AIDS patients across the globe, potential treatments appeared just around the corner.

It seemed that AIDS might be stopped.

As 1986 drew to a close, with Freddie taking refuge behind the walls of Garden Lodge, Queen released *Live Magic*, a compilation album featuring performances of 15 songs from their recent UK and European tour. Although it reached number 3 in the UK album charts, the record received strong criticism from many fans owing to the extensive editing that was evident on a number of tracks, including the removal of the opera section from 'Bohemian Rhapsody'. The UK was the only territory where the album broke into the Top 10 and it wasn't even released in the US, where the band's popularity appeared to be at an all-time low.[1]

Queen had decided to take 1987 off, to rest, recuperate, and focus on solo projects. This allowed Freddie to begin the year by throwing himself into continuing the recording sessions he had started the previous November at Townhouse Studios in west London. He began work in January on a number of songs including a cover version of 'The Great Pretender', which had been a number 1 hit for The Platters in 1956.

Freddie might not have been working with Brian, John and Roger during these sessions, but he had another close collaborator in Mike Moran. The two of them had met during the recording of material for Dave Clark's *Time* and had struck up a close friendship. Moran had been one of the most in-demand musicians and songwriters of the 1970s and 1980s and ended up writing with Freddie as well as co-producing Mercury's rendition of 'The Great Pretender'.

'He [Freddie] had been attracted to the number, because apart from really liking it, it was very him,' says Moran.[2]

'Most of the stuff I do is pretending,' said Freddie. 'It's like acting. I go on stage and pretend to be a macho man and all those things. I think *The Great Pretender* is a great title for what I do because I *am* The Great Pretender!'[3]

With the song recorded, Freddie began shooting the video at Battersea Studios. Directed by David Mallett, who had directed previous Queen videos such as 'Radio Ga Ga' and the controversial 'I Want

Mineshaft in New York was once the most notorious members-only gay sex club in history. It was open from Wednesday night through to Monday morning. After the outbreak of AIDS, Mineshaft was closed down by the city authorities.

Freddie had limited ability on the guitar, which ironically helped him to compose one of Queen's biggest hits, 'Crazy Little Thing Called Love'. It took him ten minutes to write, 'because I was restricted, knowing only a few chords… and because of that restriction I wrote a good song, I think.'

The summer of 1982 saw Queen travel to North America to promote their new album, *Hot Space*. Taking a break in New York, Freddie likely contracted HIV here.

1986 saw Queen's final tour with Freddie. He was heard to let slip the comment, 'I'm not going to be doing this forever. This is probably the last time.'

This chance encounter at the Ivor Novello Awards in 1987 would be the only time Annie Lennox would meet Freddie Mercury. His death four years later would profoundly affect her: 'He was so full of life... It made me stop and think about what is important, and what each of us could do to fight this terrible disease.'

South America saw Queen set and then break their own world record for most paying fans attending a concert. In 1985, they performed to an estimated crowd of more than 350,000, more than doubling their previous record of 131,000.

© DENIS O'REGAN

Chatting backstage with David Bowie at Live Aid in 1985. Freddie's performance helped Queen steal the show before an international audience of a billion people, and put their career firmly back on track.

© DENIS O'REGAN

'When I come off stage it takes me hours to unwind and transform back into my real self.'

Hollywood heartthrob, Rock Hudson, kept his homosexuality secret for decades, fearing that coming out would be career suicide. During Hudson's last months, Freddie had his first AIDS test. He claimed the results were negative.

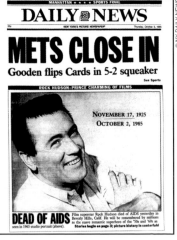

© NY DAILY NEWS

Freddie with Jim Hutton after performing at Live Aid, despite the advice of doctors. He had likely been HIV positive for three years and was now suffering from a severe throat infection.

Freddie had mentioned his admiration of Spanish opera diva, Montserrat Caballé, during a radio interview in 1986. Freddie and Mike Moran composed a number of operatic pieces that formed the programme for Freddie's final live performance in October 1988.

'I pray I'll never get AIDS. So many friends have it. Some have died, others won't last much longer. I'm terrified that I'll be the next.'

This photograph by the acclaimed photographer Richard Young is an intimate portrait of Freddie. The facial wastage is no longer apparent as he had subjected himself to injectable dermafilla, which gave him more confidence.

'In ten years' time I certainly won't be wearing the same costumes and running around on stage. I don't know what I'll be doing then, but I know one thing... I'll still be having a good time.'

Freddie's final public appearance in February 1990, at the British Phonographic Awards, shocked those watching. The only words he spoke were, 'Thank you, goodnight,' as he walked off stage for the final time.

A party to celebrate Queen's 20th anniversary was held at The Groucho Club. Freddie struggled with the attention and quickly became tired.

Following a long meeting with Queen manager Jim Beach, Freddie decided to release a statement confirming he had AIDS. Less than twenty-four hours later, Freddie Mercury was dead.

4 Sunday Sport November 24, 1991

Rock star confirms tragic secret

MERCURY: I HAVE AIDS

ROCK superstar Freddie Mercury last night finally confessed to the world that he IS suffering from AIDS.

The 45-year-old Queen lead singer issued a surprise statement to the Press Association news agency in London, ending weeks of speculation about his health.

Positive

Freddie told newsmen: "Following the enormous conjecture in the Press over the last two weeks I wish to confirm that I have tested HIV positive and have AIDS."

Freddie said he had to speak out for the sake of his millions of fans who've

> By GARY THOMPSON

dramatic weight loss over the last few months.

He has not been seen in public for the last nine weeks.

His statement went on: "I felt it correct to keep this information private to date in order to protect the privacy of those around me.

"However, the time has now come for my friends and fans around the world to know the truth and I hope that everyone will join with me, my doctors and all those worldwide in the fight against this terrible disease.

"My privacy has always been very special to me and I am famous for my lack of interviews.

'When I'm dead I want to be remembered as a musician of some worth and substance. I don't know how they will remember me... It's up to them. When I'm dead, who cares? I don't!'

In the Spring of 1991, Freddie posed for his boyfriend, Jim Hutton, in his garden. The last photo of him, Freddie would die almost six months later.

'I want to reach as many people as I can, and the more the merrier. As far as I'm concerned I'd like the whole world to listen to my music and I'd like everybody to listen to me and look at me when I'm playing on stage.'

To Break Free', the video began with Freddie emerging dramatically from behind curtains, clean-shaven and dressed in a pink suit. He then performs the song as he descends a giant stairway while scenes from previous iconic Queen videos are re-staged and inter-cut within the main body of the song. Freddie also appears in drag as one of three backing singers (the other two being Roger Taylor and Peter Straker) and the video ends with Freddie, still in his pink David Chambers suit, finishing his walk down the grand staircase, which is flanked by 100 cardboard cut-outs of himself.

The video, costing £100,000[4] took three days to film and proved to be one of Freddie's most popular videos, just as the song proved to be his biggest solo hit during his lifetime, peaking at number 4 in the UK singles chart. 'The Great Pretender' was also a record that perfectly commented on his life at that point. It couldn't have been a coincidence that Freddie chose to sing this song; he knew very well the subtext of his choice of record and was well aware that he was interpreting the lyrics in a way that differed from their original meaning. In doing so they spoke volumes about his life and circumstances.

'I thought that you could take it a lot further in, just in the word "pretender",' he told journalist and friend David Wigg in 1987. Freddie would say in the same interview that the video was 'tongue-in-cheek' and showed that 'the images I've portrayed over the years is a kind of pretense'.

But when the video is combined with the song, and its lyrics ('Oh yes, I'm the great pretender / Pretending I'm doing well / My need is such, I pretend too much / I'm lonely but no one can tell'), it's hard to escape the thought that Freddie is once more laying himself bare, and in a much less subtle way than a song such as 'Bohemian Rhapsody', in which his message of 'coming out' is layered beneath a complex masterpiece of songwriting. Here, in 'The Great Pretender', he is opening himself up, telling all who want to listen that his life has been one great deceit. But it's not only Freddie Mercury, the performer, who is 'The Great Pretender', it's Freddie Mercury, the man. After all, even his name is not his own. And he was always reluctant to discuss his upbringing in Zanzibar, almost as though it never existed. Then there's the pretence over his sexuality; his denial that he was gay, his life with

Mary Austin, his subsequent bisexuality that developed into his desire to embrace the gay scenes in cities around the world. This pretence continued with his desire for a loving relationship; yet a lifestyle that was consumed by one-night stands and promiscuity was at odds with this and, even when he was in a seemingly stable relationship with Jim Hutton, Freddie would cheat on him and demand to be photographed with Mary Austin at official functions, thereby erasing Jim's very existence publicly for the cameras.

For over a decade Freddie had kept his homosexuality secret, and had worked hard to ensure it remained so. That, up until 1986, was arguably the greatest pretence of all, and now he was faced with an even bigger secret: that he was HIV positive (in an interview in 2000, Mary Austin states that, at the time of his death, Freddie had lived with the knowledge he was HIV positive for seven years, meaning the early HIV tests he took in 1984 were definitely positive and his comments subsequently, that they were negative, were deceit and denial on his part).[5]

In 1987, 'The Great Pretender' was the one song – the *only* song – that summed up Freddie Mercury. The great irony was, just as in his final weeks with the song, 'These Are The Days Of Our Lives' written by Roger Taylor, it took somebody else to compose a song for Freddie that actually let him speak of his inner demons. Freddie Mercury could never have written 'The Great Pretender', but there was no one else for whom a song was so perfectly written.

With 'The Great Pretender' riding high in the charts, Freddie spent much of February and March in the studio working on new material with Mike Moran, rarely venturing out in public. The allegations made in *The News of the World* that he had taken an AIDS test under his birth name meant that his distrust of the British press was now at an all-time high. With the exception of an appearance on a German television show in early March, Freddie didn't undertake any publicity to promote 'The Great Pretender'. But that was the way he wanted it.

As far as Freddie was concerned, there was a much more pressing musical engagement that demanded his attention. In August of 1986, while in Spain, Freddie had mentioned his admiration of the Spanish opera singer Montserrat Caballé during a television interview. Now, in March 1987, the various cogs of the music industry had turned enough to arrange a meeting between Freddie and Caballé to discuss the possibility of working together.

'I came home late one night,' recalls Mike Moran, 'and then Fred phoned me in the early hours of the morning and said, "You'll never guess what happened. I got home and there was a message from Caballé and she wants to meet me. We're going to Barcelona next week and you're coming as well."'[6]

Freddie was extremely nervous about meeting the great operatic diva on 24th March at the Ritz Hotel in Barcelona. He had flown out the day before with Mike Moran, Peter Freestone and Jim Beach, and was so wracked with nerves that the next morning, he suggested they flee Barcelona without meeting Caballé. The opera star arrived late, a trait she was notorious for, and when the two of them were introduced there was an icy and awkward silence. At first Freddie was incredibly shy and actually intimidated by Caballé, but a glass of Louis Roederer Cristal champagne helped to get conversation flowing and they soon discovered they shared a sense of humour, which put Freddie at ease: 'I wasn't sure how to behave or what I should say to her. Thankfully she made me feel very at ease right from the start and I realized that both of us had the same kind of humour,' recalled Freddie. 'It was great. She jokes and she swears and she doesn't take herself too seriously. That really thrilled and surprised me because up until then I had been laboring under the illusion that all great opera singers were stern, aloof and quite intimidating.'[7]

Before long, Freddie took the plunge and instructed Peter Freestone to play the tape of the song, 'Exercises In Free Love', that he and Mike Moran had written for her and which he had brought with him. 'So Fred played this thing and she gave it her full attention,' recalls Moran, 'and at the end of it there was a bit of silence and then she said, "I love it and I will give it its world premiere in Covent Garden in three weeks' time," and then she smacked me on the shoulder and said, "and you will play."'[8]

True to her word, Caballé performed 'Exercises In True Love' for the first time in public at Covent Garden, with Mike Moran accompanying her on piano and with Freddie in the audience. 'We came out and did our thing and afterwards, Caballé and Carlos were invited to Garden Lodge for a dinner,' recalls Moran. 'Carlos, her brother, left, but she didn't want to leave, she was having too good a time, and as Carlos left, he said, "Look, she's got to leave for the airport at five or six in the morning as she's got to fly to Buenos Aires and please don't keep her too late."

'At one point after dinner she said, "Let's go and sing around the piano," and so I got on the piano and the two of them were warbling away and it was just a singsong, to be honest, and she said, "Shall we sing some of your music, Freddie?" So we went through a few things and then sang songs from the shows and then she said, "This is such good fun, it's not the stifling constraints I have at grand opera or a vocal recital. It would be really fabulous if we could do something together so why don't you write something for us to do together?" and so Freddie said, "I'm sure we could do that," but in the middle said, "Look, I promised your brother I wouldn't keep you too long." And she turned around and said, "Are you trying to get rid of me? I'll decide when I'm tired and I want to go." So we carried on for a bit longer and eventually she left.'[9]

'It was wonderful, a great night,' recalls Peter Straker. 'We just carried on until about six or seven in the morning. She'd had a few!'[10]

When Caballé left the following morning, Freddie and Mike Moran began work on material, with Freddie shelving plans of another solo record in favour of a potential album with the opera superstar. 'So we started out one day at Garden Lodge and I thought, how do we start this thing? I said to Freddie, "Let's just have a title," and he said, "We met in Barcelona. Let's call it Barcelona so we know what we're talking about. It was the first time we met." I said, "That's not a bad line – 'Barcelona, it was the first time that we met'. Let's make it a story about how you met." So that was how we started to do it and it took a while to refine because what people are not aware of is that there was no template for this. This was a real original. It was way before opera or classical music became populist.'[11]

Freddie and Mike spent most of April and May at Townhouse Studios, working on material for Caballé. However, their schedule was dictated by that of Caballé, who, like most great opera stars, had her diary booked up for five years in advance.

And Freddie didn't have five years.

41

After the highs of meeting Montserrat Caballé, and beginning work on music for her, in April 1987 Freddie received the shattering news he had been dreading, but had been expecting too.

Earlier in the month Freddie had had a biopsy performed on a lesion on his shoulder by his doctor. He had undergone 12 AIDS tests up to this point and while, in all likelihood, they resulted in positive outcomes, it is probable that all were blood tests in various forms and, as such, Freddie's doctors were obliged to point out, somewhat optimistically, that none were 100 per cent reliable. It had been this faint slither of doubt and hope that Mercury hung on to. But the biopsy confirmed what he must have known all along. The results showed that the lesion on Freddie's shoulder was Kaposi's sarcoma, which usually occurs no less than three years after initial infection but more likely around five to seven years, which brings us back to 1982 as the time of infection, almost certainly when he was in New York that summer.

Freddie must have known that a positive diagnosis of AIDS was inevitable. His doctors had noted for some time that his lymph nodes had become swollen and this had been accompanied by weight loss of more than 10 per cent. He had also complained of fatigue and frequent night sweats and had suffered mouth ulcers and throat infections. Everything pointed towards AIDS, but it took this biopsy to confirm it. Ultimately, his GP, Dr Gordon Atkinson, explained that the disease had progressed beyond HIV and had manifested into AIDS.

When Dr Atkinson initially told Freddie he had AIDS, he asked him how long he had known that he was positive. Freddie didn't answer but immediately sought a second opinion from another doctor, who did a blood test and another excisional biopsy of the Kaposi's sarcoma. This doctor also confirmed the same result: Freddie's HIV had developed into AIDS, the final stage of HIV infection after the immune system has become so compromised it can no longer fight off other infections. Before he left, Freddie asked how long he had left. The doctor responded by telling him there was no way of knowing for sure and said, perhaps three years, maybe a little longer.

Having received the shattering news, Mercury immediately sought the expertise of two specialists. Dr Richard C.D. Staughton, a dermatologist at the Lister Hospital on Chelsea Bridge Road, who was also the dermatologist to HRH Queen Elizabeth II, began to treat Freddie's Kaposi's sarcoma, which had spread rapidly and formed scattered skin lesions over parts of Mercury's face and body. These were treated initially by being injected with local chemotherapy, sprayed with radiation or removed through incision and extraction. As a result, these procedures would, over the next few years, subtly change the contour of his face. Alongside Dr Staughton, Freddie was looked after by Dr Brian Gazzard, one of Britain's most prominent AIDS physicians. Gazzard, who first met Mercury at his home, did not know the identity of the star, and upon his arrival famously whispered to him: 'I don't know what you do, but you are obviously quite successful at it.'[1]

Due to the veil of secrecy that shrouded his case, Mercury received medical attention outside regular hours. Terry Giddings, Freddie's chauffeur and bodyguard, provided security during those discreet hospital visits. He states: 'I used to take Fred there at six o'clock in the morning or very late at night. Obviously, Fred did not want to be seen having treatment, so I went there in advance to figure out the route and point of entry. Upon our arrival, I would park the car at the back. Fred would be wearing a big hat and coat, and we would go in through the maintenance door.'[2]

Peter Straker, a regular visitor to Garden Lodge, recalls these unusual early-morning departures by Freddie: 'When I was staying at his house a couple of times he would get up early in the morning and he would be out and I'd look down from the window and I'd see him going off with Terry in the car, so he was going off to get some blood thing and he would be there for hours and then come back in the afternoon and go to sleep. Everything was a bit secretive at this stage, with all the going off to the hospital.'[3]

While at the Chelsea & Westminster Hospital, Freddie would receive treatments to slow the rate at which his body deteriorated. Although he was aware that the treatments would not save his life, statistical data demonstrated that they had the potential to delay his death. One AIDS research specialist states: 'If we look at the clinical trial data with those drugs, they certainly provided evidence of benefit but the evidence and benefit was transient. The main measure that would be examined for treatment response at that time was to look at changes in CD4 count, a measure of the immune system's function. This is on a scale from zero, which is the lowest it can be (effectively a complete breakdown of the immune system), through to greater than 450, which is in the normal range. When someone would start one of these new medications, you would often see a rise of fifty to sixty cells, which might last for a year to eighteen months.'[4]

Freddie could not contend with the social, physical and emotional pressures that AIDS imposed upon his life alone, and therefore would later turn to his closest friends for support, people such as Jim Hutton, Peter Freestone, Mary Austin and Joe Fanelli. These people provided him with medical and nursing assistance, compassion to ease the psychological burden of being terminally ill, inspiration to create and record music, and refuge and reprieve from the menacing paparazzi.

No one had been cured of AIDS so far and the statistics were distressing. Life expectancy in 1986 was just 13 months from the onset of full-blown AIDS. A great many people don't make it that far. Someone like Freddie, with a strong constitution, access to drugs and a great diet – meaning nourishment – was more likely to make it to 18 months. The very fortunate then might last another year. To last three years would be a triumph. He was not young, but then again he was not old. However, to have AIDS was the black mark. But Freddie's lifelong inner strength and determination bought him extra time. His approach was, I'm going to beat this. He had played a role all his life: the singer, the performer, the star. So why not play a role now?

Yet the truth was that Freddie could no longer hide his condition. At least from those close to him. His Kaposi's sarcoma was now visible on his face. He was desperate to tell Jim – after all, not only was Jim his partner, but they had been having unprotected sex throughout their relationship and it was impossible to ignore the fact that Freddie had exposed him to the virus. But Jim had flown back to Ireland to spend Easter with his mother.

Jim had never told his family he was gay, let alone informed them that he was in a relationship with Freddie Mercury, and although he suspected his family knew of his sexual orientation, it was never discussed. Jim's mother lived in rural Ireland and didn't have a telephone in her house and so in a time before mobile phones if Jim wanted to phone or receive a call from Freddie it was a four-mile trek to the nearest phone box.

The day before he was due to fly back to London, Jim walked to the phone box to call Freddie and immediately sensed something was wrong: 'The doctors have just taken a big lump out of me,' Freddie told a concerned Jim, but refused to elaborate, saying he'd tell him all he needed to know once he got home.[5] The following day, when Jim arrived back at Garden Lodge, he found Freddie in bed and when they cuddled up together, he showed Jim the mark on his shoulder where the biopsies had been performed before telling him that the doctors had done a test and confirmed he had AIDS.

Jim refused to accept the news, suggesting Freddie get a second opinion, unaware that he had already *had* a second opinion and had failed 12 HIV tests over the past few years. Freddie told Jim that he understood if he wanted to leave and move out of Garden Lodge, but Jim was having none of it: 'But I love you,' he reassured Freddie. 'I'm not going to walk out on you – now or ever. Let's not talk about it any more.'[6]

Jim refused to take an AIDS test himself, despite Freddie suggesting he should, for fear of proving to be HIV positive himself and therefore making Freddie feel guilty in the knowledge he'd probably given it to his lover. It wasn't what their relationship needed at that point, and it proved to be the last time they referred directly to Freddie's AIDS condition, the only concession in their relationship being that they practised safe sex from that moment on.

Apart from Jim, Freddie only told Mary Austin, Peter Freestone and Joe Fanelli at Garden Lodge, and Queen's manager, Jim Beach, about his condition but stipulated it had to be kept secret from everybody else for the time being, including his parents: 'He protected us by never discussing these matters,' his mother, Jer Bulsara, later revealed. 'It is quite different now, but back then it would have been very hard for him to tell us and we respected his feelings.'[7]

Peter Freestone remembers: '[Once he contracted HIV] he never, ever spent time talking to me, wondering where he got it, which country, which city. It was a fact, it was happening. He knew he was going to die, so why waste time regretting?'[8]

His bandmates in Queen were another matter altogether, though. They had only just won an Ivor Novello Award for Outstanding Contribution to British Music, but Freddie took the decision to inform only Jim Beach of his condition, under the proviso it was kept a secret. Brian May, Roger Taylor and John Deacon were not told. He felt he had to tell Beach; the band were under contract for a number of albums and who knows what the reaction might have been from record companies if they knew Freddie was living on borrowed time? Then there was the public reaction. How would they receive the news that Freddie Mercury had AIDS? Would there be backlash? Would Freddie and Queen become pariahs within the music industry? Freddie had a responsibility not only to himself, but also to his three colleagues in Queen; they were a multi-million-pound business that many other employees depended upon within their organisations. If Freddie was to announce he had AIDS, which, by its very nature in 1987, would mean him revealing his homosexuality, the damage could be enormous – and not just to Freddie. The only way forward, as he saw it, was to keep his battle with AIDS a secret and hopefully find a cure somewhere in the world.

In the meantime, he would throw himself into his work, beginning with writing a number of songs for his proposed album with Montserrat Caballé, and maintain the façade of an untroubled persona to the world. Although he had somewhat hidden away from public life, always the London paparazzi were keen to photograph him, especially in light of the allegations made in *The News of the World*. It was crucial that those around him suspected nothing. As far as Freddie was concerned, he would take sanctuary either at home or in a recording studio and make the most of what time he had left out of the glare of the public eye.

'Freddie was still being seen by his inner circle,' says Paul Gambaccini, 'but people on the periphery, like myself, were jettisoned as he concentrated on the hard core. And I think he was someone who was self-conscious enough not to want to be seen past his best, unless it was someone he had to see or really wanted to see.'[9]

But if Freddie thought he could sustain staying out of the public eye, then he was wrong. On 4th May 1987, *The Sun* ran a story across three pages under the headline: 'AIDS Kills Freddie's Two Lovers'. As well as detailing the deaths of Tony Bastin and John Murphy, the story also contained a number of lurid and scandalous claims by Paul Prenter, whom Freddie had sacked just a few months previously. One of the claims was that Freddie had actually phoned Prenter late at night on 29th April in a panic that he had AIDS. Prenter also named Jim Hutton as Freddie's lover, described how the singer drank excessive amounts of vodka and took lines of cocaine with Rod Stewart and David Bowie, revealed the hundreds of men Freddie had slept with, provided photos of a number of Freddie's lovers to be splashed all over the pages and even revealed the reason for Freddie falling out with Kenny Everett. (According to Prenter, Everett had accused Freddie of overindulging too much in the comedian's hospitality, meaning cocaine, but other sources suggest it was the other way around. Everett and Freddie never made peace with each other and never saw or spoke to each other again. Everett died in 1995 like Freddie, of an AIDS-related illness.)

Freddie was furious about Prenter's betrayal of him and grew increasingly angry with each new revelation. It turned out that Prenter was paid £32,000[10] to dish the dirt and he even had the nerve to call Garden Lodge following the revelations in the hope he could convince Freddie that his excuse for selling the stories was simply that the press were hounding him. But Freddie wasn't prepared to listen to any excuses, and most certainly wasn't prepared to talk to a traitor such as Prenter.

If Freddie was already retreating behind the walls of Garden Lodge, he was now putting up barriers around himself. He wondered who he could truly trust, whom he could confide in, and from that moment on made barely any new friends for the rest of his life.

42

Despite the protection afforded by the walls of Garden Lodge, Freddie decided he needed to get away and so headed off to Ibiza in May 1987 with Jim Hutton, Peter Freestone, Joe Fanelli and Terry Giddins, as well as a supply of medicine. As usual, they all stayed at Pike's Hotel and spent the days lounging by the pool or playing tennis (during one game Freddie developed a wound on the bottom of his right foot that did not heal for the remainder of his life and would cause him excruciating pain, which made walking difficult). Even in Ibiza, *The Sun* newspaper was still stalking Freddie and managed to get a photo of him playing tennis. Yet they were unsuccessful in photographing him with Jim Hutton, which was one of their goals. The owner of Pike's Hotel, Tony Pike, remembers well this visit by Freddie and his entourage: 'By this time, rumours had begun circulating that Freddie had AIDS – but then you don't ask a friend if he is terminally ill, and no one ever spoke about it. It was just not discussed. Those around him would have categorically denied it anyway.'[1]

But Freddie wasn't simply in Ibiza to escape from the press back home in England: he had a professional engagement on the island. At the end of May, as part of the Ibiza 92 Festival, he would make a surprise appearance with Montserrat Caballé at San Antonio's Ku Club, where the two of them would treat the audience of 6,000 to a premiere, although mimed, of their new duet, 'Barcelona', which would also be filmed. 'The song "Barcelona" basically describes his [Freddie's] admiration of Montserrat, whom he saw as the embodiment of not only her native city but the spirit of a people,' recalls Peter Freestone.[2]

When Freddie and Montserrat stepped on-stage, no one in the audience quite knew what to expect, and for Freddie, he felt as though he was in a dream: 'Just before we went on-stage I couldn't help wondering if all this was really happening to me,' he said. 'And though I knew I was taking a big chance doing something like that, it gave me such a fantastic rush.'[3]

As the song began, the whole audience hushed and remained silent for the entire rendition before bursting into spontaneous applause as it ended. People rose to their feet, waved their arms and cheered loudly. It was said audience members were even heard to exclaim that it should become the new Spanish national anthem. Freddie's operatic debut with Montserrat Caballé had been an overwhelming success and it was subsequently chosen to be the anthem for the 1992 Barcelona Olympics.

But Freddie's appearance at the Ku Club attracted more speculation from old friends and colleagues. One of the groups performing was Marillion, and lead singer Fish told author Laura Jackson of the shock he felt when he paid a visit to see Freddie: 'I thought I'd go see him and say "How ya doin'?" you know, and he was, like, really drawn. There were about three or four close friends in the dressing room with him, and it was like someone had fuckin' died! I thought, something really heavy is going down here, and I'm not part of it. So I got out of there fast. At the time the people around him were saying things like, he's got a kidney complaint or a liver problem – stuff like that. But having glimpsed some of Freddie's excesses, it wasn't so hard to put two and two together.'4

Freddie was having trouble hiding the telltale signs of the Kaposi's sarcoma that was beginning to show on his hands and his face. He used make-up wherever possible, but that only drew attention to the blemishes, however well he hid them. One of those attending the after-show party at the Ku Club was Freddie's old lover and friend from Munich, Barbara Valentin. She hadn't seen him for a while but immediately observed the marks on his face and hands.

'Freddie and I never spoke about his HIV and AIDS,' she said, 'but he knew that I knew.'5 Realising what the blemishes were, Barbara did all she could to ensure other people didn't see them and draw their own conclusions: 'I said nothing but took Freddie away with me to another room and used my heavy professional make-up on him to make him look better.'6

Another person attending the party that night was the Spanish promoter, Pino Sagliocco. He had helped secure the partnership between Freddie and Caballé, but the Freddie he now saw was a man already exhibiting signs of illness: 'There was an incredible party afterwards, and everyone had a good time, but I think we already knew then that Freddie was sick. He was not telling anyone anything, but as soon as he arrived we saw that he had begun to get these strange blemishes on his face. We were told it was his liver, and, of course, he did drink too much – but all those spots?'[7]

Freddie headed back to London after the Ibiza performance and spent the rest of the summer pottering about in his home and tending to the garden with Jim Hutton, who by now had left his job at The Savoy and was officially employed as Freddie's 'gardener' on £600 per month. During the summer of 1987, Barbara Valentin visited Freddie and Jim at Garden Lodge. She was shocked to see that the blemishes from Kaposi's sarcoma were increasing in number, even though Freddie had laser treatment to try and diminish their appearance, and he also now had a painful wound on his right leg as well as the foot problem following his tennis injury in Ibiza.

All too often, when treating AIDS patients during a time when much was still unknown about the condition, certain symptoms, specifically diarrhoea, fever, weight loss and anaemia, were simply attributed to AIDS and not investigated further. In fact, such symptoms could frequently be made better and more bearable and, more often than not, they were caused by simple and treatable conditions. Freddie had access to this level of care from the doctors and specialists he surrounded himself with; they didn't steadfastly attribute the symptoms and conditions to AIDS and, therefore, did not consider them to be untreatable. Instead they sought to investigate further and do whatever they could to make any symptoms bearable, refusing to blindly associate them with AIDS. This provision of general support, including attention to nutrition and mental health and other issues, are areas of patient management that are, as a whole, extremely costly, both in terms of finance and in terms of time. While he could easily afford the treatments financially, in order to have the best treatment Freddie needed to devote his time to attending the Chelsea & Westminster Hospital. And time was what he couldn't afford. In addition was the stark reality that the more time he would spend at the hospital the greater the risk of his secret getting out. The press was already on his back, eager for any snippet of gossip and he simply couldn't take the risk of being spotted undergoing treatment at the hospital. Therefore, he restricted the amount of time he spent there, only attending when absolutely necessary.

One of the first drugs made available to him would be AZT. It was supposed to be the wonderdrug for AIDS in 1987 when it became available on prescription for the first time. AZT was a US Government approved treatment that was marketed under the name of Retrovir. It had been developed in California since 1985 and was hailed as a major breakthrough in the battle against HIV/AIDS. When licensed for use in 1987, demand for it was enormous. As the journalist Simon Garfield wrote: 'By then, Aids patients had grown so desperate that they would sample any of the bootlegged underground therapies, some of which were probably life-threatening. With the arrival of AZT, doctors who had been powerless for so long against a syndrome about which they knew so little, at last had something they could give their patients that had passed stringent official tests.'[8]

AZT didn't profess to be a cure for HIV/AIDS, but its producers did claim it could keep those with HIV/AIDS alive for longer, in which time, it was hoped, a cure or a vaccine for the disease might be found. Except AZT wasn't all it was cracked up to be. Back in 1984, when the onset of AIDS was beginning to suggest a worldwide pandemic, drugs companies around the world raced to find a drug that could fight the disease. Although only 3,000 people had been diagnosed with AIDS, predictions were suggesting that hundreds of thousands might have it and that millions were potentially at risk. For any drugs company finding a treatment or preventative medicine for this proposed pandemic, the potential financial rewards appeared astronomical.

In June 1984, Wellcome began intensive research and mass-tested numerous anti-viral compounds, but one appeared to work and inhibit viruses in animal cells. Its name was AZT. However, they needed to test it on humans, and such a procedure could be fatal. What's more, the usual testing period for a drug is around eight years, but after just 20 months, AZT was on the market. It was fast-tracked through, with the hopes of everybody connected with AIDS riding on it. However, it later emerged that the human phases of testing were a shambles, despite the fact that Wellcome stated in a press conference that they had been a huge success. Just a few months after AZT had been released, a journalist for *Native*, New York's gay newspaper, John Lauritsen, uncovered documents that showed a number of rules had been broken during the human testing of AZT and wrote, 'The trial had been "unblinded" within weeks: some patients claimed they could tell what they were taking by taste; others were so keen to have AZT that they pooled their treatment with other patients to increase their chances of receiving the drug.'[9]

But in 1987, with no knowledge of rules having been broken, AZT was heralded as the magic bullet. Filmmaker Derek Jarman took it, basketball-star Magic Johnson took it, dancer Rudolf Nureyev took it and, of course, Freddie Mercury took it. None of them knew that AZT would only work for a short while, perhaps a year at most, and then do more harm than good.[10] However, Freddie was experiencing the onset of AIDS, and the reality that the trial itself was ultimately flawed was not what people living with AIDS wanted to hear. Despite his doctors' cautionary warnings he was eager to try anything that might be of benefit.

In 1986 and 1987, before the scandal of the testing was discovered, Wellcome revelled in the part they appeared to play in the successful halt of AIDS, if not in curing the disease, then at least giving patients more time. And, financially, they did extraordinarily well out of AZT. In 1986, coincidentally the year of the AZT breakthrough, part of the Wellcome Foundation was floated on the stock market. Within a few months their share price had jumped from 73.5p to 374.5p following the news that AZT would be widely available in the US. Two years later, the share price had almost doubled to 724p and the company was making a profit of almost $10,000 per year on every patient. By 1993, their pre-tax profits were $505m.[11]

Those with AIDS weren't concerned about the money Wellcome was making from their condition; they just wanted medication. Freddie was no exception. He wanted a treatment, a cure, a vaccine... anything to stop AIDS. His fears weren't only the illness itself, but the anxiety of the public finding out. After all, as writer and political activist Susan Sontag wrote: 'It is not a mysterious affliction that seems to strike at random. Indeed, to get AIDS is precisely to be revealed, in the majority of cases so far, as a member of a certain "risk group," a community of pariahs.'[12]

In September 1987, Freddie was back in Ibiza to celebrate his 41st birthday with an extravagant party at Pike's Hotel. Freddie flew out

80 of his friends from London especially and despite the discovery that the planned Gaudí-themed birthday cake had collapsed in transit, he and his guests had a wonderful time as 350 bottles of Moët & Chandon were consumed. It was at this party that John Deacon had approached Jim Hutton to enquire, discreetly, what the marks were on Freddie's legs.

'I passed them off as nothing of importance,' recalled Hutton. '"He's allergic to the sun," I said, "they're sunspots." It was left at that. I put a brave face on it and hid my feelings so that John would not suspect that something was wrong.'[13]

Throughout the summer of 1987 there had been negotiations for Queen to get back into the studio in 1988, and none of the other members of the band had the slightest sense of Freddie's illness, despite Deacon's observations and questions at the Ibiza party. How much longer could Freddie keep his condition secret? And when, if ever, would he tell his bandmates?

'Freddie was not good with being as honest about his sexuality and his illness,' recalled Paul Gambaccini. 'He once said to me, "One day we'll do an interview that will shock the world," which I took to mean his coming-out interview, but he never gave it because Boy George came along and Boy George was open, so it wouldn't have been a big shock if Freddie had said, "Hey, hang on, I'm gay too!"'[14]

In the meantime, he had the release of 'Barcelona' on 27th October to occupy his mind. 'When we'd finished "Barcelona", he said, "Well, that's lovely, dear. I think we should put it out,"' recalls Mike Moran. 'Don't forget nothing like this had been done before and I remember saying to Fred, "Are you sure? It's a project, yes, but you want it to go out as a single?" There wasn't any question in Freddie's mind. He was proud of it; he thought it was worth the world at large listening to it. So it had to come out.'[15]

It was an unlikely Top 10 hit in the UK, reaching number 8 in the charts with John Shepherd writing of it in the *Continuum Encyclopedia of Popular Music of the World* that 'When Freddie Mercury and Montserrat Caballé duet "Barcelona", one hears not only the rock/classical dichotomy, but also the extent to which each singer can draw on elements in his/her own tradition to approach the other.'

While there might appear to be a distinctive contrast between the classical voice of Caballé and the rock voice of Mercury, a study indicates that Freddie's voice, particularly the way in which he could modulate the vibrato, was significantly faster than other rock stars and even professional classical singers. "Freddie Mercury was an incredibly skillful and versatile singer, capable of a wide range of artistic vocal expressions,"[16] says Dr. Christian Herbst who conducted the scientific study to determine why Freddie had a voice described as "a force of nature with the velocity of a hurricane."[17] The study, published in the journal *Logopedics Phoniatrics Vocology*, found that when Freddie spoke he had a median frequency of 117.3 Hz giving him a rich baritone voice, but when he sang his range went from 92.2 Hz to 784 Hz, meaning he was quite capable of hitting perfect notes from the booming low of F#2 to the high pitch G5, a range that covers a full three octaves.[18] In fact, such was the quality of Freddie's voice that Caballé even suggested a true classical duet. 'He had a baritone voice. I told him one day, "Let's do a small duet of baritone and soprano", and he said, "No, no, my fans only know me as a rock singer and they will not recognise my voice if I sing in baritone,"' said Caballé.[19]

Although not willing to contemplate this duet, for Freddie, there was no let-up in his work. Although he would sometimes slow down (Christmas and New Year of 1987 were quieter affairs than usual), he knew time was of the essence and he was determined to get in as much work as possible before he was forced to give up. The drugs and medication would give him time, but not much. His doctor said three years at the most – if he was lucky.

But Freddie appeared to also accept his mortality, as an interview with David Wigg in 1987 reveals. When Wigg asks Freddie: 'Do you ever worry that you could end up a lonely rich old man when you're seventy?' Freddie replies with, 'No, because I will be dead long before that, I tell you. I won't be there, darling. I'll be dead and gone, dear. I'll be fucking starting a new life somewhere else, dear.'[20]

But before then, Freddie had so much to do. And with the slight respite from his illness due to the AZT, it would begin with a new Queen album in 1988.

43

AIDS without end

Throughout 1987 the British Government, finally mobilised by the prospect of tens of thousands of its citizens becoming infected with AIDS, launched one of the most remarkable public health campaigns ever seen in post-war Britain. Accompanied by a chilling voice-over by actor John Hurt, the television and cinema ads were overt and threatening, characterised by the overpowering image of a tombstone inscribed with one word: AIDS. Additionally, leaflets were delivered to virtually every household in the UK.

The 'Don't Die of Ignorance' campaign attempted to make everyone in the UK in no doubt as to the dangers of unsafe sex. The first television advert in the UK for Durex condoms was broadcast the same year and, for the first time, condoms started being sold in public places. It seemed to work: from 1988 to 1992 in the UK condom use rose from 23 to 32 per cent, with the proportion of people reporting that they always used a condom with a casual partner more than doubling from 22 per cent in 1989 to 52 per cent in 1992, while across the Atlantic, data from US drug stores showed that condom sales had risen from 240m in 1986 to 299m in 1988.[1] However, one of the countries that failed to instigate a national campaign in the 1980s warning of the dangers of unprotected sex, France, was found in a 2009 UN programme to have over twice as many of its citizens living with AIDS as the UK.

It appeared that, by 1988, most of the world was waking up to AIDS.

Freddie Mercury, meanwhile, was visiting his GP, Dr Gordon Atkinson, for regular check-ups and continued seeing a number of other specialists, although he kept these details close and was reluctant to even talk to Jim Hutton about them. As it happened, thanks to his status and connections, he had fast-tracked more advanced drugs than most normal people had access to, in particular AZT. It seemed the best option open to him, perhaps in actuality the *only* option, and offered some form of hope while, at the same time, mentally dispelling despair. The main benefit of AZT, as Freddie and other users of the drug hoped, was that it would keep them alive long enough for a cure to be developed.

Freddie began taking AZT at the recommended dosage of 200mg five times a day, roughly every four hours. But this proved too high for him, as it did for many others who took AZT, some of whom died as a result of the higher dosage. Consequently, Freddie's daily dose was reduced from 1,000mg per day to 300–500mg per day. It proved just as effective and the benefits began to outweigh the side effects. AZT gave Freddie some genuine hope, as it did to most of those who took the drug, offering a tangible effect for a six- to nine-month period. It was only years later, when many of the people who had put their trust in the medication had died, that the true facts about AZT emerged.

With this initial respite, Freddie felt well enough to go back into the studio with his colleagues from Queen. The negotiations to create a new album had taken place during the latter part of 1987 when all four bandmates were coming to the end of a year off. Freddie and the rest of Queen moved into Townhouse Studios to begin work on their 13th studio album, which would be called *The Miracle*.

By the end of February, the band had recorded 22 songs, according to an interview with Roger Taylor, who went on to say, 'and it'll be the best album that Queen have done in ten years, easily. It's more back to the old style. I mean, it's almost like echoes of Led Zeppelin and everything in there. It's great and it's all live in the studio, which is great. It gives it more spark and energy, I think.'[2]

The band had also made a significant decision during the recording of the album. For the first time they decided to adopt collective writing credits to each track. 'When we came to make this album, we made a decision that we should have made fifteen years ago,' says Brian May. 'We decided that we'd write as Queen, that we would credit everything to the four of us, so that nobody would leave a song alone. It also helps when we choose singles, because it's difficult to be dispassionate about a song that's purely of your own making.'[3]

Having had such a productive January and February, Queen took March off from recording, which allowed Roger to tour with his side project The Cross and Freddie to work on more material for the Montserrat Caballé album alongside Mike Moran at Townhouse Studios. But the demands of constant recording and writing, and appointments with doctors and specialists as well as the exhausting side effects of his various treatments meant he often had to slow down.

'It was patently obvious that Fred was ill,' remembers Mike Moran. 'It became increasingly obvious that things weren't right and when something like that happens, and I've had a lot of friends that have gone through this, you do tend to go into denial and you do tend to go, "Well, he'll be alright." And honestly, all of us were like that. He would say, "I'm going to the doctor's today" and I'd never ask what it was for or about, but he went through everything, really, to try and beat this. But sometimes he'd go, "I'm not feeling that great, we'll call it a day today." But he never said it was because of his illness.'[4]

The rest of Queen were in the dark also. But how much longer could Freddie keep his condition a secret? Those around him were beginning to wonder about the nature of his illness, including former manager John Reid: 'I got a letter from Paul Prenter, must have been about '88,' recalls Reid, 'but it was a farewell letter, so when I realised he had AIDS, I started to think about Freddie, and he was being more and more reclusive.'[5]

Freddie was already beginning to develop more unpleasant side effects from AZT, such as nausea, vomiting, insomnia and headaches, and soon he couldn't stand how ill he was feeling on the drug. He felt, over the following months, as if his immune system was being damaged rather than strengthened; he came to believe he had never encountered a drug as toxic as AZT. Even on the lowest dose it began to make him ill. He continued taking the drug while working from March to June and had a beeper that ensured he would remember to take AZT every four hours, even throughout the night. Then there was a point during 1988 when Freddie stopped taking the drug, but he soon became scared that he wasn't following doctor's orders and began taking it once more.

Apart from time at the recording studios, the debilitating side effects he was suffering from AZT meant that Freddie remained within the sanctuary of Garden Lodge, where he would spend time in the garden or hosting quiet dinner parties for his increasingly smaller circle of friends, unable to welcome anybody new for fear of them betraying him, just as Prenter had done. But for those in that inner circle, Freddie ensured the warmest of welcomes.

'We became very close friends,' recalls Mike Moran, 'and the evenings at Garden Lodge are probably not what people imagine. It was just a normal home life. It was a very friendly, homely place, full of priceless antiques littered around the place and I remember when my two-year-old daughter used to go around there and my wife was petrified she would knock over a Gallio or Lalique glass. But Fred used to say, "Oh, you can't stop her playing, it doesn't matter," and you could put your feet up on the table or do what you like in his house.

'And an evening with Fred would be a bite to eat and it would usually then be watching TV – not just Fred and I, but people would drop in and out – and quite often we'd play Scrabble and Trivial Pursuit, and very competitively, I might say. And it sounds very odd, but it's home life for Freddie. The normal things that everybody does at home. And a very amusing person too, a fantastic sense of humour. And we used to have these mad drink-fuelled singsongs around the piano. That was another thing that he would love because of my varied background in music and we used to have hours and hours of this, and anyone who came was subjected to these singsongs around the piano, which was all very lovely actually. It was just good fun.'[6]

Queen resumed recording *The Miracle* in April and May of 1988, although Freddie was flitting between this project and his Montserrat Caballé, album; he also made his final live appearance in the UK on 14th April when, to the surprise of the audience and fellow cast members, he appeared for one night only in Dave Clark's *Time* at London's Dominion Theatre. The event was a charity performance for the AIDS organisation, the Terrence Higgins Trust, and Freddie, clean-shaven and wearing jeans, a black leather jacket and white T-shirt, sang four numbers during the show: 'Born to Rock 'n Roll', 'In My Defence', 'Time' and 'It's In Every One Of Us', a duet with Cliff Richard.

It was a bold gesture for Freddie to appear at such an event with speculation about his health a recurring theme in the British press and the charity benefiting from the performance being an AIDS charity. He must have known there was a distinct possibility that any questions from critics or newspapers directed to him would have focused on his health or on rumours that he might have AIDS and, for someone with a firm distrust of the British press and who had become something of a recluse, such an appearance was fraught with danger. As it turned out, he managed to avoid any press interviews and the evening passed without any problems or additional gossip or speculation.

Following a brief trip to Madrid on 22nd April 2 to attend a gala tribute concert in honour of Montserrat Caballé, Freddie headed back to Ibiza for some rest and recuperation. Keen to avoid any chance of press intrusion, he chose to stay at Roger Taylor's villa rather than his usual haunt of Pike's Hotel. By now, he was becoming visibly weaker and spent the days lying by the pool, secure in the knowledge that he was out of the way of the prying eyes of the paparazzi.

In July, Freddie returned to London to record more songs for *The Miracle* with Queen and also to complete work on his *Barcelona* album with Mike Moran and Montserrat Caballé. Still, he failed to mention anything about his illness to his bandmates and simply carried on working to the best of his abilities. However, the close working environment of a recording studio meant that anything unusual, or a change in someone's character, caused raised eyebrows, and Brian May was beginning to suspect something was amiss with Freddie. He was aware that AIDS was in the midst of ravaging the gay community, and had had a particularly tragic effect on New York's gay scene. He knew too that Freddie had spent a lot of time in the Big Apple and, by now, was aware of his bisexuality. Nevertheless, any suspicion that Freddie might have AIDS wasn't discussed within the group, although, as May admits, it wasn't hard to guess what was probably going on when Freddie announced he didn't want to tour any longer to promote new albums.

'We didn't know actually what was wrong for a very long time,' said May, a couple of years after Mercury had died. 'We never talked about it and it was a sort of unwritten law that we didn't, because Freddie didn't want to. He just told us that he wasn't up to doing tours, and that's as far as it went. Gradually, I suppose in the last year and a bit, it became obvious what the problem was, or at least fairly obvious. We didn't know for sure.'[7]

As the summer of 1988 progressed, so Freddie's appearance started to change again, owing to the medication he was taking and the minor surgery required on his lesions. He also began to lose more weight, spent more time sitting or sleeping and used more and more make-up to try to conceal any blemishes on his face or hands.

Together with Jim Hutton, Freddie flew to Montreux for a break. Renting a lakeside house called The Cygnets, which Roger Taylor nicknamed 'Duckingham Palace', he spent the time there watching old movies on television or strolling around the lake and breathing in the fresh mountain air. He needed to be revitalised because in October he would be appearing in Barcelona with Montserrat Caballé to perform their duet together as the city welcomed the Olympic flag.

Before he flew to Spain, he returned briefly to London and welcomed his parents, Bomi and Jer, to Garden Lodge. Though Freddie would try to visit them at their Feltham home every Thursday, from which he would always return with a box of his mum's homemade cheese biscuits, they were less frequent visitors to Garden Lodge.

'He kept his parents quite separate, really,' reflects Peter Straker.[1] It was during this visit to Garden Lodge in the late summer of 1988 that Jim Hutton was first introduced to Bomi and Jer. But, as always with Freddie, there was a pretence to keep up and so, for the sake of this visit, an elaborate plan was worked out where Jim would be introduced as Freddie's gardener, with no reference to their relationship, and, if asked, Jim would say he slept in the Pink Room. The plan worked and even if they suspected anything, Freddie's parents never commented on the nature of his friendship with Jim.

Over the next few months Jim would get to know Freddie's parents a little better as he would be Freddie's chauffeur for his weekly visits to their house. Entering their Feltham home, the same house they had lived in since their arrival in the UK in 1964, Jim was surprised to find no photographs of Freddie anywhere and when he found himself in the garden with Freddie's father lamenting the rose bushes that were dying, Jim felt that, perhaps, Freddie's parents were aware that their son hadn't got long left, too.

At the beginning of October 1988, following a month working in the studio with Queen on more material for *The Miracle*, Freddie flew to Barcelona to perform with Caballé. His doctors had advised against the trip. Dr Gordon Atkinson said: 'He approached his illness in his own perfectionist way, discussing pros and cons of the various forms of treatment quite objectively with the various specialists from the Westminster Hospital. He never allowed his physical condition to interfere with his professional commitments. At the time he made the video of "Barcelona" with Montserrat Caballé, his haemoglobin had fallen to 7.0 grammes [50 per cent of a normal reading] and yet he went ahead and shot "Barcelona" like the true professional he was.'

This low haemoglobin count clearly indicated he was suffering with anaemia.[2] But Freddie wasn't going to let AIDS beat him – at least, not yet. He travelled to the Catalan capital with every intention of giving the best show possible and on 8th October 1988, Mercury made his final live appearance singing 'How Can I Go On', 'The Golden Boy' and 'Barcelona' with Caballé at the Plaça de Carles Buïgas Montjuïc Park in Barcelona as part of the Olympic Committee's festivities.

Freddie and Montserrat were scheduled to close the show but as their moment on stage approached, he grew increasingly nervous. 'We kept out of his way,' recalls Tony Pike, 'but I caught sight of him – and he was pacing up and down dressed in his suit, deep in thought and lipping various phrases from the songs.'[3]

Freddie was once again suffering problems with his throat. This shouldn't have worried him too much as the plan was to mime their performance. However, when he and Caballé stepped out onto stage to perform their first number, the playback tape was playing at the wrong speed: it was too slow, so the performance had to be stopped briefly, the tape rewound, and then started all over again. For those in the audience, and the gathered press corps, it was a giveaway sign that Freddie was miming and, immediately, upon hearing he had a throat infection rumours began that he had AIDS.

At a press conference after the show, Freddie attempted to set the record straight: 'I didn't want to risk singing live. It's a very difficult thing for me because they're complex songs and we just didn't have enough rehearsal time as well. We did think we might do something live but my God, I tell you it would need a *lot* of rehearsal – weeks and weeks of it. I'm used to singing with Queen, where hiding behind their power is quite easy to do. But here, each note counts and it's a very different kind of discipline. I can do it in a studio because I can have retakes, but I wondered whether I could do it live, where you have to do it straight away. She's used to that, whereas I'm not. I've never done things with orchestras, and if my voice was not to come up to scratch I'd be letting her down. I wouldn't want to take any chances.'[4]

But, despite protestations that the performance was always going to be mimed and that the decision to do so was in no way influenced by his illness, Freddie had struggled through the songs on-stage because, beneath his tuxedo, the effects of AIDS were becoming more debilitating. He had a wound on his right calf and of course the permanent lesion on the ball of his foot; neither would ever heal properly and caused him to limp.

Montserrat Caballé recalled performing with Freddie that night and how she felt he was aware that he knew it was probably his last performance: 'While he was singing, I noticed that his eyes were shiny with tears. I gave him my hand. He clasped it and kissed it. It was clear he was suddenly aware of his own fate. They were tears of farewell. It was his goodbye, at least to the stage,' she said.[5]

Caballé was one of the few who already knew the extent of Freddie's illness. It had been revealed during one of their final recording sessions when, out of character, Freddie recoiled from their usual welcoming embrace to avoid a kiss, as she recalled in a 2012 interview: 'I said, "Sorry, Freddie, I didn't want to bother you." He said, "No, no, I have to tell you. I am HIV-positive." I said, "What does that mean?" I knew many people with HIV and they were well so I didn't think it was a problem. He said, "Well, in my case I have developed AIDS and I don't want you to catch anything." At the time nobody knew how it was transmitted and there was a chance it could be through the skin.[6] I said, "But you are so strong, and so is your voice." It was very hard for me to take everything in, though nothing like as hard as what he must have been feeling. I was just so pleased that he felt able to confide in me. It meant he must have really valued our friendship.'[7]

Two days after their final performance, Freddie and Caballé helped launch the album, *Barcelona*, in Covent Garden's Royal Opera House. The album reached number 25 in the UK album charts and, despite a lukewarm reception by the music press, it remained a highlight of Freddie's musical career: 'I didn't think I was capable of writing operatic pieces that would suit a world-renowned prima donna,' he said. 'I really didn't know I was capable of things such as that. I thought, "What else is there left for me to do?"'[8]

With his work on *Barcelona* complete, Freddie decided to take a spontaneous trip to Munich. He took Peter Freestone and Peter Straker with him, but grew increasingly impatient at the fun everyone else seemed to be having, fun in which he was unable to participate owing to fatigue and suffering from flu-like symptoms due to his severely depleted immune system. Jim Hutton flew out to join him in Germany but, even then, Freddie felt so lousy that he didn't join the rest of the group visiting the bars and clubs of the Bermuda Triangle, part of the city he had partied so hard in only a few years earlier.

Returning to London, Freddie took refuge in Garden Lodge once more and resumed his AZT course of treatment, but he soon fell into the same problem that many AIDS patients had encountered with AZT: that it worked for a short while, anywhere from four months to a year at the most, and afterwards there was no effect except for physical side effects. But, because it had worked once patients kept returning to it, and Freddie was no exception.

Towards the end of 1988, after a year on and off AZT, it was discovered that Mercury's T4 count was down significantly and, consequently, it was suggested he come off AZT completely. But AZT wasn't the only drug he was on: he had to have suppressants for toxoplasmosis and PCP along with hydrocortisone and fludrocortisone, which would keep his energy levels up. Eventually Freddie abandoned AZT altogether in favour of trying some new experimental drugs, anything that would give him hope. If he had lived longer he would have discovered that AZT didn't really work after an initial period and that all of his suffering, and that of tens of thousands of other people, would have had been avoidable.

The next drug that Freddie tried that offered hope was DDI, a drug that when taken with at least two other anti-HIV drugs suppressed HIV to low levels. He was treated with DDI when Dr Brian Gazzard gained access to it for a small group of patients at the Chelsea & Westminster Hospital (up until 1989, AZT was the only licensed drug used in the management of HIV/AIDS). Trials indicated that DDI taken alone showed greater increase in CD4 cell counts than in patients receiving no HIV treatment and the drug would eventually be approved in October 1991. But, for Freddie, the drug was still in the study phase and he took it as much in hope as anything else.

However, he had finally made the decision that he had to tell the rest of Queen about his illness and dedicate the remainder of his life to recording as many songs with his three bandmates as time and energy would allow.

The year 1989 was a seismic year in world history: the protests at Tiananamen Square in Beijing, China, the collapse of Communism in Europe, the fall of the Berlin Wall, and Ronald Reagan succeeded by George W. Bush.

Reagan had faced great criticism for the manner in which he appeared to avoid the AIDS crisis during his presidency, although there is conflicting information as to the validity of that criticism. Author Larry Kramer claimed in 1992 that, 'He had, apparently, reduced federal health budgets and even refused to utter the phrase "AIDS" in the first seven years of his tenure of the White House,' and he continued, 'Ronald Reagan may have done laudable things but he was also a monster and, in my estimation, responsible for more deaths than Adolf Hitler. He is one of the persons most responsible for allowing the plague of AIDS to grow from 41 cases in 1981 to over 70 million today.'[1]

In fact, the truth was that Reagan first mentioned AIDS, in response to a question at a press conference, on 17th September 1985, and, on 5th February 1986, he made a surprise visit to the Department of Health and Human Services, where he said, 'One of our highest public health priorities is going to be continuing to find a cure for AIDS.' The Reagan administration also increased AIDS funding requests from $8m in 1982 to $26.5m in 1983, which Congress bumped to $44m, a number that doubled every year thereafter during Reagan's presidency.[2]

But, however much funding the Reagan administration did or didn't plough into the US federal health budgets, by 1989 the number of reported AIDS cases in the US had reached over 100,000. While 50,000 cases had been reported in the six years between 1981 and 1987, the number had doubled in the 18 months from December 1987 to July 1989. Of these, 59,000 had died of AIDS-related illnesses.[3] And these were only the officially recorded cases. It was estimated up to 1.5m people were infected with HIV in the US by the end of 1988.[4]

The year 1989 was also the year when Haiti finally stopped distribution of its tainted blood products and, following two years of intensive protest, 1989 also saw Wellcome lower its price of AZT by 20 per cent. That same year saw a report published by the World Health Organization, which stated that 145 countries around the globe had reported AIDS cases within their boundaries, with over 400,000 people suffering from the condition.[5]

In the UK the annual number of AIDS-related deaths had risen to 567 by 1989, compared to 119 just four years earlier.[6] The effectiveness of the 'Don't Die of Ignorance' campaign was yet to be seen as a result of the latent period of the virus, and while the rise in HIV prevalence among GUM (Genito-Urinary Medicine) clinic attendees in London during the early 1980s was comparable to that observed in San Francisco, the subsequent behavioural change brought about by this campaign (principally a reduction in partner numbers and use of condoms, which was very high during this period in gay men) at an earlier epidemic stage in the United Kingdom, probably prevented the continued rapid rise in prevalence that was seen in the US and meant instances of HIV/AIDS in the UK over the next decade were not on the same scale as America was to experience.[7] However, in the Houses of Parliament, MPs continued to stand up and make scaremongering speeches warning of the potentially decimating effect of AIDS that would result in problems finding enough workers, nurses and soldiers for the UK to function properly.[8]

But it wasn't only politicians who were wary of the unknown surrounding HIV/AIDS in the UK; the general population, too, were still exhibiting negativity towards anybody with HIV or AIDS and there remained a huge stigma connected with the condition. Myths surrounding HIV and AIDS were still commonplace in British society, with people continuing to think AIDS could be caught from a lavatory seat, from coughing and even in public swimming pools. One of the most prevalent myths was that AIDS could be transmitted by a simple handshake and it was only in 1989 when Diana, Princess of Wales, was photographed shaking the hand of Jonathan Grimshaw, who had been HIV positive for five years, as she opened the Landmark AIDS Centre in south-east London, that attitudes began to shift. In a single gesture, Diana showed that this was a condition needing compassion and understanding, not fear and ignorance. It was also the first attempt to de-stigmatise HIV/AIDS by a high-profile member of the Royal Family.

The Royal Family had already had a brief flirtation with AIDS, although they refused to comment on the circumstances of the death of Stephen Barry, personal valet to Prince Charles for 12 years, who had died in London in 1986 at the age of 37 from an AIDS-related illness. 'He was a valet, and that's all we can say,' a spokesperson for Buckingham Palace said. 'We refuse all other comment on the matter.'⁹ However, it was reported that the nature of Barry's illness *was* known to the Royal Family.¹⁰

Although news of Stephen Barry's death from an AIDS-related illness made few newspaper inches around the world, by 1989, one by one, AIDS was claiming the lives of a number of significant figures in society, many of whom had tried to keep the nature of their illness out of the public domain. While Rock Hudson had been the first high-profile victim of AIDS, the years since his death had seen well-known figures such as writer Bruce Chatwin, musician Liberace, supermodel Gia Carangi and fashion designer Bill Gibb all succumb to AIDS, while 1989 saw Michael Vyner, the artistic director of the Royal Opera House, and photographer Robert Mapplethorpe die from AIDS-related illnesses. 'It kind of hovered like a mist,' says John Reid, Queen's former manager, 'and people were dying very quickly.'¹¹ With each death – and the world of the arts seemed particularly vulnerable – Freddie Mercury must have been made even more aware of his own mortality. However, he was determined for life to go on as normally as possible, for as long as possible.

With this in mind 4th January 1989 saw Jim Hutton's 40th birthday. Freddie made sure the occasion was celebrated in style at the Meridian in Chelsea, where guests drank champagne and witnessed a huge birthday cake, in the shape of the Garden Lodge conservatory, being wheeled in at the end of the night. January also saw the release of another Freddie Mercury and Montserrat Caballé duet from the album, *Barcelona*, but 'How Can I Go On' performed poorly, reaching number 95 in the charts. This followed the disappointing performance of Mercury and Caballé's previous single, 'The Golden Boy', which only got to number 86. These would be Freddie's final single releases, as either a solo artist or as a duet, before his death.

But Freddie's solo career was simply a distraction to him. A chance to be his own boss, an opportunity to do something he wanted to do away from his bandmates, and the space to explore musical ideas that didn't fit within Queen, whether it was the Europop disco-style of 'I Was Born To Love You' or the operatic bombast of 'Barcelona'. And Freddie was adamant that his solo work was only of benefit to Queen at the end of the day: 'I think my solo work probably brought Queen closer together and enhanced our careers. I had no doubt that Queen would come back even bigger. I have a very good outlet within the group, so I'm not stifled in any way and I'm certainly not complaining. It would have been very easy for me at one stage to become a solo artist, because the draw was there. People in the media were always asking when I would go it alone. But I was very happy with Queen, and therefore I didn't need to give my ego a boost by suddenly leaving them and becoming solo. It's a very tempting area for me but why ruin the damn thing? I feel a loyalty towards the band and I'd hate to let them down. That, to me, is too high a price.'[12]

The beginning of 1989 saw Queen back in the studio to complete *The Miracle*. Given the demands on Freddie and his inability to function fully, the time when he would have to announce his news to his bandmates was getting nearer. Until then, however, he attempted to act as though everything was normal and the four members of Queen worked together with a newfound sense of vigour after having had over a year apart.

With the album in the can in March, Freddie and the band under-took a rare group interview for BBC Radio 1 with Mike Read. By now, Freddie had adopted a new look. Struggling with the constant effort of trying to conceal the blemishes on his face with make-up as a result of his Kaposi's sarcoma, upon the suggestion of his boyfriend, Jim Hutton, he grew a beard to mask the blemishes but, despite this, rumours surrounding Freddie's health continued to arouse speculation. The interview with Read contained a number of diplomatic answers to the question of the band touring again, with Freddie acknowledging that he was the one among the four of them who didn't want to tour. 'I don't give a damn actually what they think, it's just that I don't want to do it, and I don't think I'm letting them down or anything,' he said.

At no point was there any discussion about Freddie's health or rumours about AIDS, but he was beginning to look a shadow of his former self and, with the exception of appearances in song videos, took no part in promoting the album when it was released on 22nd May, leaving the bulk of the promotional work to Roger Taylor and Brian May. It was during one of these promo sessions, in Munich of all places, that Taylor was asked if there was any truth in the rumours that Freddie Mercury had AIDS. He responded with this: 'Freddie is as healthy as ever. The reason we are not going to tour is because we can't agree on the process. Everything else is just a stupid rumour.'[13]

Freddie was at a crossroads. By revealing his condition he would not only face public excoriation on top of the disease itself, but he would also jeopardise the whole industry that Queen had become. His band members, all those people who were kept employed ... he was responsible for others, not just himself, which in itself is a state of precariousness beyond belief. He at least needed to tell the band, if no one else.

Whether or not Roger knew, and he likely did know that Freddie was ill, the extent of his illness, the charade could go on no longer. 'Freddie is as healthy as ever and sings better than ever on the new album,' Taylor told the press in 1989. 'We had a party at Brian's a few days ago, and Freddie didn't exactly give the impression he was on his death bed,' he continued.[14] But the press scrutiny was becoming intense as Roger, Brian and John were left to constantly fend off questions concerning Freddie's wellbeing, so in late-May 1989, Freddie finally decided to tell his three bandmates the truth about his condition.

According to Jim Hutton, the four members of Queen were sitting in a restaurant called The Bavaria in Montreux when Freddie finally admitted to Brian, Roger and John what was wrong with him. 'We kind of knew for a long time, very, very gradually, because the signs began to be there,' recalled Brian, 'and there came a day when he just said, "Look, you've probably figured out what I'm dealing with. I have this thing, and as far as I know there's no cure and I only have a certain amount of time left. I want to have this conversation, I want life to carry on exactly as it is, I want to make records, I don't want anyone to know, I don't want anyone to talk about it from this point forwards and that's it." That's what he said.'[15]

According to Jim Hutton, the way Freddie told the band differs from Brian's version: 'Someone at the table was suffering from a cold, and the conversation got round to the curse of illness,' said Hutton. 'It was then that Freddie, who still looked fairly well, rolled up his right trouser leg and raised his leg to the table to let the others see the painful, open wound weeping on the side of his leg. "You think you've got problems," he told them. "Well, look at this." Then just as quickly as he had mentioned it, Freddie brushed the subject aside.'[16]

Hutton wasn't at the dinner, so May's description seems more reliable but, regardless of how they were told, all three of Freddie's colleagues were devastated by the news and, according to Brian, 'all went off and got quietly sick somewhere, and that was the only conversation directly we had about it.'[17]

'We knew he was terribly ill; it was really only a confirmation of what we'd guessed,' said Roger Taylor. 'But actually hearing it was an appalling thing. For quite a long time we tried to tell ourselves it was other things.'[18]

'He never asked for sympathy from anyone else,' recalled May. 'He was a very strong person and always liked to be in control of his own destiny. He knew that if he did announce it his life would become a circus and he would be prevented from going about his business, which was making music. He wanted it to be business as usual until the end. There was no drama, no tears in his eyes. He was incredibly self-contained. We didn't feel we could speak about it to anyone. It was particularly hard lying barefacedly to our friends. And, of course, we had to stand by and watch this incredibly talented, strong man, in the prime of his life, gradually wasting away. There was a terrible feeling of helplessness.'[19]

There is a school of thought suggested to the terminally ill, in particular those with AIDS, that you might live longer than you're supposed to by telling as few as possible you are ill. Of course, the lying means you have to involve other people. Freddie had already told those close to him in Garden Lodge the secret. They became part of the lie. But then everyone lied: whether it was telling him tales of survival and assurances he would survive to how much better he was looking, how he seemed to have put on weight. Lying is encouraged as a way to make things easier for the person with AIDS.

Brian, Roger and John did what Freddie asked them to do: became part of the lie, and tried to ensure life went on as normal. The group was galvanised by the situation they found themselves in and, almost immediately, the three other members of Queen formed a protective shield around Freddie. He wanted to get back into the studio as quickly as possible and record as many songs as he could in the time he had left – however long that might be. The other three bandmates, aware of the reality facing Freddie, were desperate to do what they could.

'I think we thought *The Miracle* was going to be the last one,' said Brian. 'There were no guarantees how long Freddie was going to last at that time. So we just knew we had to press on and do what we could.'[20]

With ten tracks, all credited to Queen rather than individual writers, *The Miracle* was released on 22nd May 1989 and went straight into the UK album charts at number 1, although, in keeping with their lukewarm popularity in the US, it only reached number 24 there. And, as had followed them throughout their career, the reviews were decidedly mixed, with *The Times* writing that the album: 'addresses the question of how much bad taste is it possible to cram on to one album'[21] while *Rolling Stone* said, 'Somewhere out there, there's a cruel prankster circulating a rumor that "The Miracle" is Queen's official return to hard rock. Well, off with his head. The band hasn't been so bogged down by synthesizers and pinging drum machines since "Hot Space".'[22]

Five singles were released from the album in 1989 with two of them, 'I Want It All' and 'Breakthru', both reaching the Top 10 in the UK. But chart positions bore little relevance to Freddie now, and possibly the rest of Queen, come to that. Theirs was now a simple race against time to get as much done with Freddie as possible. He had probably entertained thoughts of recording another solo album – he had enough material left over from previous projects – but with his illness any such thoughts were quickly put out of his head. His physical and mental capability now was such that he needed people around him to make things happen, and a solo record, even if it were started, would never see completion.

As it was, Freddie Mercury began with Queen, and he would end with Queen.

But it was not all work for Freddie. He spent some of the summer of 1989 at Garden Lodge tending his garden and his growing collection of koi carp but even there he was hounded by the press, who were stalking his every move from outside the gates and constantly speculating on his health. And when they couldn't get a story, they made one up, with *The Sunday Mirror* suggesting that Freddie had made a pact with his ex-lover, Mary Austin, to 'father' a child for her. In fact, Mary was already pregnant and was in a stable relationship with the father of her child, Piers Cameron, and Freddie couldn't be happier for her. (Freddie would become the boy's godfather when he was born in 1991 and said, 'I'd love to have a baby, yes. That would be nice, but it will never happen. I'd rather have another cat.')[23]

Such press harassment resulted in Freddie frequently fleeing to Montreux throughout the year. Not only was this an effort to escape the press intrusion, it was also where Queen were working on their new album in their old haunt of Mountain Studios. They had commenced work on what would be their 14th studio album even before *The Miracle* had been released, and by decamping to Switzerland the band had a safer and more peaceful environment in which to make music. They had devised a schedule whereupon they would record for three weeks and then take two weeks off to allow Freddie to recuperate while the other members, specifically Brian and Roger, worked on other material and other projects.

'He did apply himself incredibly over the last few years because he felt he owed it to the band to leave them some kind of legacy, so a couple of albums were done very quickly,' says Mike Moran.[24] This was despite doctors telling him to slow down, to take stock, to accept the eventuality. But he wouldn't listen to people telling him that he must slow down: Freddie was not there yet, not ready to concede.

By now, he had also given up smoking on doctor's orders, and the clean mountain air proved a welcome relief from the grey skies of London and eased the AIDS-associated respiratory problems that were by this time evident. Freddie, having now shunned for good the hedonism and hectic lifestyle of Munich, grew so fond of the peace and tranquillity he found in Montreux that he was to buy a three-bedroom apartment there overlooking Lake Geneva in the last year of his life. It was a purchase that, however brief his stay, would give him enormous comfort and solace as his great force and energy ebbed away at the beginning of the new decade.

Freddie returned to Garden Lodge for Christmas 1989 and once again hosted a Boxing Day party for his small circle of closest friends but speculation continued in the British press about his condition as the decade drew to a close. When he appeared in public for a brief moment on the Cilla Black ITV show *Cilla's Goodbye to the '80s*, there could no longer be any doubts that he was seriously ill. The show saw presenter Cilla Black host a fond farewell to the 1980s with awards being presented to those who had had a major influence on society, sport and culture throughout the decade. Queen had been voted Best Band of the Decade and appeared briefly on-stage to receive the award from Jonathan Ross. Freddie walked onto the stage first, immediately followed by the rest of the band, but following a cursory wave to the audience, he shrank to the rear of the group as Brian May accepted the award and thanked everyone who had voted for Queen and supported them throughout the decade.

But it was Freddie who everyone was looking at, and they were shocked by his gaunt appearance.

During his acceptance speech, Brian said, 'We hope to be performing some more miracles for you soon, in 1990 and beyond.'

It was wishful thinking. Unless Freddie had a miracle of his own, there was little chance of him surviving long into the 1990s. Likely infection with HIV in July 1982 meant that he had survived for over nine years, an extraordinary length of time then.

But time was running out.

By the end of the 1980s, the UK had seen 848 reported cases of AIDS, of which 553 had died. But a report in 1990 suggested that anywhere between 57,000 to 91,000 people in the UK might already be infected with HIV and as many as 161,000 could be infected by 1994. The same report estimated that deaths from AIDS in the UK would peak at 17,400 annually in 2000 with almost a quarter of a million people having died from AIDS-related illnesses by 2010. The projections were shocking, as was the study indicating the median survival time of those with full-blown AIDS was one year from date of diagnosis and, more likely, just ten or 11 months.[1]

Freddie Mercury was only too aware of the scant survival time. Time was almost up, and if the figures in the report were correct then he was already on borrowed time. Given this, it's hardly surprising that January 1990 saw Queen back in the recording studio in Montreux, making the most of every hour they had. It was the perfect place of escape for the band and especially Freddie, as the press had started to camp 24 hours a day outside his London home, eager for any snippet of gossip and training their telephoto lenses on the windows of Garden Lodge for a snatched picture of Freddie that would confirm the rumours and gossip concerning his state of health.

With the band in Montreux, manager Jim Beach began work on finding Queen a new record label in the US. It was felt that a new label might help revitalise the band there as well as exploiting their extensive back catalogue, which was its main selling point across the Atlantic at that point. Capitol, who at the beginning of 1990 were Queen's US label, were more than happy for Beach to buy back the rights; after all, the band were hardly big-sellers in the States at that time, and with the news that Queen were suddenly unsigned there a number of other record companies made approaches, including a brand new company.

Hollywood Records had been founded a year earlier by Michael Eisner, then CEO of The Walt Disney Company, with the aim of the label being geared to a mainstream audience rather than children. Eisner quickly identified Queen as being the perfect band for the new label. He wasn't so interested in their new material at that point, rather it was the back catalogue that took his fancy. In 1988, *Billboard* magazine published a poll of consumers' most requested unreleased compact discs, and high on that list were virtually all of Queen's 1970s albums. This led to Eisner spearheading a bid for Hollywood Records to sign Queen in the US, a bid rumoured to be in the region of £10m (almost £22.5m in 2016). By September 1990, the deal had been signed and Queen once more had a presence in North America.

While this was going on, the band continued work on their new album in Switzerland. But these sessions drained and exhausted Freddie and required an almost superhuman effort from him to muster his trademark vocal power.

'He wanted to work,' recalls Roger Tayor, 'he wanted to occupy his mind and his days. So we spent long, cloistered periods abroad, just backing him up and forming a protective wall. It was actually a good time in a way, because we felt very close – the closest we've ever been.'[2]

While the press continued to speculate about the state of Freddie's health, the three other members of Queen were refusing to tell anyone about his condition, even to the point of lying to friends and family. Freddie had insisted this be the case and that life went on as normal. Brian, Roger and John carried out his wishes.

'We still didn't mention a word to anyone, not even our families, which is very difficult. When your friends look you in the eye and say, "What's wrong?" and you say, "Nothing," it's very hard. So it was a big strain; it did something awful to our brains for a while,' says May.[3]

On 18th February 1990, Queen were due to receive an award for their outstanding contribution to British music at the British Phonographic Awards, held at the Dominion Theatre in London. Just as with the Cilla Black show, accepting the award posed a number of issues: it was now visibly evident that Freddie was extremely ill, so for him to be on-stage with the other members of Queen would only draw attention to his swift decline and confirm to the media, and Queen fans, his dramatic health issues. But if he didn't appear, it would only fuel the rumours and lead to increased speculation. In the end, he made the courageous decision to collect the award in person, along with Brian,

Roger and John, and when he walked on-stage to the accompaniment of 'Killer Queen' his suit hanging off him, swamping his gaunt frame, his hair thinner and dyed, and his hollowed face beneath thick make-up hiding any blemishes on his skin, no one watching could be in any doubt that Freddie Mercury was extremely ill.

Watching the clip of him on the Brit Awards, you can perhaps see, in the short time he is on-stage, a traumatised child as he once was, long ago, and one who recovers, as he did, one who has a wall between him and pain and despair, between him and grief. In that momentary appearance you see the child, the adolescent man, then the young man, and now the middle-aged man with AIDS. It was to be Freddie's final public appearance and just before he walked off-stage he leant into the microphone and said, 'Thank you, goodnight.'

With his appearance at the Dominion Theatre over, Freddie and the rest of Queen shunned the party there and instead made the short journey to the Groucho Club in the heart of Soho. It had been decided that 1990 was close enough to the 20th anniversary of Queen and a party had been laid on at the Groucho for 400 guests to celebrate this landmark. While 1990 *was* the 20th anniversary of Queen – they had played their first shows billed as Queen in July 1970 – the line-up of Freddie, Brian, Roger and John hadn't come into being until 1971. However, with it appearing increasingly unlikely Freddie would be around in 1991, it was thought prescient to celebrate the anniversary as soon as possible.

The gathering at the Groucho was full of stars – Liza Minnelli, Rod Stewart and George Michael were among the guests – and a cake to celebrate the event was created in the shape of a Monopoly board with the various properties on the board being replaced with the names of Queen hits. With the party in full swing inside the club, outside a baying pack of reporters and paparazzi gathered, sniffing an opportunity to get at Freddie. They got their wish when he finally emerged to get into a waiting car that would whisk him home, but in the few paces between the door of the Groucho and the door of his car, Freddie was photographed looking tired, frail, haggard and lost in thought. It was just the photo the press were looking for and the following morning, it was splashed across the front pages of the tabloids.

One of those who was concerned about Freddie's appearance was Queen's old keyboard player, Spike Edney, but like everyone else he was met with a wall of silence: 'The first indications that something wasn't right was that Freddie looked a little thinner to me, and I called John up to see what was going on. I said, "Is something wrong with Freddie?" and he wouldn't tell me,' Edney recalls.[4]

The final public party was over.

Brian May adds: 'We hid everything. We avoided questions. We lied because we wanted to protect him.'

When people asked Roger Taylor about Freddie's health he would vehemently deny there was anything wrong and, as Paul Gambaccini observes, 'Everyone had to draw the wagons about them. At that time to become ill was to have a death sentence.'[5]

Freddie and Queen flew back to Montreux in March 1990 to escape the intense scrutiny that was following Freddie in the UK and to continue work on their new album. One of the songs they were working on was a track called 'The Show Must Go On' and the very title, let alone the lyrics, added poignancy to the recording sessions.

'That track was strange,' recalls May. 'I did most of the lyrics for Freddie to sing and you can imagine what that felt like. I did ask him at one point if he was okay about it and he said, "Yeah, totally okay about it. I will give it my all." And he did. He sang, I think, some of the best vocals of his life on that track, and most of the tracks on that album are incredible. He really was getting very weak by that time, but he could still summon up that strength to sing.'[6]

While Freddie still might be able to reach the high notes, he was finding it increasingly difficult to walk. Part of his routine in Montreux had been to get his driver, Terry Giddings, to drop him off beside the shore of the lake on the way to the recording studio. Freddie would then slowly walk to see the swans that lived there – he would call them 'my swans' – and spend some time in contemplation away from anybody else. Over the weeks that followed these walks became slower and shorter as AIDS continued to destroy Freddie's already frail body.

Another blow to hit Freddie upon his return to London in early summer 1990 was when he was given the news that his personal chef and ex-lover, Joe Fanelli, had also been diagnosed with full-blown

AIDS. Freddie was devastated but keen to look after Joe, so bought him a house in Chiswick in which Joe could see out the last months of his life once Freddie himself had died.

'We were all worried what the press would make of it if they discovered that Joe was also ill,' Jim Hutton said. 'We had visions of the sick headlines and guessed our house would be dubbed "Aids Lodge". It all made us more determined than ever to pull together and stay optimistic.'[7]

But only a few weeks later Jim, too, underwent an AIDS test in secret. 'Privately I began to get very anxious about my own health. I thought I could be HIV positive as well. The more I reluctantly thought about it, the more it seemed likely,' he reasoned.[8]

A few days later Hutton found out the results; he didn't have full-blown AIDS like Freddie and Joe, but he was HIV positive. He made the decision not to tell Freddie as he felt the singer had enough to cope with, but it was decided that they would no longer share the same bed, so Jim moved into the Pink Room. It had little effect on their relationship as any form of sexual relations had long since ceased. Instead, they would just lie together and kiss and cuddle.

'Those cuddling sessions would be as rewarding in their way as any sex we ever had,' said Hutton.[9]

In July 1990, with Freddie's health continuing to decline, Queen moved the recording of their new album to London's Metropolis Studios. Four tracks were already complete, but there was some doubt as to whether they'd have the entire album finished to release before Christmas, as EMI had hoped.

A familiar face at Metropolis Studios was engineer Gary Langan, who had worked with Queen way back in 1975 on three albums as well as 'Bohemian Rhapsody'. Langan had heard the rumours about Freddie's health but was still shocked by the change in his appearance. 'The whole thing had taken its toll,' he says. 'We bumped into each other at Metropolis and had a few words, but he was trying to be as private as possible. It wasn't a great thing to see.'[10]

The co-producer on the album, David Richards, who had been working with Queen since the 1970s, was also aware of Freddie's health problems but unlike everybody except the band had no idea what exactly was wrong: 'I knew that he was very ill,' remembers Richards.

'Amazingly his voice became better and better though. "My voice is still here," he used to say, "So I'll keep on singing 'til the end." I personally didn't know that he had AIDS: I speculated he had cancer. I think everyone involved pushed aside the fact that it was really that serious. Everyone still had that glimpse of hope that at the end maybe a miracle would happen.'[11]

By now, Freddie had had a small catheter inserted into his chest, below the left collarbone, to ease the intake of medication. It could now be administered intravenously, which was simpler for all concerned: it was not visible, and it also enabled Freddie to keep mobile, a vital requirement for a man with so much he wanted to do in so little time. And most of that involved making music.

One of the songs Queen had worked on extensively during the recording process was a track called 'Innuendo'. The song is a compli-cated composition and, although written together, it bears all the hallmarks of Freddie's writing style, with sophisticated orchestration in the bridge section in three-quarter time and a middle section featuring a flamenco guitar solo, which was performed on the record by Steve Howe from Yes. Howe had gone into the studio to catch up with Queen and ended up being played 'Innuendo' before being asked, spontaneously, to provide some additional guitar work: 'They jokingly said I could do a bit of Paco de Lucia with it,' recalls Howe. 'I could see what they were after so I did some improvising and they loved it. I was so proud to be on that record.'[12]

'Innuendo' ended up being the opening track of the album, which would share the name ("Innuendo is a word I often use in Scrabble. For Queen it's a perfect title," said Freddie[13]). But in the summer of 1990, the album was still a long way from being complete.

Freddie was becoming increasingly frail. When he found the strength, he tried to get into the studio to record, but those days came less frequently and though he was able to work, it was not with great lucidity. Still he rarely complained. Bone and intestinal biopsies were done, along with endless blood tests – and one drug was administered after another – all of which only made him feel even sicker. His doctors temporarily stopped the Interferon and replaced it with steroids, which boosted him for a short while, but then he was having trouble with his digestion, fevers of 101–102 degrees, nausea all day, and some head pains again.

With a pack of news-hungry reporters laying siege outside his Garden Lodge home, Freddie only left the house for recording sessions or to visit his doctors and relied, generally, on the small, but close-knit circle of friends around him who paid frequent visits: people such as Mary Austin, Dave Clark, Peter Straker and, throughout that summer and onwards, Elton John. He also welcomed his sister Kashmira and her husband Roger Cooke to Garden Lodge in August and it was during this visit that he finally told them he had AIDS.

'It was August 18 1990,' recalls Cooke precisely. 'We were sitting in his bedroom, having coffee when he said suddenly, "What you have to understand, my dear Kash, is that what I have is terminal. I'm going to die." We saw these marks on his ankles and knew he was ill. After that, we talked no more about it.'[14]

Although he had told his sister, Freddie insisted no word was spoken about his illness to their parents, Bomi and Jer. Like the rest of the world, they would not find out until Freddie released a statement to the press in the final hours of his life.

'At first I couldn't believe what he was telling me,' recalls Kashmira. 'Basically it was just going above my head. It was only later in the months that he deteriorated that it started to sink in. But even then I just kept on hoping that he would come out of it.'[15]

In September, Freddie celebrated his 44th birthday with a dinner for 20 of his closest friends at Garden Lodge. The friends at that last celebration party included Mary Austin and her husband Piers Cameron, Jim Beach, Peter Straker, Dr Gordon Atkinson and Mike Moran and his wife. Even Barbara Valentin flew in from Munich for the party, which was to be the final birthday Freddie celebrated with any kind of lavish event. Typical of his generosity, he gave everyone who came a memento of the occasion from Tiffany's, but over the next few months he would begin to stop seeing some of those nearest to him.

He ceased his friendship with one of his drivers, Graham Hamilton, whose boyfriend outed Jim and Freddie's relationship to total strangers one night in a gay bar in Notting Hill. He didn't see Barbara Valentin either after that party on the paranoid assumption that she was leaking information about him, and, eventually even Peter Straker, his long-term friend, was shut out. But perhaps this was because Straker was close enough to get *too close* to the truth. For a while he had been wondering about the health issues Freddie was reeling from. Not being staff (and Peter was the only one of Freddie's friends not on the payroll), Straker hadn't been told that Freddie had AIDS: 'All I got from Freddie was that he had this blood thing, and I thought it could have been leukaemia or something like that,' says Peter. 'He started to get these blotches and I asked about these and he said he had some blood condition. I knew about AIDS but it just never entered my head.

'I did have one conversation with him once after lunch because I used to go and have Sunday lunch, which was really good as we'd just sit down and talk, and I remember he said to me, "I've got a lovely bottle of great red wine for you" – we used to have our champagne first – but every time he used to have red wine or drank, he used to start scratching and I noticed this, and he said, "I can't drink today because of this blood thing that I have," but he never explained what it was.

'I went one day, around 1990, and we had lunch and he was quite blotchy and he had make-up on, and we went upstairs and we were sitting down watching telly on his bed and I said to him, "Have you got AIDS?" and he said, "No, I've got some blood condition," and I said again, "Have you got AIDS?" and he said, "No, I haven't got AIDS." And I said, "If there's anything wrong with you I'm always here for you," and we parted that evening. That was the last time I saw him.'[16]

John Reid was another cut out from Freddie's life. 'I tried to call,' remembers Reid, 'and Joe [Fanelli] or Phoebe [Peter Freestone] said he'd call me back, but they were just closing ranks and protecting him.'[17]

David Evans, a close friend of Mercury's, put it down to a condition called 'AIDS-anger' – 'where those who are terminally ill get terribly angry for no reason. It's an anger, which goes with the fact that these people are alive, and you're going to die. Maybe Barbara and Straker fell under that particular shadow because they were unable to handle his anger. Freddie cut out a lot of people at the end of his life, especially the ones who had lived with him through his hectic, wild years. He couldn't cope with the people who only adored him as that boisterous, partying, devil-may-care person. He was in incredible pain for the final twelve months of his life, yet he still had to try and keep going. So he gathered about him only the people he knew would sustain his soul, the ones he could keep up with in terms of the old days.'[18]

Freddie even had another in a series of blazing rows with Jim Hutton, which led him to tell Hutton (through intermediary, Joe Fanelli) that he should leave Garden Lodge. Such was the severity of their rift that Jim took out a six-month lease on a flat in Hammersmith and Freddie took back the Volvo car that he had given Jim as a present. But, just as he was about to move out, Freddie asked him to forget about the whole argument and to remain at Garden Lodge. Which is what Jim did until the day Freddie died.

While recording sessions continued – their schedule determined by Freddie's illness – the press remained a constant presence outside Garden Lodge. They also began hounding the other members of Queen. When Freddie failed to turn up to Cliff Richard's 50th birthday party, the press caught Brian May off-guard, who revealed that Freddie was suffering from strain and exhaustion and that the years of partying and hard living had finally caught up with him. 'It is true that he has been quite rough recently,' said Brian. 'Freddie is OK and he definitely hasn't got AIDS.'[19] But despite May's denials, it was all that was needed to keep the vultures interested, lying in wait for the perfect opportunity.

That opportunity came just a few days later when Freddie was photographed leaving Dr Gordon Atkinson's clinic on Park Lane looking frail, gaunt and struggling to simply walk comfortably. The following week, *The Sun* newspaper ran a full-page photo of Freddie, emerging from a clinic, looking cadaverous. The headline 'The Sad Face of Freddie Mercury' speculated on his illness though still failed to mention AIDS. That picture of the emaciated Mercury, dressed in a grey suit and hunched over like an old man, was soon splashed across the nation's tabloids. The first paragraph of the article, written by the now-disgraced journalist and political strategist Andy Coulson, read: 'This is the picture that proves rock superstar Freddie Mercury is battling a serious illness.'

While the picture further shocked Freddie's fans with the revelation of the extent of his illness, it also angered his bandmates, who had done so much to conceal their friend's condition. 'The thing that annoyed me more than anything,' says Roger Taylor, 'was a shot of Freddie in *The Sun*. He'd just come out of the doctor's, I think. I mean, this really grainy, full-page shot. Is this man dying? I thought, you fucking wankers.'[20]

'Living through the celebrity culture of the twenty-first century,' says writer Mark Blake, 'it's easy to forget how unusual it still was then for the press to pursue a pop star to such a degree. Queen's raised profile after Live Aid and the hysteria and misinformation surrounding AIDS proved to be a lethal combination.'[21]

The validity of any denials about the true nature of Freddie's illness were further cast into doubt when Paul Prenter surfaced once more in the US to issue a statement to *The New York Globe* following the publication of the photo of Freddie leaving his doctor's clinic: 'Freddie is just a shadow. His body is frail and stooped and he shuffles along like an old man. He used to be bouncy and vibrant, but now he looks desperately sick. He's lost an alarming amount of weight and his clothes hang on him. No matter what they say officially, he's suffering from something far worse than the flu. I am desperately afraid that it might be AIDS. Freddie has led a very wild life.'[22]

Behind the walls of Garden Lodge, the daily newspapers were vetted before Freddie read them, and in the studios at Metropolis, Brian, Roger and John once again closed ranks around him as they sought to complete their new album. 'There was a lot of joy, strangely enough,' says Brian May. 'Freddie was in pain, but inside the studio there was a sort of blanket around, and he could be happy and enjoy what he liked doing best. Sometimes it would only last a couple of hours a day because he would get very tired. But during that couple of hours, boy, would he give a lot. When he couldn't stand up, he used to prop himself up against a desk and down a vodka: "I'll sing it 'til I fucking bleed."'[23]

But the recording schedule, dictated and hampered in equal measure by Freddie's illness, meant that the album would not be ready until 1991. EMI, Queen's record label, were disappointed that they would be missing the lucrative Christmas market, but across the Atlantic, Hollywood Records had signed the deal to exploit Queen's back catalogue. Little did they know, but their decision to sign Queen had been a tragically astute one: in less than a year Freddie would be dead and, as with Elvis and John Lennon before him, join the list of artists whose death regenerates sales and interest in their work while significantly boosting the value of their estate.

Queen finally managed to complete the album, *Innuendo*, in December 1990 and it was scheduled for release in February 1991. Before that, the title track would be released as a single in the New Year, but it would require a video, and the consensus was that Freddie, given his illness, was too frail to appear on camera, so an elaborately animated video was created using illustrations and images from earlier Queen videos in a vain attempt to hide Freddie's condition.

By then, however, Freddie didn't need to tell the world what was wrong with him.

Everybody knew.

Part Four

On 26th January 1991, Queen found themselves in an unfamiliar position: they were at number 1 in the UK singles chart with 'Innuendo', the track having sold over 100,000 copies in its first week of release. The last time they'd held the top spot was almost ten years earlier with David Bowie and 'Under Pressure'. But in terms of Queen alone having a number 1, this was the first time they had reached the top of the UK singles charts since 'Bohemian Rhapsody' in December 1975. Given they were predominantly a singles band, it's a surprising statistic that they achieved the number 1 spot so rarely. During the same period Abba hit the top spot eight times, Madonna had seven number 1 singles, The Police and Blondie had five number 1s apiece, and Rod Stewart, The Jam and even Shakin' Stevens had four chart toppers each.

As well as being a number 1 in the UK, 'Innuendo', the single, was also a Top 10 hit throughout much of Europe and the album of the same name, released in February 1991, topped the charts in the UK, the Netherlands, Germany, Italy and Switzerland. Once again, as throughout Queen's career, the reviews of the album were less than positive. *Rolling Stone* wrote: '"Innuendo" is so lightweight you'll forget it as soon as it's over',[1] while *The Times* commented: 'What is astounding is that in 20 years Queen have lost none of their appetite for music of the most grandiose banality.'[2]

Quite what Michael Eisner, head of Hollywood Records, Queen's new label in the US, must have thought upon reading these reviews after splashing out £10m[3] to sign the band is open to speculation. Desperate to make the album a success the label forked out another $200,000 for a lavish launch party on board the *Queen Mary* in Longbeach, California. Only Roger Taylor and Brian May attended the launch, an extravagant party where guests and reporters were given food and drink and brief access to the two members of Queen. May was quizzed by a staff writer from the *Los Angeles Times*, who began by asking about the album, but it wasn't long before questions turned to Freddie's health.

'What about those rumours about Freddie not being healthy – specifically, that he has AIDS?' the reporter asked Brian, who responded by saying, 'Yeah, yeah, I've heard those rumours and innuendoes. I know where they came from. They were started by the English press. Those tabloids are vicious. Some of the people who write for them are a low form of life. They make up things all the time and needlessly cause all sorts of problems in the lives of celebrities – just to sell a few papers. Also, we've all been through periods when we've abused ourselves unmercifully in the outrageous ways that rock'n'rollers have always done it. Maybe the consequences of that lifestyle – what it does to you – can help start rumours. All I will say is that Freddie is healthy and fit. Listen to his singing on the album. Does it sound like someone who's sick or dying?'[4]

Freddie hadn't travelled to the launch party in California because of 'family commitments', according to the official line, but gossip persisted in the UK and his home remained besieged by paparazzi. The fact that he hadn't appeared in the video for their number 1 single 'Innuendo' only fuelled the speculation, so Freddie took the decision that he would have to appear in the next video for 'I'm Going Slightly Mad'.

Filmed in the middle of February at Limehouse Studios in London, with a closed set and tight security, it was a curious affair costing almost £200,000[5]. The song itself was quirky and humorous yet curiously odd at the same time and the video, aimed at representing madness in various forms, makes distinctly uncomfortable viewing. Filmed almost entirely in black and white, Freddie is dressed in an ill-fitting suit – padded out to conceal his weight loss – with white gloves. White make-up is caked on his face to cover his blemishes. All of this, combined with an extravagant backcombed wig to disguise his increasing hair loss, only served to accentuate how atrophied he had become. Throughout the shoot his energy levels were buoyed briefly by medication. But despite all this extra padding, and performing under huge film lights, those working on the shoot recalled how cold he was throughout the filming. The production crew had all been told Freddie had a muscle condition and that he was suffering problems with his knee. As a result, no whispers or gossip left the film studios.

The single was released on 4th March, but only reached number 22 in the UK. By that point, however, Queen were back in the recording studio working on new material. They had decided against recording in London because of the intense press scrutiny that Freddie was constantly facing and instead revisited Mountain Studios in Montreux, on the shores of Lake Geneva.

'Particularly towards the end of his life he was relentlessly pursued by the press. He just wanted peace and quiet, to be able to get on with what he did. It was very convenient in Montreux because people got used to the sight of us and nobody made a fuss,' remembers Brian May. 'Freddie wanted his life to be as normal as possible. He obviously was in a lot of pain and discomfort. For him the studio was an oasis, a place where life was just the same as it always had been. He loved making music, he lived for it.'[6]

The band all knew that there wasn't much time left and Freddie told them to write whatever they could and he would give them his vocals for them to work with at a later date. 'The sicker Freddie got, the more he seemed to need to record, to give himself something to do, some sort of reason to get up and he would make it in whenever he could so really it was a period of fairly intense work,' says Roger Taylor, while Brian May remembers: 'You know, Freddie's becoming weakened by this horrible disease and he finds it hard to stand up a lot of the time, but he'll throw a couple of vodkas down and he'd prop himself up on the mixing desk and have his mic there and go for it.'[7]

Before too long, they all realised that they might have enough material for another album, although the strain was beginning to show in Freddie's voice. 'I can hear the voice is getting thinner,' says Roger Taylor. "I think you can really tell that it's an ailing voice, although he hits the notes.'[8]

By this point Freddie had completed the purchase of the three-bedroom apartment in Montreux called La Tourelle, which had been found for him by Jim Beach. With its views across the lake, it was the perfect place for Freddie to rest. Increasingly tired, not just from the recording process, but also the very act of living itself, he knew that when he could record no more, then it would be time to go. And that moment seemed to be drawing nearer with every day.

Freddie returned to London briefly in April to visit the Chelsea & Westminster Hospital's Kobler Centre (opened by Diana, Princess of Wales in September 1988), and sometimes he would also visit the old Westminster Hospital on Horseferry Road. There was a rumour of an as yet untried drug, an inhibitor called Saquinavir, but it was not available to anyone yet. As soon as it was, they would secure it for him, he was told. It had only begun its first trial in the lab, but in truth, who was to know, inhibitors must have looked like just one more mediocre and toxic drug to Freddie.

At the end of the month, on 29th April, *The Sun* plastered a photo exclusive of Freddie over the front page of the newspaper under the headline: 'Tragic Face of Freddie Mercury'. Snapped by the paparazzi as Freddie ventured out for a rare walk with his bodyguard, the first paragraph of the news story read: 'Ailing rocker Freddie Mercury takes a rare stroll in public – a tragic shadow of the party-loving superstar his fans once knew'. Once again, tabloid intrusion forced Freddie to flee back to Montreux almost immediately, where he devoted his time to recording with Brian, Roger and John, or planning how to decorate his Montreux flat. One of Freddie's last great wishes was to spend Christmas that year in Montreux and he hired a top interior designer in Montreux to complete the renovation of the flat to his specifications with the instructions that it *must* be completed by December, when he planned to travel out to celebrate Christmas overlooking Lake Geneva.

Freddie loved to surround himself with art (he had recently taken up painting again) and his apartment in Montreux would be adorned with various objets d'art including the final painting he ever bought. 'A Type of Beauty' by Jacques Tissot, the Nantes-born artist, was purchased by Freddie from Christie's in 1991 for £160,000[9]. It depicted Kathleen Newton, a beautiful young woman whose love affair with Tissot, almost 20 years her senior, scandalised Victorian England. Moving in with Tissot in London, Newton became a pariah of the capital's society, having divorced her husband and bearing an illegitimate child. She and Newton lived together for six years, openly flouting Victorian values, but Newton's heath declined as she contracted tuberculosis. Tissot captured her fading beauty in various works. In this particular painting she is near the end of her life, her fragility apparent. While painting it,

Tissot was consumed with grief at the illness eating away at his love. Sensing his emotional demise and aware there was no cure for herself, Newton took her own life by overdosing on laudanum in November 1882, aged just 28 years old.

On 13th May, with Freddie and the band in Montreux, EMI released 'Headlong'. Most of the video for the track had been shot in November 1990 at Metropolis Studios, showing the band in various stages of 'recording' and playing around for the cameras at the mixing desk. An additional sequence with the band 'performing' the song was filmed in February 1991. The single reached number 14 in the UK charts a couple of weeks later, but by then Freddie had recorded his last vocal performance in the studio.

At some point between 13th and 16th May, Freddie was in Mountain Studios in Montreux, working with Brian May on a song that became known as 'Mother Love'. Brian, Roger and John were all now on standby in the Swiss town and ready to come into the studio at a moment's notice whenever Freddie was well enough to perform – 'We all knew there wasn't much time left,' says May.[10] By now Freddie was extremely ill; he could not stand for long, and he could only walk with a cane. Every movement was an effort, causing him great pain, and he could only be in the studio for one or two hours at a time.

'I don't know where he found the energy,' says May. 'Probably from vodka. He would get in the mood, do a little warm-up, then say, "Give me my shot." He'd swig it down, ice-cold. Stolichnaya, usually. Then he would say, "Roll the tape." He still had astonishing power in his lungs at that point. I don't know where it came from.'[11]

Brian and Freddie had been working on the song together, writing down ideas whenever they were both in the studio, or individually, and then bringing them into the session. As the recording of 'Mother Love' progressed, so Freddie drove himself to deliver the best vocal performance possible. 'The song starts low and gentle, but Mercury chose to push himself and go higher,' remembers May. 'We looked at each other and knew there was a mountain to climb. That's when the vodka really went down. He said, "I will hit these notes." And he did. It was a wonderful performance. We got as far as the penultimate verse and he said, "I'm not feeling that great, I think I should call it a day now. I'll finish it when I come back, next time." But, of course, he didn't ever come back to the studio after that.'[12]

Shortly afterwards Freddie returned to London. He had one last performance to give. At the end of the month, he joined Roger Taylor and John Deacon to film the video for their next single, 'These Are The Days Of Our Lives', a song Taylor had written about his children and life in general, but now, when sung by Freddie, a song that took on a whole new meaning. At the time Brian May was out of the country on a promotional tour, so footage of him was shot separately later and edited in.

By this point, Freddie was incredibly frail. It was decided to film the video in black and white in an attempt to hide the extent of his illness, although Jim Beach, ever the pragmatist, already had an animated video on standby in case Freddie was too ill to film. As it was, and in immense pain from the lesion on his foot, the hardened edges of it digging into his skin, he had to remain almost static throughout the video.

'He looked so ill that it was quite scary,' recalls Roger Taylor. 'I thought that was a very brave thing to do. And why not?'[13]

Wearing his favourite waistcoat, decorated with images of his cats, Freddie appeared enervated and drawn, but was determined to give a final performance of note. He accomplished this with raw emotion; it's obvious he knows this is his last time in front of the cameras, and at the end he bids farewell to his adoring fans and to the world when he looks straight into the camera with a smile and sings the final line from the song, before saying, 'I still love you.' Then, with a vaudeville swish of the hand, he exits the frame. With that gesture and those words, Freddie Mercury had said his public goodbye.

Meanwhile *The Sun* intensified their pursuit of Mercury in London as they unpityingly anticipated his death. The newspaper ran a series of headlining articles that attempted to correlate his suspected homosexuality with the deadly AIDS disease. Freddie's former chauffer Terry Giddings states: 'Fred used to love gardens and flowers. On one instance, at his request, I discreetly brought him to a garden centre for him to get out. At this point, Fred looked quite ill. The next day, on the cover of *The Sun*, was a photo of Freddie and me, with the headline: "Freddie Mercury and His New Boyfriend".'[14]

For many people the 1980s had been a brutal time and it continued as the decade ended and into the 1990s. Writers James Hogg and Robert Sellers describe it by saying: 'By 1982 the moral paradigm to which the press usually adhered seemed no longer to be valid. A new breed of editor had been created; one that would change the face of tabloid journalism forever. Profit at any cost – human included. Stylistically, things would also change. From now on it would be ignominy and loathing "masked" as consideration for the "Great British Public". Gay celebrities (not all of them openly gay at the time) would be hounded for as long as the tabloid could keep the public fearful of what they'd christened the "Gay Plague". The eighties was really the Murdoch reign of terror – the dark ages – and they (the tabloids) were trying to either expose, invent or seduce every gay person they knew.'[15]

And top of the tabloids hit list was Freddie Mercury.

48

By August 1991 Freddie had started to die again. The promising results of the latest regime of drugs had not lasted: he was at the end of the list of AIDS drugs to take. It was late August when the idea of stopping all drugs came to Freddie. He likely felt that to continue living when things are over, when things are done with, was not for him. Novelist Harold Brodkey described this state as 'The unbearable lightness of not-being.'[1] But unfortunately the absence of the will to live is insufficient to make one want to die: the stubbornness of life.

There is a photograph taken by Jim Hutton of Freddie on his 45th birthday, 5th September 1991. It is the last photograph of him. He is standing on the lawn of Garden Lodge with one of his precious cats by his feet. The photo is framed by the last of the year's orange 'Golden Lights' azalea blossoms. It is a private moment not intended to be shared. Freddie expresses no anxiety in the photograph; he does not seek the camera's approval. His high waistband reveals how thin he has become, the trouser belt sitting on his hipbone. In it we see there is something miraculous in the way the years won't wash away the evidence of that day, but will hold it fast.

Freddie was down to 140lb – almost 35lb less than before he was infected. By now, his speech was slower, too, and he was constantly struggling with walking and standing. He found it difficult to sleep at night so was continuously fatigued and he also became plagued with infections in the mouth, and on the skin.

In 1991 AIDS was still a disease that few knew anything about. People were sympathetic mainly, especially Freddie's friends, but most had no real experience or idea of how to treat a dying man, especially one who was dying of AIDS. For many it was an entirely new and uncomfortable experience and no one really knew how to deal with it.

August brought with it the news that Paul Prenter, his once-trusted friend and ally, then his greatest betrayer, had died of AIDS. The two had not spoken for some years, and though Freddie knew that Prenter had AIDS, the news that he had succumbed so quickly to the condition shocked him and, according to Jim Hutton, 'Paul's death troubled him for many weeks, and inevitably reminded him of his own fate.'[2]

On 5th September, a small birthday party was held at Garden Lodge for Freddie's 45th birthday. The quietest birthday of Freddie's adult life, it was attended by only a handful of friends, including Dave Clark and Mike Moran. It was a birthday few people had expected Freddie to see as his health was failing so dramatically. He must have imagined that there wouldn't be another. Perhaps for the first time in his adult life, it was a specific number: 45. Of course he could not know at what rate he was moving towards his death. No one knew for sure, not even the doctors – the only hard medical fact with AIDS *was* death. The hope of a cure, a half-belief in treatments that could extend his life, was gone to him.

'He got to the stage, certainly in the last six months,' recalls Mike Moran, 'where he became a bit more reclusive, and so I would phone up and Peter [Freestone] would say he's not very well today or whatever, and these periods become longer until it came to a point where I hadn't seen him for maybe a couple of months. And then the phone rang one day, and Peter said to me, "Are you okay for Saturday, Freddie's birthday? You can come, can't you?" And I was astonished that there was going to be any kind of event, and Peter said, "No, no, he definitely wants to have a party."

'Fred's birthday parties were always wonderful and we had some absolutely amazing dinner parties at Garden Lodge with just good food, lovely company, just very gentle lovely evenings, punctuated with raucous intervals. But I did think we'd seen the last one and then we were invited to the last one, and it was a very small group of people and it was just a remarkable evening and I felt very privileged to be there, and it was Fred saying goodbye and it wasn't a sad, horrible occasion. We had a lovely dinner and we chatted and we watched a couple of videos on TV and listened to some music and played a couple of games, and then Fred said, "Right, I'm knackered, I'm going to bed. You can all stay or you can all fuck off." And so we all fucked off. But I do remember going out of Garden Lodge and I was driving and my wife and I gave Dave Clark a lift home on the way back, and we all got in the car and nobody said anything, and then Dave said, "Mmm, well," and then I said, "Mmm, well, I wonder if that's the last time I'll see Fred." And it was.'[3]

Less than two weeks after his birthday, Freddie drew up his will and settled his affairs. 'I then started talking to Jim Beach,' recalls John Reid, 'and Jim told me what they were going to do after he died, and he told me that Freddie had told him (because he called Jim Beach "Sandy"), he said, "Sandy, dear, do what you like with the catalogue but never make me boring."'[4]

Freddie spent the rest of September as a recluse in his London home. Outside the press still gathered, but the message coming out from Garden Lodge was the same as it had been for months, that Freddie did not have AIDS. His parents still didn't know, although years later, his mother, Jer, said: 'He didn't want to hurt us, but we knew it all along.'[5]

'The trouble with death-at-your-doorstep is that it is happening to you. That you are no longer the hero of your own story, no longer even the narrator. It is a tale of death amid others' lives – like a rock in a garden,'[6] wrote Harold Brodkey. Freddie would not have an old age because what was happening to him now was his old age. One imagines he must have thought about wanting to end it all, as he began to get frail, hiding away as it all became too much, but somehow he was still in love with life. This happens to those who are terminally ill: they remain so much in love with life. Writer Voltaire expresses it just perfectly: 'I have wanted to kill myself a hundred times, but somehow I am still in love with life. This ridiculous weakness is perhaps one of our more stupid melancholy propensities, for is there anything more stupid than to be eager to go on carrying a burden which one would gladly throw away, to loathe one's very being and yet to hold it fast, to fondle the snake that devours us until it has eaten our hearts away?'[7]

October saw Freddie hire a private jet and fly to Montreux with Jim Hutton and Joe Fanelli. His eyesight was now failing (only a few weeks earlier he had stumbled up some stairs when on a rare trip out with Peter Freestone) and it was almost impossible for him to walk. He spent most of his days curled up on the sofa watching movies, one movie in particular. The film Freddie watched the most times is called *Imitation of Life*. Made in 1959 and starring Lana Turner, it is a tear-jerker melodrama about a struggling actress with a six-year-old daughter, who sets up housekeeping with a homeless black widow and her light-skinned eight-year-old daughter, who rejects her mother by trying to pass for white. An artificial soap opera dressed up as exquisite drama, it is colourful, glossy and unapologetically old-fashioned. It is stylistically over the top, with bold colours, a sweeping musical score, over-dramatic acting and stories of emotional anguish, love affairs that go wrong, unrequited love and life-threatening situations. It's also about our innate tendency to inadvertently drive away the ones we love the most.

The melodrama appealed to Freddie, as did the mawkish performance by the star Lana Turner, and the often arch and overblown script appealed to his sense of camp. 'It is just a camp joy,' said Freddie of the film. Calling *Imitation of Life* 'camp' is nothing new but there is something else that is important. The very title, *Imitation of Life*: the main characters all imitate each other's lives. They all have a crisis of personal identity; always, literally, looking in mirrors.

'The mirror is the imitation of life,' said the director, Douglas Sirk. 'What is interesting about a mirror is that it does not show yourself as you are, it shows you your opposite.'[8]

Perhaps Freddie could relate to this imitation. In the early 1970s he imitated a heterosexual. In the 1980s he became an imitation of an imitation of a heterosexual. And the more successful he became, the more alienated he was from himself.

When not curled up on the sofa in Montreux, Freddie was confined to his bedroom, with Jim and Joe taking turns to watch over him. Gone were Freddie's walks around the shoreline of the lake, gone were the visits to see his swans – 'my swans' – and gone too was the will to fight his illness any longer. During this trip to Switzerland, Jim finally told Freddie that he, too, was HIV positive.

'"The bastards," Freddie said, perhaps referring to whoever had given it to him, and whoever had given it to that person, and so on along the endless chain,' wrote Jim Hutton.[9]

But the two of them were merely small dots in a cluster that had arrived in North America from Haiti, and had entered Haiti through an infected worker returning from West Africa. And there it all began with a chimpanzee and a hunter in the dark depths of the Congolese jungle. Now, that long journey had arrived here, taking over 80 years to reach Freddie and Jim as they sat overlooking Lake Geneva, contemplating what little future they had left together.

With Freddie in Switzerland, EMI released Queen's next single, 'The Show Must Go On'. As the song rose to number 16 in the UK charts, it didn't take long for press and fans alike to be speculating about the lyrics and the hidden meaning of the song. Two weeks later, on 28th October, Queen released *Greatest Hits II*, an album with 17 hit singles, from 'Under Pressure' in 1981 to 'The Show Must Go On', a decade later. It went straight into the UK album charts at number 1 and stayed on the top spot for five weeks. The album would go on to sell over 23m copies worldwide, just short of the 25m that *Greatest Hits* had sold since its release in 1981. By the end of the year, Queen would have another number 1 single, and both *Greatest Hits* and *Greatest Hits II* would be back in the Top 20 of the UK album charts.

But Freddie wouldn't live to see this.

While in Switzerland he had taken the decision, one he had mulled over for a while, to finally stop the medication that was keeping him alive. He would still take painkillers, they were necessary to keep the intense pain at bay, but drugs such as Ganciclovir and Septrin would have no further place. Freddie had lived life his way, and lived it fully.

With the ability to make music gone, what more did he have left to live for?

'It was Freddie's decision to finally end it all. He chose the time to die,' recalls Mary Austin, his former lover and one of those who remained with him right to the end. 'He knew it was coming. The quality of his life had changed so dramatically and he was in more pain every day. He was losing his sight. His body became weaker as he suffered mild fits. It was so distressing to see him deteriorating in this way. One day he decided enough was enough and stopped all the medical supplements that were keeping him going. The overwhelming thing for me was that he was just so incredibly brave. He looked death in the face and said, "Fine, I'll accept it now – I'll go."'[10]

On Sunday, 10th November 1991, with arrangements having been made in Switzerland and England to allow him to be sped through customs, Freddie Mercury boarded a private jet, left Switzerland for the last time and flew back to London.

His wish to see Christmas in Montreux was not to be granted.

This is where we came in.

49

*So we have come to the edge of the light
at the end of the tunnel.*

It was a mild but grey day with a heavy envelope of rain when Freddie Mercury arrived back in the UK on Sunday, 10th November 1991 in the private jet.

Freddie knew that this was his final journey home. As his car drove through London, he gazed out of the blacked-out windows at the capital's passing streets, his mind likely a mixture of reminiscences and relief. When the gate of Garden Lodge closed behind him for the last time that day, it completed his separation from his fans and from society. He became entombed in a space that the outside world could not reach. Moving around the house and occasionally into the garden was his seeming freedom.

Freddie had lasted two or three years longer than the typical AIDS sufferer and so he had become a survivor. Standing at his bedroom window, one imagines he would stare out across the garden, to the wall, an emaciated figure staring through the wire. And when he lay in bed, death was close by. It was in the room all the time, peering from the darkest corners, and in such moments a person could easily become a child again, once more afraid of the dark.

Perhaps, like most who experience this waiting for death, he found a sense of fearlessness that bestows contentment. Those around him contend he did. And in the end, all he had experienced and achieved must have seemed as nothing, and isn't that when the old or dying become possessed by voices and events from the earliest edge of their memory and return to childhood? Perhaps in his dying Freddie returned to his youth in Zanzibar, where the six-year-old Farrokh is standing in the lush green garden, a garland of flowers hanging around his neck, playing beneath the baobab trees and feeding the red colobus monkeys unripe mangos.

But now, thousands of miles and decades from his youth, he is surrounded by his beloved cats, his Japanese art, and the handful of friends who would remain. Here, Freddie could take sanctuary in the knowledge that he was now in control again. He had decided who he would and wouldn't see, and he had not released any information to the press, who were still outside his walls and who were beginning to gather in ever-increasing numbers, like ravenous vultures circling the edges of a wounded beast waiting for its last breath, able to smell the scent of decay.

Freddie's first week off his medication appeared to be little different from how life had been for the past few months. He spent a lot of time in bed, sleeping or watching television, while Jim, Joe and Peter continued with business around the house, attempting to keep as much of an air of normality as was possible, all things considered. The three of them did whatever they could to ensure Freddie was as comfortable as possible, although by the second week he was declining much faster than anyone had expected. The medication he had stopped taking included a drug to stimulate his appetite. Without it he barely ate except for the occasional scrambled egg, washed down with water or Earl Grey tea. With few nutrients entering his body, he was wasting away and getting dangerously weak.

As well as Jim, Joe and Peter, Mary Austin and Dave Clark were frequent, almost daily, visitors to Garden Lodge, eager to offer help and support wherever possible, and there would always be someone with Freddie, keeping him company, tending to him and ensuring he was comfortable.

'He never spoke about what was going to happen to him after death,' recalls Peter Freestone. 'He was of the opinion that that was a question one worried about during the years of life. With the closeness of the inevitable, there was little point in thinking about it. Whatever was going to happen was going to happen and he knew he didn't have long to worry about it.'[1]

Another visitor to Garden Lodge was Elton John. 'Freddie told me he had AIDS soon after he was diagnosed in 1987,' says Elton (who had no reason to assume Freddie was diagnosed HIV+ years earlier). 'I was devastated. I'd seen what the disease had done to so many of my other friends. I knew exactly what it was going to do to Freddie, as did he. He knew death, agonising death, was coming. But Freddie was incredibly courageous. He kept up appearances, he kept performing with Queen, and he kept being the funny, outrageous and profoundly generous person he had always been. As Freddie deteriorated in the late 1980s and early '90s, it was almost too much to bear. It broke my heart to see this absolute light unto the world ravaged by AIDS. By the end, his body was covered with Kaposi's sarcoma lesions. He was almost blind. He was too weak to even stand.'[2]

As weeks passed, Freddie's nights became much like his days: fitful bursts of sleep in bed followed by hours in a state of being semi-awake. The painkillers did what they could but he was struggling to tolerate the diamorphine. All the while, outside the house, the press was gathering, sometimes as many as 60 or 70 reporters, aware that something was going on within Garden Lodge. They tried to get messages into the house, asking Freddie to come out for just one photo and a brief statement so that all the rumours could be laid to rest, they said, but when no response was forthcoming from within, the reporters and photographers became more brazen in their attempts to get any information – climbing onto walls to snatch a photograph, going through bins, and interrogating anyone entering or leaving the house for any snippet of gossip.

Within Garden Lodge, Freddie was fading fast. Peter Freestone had been advised by the doctors that it was a good idea to continually reassure Freddie that it was okay to 'let go', and that by telling him such it was easier for him to die, knowing that those he was leaving behind accepted it in their hearts.

'I was lying on the bed with Freddie,' says Freestone, 'and he was asking how things were in the house, if things were straight and tidy. "I feel so tired, wondering whether I will ever see any of it again. Trying to visualize what's going on. I'm so isolated up here. All of a sudden it feels a huge house." I sensed this was the only chance I would have to carry out the doctors' advice. "Everything's fine," I said. "Just as you'd like it, like always. And we're fine, too. We're coping. Don't worry about us. If you feel it's time to go, we're behind you all the way. Don't worry about us. Don't feel you're leaving us. Everything's fine."'[3]

The doctors expected Freddie to have two or three weeks left on Monday, 18th November. That week, Elton John came to visit him en route to Paris, as did Freddie's parents, Bomi and Jer, as well as his sister Kashmira and her family. The family had tea together in Freddie's bedroom while he tried to reassure them that there was nothing for them to be concerned about. As they left, Freddie's family suggested they wanted to return later in the week but he said it wasn't necessary. Little did they know, as they left, this would be the last time they saw him alive.

Later that week, Brian May visited Freddie: 'Anita [Dobson, Brian's second wife] and I went round to see him and he was in bed with the curtains open so he could see out into his garden, and I think I was talking about things that were in his garden, sort of "that's really interesting", and he said, "Guys, don't feel like you need to make conversation, I'm just so happy that you're here, you know, even if we say nothing, it's just having these moments."'[4]

On 21st November, Freddie appeared at his bedroom window for the final time, calling down briefly to Jim Hutton, who was working in the garden. That night, Jim lay in bed with him, but Freddie, according to Jim, was determined to venture downstairs one last time to see his pictures hanging on the walls. Somehow, Jim claims, he led Freddie down the stairs during the early hours of Friday morning to the lounge. He sat him down in a chair and one by one turned on the lights so Freddie could look at all the works of art he had collected.

'I think that Friday morning was the last time I could honestly say that Freddie was happy, the last time that Freddie Mercury was still there, the last time he radiated that Freddie Mercury excitement,' remembered Jim.[5]

Then on Friday, 22nd November, Freddie suddenly asked Peter Freestone to call Jim Beach, Queen's manager, and ask him to come to Garden Lodge. Beach arrived at around 10am and headed straight for Freddie's bedroom. By now Freddie had lost his sight, could barely move his muscles, had given up all solids and was surviving on the bare minimum of liquids. He was drifting in and out of consciousness, but despite this, held a long five-and-a-half hour meeting with Beach, punctuated only by Joe Fanelli entering the bedroom to deliver refreshments.

No one except Freddie and Jim knew what happened or what was said during that meeting, but when Beach finally emerged, what he said took Peter Freestone, Joe Fanelli and Jim Hutton by surprise. He told them that he and Freddie had decided to release a statement confirming that the singer had AIDS.

'Jim Beach explained the reasons behind this announcement and gave us the chance to put our point of view. None of us knew how exactly to react at that point. After all the years of having to keep this huge secret to ourselves, it was now going to be broadcast to the world,' exclaimed Peter Freestone.[6]

Laura Jackson writes: 'Roger Taylor reckons that as Mercury had often remarked that he could "pop off at any time", he hadn't wanted to be cheated of his opportunity to make an announcement'[7], but Jim Hutton felt there were other forces at play: 'I've always been very doubtful that Freddie made that statement of his own accord. He'd kept it all quiet for so long it seemed odd that he'd suddenly want to start confessing things as if he had something to be ashamed of. I'm sure he felt his fate should not become a matter for public debate. It was only a matter for him and his immediate friends. And I'm sure he didn't want to risk Joe and me being subjected to the publicity. I did not even know that Freddie was going to issue a statement. I believe Freddie was coerced into making the statement. However, once he had been persuaded I know that Freddie specifically told Jim Beach to release the statement worldwide to prevent the British gutter press from having a scoop to themselves. It was Freddie's way of saying to those eagerly awaiting his death: "Fuck the lot of you!"'[8]

Following a discussion between Jim, Peter and Joe, they decided to accept the decision, whoever made it, after being persuaded, according to Peter Freestone, that a lot of good could come out of Freddie admitting that he had AIDS while he was still alive. Roxy Meade, Queen's press officer, was tasked with releasing the statement to the press on the Friday night with Jim Beach hoping this would enable the Sunday broadsheets to reveal the news in a more responsible manner rather than leaving it to the tabloids who had hounded Freddie for so long.

At midnight on Friday, the official statement from Freddie Mercury was released to the press:

Following the enormous conjecture in the press over the last two weeks, I wish to confirm that I have been tested HIV positive and have AIDS. I felt it correct to keep this information private to date to protect the privacy of those around me. However, the time has come now for my friends and fans around the world to know the truth and I hope that everyone will join with my doctors and all those worldwide in the fight against this terrible disease. My privacy has always been very special to me and I am famous for my lack of interviews. Please understand this policy will continue.

'I remember thinking, okay, if he's making the statement he's near the end,' says Paul Gambaccini, 'because he wouldn't be doing this if there's the possibility that he's going to live, because he never had. So I was grieving before it happened. I don't think he was eager to let anything out of the bag. What they're doing is they're setting everybody up for it, they're getting everybody ready.'[9]

Peter Freestone says that Freddie had had a fairly peaceful night following the release of the statement, 'as though a weight had been lifted from his shoulder',[10] and Joe and Jim took turns in looking after Freddie on the Saturday, with Dave Clark and Mary Austin also helping whenever they could.

According to Jim Hutton, Freddie had a restless night on the Saturday and some time in the night almost choked on a piece of mango that had lodged in his throat. At 6am on the Sunday morning he was taken to the bathroom but when Jim lowered him back on the bed he heard a distressing crack, like one of Freddie's bones breaking, after which Freddie went into a fit. With the help of Joe, they calmed Freddie down and called Dr Atkinson, who promptly visited Garden Lodge and gave Freddie an injection of morphine around 7am. Atkinson would stay to monitor Freddie for the rest of the day and informed those gathered that his patient would probably last until Thursday.

Dave Clark came to Garden Lodge the minute he was called and he spent the rest of the day with Freddie. 'We made everything as comfortable as we could for Freddie,' he recalls. 'His bedroom had an adjoining lounge and looked out on to his beautiful garden. He was grateful for everything and for his friends.'[11]

There are varying accounts of who was with Freddie when he passed away early on the Sunday evening. In his book, *Mercury and Me*, Jim

Hutton writes: 'Peter started changing the bed while I took care of Freddie. As I was about to change Freddie into a clean T-shirt and a pair of boxer shorts, I asked Dave to leave the room for a few moments. It was when I was getting his shorts on that I felt him try to raise his left leg to help a little. It was the last thing he did. I looked down at him, knowing he was dead. His eyes were still open. I can remember very clearly the expression on his face and when I go to sleep at night it's still there in front of me. He looked radiant.'[12]

But Peter Freestone remembers it differently. He says he was called at 5:30am on the Sunday morning by Joe, who sounded anxious (they had tried to lower Freddie back onto his bed and heard a 'crack'), and had wanted Peter to come to Freddie's room immediately. On arrival Peter found Freddie in a coma, totally unaware of the presence of anyone in the room. When Dr Atkinson arrived soon after he told them there was nothing more medically that could be done and injected the morphine.

Later in the day, at some point between 6:30 and 6:45pm on Sunday, 24th November, Dr Atkinson, who had remained at the house for most of the afternoon, decided that, as there was nothing more he could do for the moment, he would go out and get some dinner. As he left the house, it appears that Dave Clark *was* the only person with Freddie in his bedroom. In the next few minutes, after Jim and Peter had escorted Dr Atkinson out of the house, Dave came downstairs and asked if they would help him take Freddie to the bathroom as he wanted to use the toilet once more. When they entered Freddie's bedroom, they discovered he was no longer breathing. Peter called Joe immediately, urging him to get Dr Atkinson, who had just left the house. In fact, the doctor's car was pulling away into Logan Mews and Joe, chasing him and shouting after him, alerted the press that something was happening. Joe managed to stop Dr Atkinson, who rushed back into the house and went straight to Freddie's bedroom. But there was nothing more to be done.

At 6:48pm on Sunday, 24th November 1991, Freddie Mercury was pronounced dead.

'The worse thing was I was actually on my way to see him,' remembers Roger Taylor, 'and I was actually about 300 yards away when Peter Freestone rang to tell me, "Don't bother coming, because he's gone."'[13]

'We phoned Mary [Austin] immediately,' said Dave Clark. 'She lived just round the corner. It was unexpected otherwise she would have been there. She had the terrible task of phoning Freddie's parents and sister to say he'd passed on.'[14]

The rest of the evening was an emotional blur to all within Garden Lodge. Each person had the opportunity to spend some private moments with Freddie's body before the undertakers arrived. They could only watch on in stunned silence as they placed Freddie in the black body bag before it was zipped up.

'For me it was the moment of finality,' said Peter Freestone. 'Once he was zipped inside the body bag, there was just no way he was ever coming out.'[15]

Jim Hutton had placed a little teddy bear inside the body bag before it was zipped up. Earlier, as Jim recalled, he had spent his last moments with Freddie alongside Dr Atkinson before the undertakers arrived: 'I said a little prayer. Then I looked at him and said aloud: "You bastard! Well, at least you're free now. The press can't hurt you anymore."'[16]

Freddie Mercury's body was taken from Garden Lodge in an oak coffin at midnight in an anonymous van with the local police managing to stop the press from following it to a Chapel of Rest in Ladbroke Grove. Despite Jim Beach now being in the US – he had flown out following his meeting with Freddie on the Friday – a statement was hastily constructed and released to the press:

> *We have lost the greatest and most beloved member of our family. We feel overwhelming grief that he has gone, sadness that he should be cut down at the height of his creativity, but above all, great pride in the courageous way that he lived and died. As soon as we are able we would like to celebrate his life in the style to which he was accustomed.*

It was also revealed that Freddie had died from bronchial pneumonia brought on by AIDS. As soon as the statement was released, the tributes began rolling in: *The Guardian* called him 'rock's showman incarnate,'[1] while *The New York Times* said he 'helped to forge a hugely popular hybrid of hard-rock, pop, heavy-metal, cabaret and a hint of opera.'[2] On the BBC, Paul Gambaccini praised Freddie by saying, 'he gave a form which was pretty staid and sour, a great personality,'[3] and speaking to *Rolling Stone*, the late David Bowie said, 'I only saw him in concert once, and as they say, he was definitely a man who could hold an audience in the palm of his hand.'[4]

But even in death, the tabloids couldn't let Freddie rest. *The Evening Mail* described his 'kamikaze lifestyle of sex and drugs and rock'n'roll,'[5] while *The Star* revealed that, 'His many lovers – both male and female – could have gone on to infect other unwitting victims. The worst fear is that Freddie was tangled in a lethal web of disease involving 500 people or more.'[6] *The Mirror* even quoted an apparent friend of Freddie's parents to highlight that, 'They were very unhappy about his homosexuality. Being gay is not accepted in the Zoroastrian religion.

We also have very few believers and the religion can only be passed on through the father to his children. Obviously, a gay man will have no children and this deeply upset the Bulsara family.'[7]

'Even though I'd seen some photographs where it was obvious that he was extremely unwell, I still felt very shocked when I heard that he'd passed away,' remembers Annie Lennox. 'He had always been such a larger-than-life character that you couldn't envisage him dying at such a young age. Living with the stigma and secrecy of AIDS must have been incredibly isolating for him and it made me feel particularly sad that he'd been sort of "hunted down" by the press and the media. Fame can be a savage game and it would have been nice if he could have been given more privacy, in my view.'[8]

Regardless of what the papers said, Freddie's fans began gathering outside Garden Lodge in a state of shock and sheer disbelief. No one, except those closest to him, had really been aware of the true extent of his illness. He had only issued his statement confirming he had AIDS to the press on 23rd November, yet he had died just over 24 hours later, and the swiftness of his exit, though many must have feared the worst for some time, only increased their sense of grief. Countless bouquets of flowers arrived, sent from all over the world, and there were so many that they covered the entire lawn at Garden Lodge, and could have done so again.

Freddie's funeral was arranged for Wednesday, 27th November at Kensal Green Crematorium. Although he had not followed his parents' Zoroastrian faith, his funeral plans, which he set out in precise detail, would be in keeping with Parsee tradition and his parents' wishes. The funeral began at 8:30am with white-robed Parsee priests chanting prayers. Freddie's coffin was brought in to the sound of 'You've Got A Friend' by Aretha Franklin, one of his two favourite singers. His other favourite, Montserrat Caballé, was also played during the service when a recording of her singing 'D'Amor Sull'ali Rosee' from Verdi's *Il Trovatore* filled the chapel as Freddie's coffin disappeared from view.

Writer Rick Sky described the funeral: 'Just like Mercury himself, the occasion, which the singer had spent weeks planning in meticulous detail, was a bewildering mixture of flamboyance and secrecy, witnessing the collision of two very different worlds – the modern world of rock music and the ancient world of the Zoroastrian religion, in which Mercury had been brought up.'[9]

The service was a private affair with only Freddie's parents, his sister Kashmira and her family and his closest friends attending, among them Elton John, and, naturally, the three surviving members of Queen and their partners.

'I didn't go to the funeral,' reflects Peter Straker. 'It was very sad and I miss him, but I'm quite pragmatic and I thought, "Oh well, there you are", it's very unfortunate but that was it.'[10] For him, the loss was compounded by the fact that he hadn't seen Freddie for over a year, seemingly cut off from the inner circle despite being his best friend for more than 15 years.

'When I used to telephone they would never put me through,' Peter says. 'They'd just say he was busy, he was out, but they got instructions from him and Joe followed him to the letter. Again, after he died, they all came to see me in a show in the West End and were all apologising, saying, "I wish we'd put you through." I said, "It's too fucking late now." But that's what the power thing does with people – they don't look at the fact that you've known somebody for the longest time. I spoke to Jim Beach just before Freddie died, actually, and said, "I wanted to speak to Freddie," and Jim said, "Why don't you phone him because he keeps talking about you, that he's seen all your reviews from around the country and how wonderful it all is," and I said, "You know, Jim, I can't phone him now because it's just before my birthday, which is November, and the way I think his mind works he'll think I'm phoning because it's my birthday, so I can't," and he said, "Well, you should," and of course, then he was gone.'[11]

After the service, a small reception was held in the grounds of Garden Lodge to celebrate Freddie, his life and his music, with champagne, love and laughter (although Brian, Roger and John decided to go off for lunch together instead and remember and reflect in their own company). But beneath it all, discontent was already simmering. Jim Hutton was livid that he wasn't allowed to ride in the first car of the cortège (the occupants of that car were Mary Austin and Dave Clark). Behind them, in the next car, Jim sat with Joe Fanelli and Peter Freestone.

'The three of us felt let down,' said Jim. 'We'd been the ones with Freddie through thick and thin during his illness and it seemed no sooner was he dead than we were being pushed aside.'[12]

But Jim wasn't the only one annoyed. In Munich, Barbara Valentin was ready to make the trip, she had even booked her airline ticket, when she received a phone call telling her she would not be welcome. There was only room for one 'widow' that day, and it was going to be Mary Austin. And shortly after the funeral, Jim became annoyed when Dave Clark gave a newspaper interview claiming he was alone with Freddie when he died.

However, all this paled into insignificance when Jim, Joe and Peter discovered they would no longer be allowed to live in Garden Lodge. As part of Freddie's will, the three of them would be well looked after, with Jim receiving £500,000[13] and the assurance that he, along with Joe and Peter, would be able to remain living in Garden Lodge indefinitely. But alarm bells should have been ringing earlier. A few months before, while in Montreux, Jim had had a discussion one evening with Tony King, a friend of Freddie's, who had accompanied them on that trip. During this discussion, Jim was somewhat alarmed to hear that, although Mary Austin was being left Garden Lodge in Freddie's will and he was insistent that Jim, Joe and Peter would remain living there, the impression was that Mary didn't seem to get on with Jim.

'According to Tony that night, Freddie answered: "Well, they'll just have to work it out, won't they?"'[14] Jim also claims that, 'I wasn't surprised to hear that Mary didn't like me.'[15] In the will, Mary was left Garden Lodge and a 50 per cent share of the singer's estate. However, nowhere in the will did it appear that Freddie had stipulated that Jim, Joe and Peter should be allowed to remain in Garden Lodge. They were given three months' notice to find alternative accommodation as Jim Beach confirmed to them that, although Freddie's wishes were that they should continue to live in Garden Lodge, they were not legally binding as he hadn't included them in his will: they had to be out by 1st March 1992.

'We didn't have anywhere else to go,' said Peter Freestone, 'and needed a while to sort things out. We would have left soon enough. Mary's behaviour was certainly baffling.'[16]

In an interview of 2000, Mary gave a slightly different version of events: 'I felt very much out of my depth really. Freddie's staff had been like family to me, but after his death, most of them had left because he'd been so generous to them.' She continued: 'There are those who thought they should have been left the house. It's like people begrudged me having what he left me.'[17]

Perhaps a comment given to the authors by John Reid might shed a bit more light on this sorry affair: 'I didn't go to the funeral,' Reid said. 'I saw Mary a couple of times. I bump into her now and again. She said the strangest thing to me; she said as I was trying to comfort her, because she'd been through a lot and seen a lot, and she said to me, "Well, I won in the end, didn't I? He was with me at the end." That was a bit scary.'[18]

It seems despite all of Freddie's lovers, Mary was the one he loved the most, the one that he bequeathed virtually everything to. The accounts of Jim and Mary contradict each other with regards to how Freddie catered for them both in his will. Certainly Jim was well looked after, for with his inheritance of £500,000. Perhaps he felt he should have had the house, but the one constant throughout Freddie's adult life, apart from the music, *was* Mary Austin. They had met over 20 years earlier, been lovers, and been the best of friends. She had been beside Freddie through thick and thin and they loved each other immeasurably.

Freddie said of her, 'Mary is one of my closest friends in the world. Ours is a pure friendship and a friendship of the highest standard. It's an instinctive thing. I have built up an immense bond with Mary. I open up to her more than anybody else. We have gone through a lot of ups and downs in our time together, but that has made our relationship all the stronger. I know a lot of people find it hard to understand our relationship. Other people who come into our lives just have to accept it. We love each other very much and look after each other. I don't want anybody else.'[19]

Whatever Jim thought, and whatever Jim wanted, it seemed as far as Freddie was concerned there was only one rightful heir to Garden Lodge and half of Freddie's estate, and that was Mary Austin.

And Mary was also the person responsible for Freddie's final resting place. Freddie had given her that responsibility and made her promise she would never reveal where his ashes were hidden. 'I was very neglectful over them,' Mary said in an interview in 2000. 'I left them in the Chapel of Rest for a while. I knew I had this responsibility, but I couldn't bring myself to finally part with him. I had to do it alone as he asked, and keep it a secret.'[20]

Over the years there has been much speculation about Freddie's final resting place, with locations ranging from his childhood home of Zanzibar to the shores of Lake Geneva, where he spent much of his later life. But in 1994, Jim Hutton suggested another location for Freddie's ashes, in the garden of his former home, Garden Lodge: 'It's become something of a riddle,' he said, 'but I'm pretty sure his final resting place is at the foot of the weeping cherry tree overlooking the whole place.'[21]

Beneath a weeping cherry tree would be a fitting final resting place and would complete a symmetry that likely none have considered: Gaëtan Dugas, identified wrongly as AIDS Patient Zero, was buried beneath a weeping cherry tree in Vancouver. Rock Hudson, the first high-profile celebrity to die from AIDS, had his ashes scattered at sea but his memorial stone rests beneath the cherry tree borders in Forest Lawn Cemetery, California. And quite possibly, Freddie Mercury, the greatest rock showman in history and Britain's highest-profile AIDS casualty of the time, rests beneath a weeping cherry tree in London.

For all of them, and all the victims of AIDS, it's the perfect tree to remember them by, signifying as it does the fragility and precariousness of life, symbolic of awakenings and rebirth.

They bloom at the first promise of the spring, they beautify even the most grey landscape, they scatter at the first gust of the wind, but as they hold, when you look at them, you steal a little view of paradise.[22]

Everything has a beginning.

We travel back in time to the African rainforest, but not to 1908 when our hunter became the true Patient Zero, but even further back when there was Chimp Zero. Like us humans, chimpanzees were infected by something. The virus didn't begin its life in chimpanzees at all and whatever they passed to us, something gave it to them.

New research appears to indicate that the chimpanzee virus (named SIV) is a hybrid of a virus from two different monkey species, the red-capped mangabey and the greater spot-nosed monkey. In one single moment a chimpanzee was infected with both monkey viruses and must have acted as the mixing bowl in which two viruses traded genes. Chimpanzees, on occasion, eat monkeys and it is likely that, on just one such occasion in the West and Central African jungle, a fight to the death occurred between a chimpanzee and these monkeys which resulted in the chimpanzee killing and ripping apart its prey, in the process of which it sustained bites, scratches and other wounds. Blood was mixed into these injuries as the frantic, hellish fight reached its denouement with the chimp killing its prey before devouring the flesh.

In an all but incalculably rare occurrence, pieces of two viruses combined and thrived (one from a red-capped mangabey monkey and the other a greater spot-nosed monkey) once they had entered and infected the unfortunate chimpanzee. And the odds suggest this absolutely occurred only once, and hundreds of years earlier, rather than thousands or tens of thousands. We know this because the virus is not harmless to chimps as it is to the monkeys (who have likely carried it for millions of years, allowing enough time for virus and host to accommodate each other). This hybrid virus then spread through the chimpanzee species and was later transmitted into humans to become HIV.

Despite what early scientists believed, it is now known that SIV causes Simian AIDS in chimpanzees, inducing failing health and early death. Only with the passing of time did this become apparent. It happened when a wild chimp, subsequently named Vincent, was killed by two young male chimps in Tanzania's Gombe Stream National Park in 2004. His corpse was discovered and aroused the interest of Professor Michael L. Wilson of the University of Minnesota as it was the first wild chimp known to be SIV-positive available for a post-mortem examination called a necropsy.

'We had to be very careful because he had to be treated like an AIDS patient,' Professor Wilson said. 'He had a very high level of the virus in his system. We already knew that from his faeces.'[1]

What the post-mortem showed was shocking: Vincent's immune system was damaged in a way that was similar to humans with AIDS. He also had unusually low counts of a type of T-cell white blood proteins, as had subsequent wild chimps analysed from bush meat samples. These cells are vital to immunity and their loss is a classic indicator of AIDS in humans.[2]

Since the first spillage of the virus from chimp to human, over 30m people have officially died of AIDS-related illnesses and, in a report issued in 2014, an estimated 35.3m people across the world are living with HIV.[3]

To many people, even today, HIV is thought to have started in the US in the 1980s. But it didn't. The United States *was* the first country to become aware of the condition, at the time unnamed, when a few cases of rare diseases were reported among gay men in New York and San Francisco, and in 1981, the US *was* the first country to officially recognise the condition. By 1982, the 'disease' was finally given a name: AIDS. Further research has led to the generally accepted view that the origin of AIDS lies in Africa.

However, the US *was* the first country to bring AIDS into the public consciousness and the American reaction undoubtedly contributed to the establishment of AIDS as one of the most politicised, feared and controversial diseases in the history of modern medicine.

A reputation that still stands today.

But it was the migration of the disease out of Africa that changed the nature of how AIDS was, and is, perceived. As the American writer and political activist Susan Sontag points out: 'If AIDS had remained only an African disease, however many millions were dying, few outside of Africa would be concerned with it. It would be one of those "natural" events, like famines, which periodically ravage poor, overpopulated countries and about which people in rich countries feel quite helpless. Because it is a world event, which afflicts whites too, and because it affects the West, it is no longer a natural disaster. It is filled with historical meaning. Part of the self-definition of Europe and neo-European countries is that it, the First World, is where major calamities are history-making, transformative, while in poor, African or Asian countries they are part of a cycle and therefore something like an aspect of nature. And perhaps, true to an extent, AIDS has become so publicized because, as some have suggested, in rich countries the illness first afflicted a group of people who were all men, almost all white, many of them educated, articulate, and knowledgeable about how to lobby and organize for public attention and resources devoted to the disease. And a few were famous, a couple very famous. And so through all those things AIDS occupies such a large part of our awareness because of what it has been taken to represent. It seems the very model of all the catastrophes privileged populations feel await them.'4

By Christmas 1991, just a few weeks after the death of Freddie Mercury, Queen were back at number 1 in the charts with 'Bohemian Rhapsody'. Released as a double-A side with 'These Are The Days Of Our Lives', the single went straight to the top of the charts and stayed there for five weeks. In doing so, it became the first record to be at number 1 for two Christmases. It went on to sell another 1.1m copies and the same month that saw 'Bohemian Rhapsody' top the singles charts, the band had no fewer than ten albums in the UK album charts. The rebirth of Queen had begun and it seemed that, in Britain especially, the country had fallen in love with Freddie Mercury all over again.

Even Kenny Everett, who had fallen out with Freddie so spectacularly and hadn't spoken to him for years, and who would himself die from an AIDS-related illness in 1995, was touched by his death. 'When Freddie died, I wrote to Kenny,' recalls Paul Gambaccini, 'because I thought this must have an impact on him and I'm going to show you the letter. It's January 15th, signed Ken. "Many thanks for your letter. Yes, it was quite sad and a shock, even though we knew for about five years that it was going to happen. The first thing I thought, when I heard the news, was 'bloody hell, all the places I've taken him and he pisses off somewhere without me.' After a couple of days I came to the realization that every time I thought about him he'd still be there, so it didn't hurt as much. He was a loveable rogue, and very costly to be around, always bumping into expensive things and demanding champagne, but always bright and lively and the centre of attention. Wherever he is now I'm sure he's having a good time. Thanks again for your letter, Paul. It was very sweet of you. Take care. Ken"'[1]

But not everyone was so enamoured. In an article in the *Daily Mirror* shortly after Freddie's funeral, critic Joe Haines delivered an angry sermon on the singer: 'It might have been brave to announce he had AIDS the moment it was diagnosed. It wasn't brave to conceal it until his last few hours. There was nothing flamboyant about catching AIDS and probably spreading it to others. Nothing admirable about touring the streets seeking rent boys to bugger and share drugs with. Mercury died from a disease whose main victims in the Western world are homosexuals. For his kind, AIDS is a form of suicide. His death won't help the fight against AIDS because he gave a glamour to the lifestyle which causes it. The harm he did, at a time when governments throughout the world are devoting billions to preventing the spread of the disease and drug-taking, is incalculable.'[2]

It was an inherently hateful attack by Haines, and at the heart of it is deep-rooted homophobia.

'There is not a moral judgement, there is just a quantitative judgement,' says Paul Gambaccini. 'I think we should always emphasise that people like Freddie got infected before the existence of the virus became known. So these people must not be criticised for not practising safe sex because the very concept of safe sex did not exist. There was no sex that was known to be dangerous.'[3]

Susan Sontag says: 'In the eighties it was not a surprise that many people wanted to view AIDS metaphorically – as, plague-like, a moral judgement on society. Professional fulminators could not resist the rhetorical opportunity offered by a sexually transmitted disease that is lethal. It was ammunition of bigotry who depicted it as a visitation specifically aimed at homosexuals and drug addicts. "God's Judgement."'[4]

In fact, Freddie, in death, was to do more to help fight AIDS than most of the governments of the world put together, beginning with all proceeds from the re-release of 'Bohemian Rhapsody' being donated to the Terrence Higgins Trust, over £1m, and, over the coming years, tens of millions more would be donated through the Mercury Phoenix Trust. But Mercury's death was worth much more than simply money: it offered up unprecedented global coverage in the media that spoke about a disease that many still knew very little about.

'In terms of AIDS awareness, I think it was very significant,' suggests Annie Lennox, 'because Freddie Mercury's death meant that the issue was suddenly given global headline attention. People are fascinated by fame and the facts are unfortunately that the media will give more attention to the issue of HIV and AIDS if it's in connection with a famous celebrity, otherwise it rarely reaches headline status.'[5]

Meanwhile, Brian May, Roger Taylor and John Deacon turned their attention to their final goodbye. They were planning a tribute concert called 'The Freddie Mercury Tribute: A Concert For AIDS Awareness'. It would feature some of the biggest stars in the world, all performing Queen classics in front of a, hopefully, sell-out audience. This was a pivotal point in the history of Queen. It was the moment when they ceased being simply a group and, instead, began to sow the seeds that would turn Queen into a brand and a massive corporate money-making organisation.

The date set for the show was 20th April 1992 and the location was Wembley Stadium – where else? – scene of Freddie's great triumph at Live Aid in July 1985. As it turned out, it was a show that virtually rivalled Live Aid in terms of scale and spectacle. For one night only, the worlds of rock, pop and showbiz would collide as artists as diverse as David Bowie, Liza Minnelli and Axl Rose joined Brian, Roger and John on-stage to remember Freddie and to increase AIDS awareness.

'Queen's manager, Jim Beach, took control of it all,' recalls promoter Harvey Goldsmith. 'He came to me with a proposal to do a show at Wembley Stadium. They had a wish list of artists, so we had to ring round to see who was available. Jim had already sorted out some names. Liz Taylor was one. She was involved in Aids campaigning through her friendship with Elton, so when the tribute concert came up she was already interested in the cause.'[6]

All 72,000 tickets for the show sold out within three hours, with fans, including Jim Hutton, paying £25 per ticket for the concert without knowing who would be appearing on the bill, except for the three surviving members of Queen.

'It was a massive strain on our shoulders,' remembers Brian, 'because we weren't just performing, we were also organizing everybody else. It was difficult enough just choosing the acts who would appear. We argued a lot among ourselves about the bill, but the basic criteria for the acts finally selected was their relevance to Freddie.'[7]

Slowly but surely, the list of acts was finalised: Roger Daltrey, Robert Plant, Joe Elliott, Seal, George Michael, Lisa Stansfield, Elton John, Annie Lennox and Ian Hunter were among those committed to performing.

At 5:55pm on 20th April 1991, with the show being broadcast live on radio and television to 76 countries around the world with an estimated audience of 1bn, Brian, Roger and John stepped out onto the vast Wembley stage to be greeted by a deafening roar that, at once, was filled with admiration, warmth and heartfelt love for Queen and for their missing fourth member.

'Good evening, Wembley – and the world,' Brian told the assembled mass. 'We are here today to celebrate the life and work and dreams of one Freddie Mercury. We're gonna give him the biggest send-off in history!'

Over the next few hours the world was treated to some of the top acts in the world performing Queen classics: among others Robert Plant did 'Crazy Little Thing Called Love', Lisa Stansfield came on in curlers to sing 'I Want To Break Free', George Michael stole the show with 'Somebody To Love', and 'Bohemian Rhapsody' was performed by the unlikely duo of Elton John and Axl Rose. Even veteran Hollywood actress Elizabeth Taylor appeared on-stage, saying that Freddie was 'an extraordinary rock star who rushed across our cultural landscape like a comet shooting across the sky.'

'That was quite amazing,' remembers John Reid. 'I remember sitting in the box with my mother, just weeping. The entire audience was weeping.'[8]

One of the highlights of the concert was a performance of 'Under Pressure' by David Bowie and Annie Lennox. 'I think "Under Pressure" was the song suggested by the band,' recalls Lennox, 'but I'm pretty sure that David [Bowie] must have had a hand in the choice, as it was written by him and Freddie after all. It's not the easiest song to learn or perform, but I gave it my best shot. I was so completely bowled over to be singing a duet with him that it felt like I was dreaming. Our rehearsals went very smoothly and the band sounded so powerful and polished that it felt like settling in to drive a top-of-the-range classic limousine.

'Most of the line-up for the concert was male so I stayed in my dressing room for the entire day, just waiting quietly before I was due to go on-stage. I'd asked David if he had any thoughts as to what I should wear, so I could complement him, and he said, "Why don't you have Anthony Price make you a frock?" So that's what I did. I had a very clear idea as to what kind of dress it should be: theatrical, dark and funereal. The finished dress was extraordinary, with hoops underneath to spread it out like a floating tent.

'When I walked on stage, Bowie looked genuinely taken aback. He had no idea it was going to be so strong. The performance was electrical and totally on point. It was one of the high points of my life and I earnestly hope he enjoyed the experience as much as I did! But above all that, over and above my own experience, the most significant thing was that the concert gave an unprecedented global platform to the issue of HIV and AIDS, which was boundary pushing and life saving.'[9]

Fittingly, it was Liza Minnelli who brought the concert to a close with a rousing and theatrical rendition of 'We Are The Champions' that *The Times* said 'most convincingly captured the essence of Mercury's unique and much-loved style. Combining a commanding presence with a suitably valedictory tone, she injected just the right degree of knowing burlesque into her performance. It was a touching and appropriate end to a heartfelt memorial.'[10] As she finished, Minnelli looked to the heavens and said, 'Thanks, Freddie. We just wanted to let you know, we'll be thinking of you.'

The show raised £12m for AIDS awareness and that night, after the acts had left the stage and after the sell-out crowd had disappeared into the night, an after-show party was held at Browns nightclub. It was, like the concert itself, a strange affair: celebration mixed with undeniable sadness. At the party Brian and Roger appeared vacant, according to Spike Edney, as though unable to take anything in[11] and over the next few days questions were asked about the success of the concert, with *The Times* commenting: 'While it was perfectly appropriate that surviving Queen members Brian May and Roger Taylor should host the evening, both seemed to have graduated from the "Hello London!" school of on-stage repartee. The talk was mainly of "great friends of ours" and "having a good time tonight". Cheerfulness was all. From what his old partners had to say about it, you might have thought that Freddie's absence that night was due to a temporary indisposition. AIDS being the complicated and depressing subject it is, most of the acts that flitted on and off the Wembley stage chose not to mention the theme of the concert at all. For the hard rock bands, which opened the show, singing about safe sex is pretty awkward anyway, a bit like extolling the virtues of shandy. *Guns N' Roses* duly hollered on about a place called Paradise City, where it was by no means clear whether the girls carried condoms in their handbags; and Def Leppard led a rally call of Let's Get Rocked, which seemed blissfully unaware that anything as unpleasant as AIDS might impinge on a man's urgent need for casual sex.'[12]

The same article questioned what Freddie himself would have made of it. Certainly none of his true favourites were represented; there was no Aretha Franklin, no Michael Jackson, no Montserrat Caballé. In fact it was Caballé herself that was perhaps the singular most glaring omission. And there were none of his close friends performing, people such as Elaine Paige, Tony Hadley or even his best friend Peter Straker. There was no reference to opera, to ballet, to classical works, and none of Freddie's solo work was heard. Perhaps the concert was more about Brian, Roger and John than it was about Freddie. Maybe it was their way of coming to terms with Freddie's loss, a chance to grieve publicly and get it out of their system. They needed closure, and the tribute concert may have provided it for them.

As Queen left the stage after 'We Are The Champions', Joe Elliott of Def Leppard was walking off and found himself next to Brian May. 'I grabbed his sleeve,' recalls Joe, 'and said: "Brian – turn round and look at this, because you might not ever see this again." He stood there and had a long look. And then he said: "Thanks, Joe." And he gave me a big hug and then buggered off.'[13]

Black Sabbath guitarist, Tommy Iommi, who had performed during the show likewise recalls the immediate aftermath of coming off-stage: 'Immediately after the show was over, in private, it hit Brian very hard. Hit them all. It was so, so sad. John was just in bits. It was a case of: "Right, that's it, over, final."'[14]

53

With the end of The Freddie Mercury Tribute concert, many thought the days of Queen were over. As Freddie himself said: 'If anyone left, any one of the four, that would be the end of Queen. We are four equal, interwoven parts. And the others just couldn't function the same without each quarter.'[1]

But Queen's music refused to die with Freddie. In 1992, the band's fortunes in the US were suddenly and surprisingly revived when the comedy film *Wayne's World* featured a sequence in which the two main characters were seen singing along to the operatic sections of 'Bohemian Rhapsody' before headbanging their way through the rock section of the song. 'The gleeful scene has become iconic itself, a cultural touchstone that's been parodied, copied and celebrated almost since the moment of its release back in 1992,' wrote *Rolling Stone*[2] and the movie introduced the song to a whole new generation, the MTV generation. Within weeks the song was once more being played on US radio stations forcing it to be re-released as a single in the US, where it climbed to number 2 on the Billboard charts.

While all this was going on, behind the scenes discussions were taking place about a possible 'new' Queen album. 'We thought, "OK, it'll just die away" when Freddie died, and that would be the end of it, but it didn't,' recalls Roger Taylor. 'And the interest continued. So then we found ourselves obligated to sort of keep running the whole thing, even on a business level, which sounds boring, but I mean it just needs to be done, you know. And of course we've always remained friends – you can't be friends for that long, and then just split up.'[3]

Freddie had left behind material that he had recorded at Montreux during his final weeks, material that had come about after he had urged his bandmates to write as much as they could, which he would then record against a simple drum click-track, for them to work with after he had gone. Working with producer David Richards, Brian, Roger and John began piecing together the material Freddie had recorded and reworking it as fully-fledged Queen songs.

'It's difficult in many ways,' said Brian May on the recording of the album, 'but it's gradually taking shape. There was only a certain amount of material that Freddie sang on which we can work with so there are very real limits.'[4]

With not quite enough material to make an album, the band explored unreleased material from Freddie's solo career and radically reworked it to give it a Queen identity. 'Some songs remained in the original way,' recalled producer David Richards. 'Others, like the two songs from Freddie's solo work, received a Queen arrangement which transformed them from a solo product into a Queen product. This kind of work takes a lot of time. The whole thing was a very emotional experience. The fact that Freddie wanted this album finished gave us strength.'[5]

On 6th November 1995, and almost four years after Freddie's death, Queen's 15th studio album, *Made In Heaven*, was released. Featuring 13 tracks, including Freddie's final vocal performance, 'Mother Love', it was a number 1 album in the UK and across Europe, and sold over 10m copies worldwide, generating mainly – although not exclusively – positive reviews. *The Sunday Times* said of the album: 'This rates as a superior effort and a more-than-worthy epitaph to the great entertainer himself,'[6] while *Q* magazine asked, 'What manner of tasteless, barrel-scraping exercise are the surviving members of the band involved in now?'[7] And *The Times* wrote: 'Despite its overdue delivery, "Made In Heaven" stands up remarkably well as the closing chapter in a spectacular pop odyssey.'[8]

Except the Queen pop odyssey wasn't closing.

While John Deacon had stepped out of the limelight and retreated into his own private world, Brian May and Roger Taylor kept the Queen legacy alive.

As the Millennium drew to a close, Brian and Roger performed in public on a number of occasions, playing Queen songs with a variety of guest singers, and in 1999, EMI released the album *Greatest Hits III*, which featured songs from the latter part of their career, solo hits, and collaborations with other artists.

'Eight years on from the "Greatest Hits II" package – the same amount of time since Freddie Mercury's death – perhaps the most remarkable thing about "Greatest Hits III" is that 15 of its 16 tracks were, in fact, hits,' wrote *Classic Rock*, while also saying it was 'padded out by second-division material.'[9]

Within a year, Queen had released *The Platinum Collection*, a box-set containing *Greatest Hits I, II & III* and, undeterred by the albums in their original form selling millions, fans flocked to buy the package. By now, such was Queen's success that they were the second-biggest selling artist in the UK behind The Beatles.

'We Will Rock You' had been another number 1 for Queen in 2000 when they recorded it with the boy band Five providing the vocals. For the 2001 movie, *A Knight's Tale*, Robbie Williams supplied the vocal performance, begging the question whether Queen would ever record or tour again with another vocalist. Upon hearing Williams' version of 'We Are The Champions' with Queen, John Deacon, in a rare interview, told *The Sun* that, 'It's one of the greatest songs ever written but I think they've ruined it. I don't want to be nasty but let's just say Robbie Williams is no Freddie Mercury. Freddie can never be replaced – and certainly not by him.'[10]

It appears serious conversations were had with a view to Queen – that is, Brian and Roger by now – touring North America with Robbie Williams performing vocal duties but, for whatever reason, it never came to fruition. However, Queen had another project to devote their energies to.

In 2002, *We Will Rock You* opened in London's West End. A musical based on the songs of Queen, it was written by Ben Elton. Despite almost universal panning by the critics, the show would run for a record-breaking 12 years in London to sell-out crowds, with over 13m people seeing the show worldwide.

'What would Freddie think about the musical?' Brian May laughs out loud. 'Oh, he'd be so thrilled that the music was living on in this way. He'd be happy to pass it on to the next generation, like I am. Just so proud.'[11]

With no more Mercury music to mine, record labels had to be content with repackaging solo material: first came *Solo* in 2000 and then *The Very Best of Freddie Mercury Solo* in 2006, which was a Top 10 hit, proving he had not been forgotten.

The Queen bandwagon continued to steamroll through popular culture – in fact, they could claim to be Britain's national band, perhaps.

As well as the musical *We Will Rock You*, the band had their own computer game, countless DVDs had been released of live performances, behind-the-scenes documentaries or profiles had been made, there was a Queen-branded karaoke release, a *Guitar Hero* collaboration, and their songs were used in movies and television programmes around the world in everything from *The Simpsons* to *Iron Man 2*. And if their ubiquity wasn't enough, Queen were the most licensed band for advertising purposes[12], with their songs being used to sell everything from cruise-ship shows to Hoover adverts, credit cards and cellphones, Renault cars, Walmart, Pepsi, VISA, Volkswagon, Taco Bell, brandy, cat food, crisps, beer, pot noodles, chewing gum, diapers, ice cream and even Viagra (ironically, Viagra might have been the only one Freddie would have approved of).

The band even found time to release another Queen album in 2014, featuring three previously unreleased tracks with Freddie singing, including his duet with Michael Jackson, 'There Must Be More To Life Than This', alongside other songs that illustrated the band's musical journey. 'There was a little bit more in the can that we had overlooked for a long time,' said Brian May at a press conference to announce plans for the album, 'so we have a few songs which we're working on right now. Freddie sounds as fresh as yesterday.'[13]

The album reached the Top 5 in the UK, showing that, in Britain anyway, the desire for anything Queen and Freddie Mercury-related was still strong. '"Queen Forever" is a statement of intent,' said the *Daily Mail* in its review. 'A classic act is no longer merely the sum of its parts and its works. It is an industry in itself, and self-perpetuating. Here Queen proclaim their right to live for ever – not just in popular memory, but at the tills and in the charts.'

And therein lies the rub: by 2015, Queen were more brand than band. Their back catalogue was being exploited mercilessly, any fragment of unreleased recordings being dusted off and digitally enhanced to release to the world, and live recordings repackaged, old hits remixed and albums re-mastered. While John Deacon assumed the life of a recluse, Brian May and Roger Taylor toured the world with different singers to keep the music of Queen alive. This clearly sits at odds with his comment in 1992, when May had said, 'My personal feeling is that we should never go out and try and be Queen again. It doesn't make sense without Freddie.' It was a sentiment he was to echo in a 1993 interview: 'I think that there was a kind of tacit agreement that Queen couldn't exist without any one of us, especially without Freddie, because he was so much a part of the image of the band. It wasn't like just losing a singer, it was like losing a real heart.'[14]

'Queen wouldn't be Queen if one of us left the band, or if we did things differently,' said Taylor in 1984. 'The sense of unity has kept us strong. It's the same band today that it was when we started. I think that's good. I think that's important. There's an old saying: "The whole is more than the sum of its parts". That applies to Queen.'[15]

But the above quotes withstanding, they had no intention of stopping after the death of Freddie, and it certainly paid dividends: 2014 accounts show Queen Productions Ltd was bringing in £132,000 per day and the band's earnings had more than doubled from £22m in 2013 to £48.5m a year later. Freddie had an equal share in Queen Productions and his estate would have received similar.[16] Indeed, Mercury's personal wealth since his death has been far greater than during his lifetime. It is estimated he made a fortune of around £20m before he died in 1991, but since then royalties from his music, the Queen musical and Queen tours have made another £50m for the estate and global charities.

In 1991, his death drew attention to the AIDS crisis both in the UK and abroad, and perhaps helped to reduce prejudice more than any leaflet or advertising campaign could ever do as people realised that HIV could affect anyone, including a figure whom they idolised and respected. All of this has been accomplished because Freddie Mercury's death brought AIDS into our living rooms.

And, in doing so, he became a legend.

'He becomes a bigger star with each passing year,' says Paul Gambaccini. 'It's only when the dust settled afterwards, and the people who had been buying those records became the people who were writing the histories, that it became clear how major they had been. And Freddie, for example, the fact that Mika could just refer in the song "Grace Kelly" to Freddie and everybody knew who it was, there are a million Freddies in the world but everyone knew he was talking about

Freddie Mercury. So Freddie's become the symbol of not only talent but extravagance and of burning the candle at both ends and of playing a part in history by being the most famous rock star to die of AIDS. Because it won't happen again now because of medication, and now that society feels comfortable enough to talk about it, we think, "Holy Cow, this guy was a shooting star."'[17]

'When I'm dead, I want to be remembered as a musician of some worth and substance,' said Freddie. 'I don't know how they'll remember me. I haven't thought about that – dead and gone! No, I haven't thought about it. I don't really think, "My God! When I'm dead are they going to remember me?" It's up to them. When I'm dead, who cares? I don't!'[18]

Danielle Ofri, associate professor at the New York University School of Medicine and author of *What Patients Say; What Doctors Hear*, says in an article written for the *New York Times*: 'In the worlds of both medicine and metaphor, the narrative arc of AIDS has almost no peer. The transformation from hopelessness to pragmatic optimism is – scientifically speaking – nothing short of miraculous. Potent combinations of anti-viral medications that brought patients off their deathbeds and back to life, viral load testing and HIV genotyping that helped tailor treatment regimes, screening of the blood supply, aggressive public health campaigns, prevention of maternal-fetal transmission – we could hardly have envisioned the pace of development. After years of disappointments, HIV vaccine research is heating up again as breakthroughs in the understanding of HIV immunology have identified nearly two dozen potential vaccine candidates. The apparent HIV cure as a result of a bone-marrow transplant in a man known as the 'Berlin patient' has stimulated tantalising gene therapy research. The staggering progress of these past two decades leaves us breathless, and to be honest, almost teary-eyed. For nearly every other category of disease that afflicts my patients, the treatments are largely the same as when I was an intern. Yes, we have fancier stents for our cardiac patients and more targeted chemotherapy for our cancer patients, but the overall paradigms have shifted only incrementally. HIV has been easier to target, in part, because it is caused by a single infectious agent – as opposed to the diverse factors that influence cardiovascular disease or cancer. And then there was the avalanche of resources and the galvanising of public activism that served to concentrate scientific efforts in a manner never seen before. By no means do I wish to belittle the impressive advances in other fields of medicine, but our oncology wards and cardiac wards still do brisk business. AIDS patients in the hospital are a rarity now – they are more likely to be admitted for an ulcer or a heart attack than for an HIV-related illness. The overwhelming majority receive their medical care in outpatient settings, like everyone else who is living with a disease rather than dying of a disease. AIDS has settled in next to hypertension and diabetes as one of those chronic conditions that patients deal with over the course of a lifetime.'[9]

'Over the course of a lifetime.'

Now there's a concept never thought about back then.

The great sadness with Freddie Mercury is that, had he managed to live a few years longer, he might have found himself with access to treatments that would have prolonged his life. But that wasn't to be. As it was, he became one of the millions around the globe who died from AIDS.

At the time of writing, in 2016, it is estimated that there are 43m people worldwide infected with HIV. However, the majority of people with the virus don't even know they have it. For this reason, major inaccuracies exist in certain statistics and millions of people continue to die from AIDS-related diseases every year. In Africa, the disease is particularly devastating. The continent is home to over 70 per cent of the world's infected population and will see 82 per cent of all AIDS deaths in 2016.

In the Western world, the world of the arts, culture and sport has been particularly hard hit by AIDS. Brad Davis, Miles Davis, Leigh Bowery, Yves St Laurent, Andy Warhol, Arthur Ashe, Isaac Asimov, Fela Kuti, Anthony Perkins, Herb Ritts, Rudolph Nureyev, Esteban De Jesús, John Curry, Dan Hartman, Patrick Juvet, Denholm Elliott, Chuck Holmes, Eazy-E, Jerry Herman, Klaus Nomi, Gil Scott-Heron, Scott O'Hara, Mike Beuttler, Michael Bennett, Robert R, Sylvester, Tina Chow, Derek Jarman, Jean-Paul Aron, Jaime Gil de Biedma and Freddie Mercury, among others. All connected by one inconsequential moment when a chimpanzee bit our hunter in the African jungle.

There is another connection, a connection between three men who all shared the same terrible and debilitating disease: Freddie Mercury,

Gaëtan Dugas and Rock Hudson. Mercury and Hudson were both famous; Gaëtan would become infamous. And it would be their struggle and subsequent deaths that would become a backhanded blessing, finally focusing front-page, prime-time attention on the disease, and finally bringing in additional research money and attention to and for the mortal war being waged.

While the death of Dugas was a quiet affair (he was only immortalised afterwards by Randy Shilts' book, *And the Band Played On*, and his story picked up by the American media), the significance of Mercury's death, as with Hudson's, cannot be overlooked, and it is, in many ways, as important as his achievements in life, which were almost unsurpassed. He was one of the most recognisable people in the Western world, adored and loved by millions of people, most importantly, after his death in the fight against HIV and AIDS, by a demographic indifferent at worst, ignorant at best, of the struggle to beat the disease. Even Queen fans confessed they had absolutely no idea that Mercury was gay, or that he had AIDS (right up until the announcement). This may be difficult to believe but the point is, the majority of people did not. In a career that spanned 20 years, it is reasonable to assume he was HIV positive for almost half of it. So what we were witnessing, through a time with no treatment per se, was the slow death of an individual and artist. (However much it might not be palatable to most fans, it is impossible to write about Freddie without the story of his HIV and AIDS. It was, and would be more so after his death, a defining aspect of what he was.)

In terms of Freddie's life, his death and his legacy, the single most important cover was *The Sun* newspaper with the headline, 'Freddie is Dead'. That cover marked a tangible change in attitude both in and towards the media. 'Freddie's death and that cover ended Murdoch's stranglehold on public morals,' claims Paul Gambaccini. 'Murdoch's *The Sun* under, I believe, Kelvin MacKenzie, wanted to run a three-day exposé of Freddie courtesy of the late Paul Prenter and to the shock of Rupert Murdoch, circulation went down on the first day. Freddie was on the front page, Freddie was this terrible person, whatever it said; people didn't want to know, they didn't buy it. So, I was told, word went out from Murdoch himself to downplay the last two sections and that was the first time that the homophobia of the Murdoch newspapers was toned down. It was a very useful social role to turn the tide against the homophobia of the person whom I consider to be the greatest hate-monger of the 1980s.'[20]

Even after the death of Rock Hudson, and seeing how public support had rallied to the cause on behalf of the actor, Freddie still found it impossible to come out as a person infected with the virus, just as he had found it impossible to come out as gay. For all of them, their closets were cells from which they couldn't truly escape. But we view the past from a different present. Those final public images of a pale and gaunt Freddie leaving Mayfair clinics might have told us how ill he really was, but more importantly, they reveal a deeper truth about Britain in the late 1980s and its seeming unpreparedness for a crisis so long in the making. The country was governed (through almost all the worst years of the AIDS crisis) by Margaret Thatcher, who while extolling the virtues of human rights and humanism, remained utterly resistant to the suffering of those around her and was indifferent to gay rights. Alongside the Reagan administration in the United States, this attitude ultimately jeopardised research, setting it back at least five years and costing hundreds of thousands of lives in the process.

Since the beginning of the AIDS epidemic as we know it, which is around 1980, up to 87.6m people have become infected with HIV and 40.8m have died from AIDS-related illnesses.[21] However, there are no accurate statistics to give an indication of how many people developed and died from HIV and AIDS before the 1980s and therefore, using the most basic multiple and knowing the disease began in the early part of the 20th century, the number of AIDS-related deaths could feasibly be upwards of 200m people globally.

In the years since the death of Freddie Mercury it's easy to look back upon the brilliant career and secretive life of music's most entertaining, talented and flamboyant showman only to get lost in the music and drown in sold-out stadiums of nostalgia and forget these catastrophic numbers.

But it also allows us enough time consider the question that *The Advocate* posed back in 1991 upon Mercury's death: 'Will the singer do more to battle ignorance and prejudice in death than he managed to in his lifetime?'

After 25 years, the unequivocal answer to that question is 'yes'.

Epilogue

Twenty-five years after his death, Freddie Mercury has been voted the greatest frontman of all time, he has been immortalised on British postage stamps, statues and plaques have been erected in his honour, and his posthumous magnetism appears to show no signs of slowing down, attracting fans too young to remember him in his pomp, while his music continues to echo around the world. It's a truly remarkable continuation of the story of the shy young Frederick Bulsara, who arrived in England with his parents as refugees from a civil war in 1964, went to art college, and then embarked on a career as a singer, songwriter and performer, a career that would see him dominate charts and stages all around the planet.

Some five decades after Queen formed, the band remains one of the most popular groups on Earth, despite the fact that they have been without Freddie for longer than they were with him. So why is there still so much interest in Queen and Freddie Mercury? The dance critic Mark Monahan wrote of Queen's enduring appeal that, 'In an era that saw John Lennon take on war, The Velvet Underground embrace heroin addiction, Pink Floyd probe the darker reaches of the human psyche, Queen preferred to sing about fat bottomed girls and the delights of pootling about on bicycles. In short, they seldom if ever tried to "say" anything, and so laissez-faire was their attitude to politics that, in 1984, they defied the UN's cultural boycott of apartheid-era South Africa to play several sold-out gigs in Sun City. If the latter decision was misguided at best, it has nevertheless generally been the band's very refusal to take things too seriously that has so appealed to the public (while often confounding the more po-faced elements of the music press).'[1]

Of course, it helps that Queen came up with some of the catchiest and most successful songs of the 1970s and 1980s. But there's more to Queen's enduring legacy than simply great songs and that, ultimately, is down to one man: Freddie Mercury. While Brian May, Roger Taylor and John Deacon provided the instrumentation, always firmly in the background, Freddie pranced, posed, preened and performed like no one before and no one since.

'He should be remembered as one of the iconic performers of the 20th century,' says Mike Moran. 'A great writer, and a great human being. He's just a one-off. I don't know what the epitaph should be really, but from my point of view he was just a true original. His sense of humour, his performing style, his compositions, his ambitions, his courage – a true original.'[2]

Only in his last few years, in his fight against AIDS – a fight he sought to assure us *wasn't* against AIDS, or even *his* fight – did he become a staple figure in the gossip columns and tabloids. Then he achieved by default another level of public consciousness. And with his death, it seems he rose again.

'The national wave of sadness that greeted Mercury's death hints, I think, at one of Queen's greatest assets: the band's lovability,' suggests Mark Monahan. 'For all his excess, Mercury was a hopelessly appealing, not to mention endearingly private figure whose sexuality and love life were – inconceivable as it now seems – not a matter of public record.'[3]

Freddie Mercury created the look of *Queen*; he created the crest that adorned album covers and he just happened to write most of the hits. No one in the history of pop composition has blended rock with opera, music hall with metal, Coward-esque campness with vaudevillian influences to create such a canon of work as Freddie Mercury. And while the others all composed hits of their own, only Mercury could have composed the greatest of them all, 'Bohemian Rhapsody'.

Certainly, the era into which Mercury descended helped him create his legacy. With no Internet, he was unable to destroy his own mystique through social media. He rarely gave interviews, so that helped him maintain an air of aloofness, but also mystery. It may have been no coincidence that the band had a regal name, for Freddie lived a life that was as secretive as royalty. He was a man who held court with those around him, and only a few could get close enough to touch. As Caroline Sullivan wrote: 'Mercury was a fastidious, generous man whose private life was utterly off limits to anyone outside the inner circle. For someone who sold in the neighborhood of 150 million albums, he was remarkably hard to fathom.'[4]

And what is evident, in the words of those who knew him, is how deeply he was loved, not merely by fans but by those few people he kept around him, be it employees or friends. Yet Freddie rarely talked to anyone, even his lovers, about his fears and insecurities, his inner feelings. As he said so often, 'I am lonely' – which has, in his case, nothing to do with being alone. But Freddie often felt he had to stay alone, as he had done in his childhood.

'It can be a very lonely life,' he said, 'but I choose it.'[5]

Instead of domestic refuge, Mercury sought ecstasy and restlessness for most of his life, and obviously that choice incurred a cost. But let's not overcomplicate things because in the end it isn't. He knew in the end if he revealed too much about himself the public might be 'let down'. His own stark reality was his own disappointment. On-stage he could adhere to the cliché. He could be a creation, aside from himself; he was a show-off from the 1970s who had an extraordinary voice, loved dressing up and theatrics, and adored the musical *Cabaret*. An incredibly accomplished musician, who had the ability to write infinitely clever pop songs, his common touch was the key to Queen's success. This single truth was recognised by critics who cared little for him or the band, just as that single truth was applauded by the ordinary man who bought into it.

But the Freddie Mercury story is also one of the human conditioning for survival and the joy of life: he fought to the bitter end. And while he couldn't survive, his legacy most certainly did. 'If I had to do it all again? Yes, why not?' Freddie said. 'I might do some of it differently. I have no regrets.'[6]

Peter Straker shares these views: 'I remember him as my friend and I remember him with a great capacity to enjoy life and enjoyed it when other people enjoyed it with him, and he was a very generous man in his time, energy and money. I remember him for some of the music, which I just think is tremendous, and his showmanship, which sent tingles down the back of my neck. I just remember him as one of the great people I knew and I'm grateful that we were friends.'[7]

Freddie Mercury, singer and songwriter, stood 5ft 9in tall, with black hair and dark brown eyes. He loved opera and ballet, Lana Turner was his favourite actress and Aretha Franklin just one of his many favourite singers. He liked to drink either champagne or iced vodka, smoke purple Silk Cut, and Indian food was one of his favourites.

He died on 24th November 1991, aged 45.

Acknowledgements

MARK: No biography exists in isolation, so firstly we extend our thanks to all the other biographers who have written so meticulously about Freddie Mercury, and whom we acknowledge: Lesley-Ann Jones, Laura Jackson and Mark Blake.

We acknowledge and thank all the people whose words and deeds and thoughts and expressions we used in order that we might, in some small part, bring something of their experiences to this book. Due to the sheer scale of Freddie Mercury's work, this book never sought to cover every historical aspect and musical gesture that comprised his lengthy career. Instead, our investigation explores selective elements within that extensive landscape and, in particular, Freddie Mercury himself. In so doing, we incorporate a range of divergent viewpoints held by critics of the popular tabloid press, the existing members of Queen, Freddie's household and medical advisers, the music press, staff members, devoted fans, friends, critics, gay activists and homophobes.

And extended thanks to: firstly, the remarkable Barry C. Promane, the brilliant writer David Quammen for inspiration, Liz Tray, Elisabeth Kübler-Ross, the genius that is Susan Sontag, Georgia Kakalopoulou and of course Danielle Ofri, MD, PhD, D Litt(Hon), FACP, editor-in-chief of the Bellevue Literary Review. Danielle is a doctor at New York City's Bellevue Hospital and author of several books.*

Lives lost and found, and lost once more.

In addition, this book has left a great deal out in order to get as much in as we can, and simply because you have to choose a single

---

* 'The first literary journal ever to arise from a medical setting, the Bellevue Literary Review takes a creative lens to health, healing, illness and disease. It's a journal of humanity and human experience.' The BLR website is www.BLReview.org. Donations can be made here: http://blr. med.nyu.edu/support.

What Patients Say, What Doctors Hear, by Danielle Ofri
The gulf between what patients say and what doctors hear is often wide, but Dr. Danielle Ofri proves that it doesn't have to be. Her newest book shows how refocusing conversations between doctors and patients can lead to better health outcomes for all. www.danielleofri.com

thread. Of course, this is not a history of the AIDS crisis, and never in reality comes close to understanding the threat of it, or all those who struggled against it and lost, but sometimes won. In addition, primary sources contributing to this book were obtained through extensive interviews with persons closely linked to Freddie Mercury. This is our thank you to those persons who have contributed so much to this book. To Freddie's closest friend for the longest time, Peter Straker, who contributed so generously and to whom we are eternally indebted. And to John Reid, Paul Gambaccini, Mike Moran, Paul Loasby, Mike Hodges, Annie Lennox, Lee Everett-Alkin, Marc Almond, Lucian Toplician, Tris Penna, Mike Youle, Jean Diamond, Darren Walsh, Michelle Mahlke and Roland Mouret (for his support throughout).

To our extraordinary editor Emily Thomas, who is simply brilliant and dedicated. To everyone at Blink for supporting this book, including the lovely Perminder and Kelly.

To Ink for the cover artwork.

Finally and most importantly, my personal thank you to my co-writer, Matt Richards, who is such a great talent and genuinely warm soul. I couldn't have found a more perfect co-writer, and he is an inspiration, a joy and a genuine friend. I am consistently amazed at your ability to find more compelling and intelligent arguments to my ramblings and writings.

To Robert Lang, Robert, Richie and Michael.

And to the memory of all those who have died from AIDS.

MATT: I can only echo Mark's comments and thank unreservedly all those who so willingly and generously offered up their time to talk about their memories of Freddie Mercury. Special thanks must go to Peter Straker, who, as Mark says, contributed so much. I'd also like to acknowledge the biographers, film-makers and journalists who have written, filmed and reported extensively about Freddie Mercury and Queen over the decades, thereby providing an invaluable resource, particularly biographers Mark Blake and Rupert White.

Thank you to our editor too, Emily Thomas, for her encouragement and diligent comments and to all at Blink involved in the production of this book.

Many thanks, as well, to my son, Thomas, for all his continued support and to my daughter, Rhoda, for providing me with so much happiness during the writing process.

As with previous books, there are two people who deserve special thanks: firstly, my co-author Mark, who continues to amaze me with his enthusiasm, passion, creativity and friendship. There is no better writing partner and I am proud to be associated with him, both as a co-author and as a friend. Secondly, my partner, Lucy, who throughout the writing of this book has offered continued inspiration, support and encouragement despite my often solitary existence as a writer and frequent research trips away. Her selflessness and devotion cannot be appreciated enough, and all my thanks are certainly insufficient. All I can say is I love my work but I live for her.

Thanks must also go to the genius that was Freddie Mercury. I was fortunate enough to see Queen in concert at Wembley in 1986. Watching Freddie on-stage that night, with the audience in the palm of his hand, will live with me forever.

Finally, as Mark says, this book is dedicated to the memory of all those who have lived with, through, are still living with, and have died from AIDS.

Select Bibliography

Books

Auaslander, Philip, *Performing Glam Rock: Gender And Theatricality In Popular Music* (University of Michigan Press, 2006).

Baenninger, R. (Ed.), *Targets Of Violence & Aggression* (North Holland, 1991).

Bayer, Ronald & Oppenheimer, Gerald M., *AIDS Doctors: Voice From The Epidemic: An Oral History* (Oxford University Press, 2000).

Blake, Mark, *Is This The Real Life? The Untold Story Of Queen* (Aurum Press Ltd., 2011).

Bret, David, *The Freddie Mercury Story: Living On The Edge* (Robson Books, 1999).

Brodkey, Harold, *This Wild Darkness: The Story Of My Death* (Fourth Estate, 1996).

Brooks, Greg & Lupton, Simon, *Freddie Mercury: His Life In His Own Words* (Omnibus Press, 2009).

Daniel, V.G. (Ed.), *AIDS: The Acquired Immune Deficiency Syndrome* (Springer, 1987).

Duffell, Nick, *The Making Of Them: The British Attitude To Children and the Boarding School System* (Lone Arrow Press, 2000).

Dyer, Richard, *The Culture Of Queers* (Routledge, 2001).

Evans, David & Minns, David, *This Was The Real Life: The Tale of Freddie Mercury* (Tusitala, 2001).

Fischer, Lucy (Ed.), *Imitation Of Life: Douglas Sirk, Director* (Rutgers University Press, 1991).

Freestone, Peter & Evans, David, *Freddie Mercury: An Intimate Memoir by the Man Who Knew Him Best* (Omnibus Press, 2001).

Garber, Marjorie, *Bisexuality and the Erotocism Of Everyday Life* (Routledge, 2000).

Gunn, Jacky & Jenkins, Jim, *Queen – As It Began* (Pan Books, 1993).

Hince, Peter, *Queen Unseen: My Life with the Greatest Rock Band of the 20th Century* (John Blake, 2011).

Hodkinson, Mark, *Queen – The Early Years* (Music Sales Ltd, 2004).

Hogg, James & Sellers, Richard, *Hello, Darlings!: The Autobiography of Kenny Everett* (Bantam Press, 2014).

Hudson, Rock & Davidson, Sara, *Rock Hudson: His Story* (Carroll & Graf, 2007).

Hutton, Jim with Tim Wapshott, *Mercury & Me* (Bloomsbury Publishing PLC, 1995).

Jackson, Laura, *Mercury: The King Of Queen* (Smith Gryphon, 1996).

— *Queen: The Definitive Biography* (Piaktus, 2002).

John, Elton, *Love Is The Cure: On Life, Loss and the End of AIDS* (Hodder Paperbacks, 2013).

Jones, Dylan, *The Eighties: One Day, One Decade* (Preface, 2013).

Jones, Lesley-Ann, *Freddie Mercury: The Definitive Biography* (Hodder Paperbacks, 2012).

Kübler-Ross, Elisabeth, *AIDS: The Ultimate Challenge* (Touchstone, 1997).

Marten, Neville & Hudson, Jeffrey, *Freddie Mercury & Queen* (Castle Communications, 1995).

Pepin, Jacques, *The Origin Of AIDS* (Cambridge University Press, 2011).

Plant, Moira, *Risk Takers: Alcohol, Drugs, Sex And Youth* (Routledge, 1992).

Pomane, Barry C., *Freddie Mercury & Queen: Technologies of Genre and the Poetics of Innovations* (The University of Western Ontario, 2009).

Pope, Cynthia, White, Renee T., Malow, Robert, *HIV/AIDS: Global Frontiers In Prevention/Intervention* (Routledge, 2008).

Quammen, David, *The Chimp and the River – How AIDS Emerged from an African Forest* (W.W. Norton & Co., 2015).

Reilly, Benjamin, *Disaster and Human History: Case Studies In Nature, Society and Catastrophe* (McFarland, 2009).

Rider, Stephen, *Queen: These Are The Days Of Our Lives – The Essential Queen Biography* (Sanctuary Publishing, 1993).

Schmidt, Thomas E., *Straight & Narrow?: Compassion & Clarity In The Homosexuality Debate* (IVP, 1995).

Shilts, Randy, *And The Band Played On: Politics, People, and the AIDS Epidemic* (Souvenir Press, 2011).

Siena, Kevin Patrick, *A Medical History of the Skin: Scratching The Surface* (Routledge, 2013).

Simels, Steven, *Gender Chameleons: Androgyny in Rock 'n' Roll* (Arbor House, 1985).

Sky, Rick, *The Show Must Go On: The Life of Freddie Mercury* (HarperCollins, 1994).

St. Michael, Mick, *Queen In Their Own Words* (Omnibus, 1992).

Sontag, Susan, *Illness As Metaphor And AIDS And Its Metaphors* (Penguin Classics, 2009). Quotations from *Illness as Metaphor* copyright © Susan Sontag 1977, 1978 and quotations from *Aids and Its Metaphors* copyright © Susan Sontag 1988, 1989, used by permission of The Wylie Agency (UK) Limited.

Swigonski, Mary E., Mama, Robin, Ward, Kelly (Eds.) *From Hate Crimes To Human Rights: A Tribute to Matthew Shepard* (Routledge, 2001).

White, Rupert, *Queen In Cornwall* (lulu.com, 2011).

Whiteley, Sheila & Rycenga, Jennifer, *Queering The Popular Pitch* (Routledge, 2006).

Websites

www.aidsmap.com

www.bbc.co.uk

www.billboard.com

www.comunitaqueeniana.weebly.com

www.iZotope.com

www.msnbc.com

www.officialcharts.com

www.queenarchives.com

www.queenconcerts.com

www.queenonline.com

www.queenpedia.com

www.queenzone.com

www.realclearpolitics.com

www.rollingstone.com

www.rtbf.be

www.thebody.com

www.ultimatequeen.co.uk

Radio/TV Programmes
Absolute Radio interview
America Westwood One Radio interview
BBC Breakfast Time, BBC TV
BBC Radio 1 interviews
Classic Albums, BBC TV (Isis/Eagle Rock Entertainment/NRK, 2005)
Days of Our Lives, BBC TV (Globe Productions, 2011)
Freddie's Loves, Channel 5 (North One Productions, 2004)
Freddie Mercury: The Untold Story (ZDF, Arte, DoRo Produktion, 2000)
'Frontline: The Age Of AIDS' (Prod: Renata Simone), PBS
Greatest Video Hits 2, EMI Music
KKLZ 96.3 Interviews
'Queen Story', BBC Radio 1
Queen – The Magic Years
Rock Power interviews
Team Rock interviews
The One Show, BBC TV
'The Story Of Bohemian Rhapsody', BBC TV (BBC Manchester, 2004)
Today, MBNS
University Radio Bath interviews
'Video Killed The Radio Star', Sky Arts TV
Xtraonline

Periodicals

American Journal of Public Health
American Journal of Tropical Medicine
American Songwriter
Bass & Bassist Techniques
Birmingham Evening Mail
Boyz Magazine
Cambridge University Press
Capital Gay
Circus Magazine
Creeme Magazine
Disc
Discover Magazine
Discoveries Magazine
Gay City News
Guitar Player
Guitar World
Guitarist Magazine
Innerview

Journal of Analytical Psychology
Journal of the Institute Of
  Actuaries
Journal of Urban Health
Melody Maker
Modern Drummer
Mojo Magazine
Morbidity and Mortality Weekly
  Report
Music Star
National Geographic
New Scientist
Newcastle Chronicle
Newsweek
Newswire
NME
OK! Magazine
Outlook Magazine
Oxford Journals
People Magazine
People Weekly
Psychology Today
Q Magazine
Record Collector
Record Mirror
Rhythm Magazine
Rock Magazine
Rolling Stone Magazine
Science Journal
Sound On Sound
Sounds
Superpop
The Atlantic
The British Medical Journal
The Brunei Times
The Chicago Sun Times

The Daily Express
The Daily Mail
The Daily Mirror
The Daily Telegraph
The Guardian
The Hindustan Times
The Hit
The Hollywood Reporter
The Huffington Post
The Independent
The Los Angeles Times
The Mail On Sunday
The Miami Herald
The Minneapolis Post
The New York Magazine
The New York Post
The New York Times
The People
The Quietus
The Star
The Sun
The Sunday Times
The Times
The Vancouver Sun
The Washington Post
The Washington Times
The Yorkshire Post
Therapy Today
Time Out
Ultimate Classic Rock
Uncut
United Press International
US Department Of Health And
  Human Services
WHO Publications

Endnotes

Chapter 1

1   Leopoldville was renamed Kinshasa in 1966 by Joseph-Désiré Mobutu, who had seized power in the Congo following his second coup in 1965 and initiated a policy of 'Africanising' the names and places of the country.

2   'Revealed: How the AIDs Epidemic Began in an African Rainforest in 1908' by Stephen Lynch, *The New York Post*, 24th February 2015.

Chapter 2

1   *The Chimp and the River: How AIDS Emerged from an African Forest* by David Quammen (W.W. Norton & Company, Inc., 2015).

2   *The Origins of AIDS* by Jacques Pepin (Cambridge University Press, 2011).

3   *The Chimp and the River* by David Quammen (W.W. Norton & Company, Inc., 2015).

4   'Blood Transfusions in the Early Years of AIDS in Sub-Saharan Africa' by William H. Schneider PhD and Ernest Drucker PhD (*American Journal of Public Health*, June 2006).

Chapter 3

1   *The Times*, 2nd September 2006.

2   *Freddie Mercury – The Untold Story*, ZDF, Arte, DoRo Produktion, 2000.

3   *Freddie Mercury: The Definitive Biography* by Lesley-Ann Jones (Hodder Paperbacks, 2012).

4   *The One Show*, BBC, 16th September 2011.

5   *The Mail on Sunday*, 26th November 2000.

6   *The Times*, 2nd September 2006.

7   *Daily Mail*, 11th February 2010.

8   Interview with Peter Straker by the authors, January 2016.

9   Interview with Freddie Mercury for *New Musical Express*, March 1974.

10 *Melody Maker*, December 1974.

11 'Boarding School: The Trauma of the "Privileged" Child' by Joy Schaverien (*Journal of Analytical Psychology*, 49, 2004 pp.683–705).

12 Interview with Freddie Mercury for *New Musical Express*, March 1974.

13 The *Hindustan Times*, 30th August 2008.

14 Ibid.

15 *The Show Must Go On: The Life of Freddie Mercury* by Rick Sky (Citadel Press, 1997).

16 *Queen – As It Began: The Authorized Biography* by Jacky Gunn and Jim Jenkins (Sidgwick & Jackson, 1992).

17 *Freddie Mercury – The Untold Story*, ZDF, Arte, DoRo Produktion, 2000.

18 Ibid.

19 *The Show Must Go On: The Life of Freddie Mercury* by Rick Sky (Citadel Press, 1997).

20 'Going Ga Ga' by Anvar Alikhan, *Outlook Magazine*, 14th November 2011.

Chapter 4

1 BBC Online, 20th November 2009.

2 *Freddie Mercury – The Untold Story*, ZDF, Arte, DoRo Produktion, 2000.

3 BBC Online, 20th November 2009.

4 *Freddie Mercury – The Untold Story*, ZDF, Arte, DoRo Produktion, 2000.

Chapter 5

1 'The Early Spread and Epidemic Ignition of HIV-1 in Human Populations' by Dr Nuno Faria, *Science Journal*, October 2014.

2 'HIV's Spread Traced Back to 1920s Kinshasa' by Monte Morin, *Los Angeles Times*, 10th October 2014.

3 Luckner Cambronne obituary, *The Independent*, 5th October 2006.

4 'Exodus & Genesis: The Emergence of HIV-1 Group M Subtype B', Oral presentation by Dr Michael Worobey, 14th Conference on Retroviruses & Opportunistic Infections, Los Angeles, 2007.

5 'Boy's 1969 Death Suggests AIDS Invaded US Several Times' by Gina Kolata, *The New York Times*, 28th October 1987.

6 *The Chimp and The River: How AIDS Emerged from an African Forest* by David Quammen (W.W. Norton & Company, Inc., 2015).

Chapter 6

1 *Is This The Real Life? The Untold Story of Queen* by Mark Blake (Aurum Press Ltd., 2011).

2 *Freddie Mercury – The Untold Story*, ZDF, Arte, DoRo Produktion, 2000.

3 *Freddy Mercury: The Definitive Biography* by Lesley-Ann Jones (Hodder Paperbacks, 2012).

4 'Colonial Roots of Queen's Mercurial Star Freddie' by Shekhar Bhatia, *Sunday Telegraph*, 16th October 2011.

5 *Freddie Mercury – The Untold Story*, ZDF, Arte, DoRo Produktion, 2000.

6 *Queen – The Definitive Biography* by Laura Jackson (Piatkus, 2002).

7 *Queen – These Are The Days of Our Lives, The Essential Queen Biography* by Stephen Rider (Sanctuary Publishing Ltd., 1993).

8 *Freddie Mercury – The Untold Story*, ZDF, Arte, DoRo Produktion, 2000.

9 *Queen In Cornwall* by Rupert White (lulu.com, 2011).

Chapter 7

1 Roger Taylor and Brian May interview, www.queenonline.com, 23rd March 2011.

2 *Mojo* magazine, September 1998.

3 *Is This The Real Life? The Untold Story of Queen* by Mark Blake (Aurum Press Ltd., 2011).

4 'Their Britannic Majesties Request', *Mojo* magazine, August 1999.

5 *The Sunday Times*, 27th February 2011.

6 *Queen – As It Began* by Jacky Gunn and Jim Jenkins (Hyperion, 1994).

7 *Mercury: The King of Queen* by Laura Jackson (Smith Gryphon, 1996).

8 *Queen – As It Began* by Jacky Gunn and Jim Jenkins (Hyperion, 1994).

9 'Queen Before Queen' by John Stuart and Andy Davis, *Record Collector*, March 1996.

10 *Queen In Cornwall* by Rupert White (lulu.com, 2011).

11 'Their Britannic Majesties Request', *Mojo* magazine, August 1999.

12 *Freddie Mercury – The Untold Story*, ZDF, Arte, DoRo Produktion, 2000.

13 Ibid.

14 'Queen Before Queen' by John Stuart and Andy Davis, *Record Collector*, March 1996.

15 *Freddie Mercury – The Untold Story*, ZDF, Arte, DoRo Produktion, 2000.

16 'For The Love of Freddie...', *The Yorkshire Post*, 24th October 2004.

17 Ibid.

18 *The Times*, 20th August 2004.

19 'For The Love of Freddie...', *The Yorkshire Post*, 24th October 2004.

20 Ibid.

21 *The Times*, 20th August 2004.

22 'Queen Before Queen' by John Stuart and Andy Davis, *Record Collector*, March 1996.

23 Ibid.

24 Ibid.

25 Ibid.

26 *Freddie Mercury – The Untold Story*, ZDF, Arte, DoRo Produktion, 2000.

Chapter 8

1 *The Atlantic*, 26th February 2014.

2 *Boyz Magazine*, 18th June 2009.

3 'Joel Grey and Michael York Recall Movie's Gay, Gender-bending Content' by Curtis Wong, *The Huffington Post*, 2nd June 2013.

4 'The Queen Tapes' by Don Rush, *Circus Magazine*, 17th March 1977.

5 *Gender Chameleons: Androgyny in Rock 'n' Roll* by Steven Simels (Arbor House, 1985).

6 *Bisexuality and the Eroticism of Everyday Life* by Marjorie Garber (Routledge, 2000).

7 *Performing Glam Rock: Gender and Theatricality in Popular Music* by Philip Auslander (University of Michigan Press, 2006).

8 'Classic Queen', *Rock*, 143.

9 Interview with Marc Almond by the authors, January 2016.

10 Ibid.

Chapter 9

1 'The Show Must Go On' by Jonathan Wingate, *Record Collector*, 23rd January 2009.

2 Ibid.

3 *Queen In Cornwall* by Rupert White (lulu.com, 2011).

4 'Freddie is in my Thoughts Every Day' by Neil McCormick, *The Daily Telegraph*, 9th March, 2011.

5 *Queen – The Definitive Biography* by Laura Jackson (Piatkus, 2002).

6 *Queen In Cornwall* by Rupert White (lulu.com, 2011).

7 'The Queen Tapes' by Don Rush, *Circus Magazine*, 17th March 1977.

8 *Mercury: The King of Queen* by Laura Jackson (Smith Gryphon, 1996).

9 *The Freddie Mercury Story: Living On The Edge* by David Bret (Robson Books, 1999).

10 *Queen In Cornwall* by Rupert White (lulu.com, 2011).

11 Ibid.

12 Ibid.

13 Ibid.

14 *Sounds*, December 1974.

15 *Queen: These Are The Days of Our Lives: The Essential Queen Biography* by Stephen Rider (Sanctuary Publishing Ltd., 1993).

16 *Is This the Real Life? The Untold Story of Queen* by Mark Blake (Aurum Press Ltd., 2011).

17 *The Freddie Mercury Story: Living on the Edge* by David Bret (Robson Books, 1999).

18 *Queen in Cornwall* by Rupert White (lulu.com, 2011).

19 Ibid.

20 Ibid.

21 *Queen: As it Began: The Authorized Biography* by Jacky Gunn and Jim Jenkins (Sidgwick & Jackson, 1992).

22 *Queen In Cornwall* by Rupert White (lulu.com, 2011).

23 *Freddie Mercury: His Life in His Own Words* by Greg Brooks and Simon Lupton (Omnibus Press, 2009).

24 *Queen: The Early Years* by Mark Hodkinson (Music Sales Ltd., 2004).

Chapter 10

1 *Freddie Mercury: His Life in His Own Words* by Greg Brooks and Simon Lupton (Omnibus Press, 2009).

2 *Is This the Real Life? The Untold Story of Queen* by Mark Blake (Aurum Press Ltd., 2011).

3 *Freddie Mercury: The Untold Story*, ZDF, Arte, DoRo Produktion, 2000.

4 Ibid.

5 *Daily Mail*, 31st March 2013.

6 Mary Austin interview with David Wigg, MGN Ltd., 2000.

7 *OK!* magazine, 17th March 2000.

8 Mary Austin interview with David Wigg, MGN Ltd., 2000.

9 *Mercury: The King of Queen* by Laura Jackson (Smith Gryphon, 1996).

10 *OK!* magazine, 17th March 2000.

11 *Freddie Mercury: His Life in His Own Words* by Greg Brooks and Simon Lupton (Omnibus Press, 2009).

12 *Freddie Mercury: The Untold Story*, ZDF, Arte, DoRo Produktion, 2000.

13 *Psychology Today*, 6th July 2012.

Chapter 11

1 Interview with Doug Bogie by Comunità Queenia, 14th September 2015.

2 Ibid.

3 *Queen: The Definitive Biography* by Laura Jackson (Piatkus, 2002).

4 Interview with Doug Bogie by Comunità Queenia, 14th September 2015.

5 *Queen: As It Began* by Jacky Gunn and Jim Jenkins (Hyperion Books, 1994).

6 Interview with Doug Bogie by Comunità Queenia, 14th September 2015.

7 Interview with John Deacon, *Music Star*, 24th August 1974.

8 Interview with John Deacon, *Music Star*, 24th August 1974.

9   *Queen: As It Began* by Jacky Gunn and Jim Jenkins (Hyperion Books, 1994).

10 Ibid.

11 *Is This The Real Life? The Untold Story of Queen* by Mark Blake (Aurum Press Ltd., 2011).

12 *Queen: As It Began* by Jacky Gunn and Jim Jenkins (Hyperion Books, 1994).

13 *Freddie Mercury: His Life In His Own Words* by Greg Brooks and Simon Lupton (Omnibus Press, 2009).

14 Ibid.

Chapter 12

1   'The Ultimate Rarities', *Record Collector*, January 2000.

2   *Queen: The Definitive Biography* by Laura Jackson (Piatkus, 2002).

3   *Queen: As It Began* by Jacky Gunn and Jim Jenkins (Hyperion Books, 1994).

4   *Freddie Mercury: His Life In His Own Words* by Greg Brooks and Simon Lupton (Omnibus Press, 2009).

5   Ibid.

6   *Queen In Cornwall* by Rupert White (lulu.com, 2011).

7   *Is This The Real Life? The Untold Story of Queen* by Mark Blake (Aurum Press Ltd., 2011).

8   'Freddie Mercury Felt Like A God, Then he Started Behaving Like One' by Norman Sheffield, *Daily Mail*, 20th July 2013.

9   *Freddie Mercury: His Life In His Own Words* by Greg Brooks and Simon Lupton (Omnibus Press, 2009).

10 *Record Collector*, 23rd January 2009.

11 *Is This The Real Life? The Untold Story of Queen* by Mark Blake (Aurum Press Ltd., 2011).

12 'Freddie Mercury Felt Like A God, Then he Started Behaving Like One' by Norman Sheffield, *Daily Mail*, 20th July 2013.

13 *Queen: As It Began* by Jacky Gunn and Jim Jenkins (Hyperion Books, 1994).

14 'Their Britainic Majesties', *Mojo* magazine, August 1999.

15 *Freddie Mercury: His Life In His Own Words* by Greg Brooks and Simon Lupton (Omnibus Press, 2009).

16 Ibid.

17 'Their Britainic Majesties', *Mojo* magazine, August 1999.

Chapter 13

1   *Rolling Stone*, 6th December 1973.

2   *Is This The Real Life? The Untold Story of Queen* by Mark Blake (Aurum Press Ltd., 2011).

3   *Queen: The Definitive Biography* by Laura Jackson (Piatkus, 2002).

4   *Freddie Mercury: The Definitive Biography* by Lesley-Ann Jones (Hodder Paperbacks, 2012).

5   'Standing up for Queen' by Michael Benton, *Melody Maker*, 28th July 1973.

6   'Queen II Revisited' by Daniel Ross, *The Quietus*, 2nd April 2014.

7   *Disc* magazine, 10th November 1973.

8   Interview with Marc Almond by the authors, January 2016.

9   Interview with Paul Gambaccini by the authors, January 2016.

10 Queen – Radio 1 interview, 24th December 1977.

11 Ibid.

Chapter 14

1 *OK!* magazine, 17th March 2000.

2 Ibid.

3 *Freddie's Loves*, Channel 5 (North One Productions 2004).

4 Ibid.

5 *The Show Must Go On: The Life of Freddie Mercury* by Rick Sky (Citadel Press, 1997).

6 Interview with Peter Straker by the authors, January 2016.

7 *OK!* magazine, 17th March 2000.

8 *Freddie Mercury: The Definitive Biography* by Lesley-Ann Jones (Hodder Paperbacks, 2012).

9 Mary Austin interview with David Wigg, MGN Ltd., 2000.

10 Ibid.

11 *OK!* magazine, 17th March 2000.

12 *Freddie Mercury – The Untold Story*, ZDF, Arte, DoRo Produktion, 2000.

13 David Wigg interview with Mary Austin, 15th October 2015.

14 *Freddie Mercury: His Life in His Own Words* by Greg Brooks and Simon Lupton (Omnibus Press, 2009).

Chapter 15

1 *Mercury: The King of Queen* by Laura Jackson (Smith Gryphon, 1996).

2 *Queen in Cornwall* by Rupert White (lulu.com, 2011).

3 *Rolling Stone*, 20th June 1974.

4 *Freddie Mercury: His Life In His Own Words* by Greg Brooks and Simon Lupton (Omnibus Press, 2009).

5 'We're In The Premiership At Last', Andrew Perry Interviews Ian Hunter, *The Daily Telegraph*, 5th November 2013.

6 *Melody Maker*, 21st December 1974.

7 *NME*, 2nd November 1974.

8 Ibid.

9 Interview with Mike Moran by the authors, January 2016.

10 *NME*, 2nd November 1974.

11 *Freddie's Loves*, Channel 5 (North One Productions, 2004).

12 *Mojo Collection: The Ultimate Music Companion*, Edited by Jim Irvin and Colin McLear, 2000.

13 *Rolling Stone*, 8th May 1975.

14 *Is This The Real Life? The Untold Story of Queen* by Mark Blake (Aurum Press Ltd., 2011).

15 Ibid.

16 'Freddie Mercury Felt Like a God. Then He Started Behaving Like One' by Norman Sheffield, *Daily Mail*, 20th July 2013.

17 'Sheer Heart Attack' by Ron Ross, *Circus Magazine*, March 1975.

Chapter 16

1 'The Changing Face of Gay Culture' by Philip Hensher, *The Independent*, 15th January 2010.

2   Ibid.

3   Donna Summer Obituary, *The Daily Telegraph*, 17th May 2012.

Chapter 17

1   The equivalent of £94,000 at the time of writing.

2   *NME*, 2nd November 1974.

3   *Circus Magazine*, April 1975.

4   *The Freddie Mercury Story: Living On The Edge* by David Bret (Robson Books, 1999).

5   Equivalent to almost £950,000 at the time of writing.

6   *Queen: In Their Own Words* by Mick St Michael (Omnibus Press, 1992).

7   Interview with John Reid by the authors, January 2016.

8   *Freddie Mercury: His Life In His Own Words* by Greg Brooks and Simon Lupton (Omnibus Press, 2009).

9   Interview with John Reid by the authors, January 2016.

10   *Classic Albums*, BBC, 18th December 2005.

11   Equivalent to almost £330,000 at the time of writing.

12   'The Queen Tapes', *Circus Magazine*, 17th March 1977.

13   *Classic Albums*, BBC, 18th December 2005.

14   'Freddie Mercury Felt Like A God. Then He Started Behaving Like One' by Norman Sheffield, *Daily Mail*, 20th July 2013.

15   'The Queen Tapes', *Circus Magazine*, 17th March 1977.

16   Interview with John Reid by the authors, January 2016.

17   *Freddie Mercury: His Life In His Own Words* by Greg Brooks and Simon Lupton (Omnibus Press, 2009).

18   'Queen Story' by Tom Browne, Radio 1, 24th December 1977.

19   'The Story of Bohemian Rhapsody', BBC, 4th December 2004.

20   'The Making of Queen's "Bohemian Rhapsody"' by Mark Cunningham, *Sound on Sound*, October 1995.

21   *Freddie Mercury: His Life In His Own Words* by Greg Brooks and Simon Lupton (Omnibus Press, 2009).

22   'The Story of Bohemian Rhapsody', BBC, 4th December 2004.

23   'The Making of Queen's "Bohemian Rhapsody"' by Mark Cunningham, *Sound on Sound*, October 1995.

24   Ibid.

25   Ibid.

26   'Britanic Majesties', *Mojo* magazine, August 1999.

27   Ibid.

28   John Deacon interview with *Innerview*, 1977.

29   *Freddie Mercury: His Life In His Own Words* by Greg Brooks and Simon Lupton (Omnibus Press, 2009).

30   Interview with John Reid by the authors, January 2016.

31   Ibid.

32   'The Making of Queen's "Bohemian Rhapsody"' by Mark Cunningham, *Sound on Sound*, October 1995.

33 Interview with Paul Gambaccini by the authors, January 2016.

34 *Hello, Darlings!: The Authorized Biography of Kenny Everett* by James Hogg and Robert Sellers (Bantam Press, 2014).

35 'The Making of Queen's "Bohemian Rhapsody"' by Mark Cunningham, *Sound on Sound*, October 1995.

36 Equivalent to £5,646 at the time of writing.

37 *Freddie Mercury: His Life In His Own Words* by Greg Brooks and Simon Lupton (Omnibus Press, 2009).

38 Ibid.

39 'Queen's Tragic Rhapsody' by Mikal Gilmore, *Rolling Stone*, 7th July 2014.

40 *Freddie's Loves*, Channel 5 (North One Productions 2004).

41 *Queering The Popular Pitch* by Sheila Whiteley and Jennifer Rycenga (Routledge, 2006).

42 *Freddie Mercury: The Definitive Biography* by Lesley-Ann Jones (Hodder Paperbacks, 2012).

43 'Freddie's Loves', Channel 5 (North One Productions 2004).

44 *Queering The Popular Pitch* by Sheila Whiteley and Jennifer Rycenga (Routledge, 2006).

45 'What Is "Bohemian Rhapsody"?' BBC News, 15th June 2015.

46 *Freddie Mercury: The Definitive Biography* by Lesley-Ann Jones (Hodder Paperbacks, 2012).

47 Interview with John Reid by the authors, January 2016.

48 *Rolling Stone*, 7th April 2011.

49 *Rolling Stone*, 5th September 2012.

50 *Freddie's Loves*, Channel 5 (North One Productions 2004).

Chapter 18

1 'The Sea Has Neither Sense Nor Pity' by Rebecca Kreston, *Discover Magazine*, 22nd October 2012.

2 What was to become AIDS officially began in the US on 5th June 1981 when CDC identified a cluster of five homosexual men in Los Angeles suffering from *Pneumocystis carinii*. From June 1982 the illness became known as GRID, while the name AIDS was coined a month later at a meeting in Washington of gay community leaders, federal bureaucrats and the CDC on 27th July 1982 and used for the first time in September of that year.

3 'AIDS Virus Travelled to Haiti Then USA' by Amitabh Avasthi, *National Geographic*, 29th October 2007.

4 *And The Band Played On: Politics, People, and the AIDS Epidemic* by Randy Shilts (Souvenir Press Ltd., 2011).

5 Ibid.

6 The period around childbirth, especially the five months before and one month after birth.

7 '25 Years of HIV in New York', *Journal of Urban Health*, New York Academy of Medicine, Vol. 78, No. 4, Dec 2001.

8 Interview with Marc Almond by the authors, January 2016.

Chapter 19

1 *Is This The Real Life? The Untold Story of Queen* by Mark Blake (Aurum Press Ltd., 2011).

2 *Freddie Mercury: The Definitive Biography* by Lesley-Ann Jones (Hodder Paperbacks, 2012).

3 Interview with John Reid by the authors, January 2016.

4   Ibid.

5   *Freddie Mercury: His Life In His Own Words* by Greg Brooks and Simon Lupton (Omnibus Press, 2009).

6   *Queen: The Definitive Biography* by Laura Jackson (Piatkus, 2002).

7   Interview with Annie Lennox by the authors, January 2016.

8   Interview with John Reid by the authors, January 2016.

9   *The Freddie Mercury Story: Living On The Edge* by David Bret (Robson Books, 1999).

10 Interview with Paul Gambaccini by the authors, January 2016.

11 Interview with Marc Almond by the authors, January 2016.

12 'I Was Cursed by Freddie's Fortune' by David Wigg, *Daily Mail*, 30th March 2013.

13 *Record Mirror*, 25th September 1976.

14 *The Washington Post*, 7th February 1977.

15 *Freddie Mercury: His Life In His Own Words* by Greg Brooks and Simon Lupton (Omnibus Press, 2009).

16 Ibid.

17 Ibid.

18 Ibid.

19 *Rolling Stone*, 24th February 1977.

20 *NME*, 18th December 1976.

21 *Freddie Mercury: His Life In His Own Words* by Greg Brooks and Simon Lupton (Omnibus Press, 2009).

Chapter 20

1   *Freddie Mercury: His Life In His Own Words* by Greg Brooks and Simon Lupton (Omnibus Press, 2009).

2   *Mercury: The King of Queen* by Laura Jackson (Smith Gryphon, 1996).

3   *Circus* magazine, 1977.

4   *Is This The Real Life? The Untold Story of Queen* by Mark Blake (Aurum Press Ltd., 2011).

5   'Stone Cold Crazy' by Mick Wall, *Q Classic*, March 2005.

6   '*Is This The Real Life? The Untold Story of Queen* by Mark Blake (Aurum Press Ltd., 2011).

7   Interview with John Reid by the authors, January 2016.

8   Interview with Peter Straker by the authors, January 1976.

9   Interview with John Reid by the authors, January 2016.

10 *Is This The Real Life? The Untold Story of Queen* by Mark Blake (Aurum Press Ltd., 2011).

11 *Freddie's Loves*, Channel 5 (North One Productions, 2004).

12 Ibid.

13 Ibid.

14 Ibid.

15 *Freddie Mercury: This Is The Real Life* by David Evans and David Minns (Britannia Press, 1993).

16 Ibid.

17 Equivalent to £325,000 at the time of writing.

18 *NME*, 18th June 1977.

19 Ibid.

20 Ibid.

21 Interview with Peter Straker by the authors, January 2016.

22 *NME*, 18th June 1977.

23 *American Songwriter*, 3rd February 2014.

24 *NME*, 30th September 2011.

25 'Crowning of Queen' by Tim Lott, *Daily Mail*, May 1978.

26 *Freddie's Loves*, Channel 5 (North One Productions, 2004).

27 Interview with John Reid by the authors, January 2016.

28 *Freddie's Loves*, Channel 5 (North One Productions, 2004).

29 Ibid.

30 Equivalent to £26,000 at the time of writing.

31 Interview with Paul Gambaccini by the authors, January 2016.

32 *Freddie's Loves*, Channel 5 (North One Productions, 2004).

Chapter 21

1 'Do Queen Deserve Rock's Crown?' by Rosy Horide, *Circus Magazine*, January 1978.

2 Equivalent to £560,000 at the time of writing.

3 'Crowning of Queen' by Tim Lott, *Daily Mail*, December 1978.

4 *Freddie Mercury: His Life In His Own Words* by Greg Brooks and Simon Lupton (Omnibus Press, 2009).

5 Interview with Roger Taylor by Matt Wardlaw, *Ultimate Classic Rock*, 21st October 2014.

6 'Late But Great' by Maurice Rotheroe, *Birmingham Evening Mail*, 8th May 1978.

7 *Mercury: The King of Queen* by Laura Jackson (Smith Gryphon, 1996).

8 *Is This The Real Life? The Untold Story of Queen* by Mark Blake (Aurum Press Ltd., 2011).

9 Ibid.

10 *Queen: As It Began* by Jacky Gunn and Jim Jenkins (Hyperion Books, 1994).

11 *Freddie's Loves*, Channel 5 (North One Productions, 2004).

12 *The Freddie Mercury Story: Living on the Edge* by David Bret (Robson Books, 1999).

13 Ibid.

14 'In Praise of Jazz' by Mark Mehler, *Circus Magazine*, 12th December 1978.

15 *Rolling Stone*, 8th February 1979.

16 *Creeme*, March 1979.

17 *Rolling Stone*, 8th February 1979.

18 'In Praise of Jazz' by Mark Mehler, *Circus Magazine*, 12th December 1978.

19 Equivalent to almost $750,000 at the time of writing.

20 'Queen: It Was All Like A Fantasy To See How Far We Could Go' by Jon Wilde and Nigel Williamson, *Uncut*, 6th September 2013.

21 Ibid.

22 *Queen: The Definitive Biography* by Laura Jackson (Piatkus, 2002).

23 *Freddie Mercury: An Intimate Biography* by David Bret (lulu.com, 2014).

24 *Mojo* magazine, August 1999.

25 *Freddie Mercury: The Definitive Biography* by Lesley-Ann_Jones (Hodder Paperbacks, 2012).

26   *Freddie Mercury: His Life In His Own Words* by Greg Brooks and Simon Lupton (Omnibus Press, 2009).

27   'Queen: It Was All Like A Fantasy To See How Far We Could Go' by Jon Wilde and Nigel Williamson, *Uncut*, 6th September 2013.

Chapter 22

1   *Daily Mirror*, 17th September 2015.

2   Interview with Brian May, Absolute Radio, 17th August 2011.

3   *Freddie Mercury: His Life In His Own Words* by Greg Brooks and Simon Lupton (Omnibus Press, 2009).

4   *Rolling Stone*, 6th September 1979.

5   'Stories From A Pro', interview with Reinhold Mack, iZotope.com.

6   'Queen's Tragic Rhapsody' by Mikal Gilmore, *Rolling Stone* 7th July 2014.

7   *Freddie Mercury: His Life In His Own Words* by Greg Brooks and Simon Lupton (Omnibus Press, 2009).

8   *Melody Maker*, 2nd May, 1981.

9   *Is This The Real Life? The Untold Story of Queen* by Mark Blake (Aurum Press Ltd., 2011).

10   Interview with Brian May for *Guitar Player*, January 1983.

11   *Freddie Mercury: His Life In His Own Words* by Greg Brooks and Simon Lupton (Omnibus Press, 2009).

12   Ibid.

13   *Mercury: The King of Queen* by Laura Jackson (Smith Gryphon, 1996).

14   Ibid.

15   *Freddie Mercury: His Life In His Own Words* by Greg Brooks and Simon Lupton (Omnibus Press, 2009).

16   *Mercury: The King of Queen* by Laura Jackson (Smith Gryphon, 1996).

17   *Freddie Mercury: His Life In His Own Words* by Greg Brooks and Simon Lupton (Omnibus Press, 2009).

18   *Mercury: The King of Queen* by Laura Jackson (Smith Gryphon, 1996).

19   *Freddie Mercury: His Life In His Own Words* by Greg Brooks and Simon Lupton (Omnibus Press, 2009).

20   *Superpop*, 8th December 1979.

21   Ibid.

22   *Freddie Mercury: An Intimate Memoir by the Man Who Knew Him Best* by Peter Freestone with David Evans (Omnibus Press, 2001).

Chapter 23

1   'Heroes, Heartbreak & Hope' by Denise Ryan, *The Vancouver Sun*, 6th December 2013.

2   *And The Band Played On: Politics, People, and the AIDS Epidemic* by Randy Shilts (Souvenir Press Ltd., 2011).

3   Our findings reveal a series of key founder events in the genesis of the subtype B epidemic, with a single virus moving from the African epicentre of HIV-1 group M to the Caribbean by 1967 [1964–70], a single virus moving from the Caribbean to establish an epidemic in NYC by 1971 (1969–73), and yet another single virus moving from there to San Francisco by 1975 (but with extensive geographical mixing in the US and beyond shortly thereafter).

Chapter 24

1   *Freddie Mercury: His Life In His Own Words* by Greg Brooks and Simon Lupton (Omnibus Press, 2009).

2   Equivalent to almost £2,300,000 at the time of writing.

3   *Freddie Mercury: His Life In His Own Words* by Greg Brooks and Simon Lupton (Omnibus Press, 2009).

4   Ibid.

5   Interview with Mike Hodges by the authors, January 2016.

6   Ibid.

7   Ibid.

8   Interview with Brian May for *Mojo* magazine, 1999.

9   *Freddie Mercury: The Definitive Biography* by Lesley-Ann Jones (Hodder Paperbacks, 2012).

10 *Freddie Mercury: The Definitive Biography* by Lesley-Ann Jones (Hodder Paperbacks, 2012).

11 *Therapy Today*, April 2011.

12 *Record Mirror*, 21st June 1980.

13 *Rolling Stone*, 18th September 1980.

14 *Days of Our Lives*, BBC TV (Globe Productions, 2011).

15 *Bass & Bassist Techniques*, April 1996.

16 *Queen – Greatest Video Hits 1*, 2002.

17 *Freddie Mercury: An Intimate Memoir by the Man Who Knew Him Best* by Peter Freestone with David Evans (Omnibus Press, 2001).

18 Ibid.

19 Ibid.

20 Interview with Mike Hodges by the authors, January 2016.

21 *Record Mirror*, 6th December 1980.

22 *Record Mirror*, 13th December 1980.

23 *The Guardian*, 15th December 2011.

24 *Freddie Mercury: His Life In His Own Words* by Greg Brooks and Simon Lupton (Omnibus Press, 2009).

Chapter 25

1   *Freddie Mercury: His Life in His Own Words* by Greg Brooks and Simon Lupton (Omnibus Press, 2009).

2   Equivalent to £2,700,000 at the time of writing.

3   *Freddie Mercury: His Life in His Own Words* by Greg Brooks and Simon Lupton (Omnibus Press, 2009).

4   Ibid.

5   *The Freddie Mercury Story: Living on the Edge* by David Bret (Robson Books, 1999).

6   *Queen: As It Began* by Jacky Gunn and Jim Jenkins (Hyperion Books, 1994).

7   *Q Magazine*, July 2004.

8   *Is This The Real Life? The Untold Story of Queen* by Mark Blake (Aurum Press Ltd., 2011).

9   *Freddie Mercury: His Life in His Own Words* by Greg Brooks and Simon Lupton (Omnibus Press, 2009).

10 'Brian May Tells How David Bowie And Queen Wrote Legendary Track Under Pressure' by Brian May, *Daily Mirror*, 11th January 2016.

11 *Guitar World* magazine, 18th October 2002.

12 *Mojo* magazine, October 2008.

13 *The New Yorker*, 11th January 2016.

14 Ibid.

Chapter 26

1 *The New York Magazine*, 5th June 2013.

2 Cognitive impairment is when a person has trouble remembering, learning new things, concentrating, or making decisions that affect their everyday life.

3 *AIDS Doctors: Voices From The Epidemic: An Oral History* by Ronald Bayer and Gerald M. Oppenheimer (Oxford University Press, 2002).

4 Ibid.

5 Ibid.

6 Interview with Dr. Lawrence Mass by MSNBC, 1st December 2014.

7 *The New York Times*, 3rd July 1981.

Chapter 27

1 Interview with Peter Straker by the authors, January 2016.

2 *Freddie Mercury: The Definitive Biography* by Lesley-Ann Jones (Hodder Paperbacks, 2012).

3 Interview with Robert Lang by the authors.

4 *New Scientist*, 28th March 1985.

5 *The Miami Herald*, 8th August 2014.

6 Ibid.

7 'The Age of AIDS', *Frontline*, PBS, 30th May 2006.

8 *The Show Must Go On: The Life of Freddie Mercury* by Rick Sky (Citadel Press, 1997).

9 Interview with Robert Lang by the authors.

10 Equivalent to $66,000 at the time of writing.

11 *Freddie Mercury: The Definitive Biography* by Lesley-Ann Jones (Hodder Paperbacks, 2012).

12 *Rolling Stone*, 10th June 1982.

13 *The Show Must Go On: The Life of Freddie Mercury* by Rick Sky (Citadel Press, 1997).

14 *Straight & Narrow?: Compassion & Clarity in the Homosexuality Debate* by Thomas E. Schmidt (IVP Academic, 1995).

Chapter 28

1 'Scourge of the Gays' by Brian Deer, *Time Out*, 18th December 1981.

2 'New Homosexual Disorder Worries Health Officials' by Lawrence K. Altman, *The New York Times*, 11th May 1982.

3 'AIDS: The Early Years & CDC's Response' by James W. Curran MD and Harold W. Jaffe MD, Morbidity and Mortality Weekly Report, 7th October 2011

4 *And The Band Played On: Politics, People, and the AIDS Epidemic* by Randy Shilts (Souvenir Press Ltd., 2011).

5   *A Medical History of the Skin: Scratching the Surface (Studies for the Society for the Social History of Medicine)* by Kevin Patrick Siena (Routledge, 2013).

6   'Clue Found on Homosexuals' Precancer Syndrome' by Lawrence K. Altman, *The New York Times*, 18th June 1982.

7   '1981–86: In The Beginning' by Jeff Graham, AIDS Survival Project, January/February 2006.

8   'Rodger McFarlane, AIDS Gay Community Builder, Dead at 54' by Paul Schindler, *Gay City News*, 30th May 2009.

9   *Targets of Violence & Aggression*, edited by R. Baenninger (North Holland, 1991).

10 'Older Gays & Lesbians: Surviving a Generation of Hate & Violence' by Deana F. Morrow, University of North Carolina, 2001.

11 'Rodger McFarlane, Who Led AIDS-Related Groups, Dies at 54' by Dennis Hevesi, *The New York Times*, 18th May 2009.

12 'AIDS: The Early Years & CDC's Response' by James W. Curran MD and Harold W. Jaffe MD, Morbidity and Mortality Weekly Report, 7th October 2011.

13 *Capital Gay*, 3rd September 1982.

14 'AIDS: The First 20 Years' by Simon Garfield, *The Guardian*, 3rd June 2001.

15 Ibid.

16 Ibid.

17 *And The Band Played On: Politics, People, and the AIDS Epidemic* by Randy Shilts (Souvenir Press Ltd., 2011).

18 *A Medical History of the Skin: Scratching the Surface (Studies for the Society for the Social History of Medicine)* by Kevin Patrick Siena (Routledge, 2013).

19 Ibid.

20 *And The Band Played On: Politics, People, and the AIDS Epidemic* by Randy Shilts (Souvenir Press Ltd., 2011).

21 'Hero Or Criminal', Xtraonline, 26th April 2011.

22 *And The Band Played On: Politics, People, and the AIDS Epidemic* by Randy Shilts (Souvenir Press Ltd., 2011).

23 'The Age of AIDS' by Frontline, PBS, 30th May 2006.

24 Ibid.

25 Ibid.

26 'AIDS in Europe' by Srdan Matic, Jeffrey V. Lazarus and Martin C. Donoghoe for WHO, 2006.

Chapter 29

1   *Is This The Real Life? The Untold Story of Queen* by Mark Blake (Aurum Press Ltd., 2011).

2   *Days of Our Lives*, BBC TV (Globe Productions, 2011).

3   Ibid.

4   Interview with John Reid by the authors, January 2016.

5   Interview with Mike Hodges by the authors, January 2016.

6   Interview with Paul Loasby by the authors, January 2016.

7   Ibid.

8   Ibid.

9   *Rolling Stone*, 10th June 1982.

10 *Q* magazine, July 2004.

11 Interview with Paul Loasby by the authors, January 2016.

12 *Is This The Real Life? The Untold Story of Queen* by Mark Blake (Aurum Press Ltd., 2011).

13 Mojo 'Queen Classic Edition', April 2005.

14 *Freddie Mercury: His Life in His Own Words* by Greg Brooks and Simon Lupton (Omnibus Press, 2009).

15 'Freddie Mercury & Queen: Technologies of Genre and the Poetics of Innovation' by Barry C. Pomane.

16 Interview with Marc Almond by the authors, January 2016

17 'The Discursive Nature of Masculinity' by Richard Dyer, 1995.

18 Interview with Marc Almond by the authors, January 2016.

19 *Is This The Real Life? The Untold Story of Queen* by Mark Blake (Aurum Press Ltd., 2011).

20 *Freddie Mercury: His Life in His Own Words* by Greg Brooks and Simon Lupton (Omnibus Press, 2009).

Chapter 30

1 Equivalent to $2,400,000 at the time of writing.

2 *Freddie Mercury: His Life in his Own Words* by Greg Brooks and Simon Lupton (Omnibus Press, 2009).

3 Ibid.

4 Ibid.

5 Ibid.

6 'Bubbles The Chimp Delayed Jacko and Freddie's Duet by Nearly 30 Years' by Angella Johnson, *The Mail on Sunday*, 8th November 2014.

7 'He Could Out-Party Me Says Elton John' by Stuart Kemp, *The Hollywood Reporter*, 3rd July 2012.

8 *Is This The Real Life? The Untold Story of Queen* by Mark Blake (Aurum Press Ltd., 2011).

9 *Freddie Mercury: His Life in his Own Words* by Greg Brooks and Simon Lupton (Omnibus Press, 2009).

10 *Freddie's Loves*, Channel 5 (North One Productions, 2004).

11 *Freddie Mercury: An Intimate Memoir by the Man Who Knew Him Best* by Peter Freestone with David Evans (Omnibus Press, 2001).

12 Interview with John Reid by the authors, January 2016.

13 *Freddie's Loves*, Channel 5 (North One Productions, 2004).

14 *Freddie Mercury: An Intimate Memoir by the Man Who Knew Him Best* by Peter Freestone with David Evans (Omnibus Press, 2001).

15 *Freddie Mercury: His Life in his Own Words* by Greg Brooks and Simon Lupton (Omnibus Press, 2009).

16 *Mercury and Me* by Jim Hutton with Tim Wapshott (Bloomsbury Publishing PLC, 1995).

Chapter 31

1 MBNS *Today*, February 1983.

2 'The Age of AIDS', *PBS Frontline*, May 2006.

3 Ibid.

4   *Newsweek*, 24th April 2014.

5   'Assessing the Impact of National Anti-HIV Sexual Health Campaigns' by Nicoll, Hughes, Donnelly, Livingstone, De Angelis, Fenton, Evans, Gill, Catchpole, Sexually Transmitted Infections, *British Medical Journal*, 10th April 2001.

6   'I'll Never Fall in Love Again', Burt Bacharach and Hal David, 1968.

7   'AIDS: The First 20 Years' by Simon Garfield, *The Guardian*, 3rd June 2001.

8   'The Age of AIDS', *PBS Frontline*, May 2006.

9   Ibid.

10 Interview with Paul Gambaccini by the authors, January 2016.

11 Interview with Marc Almond by the authors, January 2016.

12 *Freddie Mercury: His Life in his Own Words* by Greg Brooks and Simon Lupton (Omnibus Press, 2009).

Chapter 32

1   *Disaster and Human History: Case Studies in Nature, Society and Catastrophe* by Benjamin Reilly (McFarland, 2009).

2   'Survival & Treatment of AIDS Patients 1984–1993' by Hillman, Beck, Mandalia, Satterthwaite, Rogers, Forster, Goh, Genitourin Medical, February 1997 (US Library of Medicine).

3   'AIDS: The Acquired Immune Deficient Syndrome' by V.G. Daniels, 1985.

4   'AIDS At 30', *The Los Angeles Times*, 21st April, 2014.

5   *AIDS: The Ultimate Challenge* by Elisabeth Kübler-Ross, 2001 (Simon and Schuster, 2001).

6   Interview with Annie Lennox by the authors, January 2016.

7   'The Age of AIDS', *Frontline, PBS*, 30th May 2006.

8   Ibid.

9   Ibid.

10 Ibid.

11 *And The Band Played On: Politics, People, and the AIDS Epidemic* by Randy Shilts (Souvenir Press Ltd., 2011).

12 Ibid.

Chapter 33

1   *Freddie's Loves*, Channel 5 (North One Productions, 2004).

2   Interview with Peter Straker by the authors, January 2016.

3   *Freddie's Loves*, Channel 5 (North One Productions, 2004).

4   *The Show Must Go On: The Life of Freddie Mercury* by Rick Sky (HarperCollins, 1994).

5   Interview with Peter Straker by the authors, January 2016.

6   *The Show Must Go On: The Life of Freddie Mercury* by Rick Sky (HarperCollins, 1994).

7   *Mercury: The King of Queen* by Laura Jackson (Smith Gryphon, 1996).

8   'Freddie's Secret Lover', *Daily Mirror*, 1991.

9   Ibid.

10 *Sounds*, 25th February 1984.

11 *Rolling Stone*, 12th April 1984.

12 Interview with Freddie Mercury by Mary Turner for *America*, Westwood One, 1984.

13 *Freddie Mercury: The Definitive Biography* by Lesley-Ann Jones (Hodder Paperbacks, 2012).

14 *Video Killed The Radio Star*, Sky Arts, 2011.

15 *Freddie Mercury: His Life in his Own Words* by Greg Brooks and Simon Lupton (Omnibus Press, 2009).

16 *Is This The Real Life? The Untold Story of Queen* by Mark Blake (Aurum Press Ltd., 2011).

17 *Freddie Mercury: His Life in his Own Words* by Greg Brooks and Simon Lupton (Omnibus Press, 2009).

18 'Queen 1971–2011', *Q* magazine, 2011.

19 *Record Mirror*, 25th August 1984.

20 *Greatest Video Hits 2*, 2003.

21 Equivalent to £3,000 at the time of writing.

22 *Melody Maker*, 1984.

23 *Days of Our Lives*, BBC TV (Globe Productions, 2011),

24 'Recalling "Sin" of Shows in Apartheid South Africa' by Clare Byrne, *The Brunei Times*, 13th January 2008.

25 *Days of Our Lives*, BBC TV (Globe Productions, 2011).

26 *Freddie Mercury: His Life in his Own Words* by Greg Brooks and Simon Lupton (Omnibus Press, 2009).

Chapter 34

1 'Blame It On Rio' by Robin Smith, *Record Mirror*, 26th January 1985.

2 *People Weekly*, 11th February 1985.

3 'Blame It On Rio' by Robin Smith, *Record Mirror*, 26th January 1985.

4 *The People*, 28th January 1985.

5 *Freddie Mercury: The Definitive Biography* by Lesley-Ann Jones (Hodder Paperbacks, 2012).

6 Ibid.

7 Ibid.

8 Ibid.

9 *Is This The Real life? The Untold Story of Queen* by Mark Blake (Aurum Press Ltd., 2011).

10 'Blame It On Rio' by Robin Smith, *Record Mirror*, 26th January 1985.

Chapter 35

1 *Melody Maker*, January 1985.

2 'The Day The World Rocked' by Michael Goldberg, *Rolling Stone*, 15th August 1985.

3 *Mercury and Me* by Jim Hutton with Tim Wapshott (Bloomsbury Publishing PLC, 1995).

4 *People Weekly*, 24th June 1985.

5 *Rolling Stone*, June 1985.

6 *Freddie Mercury: His Life in His Own Words* by Greg Brooks and Simon Lupton (Omnibus Press, 2009).

7 *Freddie Mercury: The Definitive Biography* by Lesley-Ann Jones (Hodder Paperbacks, 2012).

8 *Queen: Magic Years* by Rudi Dolezal and Hannes Rossacher, 1999.

9 *The Eighties: One Day, One Decade* by Dylan Jones (Windmill Books, 2014).

10 *Mercury and Me* by Jim Hutton with Tim Wapshott (Bloomsbury Publishing PLC, 1995).

11 Ibid.

12 This was likely to be oral thrush, which is associated with being HIV positive.

13 Simon Bates interview with Freddie Mercury, BBC Radio 1, June 1985.

14 *Freddie Mercury: His Life in His Own Words* by Greg Brooks and Simon Lupton (Omnibus Press, 2009).

15 'Queen: Their Finest Moment at Live Aid' by Peter Stanford, *The Daily Telegraph*, 24th September 2011.

16 BBC *Breakfast Time*, 12th July 1985.

17 'Live Aid: 30 Years On', *NME*, 10th July 2015.

18 'Space Ships, Drugs Everywhere and Freddie Mercury Trying it on with Bono' by Dylan Jones, *Daily Mail*, 25th May 2013.

19 *Is This The Real Life? The Untold Story of Queen* by Mark Blake (Aurum Press Ltd., 2011).

20 'Live Aid: 30 Years On', *NME*, 10th July 2015.

21 'Queen Steal The Show At Live Aid' by Nick DeRiso, *Classic Rock*, 13th July 2015.

22 'Britannic Majesties', *Mojo*, 1999.

23 Interview with Paul Gambaccini by the authors, January 2016.

24 Mercury and Me by Jim Hutton with Tim Wapshott (Bloomsbury Publishing PLC, 1995).

Chapter 36

1 'New Secrets of Rock Hudson's Heartbreaking Battle With AIDS' by Liz McNeil, *People Magazine*, 16th April 2015.

2 'Doris Day on Saying Goodbye To Rock Hudson' by Liz McNeil, *People Magazine*, 18th April 2015.

3 Ibid.

4 'Nancy Reagan Refused to Help Dying Rock Hudson Get AIDS Treatment' by Alexandra Topping, *The Guardian*, 3rd February 2015.

5 Ibid

6 Ibid.

7 Ibid.

8 'Rock Hudson Announced He Had AIDS On July 25th 1985' by Christopher Rudolph, *The Huffington Post*, 25th July 2013.

9 'Airlines Refused To Fly Rock Hudson Home After His AIDS Diagnosis Became Public' by Michael Bates, *Daily Mail*, 22nd April 2015.

10 'The Long Goodbye: Rock Hudson' by Scot Haller, *People Magazine*, 21st October 1985.

11 'Rock Hudson's Secrets' by Roger Ebert, *The Chicago Sun-Times*, 20th July 1986.

12 *And The Band Played On: Politics, People, and the AIDS Epidemic* by Randy Shilts (Souvenir Press Ltd., 2011).

13 'New Secrets of Rock Hudson's Heartbreaking Battle With AIDS' by Liz McNeil, *People Magazine*, 16th April 2015.

14 Equivalent to almost $560,000 at the time of writing.

15 Equivalent to £145,000 at the time of writing.

16 'I Am The Champion' by Nick Ferrari, *The Sun*, 19th July 1985.

17 *Freddie Mercury: An Intimate Biography* by David Bret (lulu.com, 2014).

18 Interview with John Deacon for *The Hit*, 1985.

Chapter 37

1 *Mercury and Me* by Jim Hutton with Tim Wapshott (Bloomsbury Publishing PLC, 1995).
2 *Freddie Mercury: The Definitive Biography* by Lesley-Ann Jones (Hodder Paperbacks, 2012).
3 Ibid.
4 Interview with Peter Straker by the authors, January 2016.
5 Ibid.
6 *Freddie Mercury: His Life In His Own Words* by Greg Brooks and Simon Lupton (Omnibus Press, 2009).

Chapter 38

1 *Mercury and Me* by Jim Hutton with Tim Wapshott (Bloomsbury Publishing PLC, 1995).
2 Interview with John Deacon, *The Hit*, 1985.
3 Peter Freestone Blog, 20th September 2012, Freddiemercury.com.
4 Interview with John Reid by the authors, January 2016.
5 Interview with Peter Straker by the authors, January 2016.
6 *Mercury: The King of Queen* by Laura Jackson (Smith Gryphon, 1996).
7 *Is This The Real Life? The Untold Story of Queen* by Mark Blake (Aurum Press Ltd., 2011).
8 *Freddie Mercury: His Life in His Own Words* by Greg Brooks and Simon Lupton (Omnibus Press, 2009).
9 *Rolling Stone*, 9th October 1986.
10 *Freddie Mercury: His Life in His Own Words* by Greg Brooks and Simon Lupton (Omnibus Press, 2009).
11 Equivalent to almost £220,000 at the time of writing.
12 *Freddie Mercury: The Definitive Biography* by Lesley-Ann Jones (Hodder Paperbacks, 2012).
13 'Queen 1971–2011' – Interview with Brian May and Roger Taylor, queenonline.com.
14 'Queen's Tragic Rhapsody' by Mikal Gilmore, *Rolling Stone*, 7th July 2014.
15 'Brian May Discusses Queen's Greatest Moment' by Ben Mitchell, *Guitar World*, 19th July 2015.
16 'Queen's Tragic Rhapsody' by Mikal Gilmore, *Rolling Stone*, 7th July 2014.
17 'My Favourite Photography by Roger Taylor', *The Daily Express*, 9th November 2014.

Chapter 39

1 'Insurers Try to Screen Out AIDS Cases' by Bruce Keppel, *The Los Angeles Times*, 11th October 1985.
2 'Insurer Study Screening for AIDS' by James Barron, *The New York Times*, 26th September 1985.
3 'Brian May & The Queen Story' by Gal Benzler, *Discoveries Magazine*, September 1993.
4 Equivalent to almost £2,750,000 at the time of writing.
5 Equivalent to almost £700,000 at the time of writing.
6 Equivalent to almost £1,370,000 at the time of writing.
7 'Do I Look Like I'm Dying Of AIDS? Fumes Freddie' by Hugh Whittow, *The Sun*, 13th October 1986.
8 *Mercury and Me* by Jim Hutton with Tim Wapshott (Bloomsbury Publishing PLC, 1995).
9 Interview with Peter Straker by the authors, January 2016.
10 'The Rise & Fall of AZT' by Simon Garfield, *The Independent*, 23rd October 2011.

Chapter 40

1 '150 Greatest Rock Lists Ever', *Q* magazine Special Edition, July 2004.
2 *Mercury: The King of Queen* by Laura Jackson (Smith Gryphon, 1996).
3 *Freddie Mercury: His Life in His Own Words* by Greg Brooks and Simon Lupton (Omnibus Press, 2009).
4 Equivalent to £265,000 at the time of writing.
5 'Mary Austin Shares Her Memories of the Late Queen Singer Inside His Home', *OK!* magazine, 17th March 2000.
6 Interview with Mike Moran by the authors, January 2016.
7 *Freddie Mercury: His Life in His Own Words* by Greg Brooks and Simon Lupton (Omnibus Press, 2009).
8 Interview with Mike Moran by the authors, January 2016.
9 Ibid.
10 Interview with Peter Straker by the authors, January 2016.
11 Interview with Mike Moran by the authors, January 2016.

Chapter 41

1 'Freddie Mercury & Queen: Technologies of Genre and the Poetics of Innovation' by Barry C. Pomane, University of Western Ontario, 2009.
2 Ibid.
3 Interview with Peter Straker by the authors, January 2016.
4 'Freddie Mercury & Queen: Technologies of Genre and the Poetics of Innovation' by Barry C. Pomane, University of Western Ontario, 2009.
5 *Mercury and Me* by Jim Hutton with Tim Wapshott (Bloomsbury Publishing PLC, 1995).
6 Ibid.
7 'Freddie Mercury's Mother on her "Dear Boy"' by Angela Levin, *The Daily Telegraph*, 8th September 2012.
8 'Freddie Mercury: The Great Enigma' by Caroline Sullivan, *The Guardian*, 27th September 2012.
9 Interview with Paul Gambaccini by the authors, January 2016.
10 Equivalent to almost £85,000 at the time of writing.

Chapter 42

1 *Mercury: The King of Queen* by Laura Jackson (Smith Gryphon, 1996).
2 *Freddie Mercury: An Intimate Memoir by the Man Who Knew Him Best* by Peter Freestone with David Evans (Omnibus Press, 2001).
3 Ibid.
4 *Mercury: The King of Queen* by Laura Jackson (Smith Gryphon, 1996).
5 Ibid.
6 Ibid.
7 Ibid.
8 'The Rise & Fall of AZT' by Simon Garfield, *The Independent*, 23rd October 2011.
9 Ibid.
10 A trial of AZT called the Concorde Study, an Anglo-French programme, of 1,749 AIDS

patients over three years suggested that 'early intervention with AZT – for people who were HIV but had not yet developed any symptoms of Aids – was a waste of time' – 'The Rise & Fall of AZT' by Simon Garfield, *The Independent*, 23rd October 2011.

11 Ibid.

12 *Illness as Metaphor and AIDS and Its Metaphors* by Susan Sontag (Penguin Classics, 2009). Quotations from *Illness as Metaphor* copyright © Susan Sontag 1977, 1978 and quotations from *Aids and Its Metaphors* copyright © Susan Sontag 1988, 1989, used by permission of The Wylie Agency (UK) Limited.

13 *Mercury and Me* by Jim Hutton with Tim Wapshott (Bloomsbury Publishing PLC, 1995).

14 Interview with Paul Gambaccini by the authors, January 2016.

15 Interview with Mike Moran by the authors, January 2016.

16 *Science Focus*, 21st April 2016.

17 'Freddie Mercury: The Great Enigma', *The Guardian*, 27th September 2012.

18 *Logopedics Phoniatrics Vocology*, 15th April 2016.

19 Ibid.

20 'The David Wigg Interviews', *Freddie Mercury Solo* CD, Ibiza 1987.

Chapter 43

1 'Using Condom Data to Assess the Impact of HIV/AIDS Preventive Interventions' by J. Goodrich, K. Welling & D. McVey, *Oxford Journals*, Vol. 13, No. 2, 1998.

2 Interview with Roger Taylor, University Radio Bath, 2nd March 1988.

3 'Brian May Talks about Queen's Miracle' by Paul Elliott, *Team Rock*, 25th May 2014.

4 Interview with Mike Moran by the authors, January 2016.

5 Interview with Jim Reid by the authors, January 2016.

6 Interview with Mike Moran by the authors, January 2016.

7 '26 Years Ago: Queen Release "The Miracle" During Some Trying Times' by Nick DeRiso, *Ultimate Classic Rock*, 22nd May 2015.

Chapter 44

1 Interview with Peter Straker by the authors, January 2016.

2 'Freddie Mercury & Queen: Technologies of Genre and the Poetics of Innovation' by Barry C. Pomane, University of Western Ontario, 2009.

3 *Mercury: The King of Queen* by Laura Jackson (Smith Gryphon, 1996).

4 *Freddie Mercury: His Life in His Own Words* by Greg Brooks and Simon Lupton (Omnibus Press, 2009).

5 'For Me, It's The Bigger The Better, In Everything' by David Wigg, *Daily Mail*, 12th October 2012.

6 By this point in time, it was actually known HIV could only be spread through bodily fluids.

7 'For Me, It's The Bigger The Better, In Everything by David Wigg, *Daily Mail*, 12th October 2012.

8 *Freddie Mercury: His Life in His Own Words* by Greg Brooks and Simon Lupton (Omnibus Press, 2009).

Chapter 45

1 'Ronald Reagan & AIDS: Correcting The Record' by Carl M. Cannon, Real Clear Politics, 1st June 2014.

2 Ibid.

3 NCHS. Annual summary of births, marriages, divorces, and deaths: United States, 1988; Hyattsville, Maryland: US Department of Health and Human Services, Public Health Service, 1989; DHHS publication No. (PHS)89-1120 (monthly vital statistics report; Vol. 37, No. 13).

4 Office of the Assistant Secretary for Health. Report of the second Public Health Service AIDS Prevention and Control Conference. Public Health Rep 1988; 103(suppl 1):3.

5 'HIV Seropisitivity & AIDS Prevention Control' Report by WHO, 1989.

6 *Risk-Takers: Alcohol, Drugs, Sex and Youth* by Moira Plant (Routledge, 1992).

7 *HIV In Gay & Bisexual Men in the UK: 25 Years of Public Health Surveillance* by S. Dougan, B.G. Evans, N. Macdonald, D.J. Goldberg, O.N. Gill, K.A. Fenton and J. Elford, Epidemiology & Infections, Cambridge University Press, February 2008.

8 *HIV/AIDS: Global Frontiers in Prevention/Intervention* by Cythia Pope, Renee T. White and Robert Malow (Routledge, 2009).

9 *The New York Times*, 7th October 1986.

10 United Press International, 7th October 1986.

11 Interview with John Reid by the authors, January 2016.

12 *Freddie Mercury: His Life in His Own Words* by Greg Brooks and Simon Lupton (Omnibus Press, 2009).

13 *Is This The Real Life? The Untold Story of Queen* by Mark Blake (Aurum Press Ltd., 2011).

14 *Queen: In Their Own Words* by Mick St. Michael (Omnibus Press, 1992).

15 *Days of Our Lives*, BBC TV (Globe Productions, 2011).

16 *Mercury and Me* by Jim Hutton with Tim Wapshott (Bloomsbury Publishing PLC, 1995).

17 'Queen's Tragic Rhapsody' by Mikal Gilmore, *Rolling Stone*, 7th July 2014.

18 *The Washington Times*, 23rd May, 1993.

19 *The Times*, 29th September 1992.

20 *Is This The Real Life? The Untold Story of Queen* by Mark Blake (Aurum Press Ltd., 2011).

21 *The Times*, 20th May 1989.

22 *Rolling Stone*, 7th September 1989.

23 *Freddie Mercury: His Life in His Own Words* by Greg Brooks and Simon Lupton (Omnibus Press, 2009).

24 Interview with Mike Moran by the authors, January 2016.

Chapter 46

1 'Projecting The Spread of AIDS In The United Kingdom: A Sensitivity Analysis' by C.D. Daykin, P.N.S. Clark, S. Haberman, D. J. Le Grys, R.W. Michaelson, A.D. Wilkie, *Journal of the Institute of Actuaries*, Vol. 117, June 1990.

2 Interview with Roger Taylor, *Rhythm Magazine*, September 2002.

3 Interview with Brian May for *Rock Power*, 1992.

4 *Days of Our Lives*, BBC TV (Globe Productions, 2011).

5 Interview with Paul Gambaccini by the authors, January 2016.

6   Interview with Brian May for *Rock Power*, 1992.

7   *Mercury and Me* by Jim Hutton with Tim Wapshott (Bloomsbury Publishing PLC, 1995).

8   Ibid.

9   Ibid.

10 *Is This The Real Life? The Untold Story of Queen* by Mark Blake (Aurum Press Ltd., 2011).

11 Interview with David Richards, *Rolling Stone*, December 1995.

12 'Yes! We're Ready For The Challenge: We Chat To Steve Howe' by Mick Burgess, *Newcastle Chronicle*, 25th April, 2014.

13 *Freddie Mercury: His Life in His Own Words* by Greg Brooks and Simon Lupton (Omnibus Press, 2009).

14 'The Great Pretender', *The Mail on Sunday*, 26th November 2000.

15 *Days of Our Lives*, BBC TV (Globe Productions, 2011).

16 Interview with Peter Straker by the authors, January 2016.

17 Interview with John Reid by the authors, January 2016.

18 *Freddie Mercury: An Intimate Biography* by David Bret (lulu.com, 2014).

19 *Queen: In Their Own Words* by Mick St. Michael (Omnibus Press, 1992).

20 *Days of Our Lives*, BBC TV (Globe Productions, 2011).

21 *Is This The Real Life? The Untold Story of Queen* by Mark Blake (Aurum Press Ltd., 2011).

22 *Freddie Mercury: An Intimate Biography* by David Bret (Lulu Press, 2014).

23 'Queen's Tragic Rhapsody' by Mikal Gilmore, *Rolling Stone*, 7th July 2014.

Chapter 47

1   *Rolling Stone*, 7th March 1991.

2   *The Times*, 1st February, 1991.

3   Equivalent to £20,500,000 at the time of writing.

4   '10 Questions: Brian May of Queen' by Dennis Hunt, *The Los Angeles Times*, 24th February 1991.

5   Equivalent to £410,000 at the time of writing.

6   'Inside The Studio Where Freddie Mercury Sang His Last Song' by Cole Moreton, *The Daily Telegraph*, 1st December 2013.

7   *Days of Our Lives*, BBC TV (Globe Productions, 2011).

8   Ibid.

9   Equivalent to almost £330,000 at the time of writing.

10 'Inside The Studio Where Freddie Mercury Sang His Last Song' by Cole Moreton, *The Daily Telegraph*, 1st December 2013.

11 Ibid.

12 Ibid.

13 *Days Of Our Lives*, BBC TV (Globe Productions, 2011).

14 'Freddie Mercury & Queen: Technologies of Genre and the Poetics of Innovation' by Barry C. Pomane, University of Western Ontario, 2009.

15 *Hello, Darlings!: The Authorized Biography of Kenny Everett* by James Hogg and Robert Sellers (Bantam Press, 2014).

Chapter 48

1   *This Wild Darkness: The Story of My Death* by Harold Brodkey (Holt Paperbacks, 1997).

2   *Mercury and Me* by Jim Hutton with Tim Wapshott (Bloomsbury Publishing PLC, 1995).

3   Interview with Mike Moran by the authors, January 2016.

4   Interview with John Reid by the authors, January 2016.

5   'Queen's Tragic Rhapsody' by Mikel Gilmore, *Rolling Stone*, 7th July 2014.

6   *This Wild Darkness: The Story of My Death* by Harold Brodkey (Holt Paperbacks, 1997).

7   Voltaire, Candide: or, Optimism.

8   *Three-Way Mirror: Imitation of Life* by Lucy Fischer, 1991.

9   *Mercury and Me* by Jim Hutton with Tim Wapshott (Bloomsbury Publishing PLC, 1995).

10 'The Ex-Lover of Freddie Mercury Shares Her Memories of the Late Queen Singer Inside His Home', *OK!* magazine, 17th March 2000.

Chapter 49

1   *Freddie Mercury: An Intimate Memoir by the Man Who Knew Him Best* by Peter Freestone with David Evans (Omnibus Press, 2001).

2   *Love Is the Cure: On Life, Loss, and the End of AIDS* by Elton John (Little, Brown and Company, 2013).

3   *Freddie Mercury: An Intimate Memoir by the Man Who Knew Him Best* by Peter Freestone with David Evans (Omnibus Press, 2001).

4   *Days of Our Lives*, BBC TV (Globe Productions, 2011).

5   *Mercury and Me* by Jim Hutton with Tim Wapshott (Bloomsbury Publishing PLC, 1995).

6   *Freddie Mercury: An Intimate Memoir by the Man Who Knew Him Best* by Peter Freestone with David Evans (Omnibus Press, 2001).

7   *Freddie Mercury: The King of Queen* by Laura Jackson (Smith Gryphon, 1996).

8   *Mercury and Me* by Jim Hutton with Tim Wapshott (Bloomsbury Publishing PLC, 1995).

9   Interview with Paul Gambaccini by the authors, January 2016.

10 *Freddie Mercury: An Intimate Memoir by the Man Who Knew Him Best* by Peter Freestone with David Evans (Omnibus Press, 2001).

11 'Freddie Chose To Die When His Life Stopped Being Fun' by Spencer Bright, *Daily Mail*, 9th September 2011.

12 *Mercury and Me* by Jim Hutton with Tim Wapshott (Bloomsbury Publishing PLC, 1995).

13 *Days of Our Lives*, BBC TV (Globe Productions, 2011).

14 'Freddie Chose To Die When His Life Stopped Being Fun' by Spencer Bright, *Daily Mail*, 9th September 2011.

15 *Freddie Mercury: An Intimate Memoir by the Man Who Knew Him Best* by Peter Freestone with David Evans (Omnibus Press, 2001).

16 *Mercury and Me* by Jim Hutton with Tim Wapshott (Bloomsbury Publishing PLC, 1995).

Chapter 50

1   *The Guardian*, 25th November 1991.

2   *The New York Times*, 25th November 1991.

3   BBC News, 24th November 1991.

4   *Rolling Stone*, 9th January 1992.

5   *The Evening Mail*, 25th November 1991.

6   *The Star*, 26th November 1991.

7   *The Mirror*, 25th November 1991.

8   Interview with Annie Lennox by the authors, January 2016.

9   *The Show Must Go On: The Life of Freddie Mercury* by Rick Sky (Citadel Press, 1997).

10   Interview with Peter Straker by the authors, January 2016.

11   Ibid.

12   *Mercury and Me* by Jim Hutton with Tim Wapshott (Bloomsbury Publishing PLC, 1995).

13   Equivalent to £1,025,000 at the time of writing.

14   *Mercury and Me* by Jim Hutton with Tim Wapshott (Bloomsbury Publishing PLC, 1995).

15   Ibid.

16   *Freddie Mercury: The Definitive Biography* by Lesley-Ann Jones (Hodder Paperbacks, 2012).

17   'Mercury Left Me His Millions' by David Wigg, *Daily Mail*, 22nd January 2000.

18   Interview with Jim Reid by the authors, January 2016.

19   *Freddie Mercury: His Life In His Own Words* by Greg Brooks and Simon Lupton (Omnibus Press, 2009).

20   'Mercury Left Me His Millions' by David Wigg, *Daily Mail*, 22nd January, 2000.

21   'Fans of Queen Frontman Claim To Have Found Clue To Singer's Final Resting Place' by Alice Philipson, *The Telegraph*, 25th February 2013.

22   Georgia Kakalopoulou.

Chapter 51

1   'HIV Originated With Monkeys, Not Chimps, Study Finds' by Stefan Lovgren, *National Geographic*, 12th June 2003.

2   'Chimps & HIV: The Story Behind The Study' by Sharon Schmickle, *Minneapolis Post*, 28th July 2009.

3   'AIDS 2014: Stepping Up The Pace', AIDS 2014 Communications Department.

4   *Illness as Metaphor and AIDS and Its Metaphors* by Susan Sontag (Picador, 2009). Quotations from *Illness as Metaphor* copyright © Susan Sontag 1977, 1978 and quotations from *Aids and Its Metaphors* copyright © Susan Sontag 1988, 1989, used by permission of The Wylie Agency (UK) Limited.

Chapter 52

1   Interview with Paul Gambaccini by the authors, January 2016.

2   *Daily Mirror*, 28th November 1991.

3   Interview with Paul Gambaccini by the authors, January 2016.

4   *Illness as Metaphor and AIDS and Its Metaphors* by Susan Sontag (Picador, 2009). Quotations from *Illness as Metaphor* copyright © Susan Sontag 1977, 1978 and quotations from *Aids and Its Metaphors* copyright © Susan Sontag 1988, 1989, used by permission of The Wylie Agency (UK) Limited.

5   Interview with Annie Lennox by the authors, January 2016.

6   'The Freddie Mercury Tribute Concert' by Johnny Black, *Classic Rock*, 13th May 2014.

7   Ibid.

8   Interview with John Reid by the authors, January 2016.

9   Interview with Annie Lennox by the authors, January 2016.

10   *The Times*, 22nd April 1992.

11   *Freddie Mercury: The Definitive Biography* by Lesley-Ann Jones (Hodder Paperbacks, 2012).

12 *The Times*, 26th April 1992.

13 'The Freddie Mercury Tribute Concert' by Johnny Black, *Classic Rock*, 13th May 2014.

14 Ibid.

Chapter 53

1 *Freddie Mercury: His Life In His Own Words* by Greg Brooks and Simon Lupton (Omnibus Press, 2009).

2 'The Oral History of The "Wayne's World" "Bohemian Rhapsody" Scene' by David Peisner, *Rolling Stone*, 30th November 2015.

3 Interview with Roger Taylor, KKLZ 96.3, 16th December 1997.

4 Interview with Brian May, *Guitarist Magazine*, 1st October 1994.

5 Interview with David Richards, *Rolling Stone (Germany)*, December 1995.

6 *The Sunday Times*, 26th November 1995.

7 'Made in Heaven' review, *Q* magazine, December 1995.

8 *The Times*, 4th November 1995.

9 *Classic Rock*, January 2000.

10 *Is This The Real Life? The Untold Story of Queen* by Mark Blake (Aurum Press Ltd., 2011).

11 'Queen Guitarist Brian May On Love And His New Musical' by Nina Myskow, *Daily Mirror*, 16th May 2002.

12 *The Independent*, 13th July 2015.

13 'Queen Bring Back Freddie Mercury', *PR Newswire*, 19th September 2014.

14 'Brian May & The Queen Story' by Gail Benzler, *Discoveries Magazine*, September 1993.

15 *Modern Drummer*, October 1984.

16 *The Daily Record*, 5th July 2015.

17 Interview with Paul Gambaccini by the authors, January 2016.

18 *Freddie Mercury: His Life In His Own Words* by Greg Brooks and Simon Lupton (Omnibus Press, 2009).

19 'Imagine A World Without AIDS', *The New York Times*, 27th July 2012.

20 Interview with Paul Gambaccini by the authors, January 2016.

21 UN AIDS factsheet, 2016.

Epilogue

1 'Why We Still Can't Get Enough Of Queen' by Mark Monahan, *The Daily Telegraph*, 30th October 2015.

2 Interview with Mike Moran by the authors, January 2016.

3 'Why We Still Can't Get Enough Of Queen' by Mark Monahan, *The Daily Telegraph*, 30th October 2015.

4 'Freddie Mercury: The Great Enigma' by Caroline Sullivan, *The Guardian*, 27th September 2012.

5 'Queen's Tragic Rhapsody' by Mike Gilmore, *Rolling Stone*, 7th July 2014.

6 *Freddie Mercury: His Life In His Own Words* by Greg Brooks and Simon Lupton (Omnibus Press, 2009).

7 Interview with Peter Straker by the authors, January 2016.

Index